G.R.A.C.E.
Keys to
Entrepreneurship

God · Resilience · Action · Creativity · Enthusiasm

How God Turned a Schoolteacher's Hobby
Into a Multimillion-Dollar Business

MARTHA CAMPBELL PULLEN, PH.D.

Pullen Press, LLC
www.pullenbusiness.com

978-0-692-20806-9

Published by Pullen Press, LLC
Printed by Bookmasters, Ashland, OH
Cover and book design: Monica Yother,
MY Designs, www.my-designs.net

Dewey Decimal Classification: 658
Subject Heading: NEW BUSINESS ENTERPRISES—MANAGEMENT/HOME-
BASED BUSINESS/SELF-EMPLOYED
Library of congress Card Catalog Number: 98-43079

Scripture quotations are taken from the Holy Bible, New Living Translation, copyright ©1996, 2004, 2007, 2013 by Tyndale House Foundation. Used by permission of Tyndale House Publishers, Inc., Carol Stream, Illinois 60188. All rights reserved.

Library of Congress Cataloging-in-Publication Data
Pullen, Martha Campbell.
G.R.A.C.E. keys to entrepreneurship: how God turned a schoolteacher's hobby into a multimillion-dollar business / Martha Campbell Pullen

www.pullenbusiness.com
Huntsville, Alabama

ISBN 978-0-692-20806-9
1.New business enterprises—Management. 2. Small business—Management. 3. Home-based business—Management. 4. Self-employed. 5. Hobbies. I Martha Cambell Pullen. II Title
HD62.5.P79 2014
658'.041—DC21

Contents

Dedication

> *"For I know the plans I have for you," says the Lord.*
> *"They are plans for good and not for disaster, to give*
> *you a future and a hope."*
> —Jeremiah 29:11

I dedicate *G.R.A.C.E. Keys to Entrepreneurship* to my husband, Joe Ross Pullen, DMD whose encouragement inspired me to create Martha Pullen Company and Pullen Press, LLC and to persevere in opening every door we opened and in rounding every bend of this business journey. God and Joe have been my "Rocks of Gibraltar." There were so many times when I thought I could not go on—when, to me, it looked like the "Red Sea" facing my business could not open. God always knew how to open the "Red Sea" and Joe walked with me right through it. There would be no Martha Pullen Company, no Pullen Press, LLC without God and Joe Pullen. God gets all the credit and glory of course; however, coming in second is my beloved husband, Joe.

In *Huntsville Business* magazine March 1987, Dr. Joe Pullen was the cover story in an article titled "A Pioneer of Implant Dentistry." The writer, Melissa Ford Thornton, began the piece like this: "Dr. Pullen's contributions have been recognized by many very major dental organizations but his real reward is the happiness he's been able to bring to his patients."

Joe followed in the footsteps of his father, Joyce Buren Pullen, DDS who was the fourth dentist in Huntsville. His father began practice in Huntsville in 1942 when Joe was seven years old. Joe's mother (Emma Eileen Hodges Pullen) and father decided to move to Huntsville, which they felt was a town with lots of business potential since it only had three dentists! Joe's father had graduated from Vanderbilt University Dental School in 1924.

Joe graduated from the University of Alabama Dental School and began practicing with his father in 1961. Joe and his father practiced together until Pop was 78 years old. His patients simply would not let him retire. Joe retired from dentistry at age 65 to help me in my business which had become very large at that time.

Joe had an illustrious career as an implant dentist, serving as president of the American Academy of Implant Dentistry in 1983. He has taught dentistry on four continents at such exciting places as Harvard University, The Royal Academy of Medicine in London, The University of Zurich Dental School and Lariboisiere Hospital in Paris. He has conducted seminars for dentists in Brazil, Japan, Singapore and several other countries. He received the Medal of the City of Paris, France at the Hotel de Ville (the town hall) conferred by none other than the mayor of Paris. He stated when presenting the medal to Joe that the honor was in recognition of his contribution to the international health community in the area of implant dentistry where he had helped to "alleviate pain and suffering of people the world over."

Before becoming president of the American Academy of Implant Dentistry he served as treasurer, secretary, vice-president and president elect. The year he was president, he traveled to eight countries representing the organization and teaching other dentists how to place implants. He has been president of the Alabama Academy of General Dentistry and was named a fellow, an honor reserved for only one percent of the members, by the other fellows in the American Academy of Implant Dentistry. He is also a fellow of the American Academy of General Dentistry and of the Academy of Dentistry International. While his list of international and national honors and recognitions stretch beyond the limits of my imagination, his real message of implant dentistry lies in the patients he treated here in Huntsville. Patients traveled from across the United States for him to place implants.

One of the most rewarding aspects of Joe's dental life was his mission trips with our church, Whitesburg Baptist Church, in conjunction with the Southern Baptist Convention's International Mission Board. He has performed dentistry for people who had never had dental care available to them. Those trips were to Jamaica, Brazil, Togo, Benin, Brazil, and Guatemala. He went several times to each place. The conditions were primitive, to say the least, since his surgical light was a hand-held flashlight and the dental chair was a folding metal chair. He literally had to get on his knees for upper extractions and lean over for lowers. God gave him the strength to see more than 500 patients in a week. He simply said to them, "I come in the name of Jesus to relieve your pain." Four of those international trips were to Africa to serve with Suzanne and John Crocker, our son and daughter-in-law and their children who were missionaries in Togo and Benin for ten years.

By the way, in 1974 I was an emergency dental patient who had lost a crown while on a business trip to Huntsville. I was desperately hunting a dentist to "glue" the crown back on about 7 o'clock at night. Joe's office "just happened to be open." We both know that did not just happen. God was, in his infinite love for us, showing us what he had planned for our lives. Oh, how I thank God for that crown that fell off that night when I was in Huntsville on business while I was living in Tuscaloosa. After all, I was from out of town and did not know a dentist in Huntsville. Wouldn't you know Joe's office was the only one in Huntsville open that late at night? I begged his receptionist for an appointment as I stood at her window. The rest is history.

We each had two wonderful boys when we married. I had always said I wanted five children when I grew up. We now had four and we had Joanna fourteen months after we married. Many of you know that the birth of our daughter, Joanna, was the beginning of my wonderful heirloom sewing career! Joe is an incredible father and grandfather to our five children and eighteen grandchildren! He worked in the dental office for many years longer than possibly other men might have worked to provide the finest private college educations for them. He provided the finest of everything materially for them and, more importantly, he loved them.

Joe and I became born again Christians many, many years ago. During the years he practiced dentistry he did free dental work nearly every day on a homeless individual living in a shelter or on a kid living in another type of shelter. He would go to the office in the middle of the night to relieve pain knowing full well that he would never be paid for this trip.

There would be no Martha Pullen Company, no *Sew Beautiful* magazine, no Pullen Press, no books, no nothing I call my business if not for God first and then for Joe. Joe gave me the courage to start the business, and he and God together have kept my strength going while we built the business. From the time Joe and I first married I had made the statement that I was an entrepreneur at heart and that "I would rather try and fail than never try at all." Joe kept reminding me of this statement when I would fantasize about starting my own business. I might add that he insisted that I finish my Ph.D. after Joanna was born. I was enjoying her so much that I thought it really did not matter whether I finished the dissertation or not. He insisted that I go the final mile, reminding me that winners do not quit.

Joe furnished, along with a significant contribution from my mother, the startup funds for my first retail store. He sold property on two occasions to pay my bills to keep this business going. As I have sat and cried saying, "It's not worth it—the business pressure isn't worth it," he has reminded me of the joy that I have brought to people. He literally supported the family, alone, for the first four years that I was in business. We were well into the fifth year before I could draw even a tiny little salary out of the company. He always reminded me that we would not starve if I lost all of the money and time that we had invested in the business. He has always reminded me that he values me just as much as a wife and a mother as he does as a business woman.

Joe and I love our children and grandchildren so very much and are proud of them. Our most enjoyable evenings are spent cooking on our grill and having them over to eat with us. We love decorating our dining room table (plus several card tables since the family is now so big) for Thanksgiving, Christmas, birthdays, Easter, Mother's Day and Father's Day and having family celebrations using our beautiful china mostly inherited from my mama and Joe's mama. My sister, Mary Nixon, and her family come for these occasions, too. On those occasions, we all cook the traditional dishes that our mothers and grandmothers cooked for those occasions and we really have a feast. It is such a fun time to talk with great love about our beloved ones who are no longer with us for the celebrations. We love to tell "Do you remember when?" happy times stories centered around family celebrations. Joe loves these family meals.

Joe and I are so proud of our children, their spouses and our grandchildren. Mark is a successful dentist who started practicing with Joe. He now has not only his main practice but also several others with other dentists working with him. May I brag a little bit? You cannot feel his shots!!!! TRULY cannot feel his shots!!! His wife Sherry Ann, who always brought the children to model in my magazine and for our fashion shows for my business, works part time in the dental office. Sherry Ann does so many sweet things to help Joe and me. Jeff works for the Publix corporation. His wife, Steinunn, is a great help to Jeff as well as to us and moved from Florida to Huntsville with Jeff so he could be closer to Emma, his only daughter. Camp is very famous in the automotive business in Arizona, converting Jeeps into fabulous custom vehicles which he sells all over the world. In addition to this conversion business, he also has a school through which he teaches young people how to do these conversions. He also owns WC Caddy, a wheelchair cover used mainly by United Airlines to protect wheelchairs while in airplanes. His wife, Charisse, was a great help to me working in my business while they were in Huntsville. She always brought the little boys to photo shoots, and they modeled for our fashion shows. She is busy with the little girls, born after they moved to Arizona, in school, gymnastics, swimming and other activities.

Our son, John Crocker, is Missions Pastor of Whitesburg Baptist Church, our church for the past thirty years. His wife, Suzanne, is finishing her degree to become a nurse practitioner. John and Suzanne were missionaries with the Southern Baptist Convention's International Mission Board in Africa for ten years. Joe and I traveled four times to work with them while they were in Africa. Suzanne and John wrote many stories about their adventures in Africa for my email newsletter which went to 40,000 people in my business. My "sewing ladies" absolutely could not wait to get more news from John and Suzanne and the family in Africa. Although the children were not here to model very much, they occasionally were featured in *Sew Beautiful* magazine. It is a joy to have them living back in Huntsville after so many years in Africa.

Our daughter, Joanna is the reason my business was started. She grew up in *Sew Beautiful* magazine. She is married to Dr. Ronald Collins, an anesthesiologist who specializes in pain management at Tennessee Valley Pain Consultants. Joanna is a very successful realtor and they are the parents of six children who are all involved in many activities! Joanna has brought all of her babies to many photo shoots for *Sew Beautiful* as well as for my books. Joanna worked for my business for several years and was featured in many segments on the PBS television series *Martha's Sewing Room*. Ron has traveled on two medical mission trips with John, and Mark has traveled on one dental mission trip with John. Joe loves knowing that our children are carrying on his international medical/dental mission work with John and Whitesburg Baptist Church.

Our GRANDCHILDREN ARE JUST SPECTACULAR!! They range in age from 22 to 5! Campbell and Morgan are graduating from college this year. Sarah Joy, Marshall, Bradley and Rebekah are in college. Christopher, Emma, Peyton, Cecil and Ward are in high school. Chase and Garrin are in middle school. Houston, Ben, Sophie-Reese, William and Walter are in elementary school. Joe and I love them all dearly!

Joe, I will never be able to thank you enough for all you are, have been and will be to me. I love you with all of my heart, and I thank God for that day, many years ago, when the crown fell off my tooth and I started searching for a dentist in Huntsville. Looking at our lives as they unfold daily, I know it "didn't just happen." I thank God for you for and for planning the rest of my life to be with you. This book is for you, my darling Joe. I love you.

Foreword

Thinking of starting a business? Look no further. In the following pages, business veteran Martha Pullen outlines your road map to success. Each page is thoughtfully filled with tips and pointers learned through years of hard work and dedication. Martha Pullen does not just write about building a successful business, she has actually done it.

I have been fortunate to have known Martha Pullen personally for nearly 26 years. For those of you that have met Martha, you know well that her energy and enthusiasm are unmatched. You now know from reading the back cover of this book that Martha was actually a cheerleader at the University of Alabama. I have been told that young men drove long distances to catch of glimpse of the fetching red head. If you know Martha though, this makes total sense. Since the day I met her I feel like she has been cheering for me, my own personal cheerleader. I have to remind myself though that Martha cheers for everyone. There is no doubt in my mind that she prays for each of her customers daily. Once you meet her you will feel assured she is rooting for you too. It is with this careful approach that she has written this book. Martha no doubt wants you to succeed and through these pages, she will serve as your personal guide. Why not learn from the best?

It is her unique perspective which lends itself so well to business. Martha is not enthusiastic about business per se; she is enthusiastic about serving others. When Martha asked me to write this foreword, I was flattered and spent a good amount of time thinking about how to convey her talents and message. Servant leadership kept coming to mind again and again. I was not surprised at all when I ran across the following mission statement for the Martha Pullen Company: *To serve the sewing public in such a gracious manner that it brings glory to God, profit to the business, respect and admiration to Martha Pullen Company and joy and enthusiasm to those who participate.*

Over the years I have had the opportunity to interview many business leaders. I am an investment manager and my firm has interviewed management teams at hundreds of businesses. There are a few qualities that successful business leaders all have in common. First, successful business leaders are humble. You do not get to the top without learning some hard lessons along the way. This alone teaches humility. Second, successful business leaders are outwardly focused. Put another way, they are focused on what they have to give, not what they can get. My great uncle Sir John Templeton notably pioneered global investing through mutual funds, and along the way he wrote extensively about serving others. Uncle John wrote that, "Every successful entrepreneur is a servant. He or she must be oriented to matters outside of himself. He must look to consumers and their needs. He must rely on consumer's voluntary patronage to bring about his or her own goals. That is service. Voluntary exchange and profit is about serving others. When the businessman becomes too internal he loses his customer base and ceases to anticipate the future. He loses profits."

Martha Pullen effortlessly models this approach to business. When launching a business you might start by asking yourself, "what do I have to offer to others?" No doubt, this is what Martha did in 1981 when she began importing laces and fabrics to sell mail-order, both wholesale and retail. The success of her first book prompted the writing of over fifty more sewing books over the next 30 years. Shortly after opening the doors of her retail shop came the Martha Pullen School of Art Fashion, which now attracts hundreds of women to Huntsville twice a year. The school's success prompted Martha to venture out of her local market, conducting full-scale Martha Pullen schools in Australia, England, Sweden, Canada, Mexico, and New Zealand. She has personally taught workshops in 47 of the 50 states and Puerto Rico. To further share her love of heirloom sewing she started *Sew Beautiful* magazine in 1987; it is distributed worldwide. Her PBS TV series, *Martha's Sewing Room*, aired in all 50 states, Canada and Puerto Rico for 17 years. Thirteen episodes were translated into Japanese for Japanese Public Television. On mission trips with her church she has taught sewing in Jamaica, South America and Africa. There are Martha Pullen Licensed Teachers sharing heirloom sewing all over the world. Martha Pullen not only understands business, she has built a sewing empire all while humbly serving her customers. It is with knowledge and enthusiasm that she wrote this book for your benefit.

In conclusion, I am privileged to know Martha Pullen personally and now you can too. Let this book serve as your guide and know that now you have your own personal cheerleader..... Martha Pullen.

Lauren Templeton
Principal
Lauren Templeton Capital Management, LLC

Preface

> *Now all glory to God, who is able, through his mighty power at work within us, to accomplish infinitely more than we might ask or think.*
> —Ephesians 3:20

> *...our God whom we serve is able ....and he will ...*
> —Daniel 3:17

> *You will not leave in a hurry, running for your lives. For the LORD will go ahead of you, and the God of Israel will protect you from behind.*
> —Isaiah 52:12

Run your business in harmony with God's laws. This will keep you on an ethical footing. Seek to please God in everything you do.
—David Green, Founder Hobby Lobby

I want to be the very best competitor I can be. The Bible says, "Whatever your hand finds to do, do it with all your might, for in the grave, where you are going, there is neither working nor planning nor knowledge nor wisdom." (Ecclesiastes 9:10).
—David Green, Founder Hobby Lobby

I thought, I'm only going to be on this planet once, and only for a short time. What can I do with my life that will lead to permanent benefits?

—Henry T. Blackaby

Anything significant that happens in your life will be a result of God's activity in your life. He is infinitely more interested in your life than you or I could possibly be.

—Sir John Templeton

God always has something for you. A key for every problem, a light for every shadow and a relief for every sorrow. Stay in faith.

—Julie Ziglar Norman, (Zig Ziglar's daughter)

It shows us how much God loves us. The love he gave us, by giving us his only son, Jesus, was so unbelievable to me. I hoped others would learn of God's love. So that's why I put it there.

—Do Won Chang, Founder Forever 21

The Do Won Chang quote above was in answer to the question concerning why Forever 21 prints John 3:16 on the bottom of their trademark yellow bags.

To glorify God by being a faithful steward of all that is entrusted to us and to have a positive influence on all who come into contact with Chick-fil-A.

—Chick-fil-A Corporate Purpose

Hobby Lobby Stores, Inc.'s true owner, Mr. Green says, is God.

—David Green

Wall Street Journal (Weekend), March 22-23, 2014

Two Main Ideas to Share

Before I get into "how to create and run a business" I have two main ideas which are very important for me to share. First, I am a devout Christian and I give God all the credit for Martha Pullen Company and Pullen Press. God has parted "Red Sea" after "Red Sea" for me and my businesses. He is still in the miracle business. It is by the grace of God that I have a business. **G.R.A.C.E.** is my business philosophy. **G** stands for God. **R** stands for resilience. **A** stands for action. **C** stands for creativity. **E** stands for enthusiasm. We will explore **G.R.A.C.E.** all through this book.

Second, I am an American and I am enormously grateful for the freedoms we have in this country that allow entrepreneurship to really happen. What a great privilege we have to be able to worship in the way we choose. I am grateful for the men and women who have fought and died defending these freedoms. I am equally appreciative for those defending this country right now as you read this page. I love America. I thank God that I was born in America and I assure you that is a gift from God. America isn't perfect but compared to any other country I have ever visited or heard about it is almost perfect. God has truly blessed America.

God Gets the Credit

Exodus 14 (Several verses) -Parting the Red Sea

⁵When word reached the king of Egypt that the Israelites had fled, Pharoah and his officials changed their minds. "What have we done, letting all those Israelite slaves get away?" they asked.

⁶So Pharoah harnessed his chariot and called up his troops.

⁷He took with him 600 of Egypt's best chariots, along with the rest of the chariots of Egypt, each with its commander.

¹⁰As Pharoah approached, the people of Israel looked up and panicked when they saw the Egyptians overtaking them. They cried out to the LORD,

¹¹and they said to Moses, "Why did you bring us out here to die in the wilderness?"

¹³But Moses told the people, "Don't be afraid. Just stand still and watch the LORD rescue you today. The Egyptians you see today will never be seen again.

¹⁴The LORD himself will fight for you. Just stay calm."

¹⁵Then the LORD said to Moses, "Why are you crying out to me? Tell the people to get moving!

¹⁶Pick up your staff and raise your hand over the sea. Divide the water so the Israelites can walk through the middle of the sea on dry ground.

¹⁷And I will harden the hearts of the Egyptians, and they will charge in after the Israelites."

²¹Then Moses raised his hand over the sea, and the LORD opened up a path through the water with a strong east wind. The wind blew all that night, turning the seabed into dry land.

²²So the people of Israel walked through the middle of the sea on dry ground, with walls of water on each side!

²⁶When all the Israelites had reached the other side, the LORD said to Moses, "Raise your hand over the sea again. Then the waters will rush back and cover the Egyptians and their chariots and charioteers."

³¹When the people of Israel saw the mighty power that the LORD had unleashed against the Egyptians, they were filled with awe before him. They put their faith in the LORD and in his servant Moses.

God has parted the "Red Sea" so many times in my business. He has led me successfully through one difficult business situation after another. I will share many of these "Red Sea" experiences in this book. By sharing many of my mistakes, I also pray that you will be able to avoid them! God has known how to keep my company afloat even when I saw nothing but drowning in our future. Especially in the earlier years many is the time I said to Joe, "We just need to sell our house, pay the bills and close the business." God had other plans; He opened the "Red Sea" over and over again to reveal His plans to me. It was always to keep going since He knew how to pay the bills and keep the doors open. He has sent loyal customers. He has sent the right team members to help build the company. He has sent mentors to me personally and large and small companies to partner with us. Joe told me many times that he knew God had a plan for us and that I must not quit.

God has always been in the miracle business and He has performed one miracle after another in my company. It is through God's miracles, love and care that Martha Pullen Company is now celebrating 32 years of business. Pullen Press is celebrating four years. God has allowed a way when I saw no way. As promised in Isaiah 52:12, the LORD has gone before me and will continue to do so. The God of Israel has been my rear guard and will continue to serve in that capacity. Praise be to God. Great things He has done.

I Praise God for America

IN CONGRESS, JULY 4, 1776
The unanimous Declaration of the thirteen united States of America

The Declaration of Independence represented the want, will and hopes of the people of this great United States of America on July 4, 1776! They wanted to be free. There is the freedom we speak of in being an American but there are other types of freedom we have the right to pursue in this country. Possibly you, reading this book right now want to have the freedom to own your own business. How well I remember that dream from the time I was a child. I was born an entrepreneur even though I certainly did not know that word. Please read the following words from the second paragraph of the Declaration of Independence.

"We hold these truths to be self-evident, that all men are created equal, that they are endowed by their Creator with certain unalienable Rights, that among these are Life, Liberty, and the pursuit of Happiness."

I love this sentence from the Declaration of Independence. As I look at the world today just thinking about the fact that we have life, liberty and the pursuit of happiness gives me great joy. These are the most well-known lines in the Declaration of Independence, and are among the most important lines ever written in the history of mankind. With these words, the American government was established on a foundation that in earlier centuries, only visionaries could have imagined would ever become reality.

My business journey has always been the pursuit of happiness. I have had the happiness of being independent. I have had the happiness of creating beautiful things for others to enjoy and of teaching them how to sew. I have had the happiness of helping others plan their own businesses. I have had the opportunity to tell others about God in a business setting. This has been and continues to be a remarkable, miraculous journey filled with every emotion imaginable. It has been my "pursuit of happiness" although my preferred word is joy. I have had the joy of seeing God put the pieces together when I saw no way to go on. God has opened the "Red Sea" over and over and our company walked through on dry land. Did I still love my business even during the hardest financial times? Yes.

The words to the Declaration of Independence still remain an inspiration today not only to Americans, but to people around the world. So many in the world know nothing of a government with any foundation like ours. Thank you God that I am an American.

Does Your Life Need a Do-Over?

By purchasing this book my guess would be that you are thinking about becoming an entrepreneur. Maybe you already have a business and you want to grow that business or revamp that business into something more successful. Martha Pullen Company changed my life from one of working creatively for someone else to working creatively for myself. I loved my job as a college professor/educational consultant. I loved my students. However......... I was not my own boss. My income was dependent on "the number of years of teaching" and someone else's decisions. My income was greatly limited simply because I was in public school education. My schedule was dependent on someone else's decisions. No matter how outstanding I was, my income was still the same. I had very little flexibility. No matter how creative my ideas were others could squash them. I could not plan my own schedule around my family's needs. On and on and on.

My senior year in high school I was head majorette. I kept remembering how I loved to lead the band. I kept remembering how I loved having my own dancing school in high school. To make more money I simply had to work more hours. I started teaching baton in addition to dance. I made more money based on my efforts not on someone else's decisions. I remembered the creativity of planning the dance recital and designing the costumes for my students. Please remember that I was only 14 when I started my first business.

Martha's Entrepreneur Zone

Let's face it. My life needed a do-over which involved quitting my really good, secure job which had a great deal of enjoyment. It was time for me to follow my passion and become an entrepreneur. It was time for me to go back to one of my first childhood loves, sewing. It was time for me to incorporate my love of teaching with my love of sewing. As you will read about later in this book one of my childhood passions was also selling. I was the top magazine salesman in elementary school two years in a row. I started selling in my Uncle Albert and Aunt Eva's store when I was 12 years old. I loved selling in addition to teaching and sewing.

If your life needs a do-over you have bought the right book. Transforming thoughts and dreams into workable ideas is what this book is all about. Enter the Entrepreneur Zone with me and let's work together to see if this is what you really want.

My "I Love You" Book

Where do I begin to introduce this book to you? I was born in Morristown, New Jersey and was named Martha Elizabeth Campbell. That might be a start but I did not write this book for me. I wrote it for you. This book is an "I Love You" book, born from my true love and desire to help YOU achieve your dreams of turning your hobby into a profitable business. Actually the ideas in this book will apply to any type of business, not just a hobby based one. Owning my own business was always my dream. God allowed it to happen for me and it worked. God gave me Martha Pullen Company, Pullen Press, LLC and **www.pullenbusiness.com** a division of Pullen Press,LLC.

I have learned so much and I have a giant sized dream of helping you

Although until recent years I have never had a home based business I am a genuine advocate of home based. My Pullen Press, LLC , at this time is home based. There are some very interesting statistics on home based businesses in America.

According to The *Wall Street Journal*, 9/20/2012, the Babson and Baruch colleges poll of 5,542 adults conducted June/July 2012 69% of new businesses start at home. 59% of established business owners are home-based. 13% of U.S. adult population is engaged in entrepreneurship, the highest level in at least a decade. According to the Small Business Administration, the weekly pace of new business creation has doubled over the past three years and many of those businesses are opening in people's homes.

Are you ready for more interesting facts from that same *Wall Street Journal*? Once again these facts are from the same Babson and Baruch colleges' poll. 55.9% of Americans, who thought they were capable of launching a company, was essentially the same as 55.7% in 2008. 32.3% of Americans, who didn't launch a business because they feared failure, was up from 24.5% in 2008. 12.5% of Americans who intended to start a business in the next three years was up from 7.0% in 2008. 8.9% of Americans who took material steps to start a business was up from 5.9% in 2008. 4.1% of Americans who were running a new business, was down from 5.0% in 2005. 8.6% of Americans who owned an established business was up from 8.3% in 2008 and 5.9% in 2009.

According to James Duncan, Duncan Associates in Austin, Texas, "Home business rules are one of the things that have changed the most over the past decade. Almost all communities are loosening their regulations on home businesses." Louisiana recently passed a "cottage food" law, which allows individuals to sell food products from their homes. But the state also set a revenue cap of $20,000 to make sure businesses don't produce mass quantities of food at home without a commercial kitchen license.

So many people are wondering if they could work from home and earn real money from a job which is satisfying, exciting and profitable. So many women have told me about endless meetings, a difficult boss or coworkers, child care problems, someone else's schedule, boring projects, and a grind that leaves one wondering if these words from the Declaration of Independence,"the pursuit of happiness,"can ever belong to her. Look at the statistics. This is the perfect time to wonder about all of those issues. I too wanted more control over my personal life and greater satisfaction in my with your dreams. I have a urgent dream of helping you not make many of the mistakes that I made. In other words, my dream is now to help others develop their dreams of business ownership. I have used the word "dream" a lot haven't I? The most important first fact to think about is "dreaming is not enough." Without written plans your business will not work! Ask me how I know!

I have worked with many people over the last 30 years giving seminars on "Turning Your Hobby into a Business." I have worked with individuals helping them plan businesses in 47 of the 50 states, Canada, England, Sweden, Mexico, Australia and New Zealand. I have taught actual sewing classes on six of the seven continents. Individuals from all over the world have taken my business seminars here in Huntsville and at sewing machine conventions. The desire to own a business is certainly not limited to the "American Dream."

Since my business is a sewing business most of my seminars have been geared to women and men who wanted to have a sewing business of some kind. I have worked with individuals who wanted a home based business of many kinds-both traditional and online. I have worked with some who planned to open a bricks and mortar store front. Many of my students desired a business on eBay or Etsy. I have worked with many who wanted ideas for growing their current businesses. The principles of a successful hobby based business are the same no matter what the hobby.

Martha Pullen Company was opened August 1, 1981 and it still is alive and well today although I no longer own the business. My current business is Pullen Press, LLC, a publishing, ecommerce (**pullenbusiness.com**) and business consulting firm. This book is my story—my journey with entrepreneurship. Many people have helped me with this journey. Most importantly I will tell you that this business belongs to God and without His leading and strength for me, my family and our team there would be neither Martha Pullen Company nor Pullen Press, LLC today. I will add here that Joe, my incredible husband of four decades, has been second in importance to God in making this business survive.

Home Based Business Statistics

I am a real advocate of home based businesses. I have worked with many people who are homeschooling moms, retirees, full time employees, full time home makers (both men and women), and part time employees.

work. I also wanted to make more money. I wanted financial independence for my family and me.

Homeschooling Moms

I have had many home schooling moms come to my seminars with the desire to start a home based business to earn money at home. Many have stated the need for extra income; others have stated they would like something which is "my own." Some have stated they would like to build a home based business which eventually would allow Dad to work from home, too.

Many homeschooling moms have started teaching sewing to other children and also to other moms. Many have Etsy businesses selling a variety of products. Many have a home embroidery business embroidering gifts, baby gifts, bridal gifts, christening gifts, towels, tea towels, sheets, pillowcases, pillow shams, decorative pillows, purses, t-shirts, school logos on uniform shirts, cheerleader outfits, business logo t-shirts, t-shirts for zoos and museums to sell in the gift shops, physician's lab coats or nurses uniforms. The list is endless. Some have told me that a home based business is the perfect way for them to teach their teens practical things. What better way to teach business subjects and entrepreneurial skills than to be involved in an actual, live business? What valuable skills they would have in developing a web site, updating a web site, packing orders, handling customer service correspondence, entering business information into Quick Books—the list goes on. I know of homeschooled teens who have started their own businesses. One that comes to mind is a teen who sells his friends' older electronic equipment on eBay for a commission. I know another who makes t-shirt quilts. I cannot think of a better way for a homeschooled teen to learn time management and business skills than working for a parent's home based business or having his/her own. Of course the business is in addition to all of the academics that are required. What an education this would be!

Let's Get Started

This is going to be an incredible journey for you and me. I'm glad you are a part of my team. Enjoy this book and remember that much more is available on **www.pullenbusiness.com.**

For just as the heavens are higher than the earth, so my ways are higher than your ways and my thoughts higher than your thoughts. The rain and snow come down from the heavens and stay on the ground to water the earth.
They cause the grain to grow, producing seed for the farmer and bread for the hungry. It is the same with my word. I send it out, and it always produces fruit. It will accomplish all I want it to, and it will prosper everywhere I send it.
—Isaiah 55:9-11

Introduction

For nothing is impossible with God.

—Luke 1:37

May the LORD bless you
And protect you.
May the LORD smile on you
And be gracious to you.
May the LORD show you his favor
And give you his peace.

—Numbers 6:24-26

For I hold you by your right hand—
I, the Lord your God.
And I say to you,
'Don't be afraid. I am here to help you.'

—Isaiah 41:13

~ Chapter One ~

The Possibilities with G.R.A.C.E.

Martha's Story: Good Times, Bad Times

I looked out the window onto the morning traffic of Madison Street, August 1, 1981, whispering prayers to calm my nerves. Looking across the street, I watched nurses and physicians hurry into Huntsville Hospital to begin working. A couple of businessmen walked past, dressed in suits and ties, already wiping their foreheads from the August Alabama heat. Inside the shop, the air conditioner could not quite overpower the rising humidity, and every minute passed like an hour.

The green carpet had not been completed until about 2 a.m. that same morning, so I was working on very little sleep. Was it possible that in a couple of hours my dream store, devoted to smocking and heirloom sewing, would open? Once again I walked through the three rooms to admire the Laura Ashley wallpaper, covered with little pink roses. I felt ever so grateful that the carpet had been finished in time for the 10 a.m. opening. Everything looked so pretty, and my heart felt happy.

I turned back to the tiny showroom and busied myself with rearranging the twenty bolts of French lace I had brought back from New York City, hoping to make them look more like forty! Three new sewing machines were back in the tiny, middle room that would serve as my teaching salon, and beautiful bolts of fabrics were neatly arranged and color-coded on the freshly painted white shelves.

I thought back to the ads that we had run in the newspaper for weeks prior to the shop's opening, which simply read, "Smocking is coming" and showed a cute illustration of a little girl in an antique dress. It was only two weeks before the actual opening that we put the location and the name— The Heirloom Shop, 805 Madison Street, Huntsville, Alabama.

The day had finally arrived. Alone in the shop, I smiled and briefly allowed myself to enjoy the moment. My dream had come true. After weeks of endless work, months of preparation, and years of dreaming, I had finally, at the age of thirty-seven, realized one of my greatest dreams: to open my very own business dedicated to heirloom sewing. I was an entrepreneur. Even today, more than thirty years later, I still drive past that location and feel a deep sense of joy, gratitude, and thankfulness to God to think that my entire sewing business career began when Joe and I took that first great risk, and invested our life savings in turning my hobby into a business.

Perhaps it is more accurate to say that God has given me the chance to turn my passion into a business. I am and have always been passionate about sewing. I am equally passionate about teaching sewing to others so that they might feel the joy of making something for someone they love. I am passionate about helping others dream their dreams, accompanied by a "boots on the ground" plan for earning money through their hobbies. I believe the main reason that I have written the book you now hold in your hands is my overwhelming desire to help you and thousands like you develop your dreams of becoming an entrepreneur and live your dreams of owning your business. I want your business to be successful; I want you to avoid many of the mistakes that I made. I am passionate about helping you do this.

At this point in my life, I get far more pleasure helping others become successful in their "passion business" than I am about actually sewing more gorgeous heirloom clothes myself. I never intend to retire from the business world, but I suppose if I should change my mind further down the road, I will have lots of sewing projects to which I can return. I still love to sew.

> *Pay careful attention to your own work, for then you will get the satisfaction of a job well done, and you won't need to compare yourself to anyone else. For we are each responsible for our own conduct.*
> —Galatians 6:4-5

A Childhood Passion

The art of sewing traveled down many generations in my family before I began to learn to sew at age five from Mama and Aunt Christine Jenkins. As a seamstress, Mama was a perfectionist. As I became older and more serious about sewing, she helped me learn proper, precise methods. On the other hand, Aunt Chris just loved the creativity expressed through sewing. When she helped me make felt Christmas stockings and doll clothes she never cared about the quality of the construction—she thought they looked gorgeous and so did I! Aunt Chris and I both loved sequins and glitter and "fancy" things. She taught me how to hand stitch sequins, one by one, on my Christmas stockings and I "hand embroidered" the little cut out felt lambs and bells. I feel pretty sure that my "hand embroidery" at age five left a lot to be desired, but it was perfect to Aunt Chris and to me. I simply loved sewing. The passion was always there and it filled my heart.

I made some of my clothes in high school, but my mother made the truly special outfits for me. I can vividly remember the joy of going to the fabric store with Mama, choosing a pattern and fabric, and returning home where she would begin the process of making something beautiful for me to wear.

Mama loved Vogue patterns and since I was tall and thin she had to do some mighty pattern drafting to make it fit perfectly. But fit perfectly it always did. She paid careful attention to detail with everything she made. She believed bound buttonholes were the prettiest and she spent hours making them. She lined the skirts with silk on straight wool dresses. She truly was a tailor.

Before I went to college, Mama took me to Burger Phillips fabric department in Birmingham. We bought the finest black silk and a designer Vogue pattern for the dress I would wear to sorority rush formal night. When the night finally arrived, and I sat in the Chi Omega house hoping to receive a bid from that sorority, I felt perfectly dressed. It was a very important occasion to me, and my beautiful black silk dress that Mama made for me was my "security blanket." I did get the bid and joined Chi Omega sorority at the University of Alabama in 1961.

Sewing From Necessity

She makes sure her dealings are profitable; her lamp burns late into the night.
—Proverbs 31:18

As a young bride, I had little money, so my Singer Touch and Sew machine—a gift from Aunt Chris—was a very dear friend. I made all of my two little boys' clothes, with the exception of their coats and shoes. I made most of my own clothes. When I went shopping for fabrics, the "remnant table" was my destination. The fabrics there were very inexpensive and I could always find a treasure if I looked hard enough. I even made all of my Christmas presents on that trusty little machine and wrapped each one carefully in the Sunday comic papers that I had been saving for months. We certainly had no money for purchased Christmas wrapping paper. I actually remember those Christmas years as some of my very best. I put much time and thought into every gift since I had almost no money.

After I became a divorced mother with two little boys to clothe, my sewing took on even greater importance. I had virtually no money and I needed clothes for all of us. My trusty little machine sat on a card table in our $61 a month student housing apartment at Northington Apartments on the University of Alabama campus. I had started back to graduate school full time to finish my Ph.D. I sewed not only our clothes but also costumes for a Cub Scout Indian Dance program. I was the Cub Scout leader for one semester! After one semester in that apartment I married Joe and we moved to Huntsville. Wow! What happiness! It still is!

I made it through those difficult times with God's help, but I might have left sewing behind entirely, had I not rediscovered my love for sewing in 1976. The birth of our youngest set me off on a passionate bout of dress making, so happy I felt to have a beautiful little girl in the family. You see, our daughter Joanna was an answer to many prayers, not the least of which was God's decision to give Joe and me a little girl when we were fully expecting a fifth boy. When Joe and I married we brought together two boys from each of our families, making us a very happy family with four little boys ages 10, 9, 9, and 8. Little did I know that God's will was not simply to bring us the joy of a lovely daughter, but by allowing me to reconnect with a forgotten passion, it would start me upon a journey toward a completely new way of life—my sewing business.

For more than a decade before I opened The Heirloom Shop, I had unswervingly pursued the dream of becoming a teacher, just like Mama and my grandmother. I had shuffled our young family from one university town to another, from Athens, Georgia to Gainesville, Florida, then back to Tuscaloosa, Alabama in pursuit of my Ph.D. in Educational Administration and Management, which I did receive in 1977.

There were moments during that part of my life that I was a single mom, recently divorced and living from month to month, so that any hobby besides cooking, cleaning, teaching or sleeping was completely out of the question. When I did sew, it was entirely out of the necessity of saving a little money. Even after I met and married Joe, I barely had enough time to feed the children, pack them off to school, and continue my weekly commute to Tuscaloosa to finalize my classwork and later my dissertation. By this time I had stopped sewing altogether.

Joanna's Birth Awakened My Sewing Passion

The birth of Joanna reawakened my joy, passion, and love for sewing. I can distinctly remember as I lay in my hospital bed, contemplating the joy of having a daughter, how much I wanted to sew beautiful clothes for her. By the time she was four years old, I had already made five white heirloom dresses whose complexity and embellishments increased with each new effort. Something about sewing pushed me to go further and further, and it was not just the friendly admiration I received from other members of the congregation when I brought my daughter to a Sunday service all dressed in her finest, although their compliments certainly encouraged me.

No, it was much more than just showing off. My attraction to sewing came from the way it made me feel inside. I felt a connection with all those quiet afternoons I spent as a child making doll clothes beside my aunt and mother, while they looked on and made new dresses for the family. Sewing made me feel totally domestic as if I were creating a true home full of love and caring. It brought out all my best maternal instincts. Sewing made me feel inventive, creative, and talented, because I was good at it and it came from my heart. Sewing to me means love. It always has and always will.

> *She is energetic and strong, a hard worker.*
> —Proverbs 31:17

Joe's Encouragement

Joe certainly noticed my blossoming interest in sewing, and he began to gently encourage me to start a business. After having finished my Ph. D. I was teaching at Athens State College, which was about an hour away from our house. My classes were primarily in the afternoon and evenings. With his busy schedule as an implant dentist, five children, meals to cook and a home to care for, we both knew that this schedule would not work for our family. I am certainly not a wonder woman and could not take care of everything. Although we hired a wonderful nanny to help me with little Joanna and take care of the house, we both felt that our life was too hectic while I commuted so far away.

When we decided that I needed to stop teaching, we also realized that I needed to keep my mind fully occupied, or I might start thinking myself qualified to teach Joe how to be a better dental surgeon. Besides which, Joe could read my feelings quite well, and he already sensed my strong connection with my hobby of sewing. He also knew I was an entrepreneur at heart.

"How much longer are you going to drive all the way down to Birmingham to buy ten yards of lace and batiste and all those smocking supplies," asked Joe, "when you could be selling it yourself to the ladies of Huntsville? Half of your friends are begging you to share your sewing secrets, and there is not a store within two hours offering any half-decent supplies."

In my heart, I knew he was right, but it took months of his wheedling about my so-called talents to finally give me the courage to start my business. Fear had me paralyzed. "What if? What if? What if?" I asked Joe over and over.

Joe finally said to me "Martha we are going to put $23,000 into this business. That is our retirement savings. Your building will be free since it is part of my office building. We are not going to starve if we lose all of this money. Most importantly, I don't want you to wake up when you are 65 years of age and wish you had started your sewing business." So right then and there, we decided to open the shop.

Twenty years from now you will be more disappointed by the things you didn't do than by the ones you did do. So throw off the bowlines. Sail away from the safe harbor. Catch the trade winds in your sails. Explore. Dream. Discover.

—Mark Twain

Joe supported me both emotionally and financially through those difficult weeks that soon stretched into months, which stretched into about 10 years, when despite my efforts, the balance sheet remained decidedly in the red. His confidence and encouragement meant so much to me during those times. As much as I appreciated knowing that his dental salary could support us until the fledgling business found its legs, I felt even more reassured that someone truly believed in me.

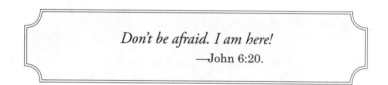

Don't be afraid. I am here!
—John 6:20.

I look back fondly on those early stages of the business, which were very memorable times for me, although each day had its highs and lows. I might have felt a burning thrill each day that I taught a class and sold more supplies, but my excitement would be quickly tempered by a dull, hollow worry as I calculated my financials for the month's end. I suppose it is that potent mix of uncertainty and daring that makes the early days of any new business so thrilling and frightening. As Henry Ford said, "Failure is simply the opportunity to begin again, this time more intelligently." Indeed, every new morning felt like a new beginning, picking up from yesterday's mistakes.

What is amazing to me now, over thirty years later, is that even today I still get the same thrill of going to work. Running a business is an exciting and fulfilling everyday adventure. Looking back on my path, I can say with complete assurance that there is nothing I would rather have done with my life, and I thank God for guiding me here. Through heirloom sewing, and the chance to share its joys with others, I found my true calling. It was my job and my ministry.

Every single day, I got to bring the joy of sewing to my dear friends all over the world. I have had the blessed fortune to touch many lives through my teaching and travels, and I have worked with some of the finest people I know. We created an immensely popular PBS television show (*Martha's Sewing Room*), an internationally read magazine (*Sew Beautiful*), scores of books (about 55), and a worldwide following for the Martha Pullen School of Art Fashion conferences. I have had the great privilege of teaching sewing on six of the seven continents. Some of my greatest sewing teaching events have been on mission trips in Jamaica, Brazil and Africa with my church. Our wholesale/retail business reaches all over the world. After helping pack some boxes one day Joe told me, "Martha I packed one box for Iceland and one for Israel today. Never would I have dreamed that our little shop would have grown to a business that would reach all over the world."

Passion is Not Enough

I am quite a fan of Michael Gerber's books centered on the E-Myth. He has worked trying to discover why "people start companies, why so few succeed, what those that do succeed have in common, and what lessons others can learn from the dialogue I've been engaged in with these owners." Knowing how many mistakes I made over the years has made me passionate about sharing ideas that I know will work to help others avoid some of these mistakes. Knowing "things which have worked for me and many others" makes me passionate about sharing these ideas and techniques also.

In fact, entrepreneurship, once discovered, is a way of life. Once you open the doors to the creative entrepreneurial energy within you, it just keeps rolling out, in continuous joy, misery, joy, joy, misery, joy, joy and joy.

—Michael Gerber

You might say that my example, Martha Pullen Company, is an exceptional one, and I would agree that not everyone is quite as blessed or crazy as I have been. With that being said I personally know hundreds of people just like me who have been extremely successful in deciding to turn their hobbies into some sort of business—large or small. I can say that many of them love their jobs and what they have created for themselves and their families. I might also add that some did not plan carefully enough to know what they were getting into and their business dreams did not work out at all. Writing this book was critical for me because of the passion I have in describing the written planning process which I believe is necessary before one even decides if a dream can become a miracle called a business. If their dreams are only going to be in their heads then I have no help for them.

One of the questions I ask everyone is about his/her business idea. Is it a good idea? Is it a bad idea? Michael Gerber says, "There are no other ideas worth talking about. If it's a good idea it's worth doing. If it's a bad idea, get out as quickly as you can." I believe sometimes one does not really know the answer to that question until one gets into the written business plan.

I must say again that passion is not enough. Passion is only the very beginning. That is one of the main reasons I wrote this book. I truly do care about others who dream about starting and growing a business. I want them to try to understand the realities of starting and running a small business and why it might or might not be a good idea for them personally. Through exercises in this book I believe these concepts can be examined completely so an intelligent decision can be made. I must say that I am regularly astonished to discover the number of people who carry in their hearts the very same dream of starting a business. Hardly a month passes without some hopeful young mother or grandmother asking me for advice. So many people are secretly considering what sort of business they might open as soon as possible. The whole prospect of starting a business can feel so unfamiliar that even approaching the topic feels bewildering. If you have little more than your own personal instincts to rely upon, coupled with bits of advice from friends or magazines, you might feel like a weathervane in a windstorm as you try to decide where to start.

Thankfully, that doesn't discourage most people from continuing to dream. Dreams need prayer, legs and massive written planning. Most people believe that becoming your own boss feels like a dream come true, and I know they are right—if the business works successfully. I am the last person in the world who will deny that the chance to combine a personal passion with financial gain, and build something personally meaningful by working with what you love, has been one of the most rewarding parts of my life, after God and my family. Without any reserve, I encourage anyone who dreams of starting his/her own business to go right ahead and start massive written planning. They should open the business only after they have fully considered their plans and understand many of the possibilities—both good and bad-that lay ahead.

I Jumped Right In—Not Much Planning

Of course, I did not quite follow that advice back when I began, and my early experiences in business were rocky to say the least. I think if people knew how many blunders, both big and small, I have made on my journey to building a business, they might think twice about coming to me for advice on how to sell a simple pitcher of lemonade. I have made lots of stupid mistakes! You can be quite certain that when I first hung that "Open" sign on the front door, I had no idea how much work lay ahead of me.

Only by the grace of God, the support of my husband and family, the help of a very dedicated team at Martha Pullen Company, some long hours and very hard but fulfilling work, and perhaps a certain amount of stubborn determination, we have been very successful. All along the way, our team, customers, and mentors have taught me so much about what it means to run a successful business. For that reason, I have decided to dispense a little advice of my own. My sincere hope is to try to pass along the lessons that I have learned along the way, to save others a lot of grief and I might add wasted money and time, so they can achieve personal success that much quicker — and with far fewer bumps than I encountered.

Critical Advice for You if You Are Thinking About Opening a Business Based on Your Passion

One of the first New York City Broadway plays that I ever saw when I was a little girl was *The Sound of Music*. Oh how I loved the words of the song, "Climb every mountain, Ford every stream, Follow every rainbow, Till you find your dream." Sounds quite romantic and inspirational, doesn't it?

Napoleon Hill was quite a popular "business writer" a number of years ago. One of his most quoted statements from his book *Think and Grow Rich* was "Whatever the mind can conceive and believe, it can achieve." That is almost as bad as "climb every mountain and follow every rainbow" to be sure of business success! Climbing mountains and dreaming big dreams are not the keys to success in business. If you are going to climb Pike's Peak to find your business dream just go ahead and jump off while you are at the top since that will do about as much for your business success as that climb did. Sound harsh? Great passion, ability and dreams are not enough for business success. Even achieving a lot of public acclaim for your hobby is not enough for business success. Now that I have burst your fantasy bubble let's get down to some very hard work to see if your dream can become a reality.

"Half-Time Work" and Other Important Questions

Being willing to work "half time" is critical. Now what is "half time?" Choose whichever 12 hours of every day you want to work—7 days a week. Owning your own business is totally consuming and there is no such thing as "work-life" balance which one reads so much about. Tradeoffs are necessary. Do you love giving dinner parties? Travel for fun and recreation? Participating in lots of clubs and school activities? Attending every little league ball game or practice? Shopping except for necessities? Lunch with friends? Long phone conversations? Evenings watching lots of television? Reading the latest fiction novel? Juggle those right on out of your life. You cannot be perfect and do it all. Even if you are a woman! I think it is necessary to have the whole family's approval for this business because everyone is going to get less of your time. Everyone needs to learn how to independently do homework, dishes, and even meal preparation for the whole family. No one older than six years old is "too young" to run the washing machine, dryer or vacuum cleaner. Are you still interested in that "passion" business? My story is yet to come in this book you are now holding. This book is as much a warning label as it is anything else. I do not want to mislead anyone about the journey God led me through to build this multimillion-dollar a year company. I also do not want to tell you it cannot be done! God did do it through me, my family and an incredible team of people who helped me all along the way. With major work there is a great possibility that you and God can do it too. I am attempting throughout this book to keep you from making some of the mistakes I made.

Small Business: Hard Realities

I know it is not easy. According to the SBA, almost half of all small businesses fail in their first five years. Some of those businesses were simply in the wrong place at the wrong time, and others invested unwisely in too much equipment or inventory. I would guess that a majority of those business owners were simply unprepared. They had not fully considered their plans, or they had no idea what lay ahead. I have to add here that my guess would be that prayer was not a regular part of their planning. I believe with all of my heart that they had no written plan or a very incomplete written plan. I had no written plan for ten years. Almost every business owner that I have spoken with has no written plan!

I believe that such oversights happen with greater frequency among those of us who have decided to turn our hobbies into a business. There is something intriguing about following your passion and making money that blinds us to the thornier realities of business. You become so enamored of your hobby, for one reason or another, that you are biased to make bad decisions, putting your business at risk right from the start. It might be a simple failure to recognize that everyone may not appreciate what you find so compelling about your hobby.

You might even say that a hobbyist is like a dewy-eyed mother who can't imagine how anyone else could not find her baby the most uniquely delightful creature ever born. The problem is not that anyone thinks the baby is unattractive or bothersome. On the contrary, most people agree that babies are generally very cute. Here is the key—for everyone except her closest friends and family, there are a whole lot of babies out there, and when push comes to shove, it is hard for most to see the difference between them.

The same holds true for most early hobby-into-business dreams. The key is to maintain a proper perspective on your hobby, looking closely and objectively at your own attitudes and assumptions about your business ideas. The most common delusions that hobbyists fall into can be neatly grouped into two categories: the "everyone is going to love my idea" fantasy, as well as the "this will be easy" fallacy. I have fallen victim to both on occasion. As you will find out during this book one of the main reason businesses fail is because of a lack of major written planning in the beginning. I think this was the main reason I made no money in the first ten years of my business. Because of the grace of God and Joe Pullen's working six days a week in the dental office to pay our bills, we were able to survive until we got help, figured out that we had to do some major planning, and made some major changes to survive.

One of My Many Failures

There isn't one senior manager in this company who hasn't been associated with a product that flopped. That includes me. It's like learning to ski. If you're not falling down, you're not leaning.
—William Smithburg

All throughout this book I plan to share my failures with you as well as my successes. I have had lots of both! I tried to launch a magazine based on my own personal attraction to an idea, without thinking through whether others would really respond to it. This failure began through my daughter Joanna, who had begun participating in pageants, and especially loved the talent and speech competitions. I noticed that my boys could compete in football, basketball, and soccer and Joanna loved to compete in dance and speech. It seemed pageants were the only place to compete in those areas. I had entered many pageants in high school and college with the idea of getting scholarship money. When combined my winnings from pageants actually paid for over a year of my college expenses at the University of Alabama. One of my childhood dreams was to be Miss America and the closest I ever got was as a talent scholarship winner in a Miss Alabama preliminary! I won $300 which was a lot of money in 1962! I did a song/dance from the Broadway play, *The Unsinkable Molly Brown*. Now back to my failing magazine venture.

I was thrilled to share my own lifelong love for dance and theater with Joanna, and make her beautiful evening gowns. Flush with the growing success of my sewing business, I decided that I would start a magazine dedicated to pageants and talent contests, focusing on dance costumes, evening wear designs and patterns, manners, interview skills and public speaking. Have I shared with you yet that my undergraduate degree was in speech and theatre? This seemed the perfect place to combine my love of sewing, theatre and speaking! *Pageants and Talent* did not succeed! It cost me a lot of money.

I thought the idea was absolutely brilliant. We would cover the biggest pageants, write stories about the latest trends, and offer patterns for mothers to make their children's dresses. I especially enjoyed sitting in the "press runway" section at the Miss America pageant! I guess that was one of the nicest things about this financial disaster magazine. I finally got to the Miss America pageant!

The only problem was that I had not researched whether any customers were interested in the same thing. What I quickly discovered was that many of the designer costume patterns we offered were carried as completed costumes by New York houses for about $50, while our intricate ones could cost up to $500 to make. I ended up folding the entire magazine venture as a costly mistake, but I learned an important lesson. In the future do a survey to find out if anyone other than Martha would like a product!! I did absolutely no market research on this subject nor did I even call my *Sew Beautiful* magazine advertisers to see if they were interested in advertising in this new magazine. I just did it! It failed! I had a lot of fun producing the magazine but I did not have a lot of fun paying the bills!

The Second Failing Magazine

Sew Beautiful, our very successful magazine was thriving. Once again I thought about a second magazine. We started *Fancywork* which was to feature more hand embroidery and let *Sew Beautiful* feature more smocking and machine work. My incorrect reasoning was that people would buy *Sew Beautiful* AND *Fancywork* since I knew our customers loved both hand and machine work. WRONG! They began to choose whether to subscribe to either *Sew Beautiful* or *Fancywork* depending on which area of heirloom sewing they really liked best! *Fancywork* was a gorgeous publication. *Sew Beautiful* was and is still a gorgeous publication. Our readers only wanted one! You might remember some words from the poem of Robert Burns written in 1785, *To A Mouse on Turning Up in Her Nest with the Plough.*

> *But little Mouse, you are not alone,*
> *In proving foresight may be vain:*
> *The best laid schemes of mice and men*
> *Go often awry,*

And leave us nothing but grief and pain,
For promised joy!

We closed *Fancywork* fulfilling those subscriptions with issues of *Sew Beautiful* magazine. More is not necessarily better. I learned to do well what was successful and not water down success trying to do something else. Well, hopefully I learned that!

It Is Not Easy To Run a Business!

The wise are cautious and avoid danger; fools plunge ahead
with reckless confidence.
—Proverbs 14:16

I also quickly learned how "not so easy" it is to run a business, even though it felt wonderfully easy while it was my hobby. When you decide to start a business, it will very selfishly demand almost all of your time, only a small portion of which will be in any way related to all the things that make your hobby such a personal pleasure.

To be very blunt, once you decide to make your hobby into a business, you may actually end up sacrificing, or at a minimum transforming, the type of relaxation and fun that your hobby once provided you. The reasons are simple and plain. First of all, in order to make a profit, you will need to change your approach to the craft by giving yourself enough time to handle the bookkeeping and business demands it will require. That can be an unexpected disappointment to anyone who thought she was going to be able to knit beautiful sweaters all day. You may instead find that your hobby time is going to have to bump into what you formerly called "time off," when you watched television or socialized with friends. Even worse, you may quickly find that the very thing you love to do most is precisely what you have the least time to perform. Have you ever heard the statement, "The cobbler's children have no shoes?" Well craft business owners many times have none of the products for themselves personally that they lovingly teach others how to do.

Pretty quickly into the course of my business, I stopped almost all sewing for pleasure. There were simply not enough hours in the day for me to devote to my family while maintaining the daily operations of my store. When I did any heirloom sewing, it was simply to try out a new technique in preparation for a teaching class. The rest of the time, I was either teaching classes or tracking down inventory for my shop or managing the books or working with clients or writing new directions or writing for our magazine or traveling all over the world drumming up new interest and new customers to love heirloom sewing. At this time I have taught sewing on six of the seven continents and I do not intend to go to the South Pole to teach penguins how to sew!

Genius is 1% inspiration, and 99% perspiration.
—Thomas Edison

I'm convinced that about half of what separates the successful entrepreneurs from the non-successful ones is pure perseverance.
—Steve Jobs

Not Much Time for Your Craft, Personally, However....

Now let me take one small moment to temper my words, and make sure you clearly understand the flip side of all this. If your heart is invested in your business, and you believe in what you are doing, there is no "net loss" in any of the supposed sacrifices that you are making. The transformation of your hobby into a business is nothing less than the conversion of your passion into something bigger, broader, and many times better. There may be some awkward adjustments along the way because you have grown attached to the joy your hobby offered to you personally. Possibly you might discover that you have taken your hobby, and used it as a vehicle to revolutionize your entire life and the lives of many others!

I can truly say that teaching others to sew, embroider and machine embroider is actually more fun than my taking the time to sew myself. I am a third generation school teacher and teaching others and seeing the lights in their eyes over the new found pleasure of heirloom sewing is more joyful than a whole day at the sewing machine for me. One day I intend to sew again just for fun. Right now I am having too much joy to fill my life sharing the joy of sewing through many avenues.

People rarely succeed unless they have fun in what they are doing.
— Dale Carnegie

That is the true payoff for all the discipline and determination that you will need to exercise. Of course, over time, as you continue to invest effort into your business, it hopefully, will start to actually earn you money, and that is a feeling of incredible accomplishment. It is also just plain smart. By taking the time now to create a whole new revenue stream in your life, you are investing in your future and your eventual retirement.

Even more fulfilling is the sense of empowerment. When you are working hard to build something that is personally important, it feels great. You feel confident and independent, knowing that your effort is creating something meaningful and real. Instead of just going through the motions to pull down a paycheck, you will be doing something that you truly believe in, and which will bring you satisfaction in all kinds of ways. It will literally feed your soul. I love earning my living in the sewing industry. I earn more money in this business than I ever could have earned teaching school. I love knowing that the harder I work the more money I can make. I have been able to do so much more financially for other people and organizations than I ever could have done teaching school. I have been able to travel more and to send others on mission trips. Financially this business has been good to me. I do not want to understate the importance of working this hard to have financial independence. God provided this for me through this company. I also know how many jobs I have been able to provide for other people. All of these things feel right to me.

Lastly, and just as important on a day-to-day level, you will really be able to gain more control over your own life. You can own your own hours and have a greater control over your day. If you want to stop in the middle of the day and go for a walk to clear your head, the only person stopping you is you. You will find yourself with a big personal stake in your own everyday life. For me and so many others, especially home based business owners, I wanted to be able to be free to pick up my children from school and to go to any meetings or games or rehearsals they had. I wanted to be able work at home when they were sick or just when I wanted to. I did not want to follow some one else's "hours in a building" requirements.

G.R.A.C.E. in My Life

> *Whatever is good and perfect comes down to us from God our Father, who created all the lights in the heavens. He never changes or casts a shifting shadow.*
> —James 1:17

These days, after more than thirty years of hard work, I have reached a point in my career where people look at all that I have accomplished and ask me with a certain amount of astonishment, as if I had somehow launched everything in one month's time, "How in the world did you do all this?"

The answer, of course, is that God gets all the credit. I could never have done any of it without His guidance and help. In times of great difficulty, the Bible is my number one comfort, and I always fare much better when I have enough sense to pray for His assistance, rather than spinning in circles trying to work things out in isolation from Him. My major problem is that I do not pray more and spend more time with God. I need to spend a lot more time reading my Bible. I will not deny that there are hundreds of different ways to be successful starting a business and I certainly have not cornered the market on common sense. I also believe that there are some basic principles, values, and methods that hold true under any circumstance.

I mention them because I want to deliver courage to those who are still undecided or hesitating at the cusp of a big decision, and let them know that while there are lots of details that they must master, and lots of specifics to always keep in mind—there are always some fundamentals they can follow, which will allow them to trust in themselves and their dreams. The planning chapter of this book is the most important place to start if you are truly thinking about a business. A written plan is beyond critical before you even think about opening your doors whatever kind of doors those are.

Let's dwell upon this idea for a moment, because so often, behind all those specific business advice questions I am asked by hopeful entrepreneurs, I hear a deeper question about whether I believe their dreams can really come true. When they ask me about my own story, or how to open a store, or if I think their designs might sell, what I really hear them asking is, "Should I believe in myself and take that first step?" My heartfelt answer to that deeper question is always, "Absolutely!" Far too often, I have met people who would make fantastic entrepreneurs, but they simply do not dare to take the first steps. Those first steps are ALWAYS prayer and a written plan—an extensive written plan.

This book is for everyone who is ready to take those first steps, but feels as though he/she needs guidance. I cannot help you see exactly what is ahead of course, but I can at least help you to begin to prepare for the challenges ahead. Planning and running a business is an everyday challenge, and I mean every single day. When you decide to start a business, you are making a choice to attempt to transform a part of your life into something better. That is how you should understand it from the start. Your new business will confront you with a set of choices and decisions that you will need to navigate. Even with major written plans all along the way you will be forced to make business choices without enough information, and decisions based partly on data, but largely on intuition. If you feel unprepared and hesitant, because you do not have enough context to make the choice, it can be agonizing. Joe has always said, "Martha after much prayer and planning you simply have to choose and decide."

Joe was right. From deciding to start the television show, and on past *Sew Beautiful* magazine, the Internet business, through every decision and challenge, there have always been a few basic business virtues that I have relied upon. Without these virtues, I would not have made it. They are the most important tools I possess, because in any situation I can turn to them and get through any difficulty.

I have believed so much in these fundamentals, I have created an acronym to help me remember them. These business virtues are based on my own personal experiences, and underscored by a solemn belief in what the Bible teaches us, along with timeless wisdom from some of America's greatest entrepreneurs. As you think about starting a business, I pray that you consider them closely.

I sincerely believe that the most powerful way to build a business is with **G.R.A.C.E.** It allows you to overcome obstacles and properly count your blessings. The reason is very simple—practicing these virtues every day will make you a better person, and the better a person you are, the better a business you will run. If you can run your business with **G.R.A.C.E.**, then you will be successful—no matter what the financial outcomes. Of course I want you to be financially successful but there are other successes in business in addition to money. **G.R.A.C.E.** is really my business philosophy and has been for many years.

Within **G.R.A.C.E.** are the five essential ingredients, the five basic personal qualities that you will consistently need to return to and cultivate.
God: God owns the business. He is the CEO as well as the CFO.
Resilience: An ability to bounce back from any setback.
Action: A passion for the boldness of doing over talking.
Creativity: Let yourself see things through your own unique perspective.
Enthusiasm: A joyful willingness to go the extra mile.

Of course, no one has monopolized these virtues. Every day I learn a little more about what it means to practice them. Truly making these qualities a part of your business means much more than just crossing them off your checklist, like paying bills each month. It means dedicating yourself to trying to make improvements in these areas, to pushing yourself in little ways to getting better and better every day.

G for God

God is the CEO and the CFO of my company. I place God before all else in my business. Every inventory slip, every receipt and every check belongs to God. Many people have written me letters of appreciation for the devotionals that I send out weekly in my newsletter. They find inspiration in my scripture selections and my thoughts for them. They especially like knowing that they are purchasing products from a Christian business. God does not need me but He can use me if I choose to be used.

Bringing the word of God openly into our business has allowed us to minister to many people. Let me carefully add that I did not become an openly Christian company simply in order to gain customers or for any financial gains. I began to share the good news with my customers because I reached a point in my life, at age 39, when God had become the focal point of my whole life, and that included my business. I felt and still feel that this business is my ministry in sharing the Gospel and in bringing encouragement as well as the joy of sewing to women all over the world.

> *Jesus came and told his disciples, "I have been given all authority in heaven and on earth. Therefore, go and make disciples of all the nations, baptizing them in the name of the Father and the Son and the Holy Spirit. Teach these new disciples to obey all the commands I have given you. And be sure of this. I am with you always, even to the end of the age."*
> —Matthew 28:18-20

I have always said that all the credit for my success goes entirely to God. The Bible is an endless source of comfort to me, as is knowing that God's hand has determined the path of my business from its early days—even before I began giving Him the credit. Running an effective business means praying and thinking, and then praying some more. There are many who say that entering business means joining all the others who run the "rat race." Well my response is that by allowing God into my business, I have transformed that "race" into "**G.R.A.C.E.**"

God Owns All the Checkbooks In the World

I should mention that God was not always an acknowledged part of my business. He certainly owned my business as God owns all businesses. He owned my checkbook and He knew exactly what was going to happen to my business. By the way, He owns all checkbooks! It was simply that I did not understand that fully yet. Although I had been a member of the church my whole life and I loved the church and God, I did not really hear the true message of God's Word until my middle years. I remember very clearly the day that I turned over my business completely to God.

> *This is what the Lord says: "Stop at the crossroads and look around. Ask for the old, godly way, and walk in it. Travel its path, and you will find rest for your souls."*
> —Jeremiah 6:16

I was still what some might call a "baby" Christian. It was only one year earlier that I had asked Jesus Christ to become the Lord and Master of my life, and to live in my heart as "CEO." My business was growing and our sales were expanding, but I had cash flow problems that left us more financially stretched than ever. My husband, Joe, who ran a very successful dental practice, could help us cover bills during the difficult months, but we had reached a crossroads. Enough time had passed, where we could no longer fool ourselves into claiming that the business was still in "start-up" mode, and I had decided that I could no longer keep sinking our own personal money into the business. Moreover, I was not willing to allow us to go into significant debt. The business needed to stay afloat on its own, or I was going to quit.

Do you remember in the introduction of this book where I shared the story of God's parting the Red Sea for the Israelites to go through to safety? This story I am about to tell you is just one of my "Red Sea" experiences in my business. There have been so many.

I owed the Swiss fabric company that supplied our fabrics and embroideries almost $23,000, and I could not order anything more until I had settled that debt. On the books, I had over $50,000 in accounts receivable, but only $100 in my bank account. The month was late December, and I could not count on receiving even a fraction of those payments, because they would not come due until late January. Even then people would not pay until several weeks later if I were very lucky. My situation was precarious—I had to have my Swiss order in order to satisfy Easter demand, and if I waited until late January to pay, the order would not come on time. I needed to pay no later than January 15 for the order to arrive about a week later. I was not willing to borrow any more money.

At church that Sunday, our pastor stated that we should give to God not only our successes, but also our failures. "He will take them," said our pastor, "both the good and the bad, strength and weakness, and transform them into something greater." That felt like a revelation. Did that mean I could give him my entire business—the disappointments and mistakes included? Joe encouraged me to offer the whole business to God, including my failures, and place its future entirely in His hands.

> *Give all your worries and cares to God,*
> *for he cares about you.*
> —1 Peter 5:7

The very next day, I gave my business to God, fully and completely, in the very same way that I had completely opened my heart to allow God to truly enter my life. I gave God all the joy of sharing my favorite things with my dearest customers, and I gave God the happiness of bringing together so many people in a community of sewing, but most importantly at that very minute, I gave Him the complete financial disaster that my business faced that month.

I had agonized for days over the problem, but as I placed the matter entirely in God's hands, a weight suddenly lifted from my chest, and I felt better. I knew at that moment that by placing the business in God's hands, and trusting God totally, that I could live with whatever He decided.

I was a young Christian, and foolishly tried to tell God what He already knew. "Please God," I prayed, "I need $23,000 so I can wire Switzerland to release my new order for fabric. I need my customers to pay me now." I did not ask for a miracle streak of new sales, just that my business customers would settle up what they already owed me, rather than waiting until late January or February.

> *Morning, noon, and night I cry out in my distress, and the*
> *LORD hears my voice.*
> —Psalm 55:17

It turned out that God had much more in store for me than simply having me fold up the shop and walk away. Within a week (early in January) and completely beyond my wildest speculation, I had received over $25,000 from my various customers. As my bookkeeper told me the unexpected news, I felt chills up my spine. God had decided to keep the business afloat as part of His plan. I was jumping up and down thanking God. He had opened the "Red Sea" for me and my busines!

> *Be courageous! Let us fight bravely to save our people and the cities of our God. May the LORD's will be done.*
> —2 Samuel 10:12

From that moment forward, I have celebrated every success in His name, and trusted each crisis to His guidance. To run a Christian business serves both as an inspiration to others, and a comfort to yourself, knowing that God is providing His influence to bear on the business. Let me state here that I know that God might not always keep my business running as I pray. I just know that it is running according to His will whatever that might be.

R for Resilience

Many of life's failures are people who did not realize how close they were to success when they gave up.
—Thomas Edison

Everyone falls down and everyone has setbacks. What counts far more than avoiding mistakes, is your ability to recover and bounce back from them. The moment you start feeling sorry for yourself, or question yourself, you have submitted to defeat. A mistake only becomes a failure after you have decided to quit.

> *So let us come boldly to the throne of our gracious God. There we will receive his mercy, and we will find grace to help us when we need it most.*
> —Hebrews 4:16

I heard a wonderful story about the start of the L.L.Bean Company, a business whose customer service philosophy I absolutely love. It turns out that L.L.Bean had a very shaky start, but its owner demonstrated the kind of resilience and confidence that is crucial to success. After years of duck hunting in the woods and marshes of Maine, the company's founder, Mr. Leon Leonwood Bean, was tired of having cold, wet feet, so in 1901 he designed a new kind of rubber-soled boot to keep feet perfectly dry. He felt so sure about his idea that he immediately commissioned one hundred pairs and sent an advertisement to a list of Maine-licensed hunters. Every pair sold almost immediately, but just as quickly, to his horror, 90 pairs were returned when the rubber sole separated from the upper leather.

Given the emerging state of his business, L.L. Bean might have decided to close up his shop, simply figuring that he was not a good businessman. Instead, he did something so remarkable that it has become the trademark of his company to this very day. He immediately refunded everyone's money—every single dime to each customer—and went back to the drawing board. He quickly corrected the problem and created an even better boot, this time making sure to thoroughly test it himself. He sent out another mailing, unconditionally guaranteeing his boots' quality, and the rest is history. His famous "Bean's Hunting Shoe" and his unconditional money-back guarantee quickly earned the respect of hunters everywhere. Today, his company earns almost $1.4 billion per year.

You conquer by continuing. At every stage of your business, you will experience setbacks. Friends and family may question your ideas, deals will fall through, inventory won't sell and products will break. The only important question is how you decide to handle it. Behind every great success story are a dozen stories about persevering through difficult times. Bouncing back is the key. Pray hard for God to help you.

It is not whether you get knocked down, it is whether you get up again.
—Vince Lombardi

That does not mean that resilience just adds up to being so completely thick-skinned that nothing can possibly faze you. On the contrary, you can't just bulldoze your way into business, disregarding the opinions of colleagues and customers alike. True resilience means staying sensitive to the mistakes you make—studying and learning from them—and bouncing back anyway.

L.L. Bean knew he had a great idea, and that simply failing to build his boot properly was not a true failure. He understood the lesson for exactly what it was—a chance to improve the product, bounce back, and make his business even better.

Resilience mean listening to you customers, adapting to good suggestions, and making your business better and better. The strength to face up to your mistakes, dust yourself off, and start over again is essential.

It Couldn't Be Done

Somebody said it couldn't be done,
but he with a chuckle replied
that "maybe it couldn't ," but he would be one who
wouldn't say so till he'd tried.
So he buckled right in with the trace of a grin
on his face. If he worried he hid it.
He started to sing as he tackled the thing
that couldn't be done, and he did it.
Somebody scoffed: "Oh, you'll never do that;
at least no one ever has done it;"
But he took off his coat and he took off his hat,
and the first thing we knew he'd begun it.
With a lift of his chin and a bit of a grin,
without any doubting or quiddit,
he started to sing as he tackled the thing
that couldn't be done and he did it.
There are thousands to tell you it cannot be done
there are thousands to prophesy failure;
there are thousands to point out to you, one by one,
the dangers that wait to assail you.
But just buckle in with a bit of a grin,
just take off your coat and go to it;
Just start to sing as you tackle the thing
that "cannot be done," and you'll do it.

—Edgar A. Guest

A for Action

In life, dreaming does not count. Taking action makes things happen. In the business world action means written plans. I have a very long section in this book on planning. A very dear friend of mine has always told me, "The harder I work, the luckier I get," and I know exactly what she means. I have been very blessed in my life—but I also know why. God has control of all of the blessings and He has showered them on me for sure.

What some consider "good luck" often has a lot more to do with placing yourself in the right place at the right time. I don't believe in "luck" but rather in blessings. I considered myself the most fortunate young woman in all of the country the day I got to meet President John F. Kennedy. The event was the 1963 Orange Bowl, and I was a cheerleader for the Crimson Tide (University of Alabama). I was thrilled beyond thrilled to be a part of the Orange Bowl not only getting to cheer at the game but also getting to march in the parade the night before in Miami. When I learned from listening to the radio on the long drive to Miami, Florida that President Kennedy would be in the stands, on the Oklahoma side, I made a firm resolution in my mind. I was determined that somehow I would meet him. This was going to take some action of a very creative nature.

The game began. Halftime came, and I slipped away from my cheerleading squad, and ran as fast as I could across the Oklahoma end zone onto our rival's sideline, to get a closer look at the President. I meant to just look at him but upon seeing him up close I began to sob. Big sobs required me to wipe my eyes while holding my crepe paper pom-poms. Since they were red you can imagine the red streaks on my face. President Kennedy must have felt sorry for me because he whispered something to his secret service men who travelled down the bleachers to greet me. Their words, "The President has invited you up to meet him," were magical to a nineteen year's old heart.

They grasped me firmly by each arm and led me to the President for an introduction. I felt so surprised and stunned that he had to ask my name. By the time he introduced me to guests in the box-the governor of Florida, Peter Lawford and others, I realized that I was still sobbing. He said, "What is your name?" I also realized that I could not remember my name! Since I was a speech major, that was especially funny to the press corps that began interviewing me as soon as I went back down to the field. I finally realized that President Kennedy had been standing paying attention to me for a while and that I really needed to go back down to the field. I finally blurted out, "Thank you Mr. President for allowing me to come up to meet you." I never told him my name. Before I thanked him he said, "Your team is doing well out there." Indeed we did. We beat Oklahoma 17-3 and once again became the national football champions. I might add that two high achieving people led Alabama to that title—Coach Bear Bryant and Joe Namath.

I think every photographer covering the Orange Bowl was there to snap a picture of me with the President and most reporters were there to interview me upon my arrival back on the field from the box. The next day the photograph of my wiping my eyes and President Kennedy's leaning over to smile at me was sent over AP and UP; that picture made many of the front pages of newspapers around the country. *The New York Times* was on strike at that time so that picture was on the front page of a Long Island paper which was serving as the main paper in the greater New York City area. When the Orange Bowl special edition came out in Miami the day following the Orange Bowl guess who had a half page doing a cheerleading jump? You guessed it. When I arrived back at the University of Alabama for the January semester to begin, letters came from all over the country simply addressed, Martha Campbell, University of Alabama cheerleader, Tuscaloosa, AL. Most included a picture cut out from a local newspaper.

I still enjoy reading some of the captions underneath the various pictures of President Kennedy and me from various parts of the Orange Bowl edition of the *Miami Herald* and *The Miami News*.

"Alabama Cheer Leader Martha Campbell Had Plenty to Cheer About...She Met The President And Her Team Won." "Everybody Falls Apart—-It's rough when both the winners and losers get all shook up-but that's exactly what happened at yesterday's Orange Bowl game. Three pictures at top show how Alabama cheerleader Martha Campbell simply disintegrated (with joy, or something) after President Kennedy summoned her to his box for personal greetings. Martha's team won."

"'Bama Cheerleader Martha Campbell Meets the President....Then The First Shock Wave Hits. She Bursts Into Tears. After All, Very Few Cheerleaders Get To Shake Hands with JFK."

"Now Who Could Resist A Strawberry Blonde? There stood the strawberry blonde, waving her Alabama pom-pom for the President of the United States. Even Presidents notice strawberry blondes and thus John Fitzgerald Kennedy beckoned to Martha Campbell, 19, an Alabama Cheerleader from Scottsboro, Alabama. 'Who me?' said Martha and the President was smiling. 'Come up.' He said. From nowhere, a policeman gently took her arm and escorted her upward into the stadium. Martha was a very happy girl. Very happy girls cry. Suddenly she was weeping big soggy tears. 'Hello,' said the President. 'Your team is doing mighty well, isn't it?' They shook hands. That's precisely when Martha began to blubber. A sophomore speech major at the University of Alabama she was absolutely speechless. Not unkindly, the President laughed."

"'I could not even remember my name,' she bawled a few minutes later, jumping up and down excitedly, which is the fashion of cheerleaders. 'This is so silly. I just looked at him and started crying.' It took her six minutes to dry her eyes." (*The Miami Herald,* Wednesday, January 2, 1963)

"One Touch of JFK Starts Happy Tears...The President made a pretty girl cry—but it wasn't his fault. She just gave way emotionally under the strain of shaking his hand. It all happened spontaneously... Martha Campbell a blonde 19 year old Alabama cheerleader was on the 50 yard line facing the south stands. She looked up at the Presidential box and waved a pom-pom that was part of her costume at him and happened to catch his eye. 'He beckoned me to come up,' she related ecstatically. She shook hands with the President and then with Florida Governor Farris Bryant. On the way down the steps to the sidelines, she suddenly dissolved into tears, and when she reached the other cheerleaders-who clustered around her she was shaking uncontrollably. Tears coursed down her cheeks and she was too overcome to talk. Finally she managed to gasp out, 'I don't know what came over me but suddenly I got so weak I started to cry. I don't know why,' said Martha. 'He was very nice. He shook my hand and said he was glad to meet me.'" (*The Miami News,* January 2, 1963)

I would like to include one more newspaper article that appeared in *The Anniston Star* after that event. It was written by Dr. Harry Lang who was a friend of mine and a retired professor from the University of Alabama. I would suppose this would be considered a press release. For your business writing a poetic story about an event surely might be included in your newspaper. It certainly would not hurt to try. I loved this story about my meeting the President.

That Heroine at Miami

In the mountainous highlands of Western Scotland there is a haunt known as the Valley of Glencoe. It was the home valley of the Campbell Clan, and the tradition glorifies the clan for its courage and it unhesitant response to the challenge from the South when Celtic possession was endangered by foreign foes.

Surrounding the quiet valley are the high mountains one of which, Buachaille Evite Mor, which being translated means "The Great Shepherd of Etive," in Summer or Winter guards the quiet homes of a peace loving people.

From all over the world tourists come year by year to stop at Oban for the wonders of a Western sunset, and go on to Fort William to rest under the shadow of Ben Nevis, but the climax is the Valley of Glencoe, where one may still feel the refrain of one of its famous songs: "The Campbells are coming!"

So it was at Miami. The Campbells were there in the person of one of true descent from the Valley of Glencoe. She is a University of Alabama Co-ed and a Chi Omega girl, her name being Martha Campbell.

From the threatening west strong, brave citizens from the plains of Oklahoma came dashing at Coach Paul Bryant's defending team of players. They deserved applause and even pride at risking battle with the University of Alabama team.

But they were plainsmen, notoriously unpoetic, and defective in the mystique of spiritual vision which belongs so obviously to the people of the hills and mountains.

So, they did not think to discover whether there might be a young lady descendant of one of the Campbells from the Valley of Glencoe. But Martha Campbell was there as a cheerleader for the braves of Alabama.

Forgetful of her name, remembering only that she was a Campbell, and with tears of dedication and the joy of victory to shake the hand of a fellow-Celtic, President Kennedy-for the Irish were Celts also-that accounted for victory for the Valley of Glencoe.

All Alabama hails that fine Celt from Scottsboro and with her we may have shed a tear of joy. For we too may forget the name but we shall not forget what was the Valley of Glencoe for Oklahoma!

—The Anniston Star

Looking back, I suppose that moment did not actually change my life in any particular way besides briefly making me the envy of all my friends, but it has had a lasting impact on my personal feelings. I felt intensely grateful to have been noticed by the President of the United States, and I believe that episode truly gave me a new sort of confidence. Crossing the field to the other side taught me that if I dared to do something about my dreams, I might actually succeed.

Action starts wheels moving toward making something happen. This is a very important personal quality that many acknowledge. Action is essential to any business. It is the antithesis of procrastination. It is the opposite of avoidance. Action means sweeping in when you realize that there is something missing, and doing it.

It means setting the example for others around you. Action is tremendously inspiring in its pure form. Most people are habituated to a world in which people put things off. Some call it procrastination—I call it lazy. Action means doing something when it is needed, not when it is convenient. In this way, it is an attitude toward what needs to get done. It is the opposite for the all-too-common practice of hoping that if you wait long enough, a problem will solve itself. Boldness is the key. Striking while the moment is right will bring a tremendous amount of energy and blessings your way. Action many times actually creates opportunities.

We have too many high sounding words, and too few actions that correspond with them.
—Warren Buffett

C for Creativity

Then the Lord said to Moses, "Look, I have specifically chosen Bezalel son of Uri, grandson of Hur, of the tribe of Judah. I have filled him with the Spirit of God, giving him great wisdom, ability, and expertise in all kinds of crafts. He is a master craftsman, expert in working with gold, silver, and bronze. He is skilled in engraving and mounting gemstones and in carving wood. He is a master at every craft! "And I have personally appointed Oholiab son of Ahisamach, of the tribe of Dan, to be his assistant. Moreover, I have given special skill to all the gifted craftsmen so they can make all the things I have commanded you to make:
—Exodus 31:1-6

God gives us creative abilities. Think of your creative knowledge in one specific area. Where are your special abilities? What skills have you been able to really develop? What skills would you really like to develop but you have simply not had the time to do so? Do you realize that God gave you all of your abilities? Do you know without a doubt that you are very creative? Everyone is creative. We are all creative in different ways but every person

Every child is an artist. The problem is how to remain an artist once we grow up.
—Pablo Picasso

is creative. God has given this gift and it is real for every person.

When it comes to business, creativity is nothing more than a talent for looking at things differently. The word "creative" intimidates so many people because they think it means the ability to paint beautiful watercolors or design a dress from scratch. Some of the most creative business ideas I have seen have come from people who simply had the cleverness to turn an idea on its head.

Truly creative people have mastered the art of looking at things like a child. Just like children, they try to see the fun in everything. Look around you. Your next business idea might be right at your feet, waiting for you to discover it.

Nimble thought can jump both sea and land.
—William Shakespeare

Sometimes a problem does not need more hard work; it simply needs a new perspective. When you bring creativity to your work, you will begin to discover new and exciting ways to approach a problem. Always nourish creativity as a discipline in your work—both in yourself and others. The playfulness that creativity requires helps to guarantee that you will not let your business go stale. Remember imagination is free. It shows us how to make reality out of possibilities or dreams.

Creativity is a skill that will serve you throughout your business, and help keep you on the path to discovery. If you are already doing something as a hobby/craft, you need to channel that same energy into your business. What you will discover is that as your business proceeds, you will need to constantly adjust to the situation, no matter how brilliant your plan may be. Creativity allows you to always reach for another star. Remember to plan in writing those creative thoughts and ideas. Creative thoughts without a written plan are truly not good in the business world. In fact they probably will not work. Write down how they will work in the business setting to see if they will make money or if they should just be wonderfully creative thoughts in your head!

Look sharply after your thoughts. They come unlooked for, like a new bird seen on your trees, and, if you turn to your usual task, disappear; and you shall never find that perception again; never, I say—but perhaps years, ages, and I know not what events and worlds may lie between you and its return.
—Ralph Waldo Emerson

If you think of an idea, WRITE IT DOWN! Always, always, keep a little notebook with you. Always make lists of ideas when they come to your brain. You never know when that creative thought might turn into something great.

I think keeping a brain bank is a great idea. I have kept "ideas" in a drawer as well as in a notebook. I have a plastic zip up pouch in my purse where I keep my receipts. I also put written ideas in that pouch. When you get home take those pages from your pocket notebook, tear them out and put them in your brain bank whatever that might be. Where can you get more ideas? I have torn out ads from magazines, written down thoughts from everywhere, torn out pages from books (those I was not going to keep), written down quotes, printed out things from my computer, photo copied sections of a book, torn out cartoons from newspapers, torn out articles from a newspaper or a magazine, printed out articles from the Internet, taken pictures many different places—the list goes on and on. I like a notebook with clear pages that I can drop items in from the top. They are easy to use and always easy to see. You can use a coffee can in your kitchen if you get lots of ideas while in the kitchen. I knew one person who kept an open kitchen drawer for an "idea drawer." Of course you can scan everything and have a computer brain bank too!

Creativity is something that you can easily develop, and we will cover some steps later in the book. It is an innate talent that all of us have in some form, and we simply need to work to allow it to express itself. Give yourself the chance to be creative. Ask God to help you. Remember God gave you that creativity in the first place.

When I am.....completely myself, entirely alone.....or during the night when I cannot sleep, it is on such occasions that my ideas flow best and most abundantly. Whence and how these ideas come I know not nor can I force them.
—Wolfgang Amadeus Mozart

E for Enthusiasm

In all that he did in the service of the Temple of God and in his efforts to follow the law and the commands, Hezekiah sought his God wholeheartedly. As a result, he was very successful.
—2 Chronicles 31:21

Allow the spirit of excitement to fill you and spread to your friends. It is contagious and delightfully enriching. Andrew Carnegie wrote, "People who are unable to motivate themselves must be content with mediocrity, no matter how impressive their other talents."

Some of our best examples of enthusiasm come from those teachers and mentors who managed to spark our own interest. To this day I cherish the memory of my high school Home Economics teacher, Mrs. Ingram. Now if the truth be told, Mrs.Ingram might not have been the most skilled seamstress, but she knew how to energize her students. I remember one day she announced that our final class project would be to create some drapes for the windows of our classroom. She gave us some rudimentary instructions on how to make drapes, and then sent us off to begin work. Of course we came back with questions, because we did not want to make any mistakes. "Girls," she said, with her bright eyes and broad smile, "you do not need to worry about that. You just go out there and do it!"

And do it we did. We bought some fabric from the Mill Ends Store with money the class had earned from a bake sale, and set to work. I am sure there were some problems with our design, but I do not remember any of that. All I remember is Mrs. Ingram's bragging on us to the entire school, saying what talented young girls we were.

For me, that is a true mentor. It is not necessarily someone who helps you develop any kind of expertise, but rather someone who lights a spark inside you. Mrs. Ingram, along with many other people along the way, awakened my own enthusiasm for sewing. I have been blessed to have many mentors!

Tell me and I forget, teach me and I may remember, involve me and I learn.
—Benjamin Franklin

When you decide to start your own business, you will need to harness your own personal enthusiasm. There will be times when the tedium of running a business, or the boredom of balancing the books will seem to have taken away all the fun from your work. The key to enthusiasm is keeping your eyes on the horizon—and knowing that all your hard work is leading to something wonderful. Always keep your dreams alive and active —make them a part of your daily life. Pray hard. When you feel a genuine enthusiasm, you can enjoy the moment and take pleasure in whatever work is in front of you. That kind of spirit is contagious and spreads naturally to both your employees and customers. People love to be around enthusiastic people, because they are full of cheer and energy. They tend to motivate others to go the extra mile, when they might be ready to quit.

Overview of G.R.A.C.E.

Now let's take a step back once more and try to put it all together. For me, the five ingredients of **G.R.A.C.E.** all fit together perfectly in the shape of a cross, like this:

G

R A C

E

God stands over everything and comes before all else. His influence shines down upon the business, and His glory is a crown over the business. He guides the business.

> *For I hold you by your right hand—I, the LORD your God.*
> *And I say to you, "Do not be afraid. I am here to help you."*
> —Isaiah 41:13

Action is at the center of the business. Without action, nothing happens. But blind or halfhearted action is just wasted effort. That is why Action is surrounded by the three other virtues that must infuse it.

> *We can make our plans, but the LORD determines our steps.*
> —Proverbs 16:9

Resilience stands beside Action and protects it like a shield, to ensure that today's disappointments and setbacks never stop you from taking Action again tomorrow.

> *And we know that God causes everything to work together for the good of those who love God and are called according to his purpose for them.*
> —Romans 8:28

Creativity stands beside Action like a lens to focus Action, showing it new ideas to develop. Creativity reveals perspectives that push Action into new directions.

> *For I can do everything through Christ who gives me strength.*
> —Philippians 4:13

Enthusiasm stands beneath Action like an underground spring that flows upward to energize it. Enthusiasm is the fuel that drives Action.

If you can bring all these qualities together in your heart, your business will have a chance of being successful. Everyone can choose to have these qualities—and I mean everyone. If you are ready to exercise these virtues, then you are possibly ready for the challenge of beginning to seriously plan a business. Notice I said plan. That means a written plan.

I have to add that you must act enthusiastically whether you feel like it or not. One of my important mentors, Sue Hausmann, the most enthusiastic person I know, was Senior Vice President of Viking/Husqvarna Sewing Machine Company. I might add that she and Herb are two of the most devout Christians I have ever know. She traveled 50 weeks out of the year either teaching sewing or going to Sweden to plan new machines and write guide books and directions. She once told me something I will never forget. She said, "Martha sometimes when I am very tired in an airport, anywhere in the world, and the planes are late or the gate has changed, I sometimes chant to myself, 'I like my job. I like my job. I love my job' as I try to run to the next gate and attempt to catch the flight. I think repeating 'I love my job' on the hard days is critical. Some days I like my job and some days I don't like it as much. It is important for me to remember that 99% of the time I do love my job."

Many of the business publications you might read will tend to obscure the basics with detailed discussion about strategy and marketing. I believe all of that is important—in the same way that it is important to balance and budget your bank account—but those are just details. If you can carry **G.R.A.C.E.** in your heart, you are ready for business. This book is my story—my journey in the business world. It is the kind of book I wish I had read before I began my business. I hope you like it and can learn from my successes as well as my failures.

> *Instead, let the Spirit renew your thoughts and attitudes.*
> —Ephesians 4:23

~ Chapter Two ~

How to Discover Your Personal Enthusiasms

> *Don't just pretend to love others. Really love them. Hate what is wrong. Hold tightly to what is good. Love each other with genuine affection, and take delight in honoring each other. Never be lazy, but work hard and serve the Lord enthusiastically.*
> —Romans 12:9-11

So we must learn how to utilize enthusiasm in order to move into that exciting and creative segment of the human race— the achievers. You will find among them total agreement that enthusiasm is the priceless ingredient of personality that helps to achieve happiness and self-fulfillment.
—Norman Vincent Peale

From the glow of enthusiasm I let the melody escape. I persue it. Breathless I catch up with it. It flies again, it disappears, it plunges into a chaos of diverse emotions. I catch it again. I seize it, I embrace it with delight...I multiply it by modulations, and at last I triumph in the first theme. There is the whole symphony.
—Ludwig Van Beethoven

The ABCD's of Following Your Dreams

How far that little candle throws its beams! So shines a good deed in a naughty world.

—Shakespeare

I sat on the wooden foldout seat in the Scottsboro Elementary School auditorium, fidgeting as the rest of the school slowly filed in. I can still recall the pleasant smell of the well-oiled wooden floors. It was early spring, and the sun had just broken through the cloudy morning sky, so school assembly felt like an unfair obstacle to recess. My fifth grade teacher, Mrs. Kent, had dryly mentioned that today's speaker was talking about magazines, so I steeled myself for another dull lecture. Although I was an attentive student, I disliked school assemblies, and although Mama always said that I was a born actress, I felt that I could hardly sit through one without melting into a puddle of frustrated boredom. One of the "tricks" that Mama taught me was that no matter how uninterested I was in a subject I could always act interested. She said this was not only good manners but it was good business. She said, "Losers act bored. Winners act interested."

As the last few classes noisily filled the auditorium, I noticed a tall gentleman onstage, seated next to Mr. Dean, our school principal. This stranger dressed with a bit of city flair, I thought, just like my father, who had spent most of his early career as a successful salesman in New York City. I observed the stranger carefully and decided that I liked his appearance and manners, for he waited quietly and watched us like a genuine audience, rather than the loud and rambunctious children we actually were.

I liked him even more when he approached the podium without introduction, and spoke with a clear and energetic voice that immediately silenced the auditorium, saying in what sounded like a single, continuous breath, "Children, let me introduce myself. I'm Mr. Curtis, and I am here to tell you all about my vocation, which is the simple business of selling magazines both educational and entertaining. Along the way I hope you will learn a few things, too, so that when you walk out of these doors this afternoon after school, you will feel both qualified and able to sell magazine subscriptions, so that you can not only help your school expand its library but equally gain the opportunity to earn prizes for yourselves — now how does that strike you?"

Well, I suddenly sat bolt upright in my chair and listened to him very closely, as if he had actually called my name out loud. I looked around to the right and left, to share my astonishment and enthusiasm, but the other children were equally rapt.

Needless to say, I was hooked. He continued in what I considered his very charismatic way to deliver a rousing speech about the art of salesmanship, then walked us through the rules of our prizes and the points we might earn by selling magazine subscriptions to our friends and neighbors.

After the assembly, back in class, each student received a prize catalogue that featured such wonders as a football, a baseball and bat, a basketball, a radio, a comb and brush set, and so forth. By this point all the children were starting to wildly consider the possibilities. The book was colorful and it felt magical in my hands. I thought "Now I will have my own business." He had shared with us how to go door to door and ask all of our friends and neighbors to buy magazines from us. He shared the technique of "telephone sales" by telling us to call all of our friends that we knew, as well as family members in town and out of town. He asked us to get our parents to sell for us at their places of business. He even told us to take our books to meetings and church. Mr. Curtis showed us how to knock on doors, how to open the sales pitch, and how to be prepared by taking pencils, order pads, and a smile. I smile today remembering the statement that really stuck in my mind. Mr. Curtis said, "Now students, the one thing that you do not want to say is, 'You don't want to buy any magazines, do you?'"

The impact of a lifetime came, however, when he told us "One of you sitting in this auditorium today will be the top salesman for the whole school. I wonder who it will be?" My heart beat faster and faster as I started to consider the possibility that it would be me. Do you want to know the truth? It was all I could do to keep from standing up and shouting, "It's going to be me!" Since Mama insisted on good manners that action would not have gone over very well, now would it? Well you can bet that I ran home that afternoon and told my mother to quickly call all the neighbors as well as her friends around the rest of the town and tell them that I would be coming by later, and to please not buy any magazine subscriptions from anyone else.

Call it the competitive spirit, call it ambition, call it whatever you please, I was born with the desire to win and to achieve. Second best wasn't good enough at my house if we could be first. Sloppy wasn't accepted. B's weren't good enough for my mother when she knew I could make A's without much more effort.

Roller Skate Selling-That Means Find Your Customers FAST!

I decided to roller skate up and down the street until dinnertime, and I planned to cover the other side the day following. It seemed to me that roller skates would help me to be more efficient in reaching the most number of customers in record time. Somehow I realized that just knocking on the door was not enough. I had to sell. I am reminded of a statement I love by Thomas Barratt, the founder of Pears' soap, and considered by many as the father of modern advertising. He said, "Any fool can make soap. It takes a clever man to sell it."

As I tightened my roller skates onto my shoes, I thought about ways to sell several subscriptions in each home. The brochure mentioned "bundling" packages, as well as discounts on certain magazines. I knew how much my family enjoyed *Life* magazine as well as *Colliers*. Of course Mama and I loved *McCall's*.

As I went door to door, I reminded each potential customer about the paper dolls included in each issue of *McCall's*—little Betsy McCall and her family. I mentioned how much I loved paper dolls, and supposed that their children or grandchildren would feel the same way. My enthusiasm grew for those magazines with each sale. It seemed that just by talking about the joy that these magazines brought to my family and me, the customers were more inclined to sign up. It's worth noting that all the magazines I praised so enthusiastically were the ones that I truly loved to read myself. Through my "verbal advertising" of these magazines, which we genuinely loved in our family, I would suppose that I was applying the advertising formula of AIDA which is now over 100 years old-Attention, Interest, Desire and Action.

I.A.S.M. I am Sold Myself

Perhaps an even simpler way of looking at my success was that I was just very enthusiastic about what I was selling, and my enthusiasm inspired others. I heard a speech once by Dr. Dennis O'Nan which opened new avenues in my heart concerning enthusiasm. He said, "Look at the last four letters of the word enthusiasm: i-a-s-m. I like to say they stand for 'I Am Sold Myself.'" That, I understood.

For instance, I am absolutely enthusiastic about sewing. I love it. I get excited about it. If someone with just a little interest in sewing asks me about it, I can easily sell them on the joy of it, the sisterhood of the people involved, the passion, the history. I can sell you on the benefits of sewing because "I am sold myself."

Let us put the shoe on the other foot, however, and take another person's hobby, such as baseball card collecting. Could I have enthusiasm for that? Could I sell others on the purchase of baseball cards? I probably could not because I don't love baseball cards, nor frankly the game of baseball. The enthusiasm that I can inspire in others can only come from things for which I am already sold, like doing mission work with my church. The key to any kind of success is to find and embrace our God-given talents and concentrate on sharing them with others.

The famous public speaker, Dottie Walters, puts it another way, "Go beyond simmering, even to boiling, and you will discover talents and powers you never dreamed were yours."

I don't recall exactly how many subscriptions I sold. With a lot of help and support from my mother, however, I certainly went the extra mile. Do you want to know a secret? I ended up winning the grand prize in both fifth and sixth grades, for most subscriptions sold. It wasn't because of any special interest or talent in sales (I was only ten years old). The simple truth was that I truly loved to read magazines and I was motivated to be the best. I wanted to win the contest. My ambition seized the challenge, and I pursued it with single-minded determination.

Let me hasten to add that I had my mother's advice and encouragement working for me, and she was a "full steam ahead" kind of woman! With this early experience I got my pieces in place. Today, at this stage of my business and personal life, as I get my pieces in place, I know with complete faith that God is the leader of my efforts and to Him goes the glory.

> *I planted the seed in your hearts, and Apollos watered it, but it was God who made it grow. It's not important who does the planting, or who does the watering. What's important is that God makes the seed grow.*
> —1 Corinthians 3:6-7

Many years later, as I taught literature in high school, I realized that the poem *No Man is an Island* by John Donne states very clearly how critical other people are to any success, which would certainly include business success. One of the most exciting pleasures of this stage of my life is seeing more clearly every day how life experiences, people, books, and most especially, my faith are all intertwined together. They have been all along, whether I knew it or not. I pray that I am always thankful for all the members of my team, and remember to give full credit not only to them but also to God who makes all things happen.

No Man is an Island

No man is an island entire of itself; every man
is a piece of the continent, a part of the main;
if a clod be washed away by the sea, Europe
is the less, as well as if a promontory were, as
well as any manner of thy friends or of thine
own were; any man's death diminishes me,
because I am involved in mankind.
And therefore never send to know for whom
the bell tolls; it tolls for thee.

—John Donne

As you start to consider the process of transforming your hobby/ craft into a business, you need to take account of your own aspirations. The success of your business will entirely depend on a combination of factors, and your emotional investment weighs very heavily in the formula. Sometimes people believe that the products of their hobby will somehow sell themselves — that talent, creativity, and quality will do all the work. These are essential ingredients, but if you have not added the energy of an entrepreneurial spirit to the venture and massive written planning, then you are on the wrong track. On the other hand, all the brute force work in the world won't help sell a product that does not stand out from the rest.

In this chapter, we will review the emotional investment you need to make into your chosen hobby in order to transform it into a business. I believe there are four important ingredients to be considered: **A, B, C** and **D**.

<u>A</u>spire

Life is a glorious adventure. Face problems aggressively-opportunities do not come to those who wait. They are captured by those who attack. I am daring you to think bigger, to act bigger, and to be bigger. I promise you a richer life and more exciting life if you do. I am showing you a world teeming with opportunity.
—William Danforth

My First Business at Age Fourteen

When I was in grade school, my mother travelled by automobile each weekend with several of her friends to Nashville, TN to work on advanced degrees at George Peabody which is now part of Vanderbilt University. I was allowed to come along, and take dance lessons nearby, while the adults attended their graduate courses. I loved dance and all the dramatic arts, and often rehearsed what I had learned in the privacy of my room, until soon enough I had acquired what could have been considered in Scottsboro something of an expertise in dance.

The other mothers in town were interested in having their children dance, so a few of them asked my mother if I would start a dance school. Of course, our answer was a resounding, "Yes, I would love to!"

Mama helped me obtain the space, then structure and plan my lessons. I would teach and she would play the piano for accompaniment. We started with a small group of younger dancers, who might not notice any early mistakes I made in teaching, but within a few years, I was teaching every grade level. I started to diversify the classes and teach different styles of dance. The kids found out that I was a majorette, and asked for baton lessons. Before I could drive a car, my business was thriving with a full day of classes every Saturday from 8 to 5. By my senior year in high school, I had one hundred dance students per week and fifty baton students. I loved teaching dance and the students seemed to love me, and best of all, the money that I earned completely covered all my expenses for a year and a half of my college education. I might add that all of that money had to be put into the "college fund" at a local bank. Mama did not allow "throwing away money" just because I was earning it. Mama and Daddy continued to support me and gave me only the allowance they wanted me to have.

When any hobby, like dance, connects with someone's deeper aspirations, like starting a teaching business, the results are dramatic. Your hobby may be a source of comfort and relaxation, but in order to turn it into a successful business, there needs to be a deeper set of personal motivations driving you.

Now I will be the first to admit that I was a pretty industrious youngster. By the time I reached high school, I had elaborate dreams about getting my degree and opening a professional children's school to teach dance, drama, baton, and other related arts. I am not suggesting that your ambitions needed to be so clear and irrepressible at a very young age. Truthfully that was my second plan while I was in high school. I really wanted to go to New York and become a Broadway actress. Even at that age I knew I needed a secondary plan for my life "just in case" I did not become a Broadway star! I have to add here that I was almost never able to attend sleep overs on Friday night with friends, never able to sleep in after having arrived home from a ball game after midnight Friday night, and never able to hang out with friends on a Saturday. There were sacrifices accompanying my entrepreneurship even at age 14. Somehow I loved my business so much that I did not care. Always remember that week-ends are many times the exact hours that people have to take advantage of your hobby. If you love free weekends and lots of leisure time probably a business is not really for you.

Invest Major Emotional Energy and Time Into a Business

> *Lazy people want much but get little, but those who work hard will prosper.*
> —Proverbs 13:4

If you want to make your hobby into a true business, you need to invest some real emotional energy into it. I always worry when someone tells me that she loves her hobby so much, she simply wants to hide away and practice it all day long. That kind of thinking has always sounded a little escapist to me.

Your hobby is going to become a vehicle for your business, and I am not talking about a magical pumpkin carriage to whisk you away to the royal ball. You are not Cinderella and there is no lost slipper! This is real work. If you are going to get any mileage out of it, there has to be fuel in the tank. You need to fill your hobby with all the aspirations for success you have carried in your heart.

Whether your plans are to just start a sideline business for a few extra thousand dollars a year, or to begin a full-time career, I can guarantee that your business will require a lot more effort than you believe. A lukewarm emotional investment will return equally mediocre results. The deeper your motivations and the stronger your aspirations, the more likely you will achieve real success.

If you are feeling even a little bit flat about your business prospects, try to get to the bottom of it before you launch into anything. Sometimes a fear of failure deflates our ambitions in advance. We lower our expectations so we don't have to disappoint ourselves later. In other cases, we anticipate the challenge and settle for less. We would rather give up on ourselves than face an uphill struggle.

Either way, please don't give up on yourself—instead place your faith in God and find courage through Him, for He will never disappoint you. Your aspirations are your dreams, and far too often we let life get in the way of them. If you take a smart and sensible approach to your dreams, with a combination of faith and major written planning, you can have a chance of making your dreams come true. Do the work involved to truly evaluate if this plan can indeed be a viable one. Pray hard and work hard. So don't abandon your aspirations just because you're afraid of the difficulties ahead. If you have examined your written plans carefully and through prayer have much peace then you just might be ready to follow your dreams. Next you have believing in your hobby and building your emotional connection to it—your "B's and C's."

That is precisely what allowed me, after many years, to rediscover heirloom sewing. After marriage, children, and graduate school, I finally rediscovered a hobby that quite naturally became the focus of my career dreams.

Don't be too timid and squeamish about your actions. All life is an experiment. The more experiments you make the better.

—Ralph Waldo Emerson

<u>B</u>elieve

One person with a belief is equal to a force of 99 who have only interest.
—John Stuart Mill

In a world where almost everything is made by machine, the few items that are made by hand are that much more precious. The true value of a handmade jar of strawberry jam, or a beautiful handmade dress, is inestimable. The mere fact that you cared enough to learn a skill, or preserve a half-forgotten technique, is a marvelous offering to the world. It says just as much about its creator as anyone who cares to own or taste or wear it.

Believing in your work invests it with life, and the degree to which you believe in your work will make a vital difference in your path to success. First of all, it will nourish your spirit, especially in the early days when times are difficult and there is very little financial reward. Secondly, the joy you feel in your work will shine through in your products and your demeanor, and make your business that much more attractive to others.

Believing in your work cannot really be faked. All of us at one time or another have worked behind the desk or counter of a company whose mission left us completely cold. The boredom, disinterest and frustration that we feel, can weigh on our souls so heavily that we end up dreading going to work each day, no matter how well we are paid. To summon a smile under those circumstances feels like lifting a watermelon, and in the corners of our eyes, the strain always shows through.

On the other hand, have you ever noticed that when you are doing work for something in which you believe, whether it is baking a birthday cake for a friend, or volunteering for the church, the work hardly feels like a chore? Despite the fact that you are not getting paid in any way, your motivation is stronger than ever. I might share here that I have led several Christian women's conferences in both Alabama and Texas. They required a lot of preparation. Some required travel. The time I spent in preparation and in travel was pure joy. The time I spent presenting was pure joy. The heartfelt happiness I felt after talking with the ladies after it was over was overwhelming. I was only paid expenses. These were some of the best experiences of my life. I was asked to speak on behalf of St. Jude

Children's Research Hospital at a large meeting in Arizona several years ago. For that I paid my own expenses and of course got no pay. That was one of the most joyful weekends of my life. There was no way to describe my joy. Although lots of time and energy went into all of these events money was totally not a factor in my "beyond full heart of joy."

My grandmother taught for Alabama Public School system for 44 years, the majority of her adult life. She passed the Alabama teacher's test at age 16, in 1908, and started teaching five grades of children in Scottsboro from a one-room schoolhouse with fifty students.

You can be certain that my grandmother was a stern disciplinarian, and brooked no argument from any children who misbehaved, but she had one of the kindest and most generous hearts I have ever known. For example, during the height of the Great Depression, when the state could no longer pay her salary, she continued to teach from her schoolhouse. When she discovered that some of the children were coming to class hungry, she rallied a few local farmers to supply some food, and made sure that everyone had a hearty bowl of soup every day for lunch. She cooked the soup in the back of the room on the pot bellied stove which also supplied the heat for the room.

I once innocently asked her why she worked so long—almost three years!—without pay, and she scolded me, answering, "Why, the state of Alabama had no money, Martha, and those children had to have an education. There were no two ways about it." Actually she shook her finger at me while telling me those words. I never asked her that question again!

My grandmother taught from the heart. Teaching was not so much a career as a duty to pass along what she knew, because it helped improve and enrich people's lives. She believed in her work, and invested all her heart and soul into its performance. My grandmother loved teaching. My mother loved teaching. I have always tried to follow their examples, and indeed I feel the same sense of joy in knowing how often the sewing skills I have taught are used to create long-lasting gifts from the heart, that are passed along from mother to daughter to granddaughter.

Be sure to take a moment, as you start planning your business to fix your ideas around a particular plan for making your hobby into a business, that you will be able to maintain a sense of joy and integrity as you think about the products and services you will offer. Be certain that you carefully balance the profit motive against your personal values. To work hard at something without some reward is unsustainable, but there are many kinds of rewards that you can derive from a business, and not all of them are financial.

Whether it is because you are making someone's living room look beautiful, or because your products are environmentally sustainable, or because they are made of the finest possible quality, a sense of self-satisfaction in your craft will buoy your business and serve as a very strong lifeboat during those inevitable moments when you feel a bit lost at sea.

There will come moments of doubt in every stage of your maturing business. I have received countless letters from my customers, who tell me how much they appreciate what they have learned from our magazine, classes, books and television shows. These kind words have a way of staying in my heart for a very long time. Many days I have bounced back from a discouraging setback simply by reading a thank you note, because it reassures me that my work has made a difference. Without these warmhearted sentiments to encourage me, there are many days I might have given up hope.

Like any charitable action, believing in your hobby creates what I call a virtuous circle. The more you believe in it, the more your love, joy and excitement will shine through, which naturally brings success and admiration from others, so that you feel even more happiness in your work than ever before.

Find something about your hobby that you can truly believe in— whether it is the smile on a child's face as he takes a bite into your cupcakes, or cooing of a baby wrapped snugly in one of your quilts—for that feeling of joy will last much longer than money in the bank.

Connect

Why does it take us so long to follow our heart's desires? All of us probably should go into a profession for which we showed talent and interest as a child, but the truth is that we rarely do. Safety and convenience shuffle us into other pathways, and we soon forget the pastimes that fascinated us as a child. We lose our natural connection to what made us truly happy.

When I was only five or six years old, my Aunt Chris began to let me make Christmas stockings and doll clothes under her supervision. To this very day, I can remember the feeling of warmth and excitement that I felt sitting beside her on the couch, as delicious Christmas smells of gingerbread came from the kitchen, while her nimble fingers helped me guide stitches in the stocking that I knew would soon be filled with presents from Santa

Claus. I remember sitting with Mama as she worked long hours sewing pretty clothes for me. She truly wanted me to be the best dressed girl in town and we certainly could not afford many store bought clothes. She loved having new dresses for me. I still feel love out of a sewing machine.

In fact, I think this might be one of the real secret of hobbies—the connection they offer us to our past. By bringing us back in touch with some of our oldest memories and feelings, they open up our hearts to some of the simplest joys of childhood. We may not even recall a specific memory, or the connection might be quite loose, but we still feel a deep sense of comfort and reassurance when we practice the hobby, and that keeps us coming back for more. Somehow we relive a part of our past every time we practice it. This certainly is true for me with my sewing career.

I am sure that is what many of my close friends are experiencing when they describe that occasional feeling, while practicing their hobby, of time's seeming to pass without their awareness. They describe a feeling of total immersion, in which they are completely focused, and the hours fly by. That is what a real connection with your hobby can offer, and it is exactly what can make the potentially long hours of starting a business seem not so difficult.

If you are still struggling to make a connection with "your hobby" or you have not yet discovered your calling, that is no reason to feel anxious. Give yourself the time and the space to stumble upon it. Start with your childhood, and return to the simple pleasures you once enjoyed. Awaken your memories by revisiting any old books or photographs you might have left in the attic. Pursue your own remembrances of enjoyable times when you felt peaceful. Maybe it was a particular time of year, like the summer, when you visited camp or planted a garden. Maybe it was during Christmas, when you baked treats with your mother or made handmade Christmas ornaments.

Trust your instincts. Sometimes your true connection lies ahead of you. Take classes and courses you have never tried. A hobby is a way of cultivating yourself, and actively investing your creative energy in something personally meaningful. We all know how ready the world is to distract us with any number of television channels, movies, and Internet sites. Nobody likes that "blah" feeling of having wasted an evening or a whole weekend on too much television. Spending your time on a hobby presents a stark contrast. You are putting your personal energy and thought into something unique. So turn off all distractions for a while, and wander around the house to see what grabs your attention.

If you are one of those people who has a wandering creativity, and you seem to drift from hobby to hobby, that is fine too. You may want to think about any common connections between your various creative pursuits. What attracted to you to each of these hobbies, and why did you move on? As with any big decision, I do not recommend diving into something that you have only recently discovered. Give yourself time to really understand what you love about a hobby.

Over time, you may discover your connection with your original hobby changes too. The truth is that I do not sew nearly as much as I used to. The demands of my business have taken over. I don't mind at all, because I am still following my passion, and I still feel deeply connected to what brought me into this business. As a sewing teacher I feel major happiness when I see that our business brings sewing happiness to thousands of people. I feel that our products and events help spread the joy of sewing around the world. I love knowing that our television series, *Martha's Sewing Room*, aired in every state in the United States and was even translated into Japanese! That makes me very happy. Sewing connects me with my childhood, and all the feelings of motherhood and love that I cherished. What I discovered is that as the business grew, I found new connections with my business and all the new creative outlets it offered. I recognized, as do all successful entrepreneurs, that as my hobby became a business, the business became my hobby. By the way, a business is a fabulous hobby to have! I love it!

The high prize in life, the crowning fortune of man, is to be born with a bias to some pursuit which finds him in employment and happiness.
—Ralph Waldo Emerson

<u>D</u>ifferentiate

Up to this point, the rules for finding your hobby are instinctively simple: Aspire to your dreams, Believe in your mission, and Connect with your feelings. If your only goal were to find the perfect hobby, that might be enough. But if you want to turn your hobby into a business, things get much more interesting. The moment you decide to make your hobby profitable, you have entered the marketplace, and that means you need to distinguish yourself from everyone else. This final ingredient is the toughest, because it is about discovering what specific innovation in your hobby is going to attract customers.

One of the biggest breaks in my business career came during that first weekend that Joe and I went to New York City to buy supplies and inventory for the grand opening of our little shop. I have always loved New York, which was the city where my own father built his career and spent a good part of his adult life before coming back South to raise a family in Scottsboro. During my early teens, my father took us on annual trips to New York City, and I have many fond memories of Broadway musicals we used to see. I had always known and accepted that New Yorkers did business a little differently than someone from Alabama. In the South, when someone decides to buy something from a store, we make polite and cheerful conversation while the customer writes a check. In New York, they move faster and talk faster, while we Southern folk take pride in our etiquette, civility and patience. Despite the differences, however, I thought that merchants followed more or less the same script, but I guess that I had never before visited the garment district in New York City, because Joe and I have never been treated so rudely in all our lives.

A few months before we opened our shop, we went there there to spend our life-savings on lace and batiste for The Heirloom Shop, but one business owner treated us as though we were a complete waste of time. We were rushed and insulted at every step of the way, and I even broke down crying after leaving another wholesaler. I felt even worse when we returned home and realized that all our purchases, which were intended to fill an entire store, could easily fit on a twin bed. After only one visit to those New York wholesalers, I was already sick of their rudeness.

That whole awful experience made Joe and me decide that we could do it better. We could buy cotton lace directly from France, where all the lace was made, and sell it ourselves through the shop, and at various sewing trade shows. We could buy batiste and embroideries directly from Switzerland. We decided to make our courteous customer service, what truly differentiated our business from the rest. We knew how to say "thank you for your business. We appreciate it."

It worked. Through Joe's relationships with Swiss and French implant dentists, we made contact with the top suppliers in Europe, got on a plane and went to France and Switzerland to place our orders. This happened six weeks after we opened the shop. We wasted no time. We then created a homemade, very crude catalog for US distribution. We simply photo copied laces and embroideries taped down on a black piece of construction paper with the prices typed on a white piece of paper underneath! It worked! Cut and paste and glue and copy! Within months we had created a new channel for the business, and were taking orders. We found out where the wholesale shows were and bought booths. We mailed our "homemade catalogue" to every shop we could find along with a nice letter. Our wholesale business started booming. We called each shop who ordered from us to thank them for their business as soon as their order arrived in the door. We shipped the orders very quickly. Mainly we thanked them.

Figuring out ways to differentiate yourself can be a creative challenge because it requires a combination of hard earned experience and naive audacity. You need to have the hardened expertise that comes from practical knowledge, and at the same time, a fresh perspective that is ready to challenge conventional wisdom. As anyone who has tried to "teach an old dog new tricks" knows, these two qualities are often mutually exclusive. The magic of innovation is finding a way to balance the two.

Differentiation will be the cornerstone of your business, and it is a skill that will serve you throughout your career. Your business will undoubtedly go through several major transformations in your mind before you strike on the right formula. Even after it is formed, you will need to keep evolving the business to keep your ideas fresh. As you start to articulate what will make your business special, do not fall back on empty clichés. "Quality customer service" and "reliable products" do not allow you or anyone else to focus on the important details. Make a point to speak directly and specifically to what will make your business unique. Saying thank you always makes you unique! Trust me!

It is hard work, so give yourself lots of time to ponder the options. There is no quick and easy path. Just keep your eyes open and observe everything, even when it is outside the particular market that you are considering. Just because you want to start an artisanal bakery, does not mean you can not learn something from a clever software company. Listen for products and experiences that people rave about, and try to isolate exactly what made them like it so much—was it the service, or the packaging, or the product? Keep your ears especially tuned when you hear people complain about a customer experience, and try to figure out what actually bothered them. Ask for customer evaluations and then carefully evaluate each. Change what needs to be changed.

Building an expertise in your hobby will always help you learn how to differentiate yourself. By learning your hobby inside out, you will start to notice many different avenues for bringing your creativity into play. Even if you have been practicing your hobby for a very long time, do not assume that you know everything. By exploring your hobby all over again, you may discover an inspiring new creative angle that you've never imagined before—which is precisely the point.

As you immerse yourself in some of the finer details of your hobby, take care that you are taking notes about everything interesting that you discover. Find every website and blog that covers the subject, and read them thoroughly. Remember that every hobby has lots of variations—for example, there is still photography, nature photography, portrait photography, sports photography, fashion photography and more. Combining elements from supposedly distinct hobby types can create some interesting results. Find the names of the state and national associations and conferences that support your hobby, and join them.

Most importantly, practice your hobby and start to experiment, especially if you have become set in your ways over time. The more you understand about your hobby, the more you can find ways to creatively combine different elements, and even break the rules. Try new things, learn what works and more importantly, what does not work! Don't always obey conventional wisdom. Instead, look for ways to introduce new variations into your old habits. Explore all the different types of materials and techniques that people are using, so you can form your own opinions about what works and what does not work! Make written plans before implementing new ideas. Evaluate carefully the pros and cons of new ideas.

I know a letterpress printer who has been making beautiful, handmade wedding invitations and baby announcements, and all sorts of beautiful paper products for twenty years. These are the kinds of things you want to frame forever as soon as you see them, and in fact a few of my friends have done just that. Obviously, he is a bit of a purist and a perfectionist. He has always insisted that using old-fashioned, handset lead type was the only proper way to print these beautiful invitations. To use the more modern techniques, he felt, which rely on plastic polymer plates and modern technologies would be a complete sacrilege and create a vastly inferior product. One summer he hired a young graphic design intern who persuaded him to try the new printing methods, and he discovered that the modern methods really did work quite well. As a result, he has expanded the range of products he is offering, and has won all sorts of new customers.

Do not get stuck in your ways and cut off your options. Even if your hobby is about preservation and traditional methods, you should constantly be on the lookout for innovations and new techniques. They can save you valuable time and effort without necessarily reducing the quality of your work. They can also serve as the perfect way to start personalizing your hobby into something both unique and valuable to the customer.

When I started learning heirloom sewing, I got my hands on everything I could learn about it. It was way back in the Stone Age of digital technology, so I learned everything from all the books I could check out of the library. I learned about different types of stitches and fabrics. I took every class I could find. I read about the various histories behind different styles of lace. All of this information went into my hobby, and influenced the dresses I made. I also knew that most of the information was about heirloom sewing by hand. I knew for sure that most people had no time to make elaborate dresses by hand. I quickly began to try to figure out how to make these gorgeous dresses on the machine. Writing the first book on heirloom sewing by machine was my really big entry into the sewing world. My first two books on this subject sold over 100,000 and we were on the way to a totally new business.

I knew that I was onto something when people started to comment on my work. If people notice your work, be sure to pay close attention, and jump on the occasion. Don't bother acting shy or modest—ask more questions. What did you like about it? What would you like to see different? Did anything bother you? Let them know that you are thinking about starting a business from your hobby, and solicit their suggestions.

The same thing goes for people asking you for help or advice. It means they've already heard about your reputation or noticed your skill, and they have decided that you have a valuable talent to offer. Let them know that you are glad to help, and you would like to try to make a living this way. You should consider everyone who is interested in your hobby as a potential customer. Ask them how much they might be willing to pay for your services, and what might make it especially valuable to them.

*Do not go where the path may lead, go instead where there is no path
and leave a trail.*

—Martin Luther King, Jr.

Do What You Love

If you are doing what you love, you can not help but work hard, simply because you are enjoying yourself. To love what you do is to do what you love. I love teaching sewing and I love doing seminars. Everyone in my business loves the thought and care that goes into producing publications for people to buy and appreciate. Because we all share a common love for our hobby, we seem to share much more of a friendship than a business/customer relationship. In short, I adore my business, our team, our customers, our business colleagues, and my lifestyle. That is a true blessing from God.

If someone offered me a seven-figure salary to run another company, I would not even consider taking it. When I wake up every morning, I do not feel like I am going to work; I think about all the exciting projects I am going to create—it feels like play. To share new and exciting sewing skills makes me feel that I am living in God's will for my life. Besides which, I am quite certain that I would hate the kind of pressure that comes from managing an enormous corporation, and I would undoubtedly get fired before I got to draw even one year's pay.

My sincere hope is that you find a way to find happiness through your hobby, and discover the path to making it a business. By following the **A,B,C,D**'s, you will hopefully learn how to invest your full energy into your hobby, discover your goals and learn your limits. That just might be where you will be most content—living out your fullest dreams, instead of wishing. All along the way, pray for a deeper connection with God and the life He has chosen for you.

*I think the most important thing for anybody is to fall in love with
what they are doing for a living. I fell in love with show business when
I was eight years old, and I love it as much today as I did then.*

—George Burns

Connect to Your Dreams with G.R.A.C.E.

God: first in all things: Add God to that "RACE" and you achieve G.R.A.C.E.
Resilience: Get up when you're down. You conquer by continuing.

> *So let's not get tired of doing what is good. At just the right time we will reap a harvest of blessing if we do not give up.*
> —Galatians 6:9

Action: It is not enough to dream; wake up and work at it!

> *The heights by great men reached and kept*
> *Were not attained by sudden flight,*
> *But they, while their companions slept,*
> *Were toiling upward in the night.*
>
> —Henry Wadsworth Longfellow

Creativity: Allow the unusual to happen, God gives us no linen, but he does give us flax to spin. Open your mind's eye.

Enthusiasm: Allow the spirit of excitement to fill you and spread to your friends. It is contagious and delightfully enriching.

> *...for I know your readiness, of which I boast about you to the people of Macedonia, saying that Achaia has been ready since last year. And your zeal has stirred up most of them.*
> —2 Corinthians 9:2

~ Chapter Three ~

Dreams into Reality

She asked me this morning if she could gather grain behind the harvesters. She has been hard at work ever since, except for a few minutes' rest over there in the shelter.

—Ruth 2:7

If you want to succeed you should strike out on new paths, rather than travel the worn paths of accepted success.

—John D. Rockefeller

To map out a course of action and follow it to an end requires some of the same courage that a soldier needs.

—Ralph Waldo Emerson

Vision without execution is hallucination.

—Thomas Edison

Do You Have What it Takes?

In my planning stage I loved imagining that if I had my own business, I could do anything I wanted to at any time I deemed necessary! I would not have to go to another town to work, and would be close to my five children, ages fifteen, fourteen, fourteen, thirteen, and four. I would have all the time I needed to be a mother and attend plays, teacher's conferences, and other events. I would have time to take my children to their physician's appointments, orthodontist's appointments, and other appointments. I could again "do" lovely little dinner parties for eight.

Ah well, so much for the fantasy.

You will not become an entrepreneur to work less—you will work more, much more. The difference will be you are doing what you love!

Later we will discuss ways to keep your family loved and secure, a happy part of your new lifestyle.

Do you have what it takes? Ask yourself these questions:

- Do I spend my free time looking for tasks to do?
- Do I plunge right in when something needs to be done and disdain the need to talk things over with friends before I make a decision?
- Do I enjoy physical and emotional exhaustion?
- Do I have the energy to work long hours?
- Do I enjoy chaos?
- Do I love to do ten things at once?
- Can I be nice to people who are not nice to me?
- Am I organized?
- Can I handle stress?
- Do I have a competitive spirit?
- Am I prepared to make financial sacrifices for several years or more?
- Do I have the skills/background?
- Do I know how to sell my product?
- Do I love my product?
- Am I a great communicator and generally find people attracted to me?
- Do I enjoy (or tolerate) planning ahead—a week, a month, a year?
- Have I always been considered a leader?
- Do I have a burning desire to be my own boss?

- Do I think I can't live much longer if I don't start my own business?
- Am I disciplined in finishing tasks?
- Am I optimistic? Do I think positively, consider problems challenges rather than problems?
- Am I a confident person?
- Can I stand risk-taking?
- Can I stand the thought of bookkeeping, raising money, and juggling cash flow?
- Do workers like to work with and for me?
- Do I really like working with people and talking with people?
- Am I willing to travel excessively if necessary?
- Am I willing to take classes to learn accounting and computer skills if necessary?
- Do I really like to sell?
- Have I had success in the past in selling?
- Do I have enough money to pay the bills for a long period of time?
- Am I willing to use my savings to get this venture off the ground?
- Is my spouse willing to do without my salary to help me get this business off the ground?
- Am I willing to work without a paycheck for weeks, months, maybe years?
- Am I willing to give up my weekends?
- Is my spouse supportive of this venture?
- Are my children and spouse willing to help me do whatever is necessary as far as helping with business chores, household chores, and other things?
- Do I want to change the world? (Most entrepreneurs really do want to change the world in some way.)
- Am I willing to move into a "New Normal" in my life?

If you answered yes to at least twenty-five of these questions, you might have what it takes to turn your hobby to profit. You just might have what it takes to be an entrepreneur. One of my favorite scriptures on faith and endurance is James 1:2-4. I quote it often on my entrepreneurial journey.

> *Dear brothers and sisters, when troubles come your way,*
> *consider it an opportunity for great joy. For you know*
> *that when your faith is tested, your endurance has a*
> *chance to grow. So let it grow, for when your endurance*
> *is fully developed, you will be perfect and complete,*
> *needing nothing.*
> —James 1:2-4

Want Some Ideas?

You are in college and you are an All American cheerleader. The middle school cheer squad needs a coach. Why not start coaching them? This happened to our daughter, Joanna when she was in school at Mississippi State. She also used her other hobby, dance, to work at a local dance studio. She ended up earning all of her spending money through her two hobbies.

You are a dance teacher and your students cannot find the right dancewear or shoes. Why not order some and create a small retail outlet at your dance studio?

You hear people say at a dog show that they just cannot find those lovely colors anywhere for a special dog bed. Why not find a manufacturer and sell them yourself? You pick up your dog from the dog groomer and see a really awful dog scarf tied around your dog's neck. Why not show your groomer a beautifully made dog scarf with a serged edge that you could make for her/him to have for the dogs when they leave?

You are retired. You love dogs. Many of your friends do not want to leave their dogs in a kennel when they travel. Why not start a dog sitting "bed and breakfast" for dogs in your home? Most charge extra for pick up and delivery. Remember people will pay more for services for their dogs than almost anything else I have found!

You are skiing and you find out that many older people don't ski anymore. Let me share a little story with you about two of the most incredible hobby based entrepreneurs in the world today, Kay and Ricky Brooks. They have started so many successful hobby based businesses! Kay and Ricky discovered "bicycle skis" called ski bikes in Europe and began importing them. They rent them, sell them and even carry replacement parts. Ricky and Kay have another very successful business

RNK Distributing (Embroidery, Sewing and Quilting Products). They love Colorado and seized this opportunity for another successful business. By the way Ricky and Kay have been two of my main mentors in Martha Pullen Company. They are the most loving, giving people you will ever meet. Their website is www.snowfunbikes.com. They write on their website:

After riding my bike for a week, I wanted to share my discovery of this new found winter sport with others. I decided to become the Snowbike Representative for Steamboat and I'm extremely happy to report we now have a large fleet of Snowbikes (in 5 sizes) available for rent to any Steamboat skier/boarder age 9 to 99.

Snowbike rentals or purchase are available online at www. steamboatsnowbikes.com or directly from our shop at Powder Pursuits located street side in the bottom of the Grand at 2300 Mt. Werner Circle in Steamboat Springs.

Ricky Brooks

Do you know how to dance and twirl a baton? If there is no dance teacher or baton teacher in your town why not start teaching lessons, even if you are only 14 years old? I started my dance school when I was fourteen years old because so many parents asked me to teach their children dancing. Because I was also a majorette, parents asked me to also teach baton. During my senior year in high school, I had one hundred dance pupils and fifty baton pupils.

Are you a homeschooling mom who loves to sew and you notice that many homeschooling families would love for their children to love to sew? Why not start kid's sewing lessons for other homeschooling families? Actually many home schooling moms have found that other homeschooling moms want to learn to sew also.

Homeschooling moms are some of the world's greatest entrepreneurs! They can teach several grades at one time, run a household with all that entails, have a home cooked dinner on the table at night and run a successful business all at the same time.

My Sister's 125 Letters Opened Her Real Estate Business

Do you love houses and watch all of the home shows on the Home and Garden Television network? Why not study for your realtor's license and become a realtor. Our daughter Joanna Collins did this and is now a successful realtor in Huntsville. My sister, Mary Nixon, got her realtor's license after retiring from 25 years of social work. Both of them LOVE real estate and are doing very well. Mary had an interesting way of introducing herself in real estate. She made a list of 125 friends from her social work contacts, her church friends, her lifelong friends, her business friends and others she had contact with in Scottsboro, Alabama where we grew up and where she lives. She wrote a letter telling them that she had retired from social work and that she was now a realtor. She shared that if any of them had any real estate needs she would love to talk with them. From those 125 original letters she got several listings immediately.

People love Mary and wanted to see her succeed. Mary is very smart and detail oriented and does a superb job in all of the details that a realtor needs to do like market analysis, follow up, availability, etc. Her new found customers have referred her over and over because they were so happy with the way she treated them. Likewise Joanna bends over backward to take care of her clients and has received many, many referrals from satisfied customers. Both Mary and Joanna answer their phone calls immediately and follow up quickly with answers to client's questions. They are very active in taking care of their customers.

Once you have decided on your hobby, and decided that you are going to try to make it into a business, you should also take a moment and be certain that you feel peace about this big step. Major written plans should have been made before you even begin to charge out into this next step. You should think and reflect, and pray hard that this is the Lord's will for your life. It is very important that you feel that practicing your hobby, and turning it into a business, is the sort of decision that brings both peace and excitement to your heart. Peace comes from knowing and believing that you are following with the Lord's blessing, excitement from knowing that you will be making a dream come true.

> *May the LORD bless you and protect you.*
> *May the LORD smile on you and be gracious to you.*
> *May the LORD show you his favor and give you his peace.*
> —Numbers 6:24-26

Pick Your Business Model

Commit your actions to the Lord,
and your plans will succeed.
—Proverbs 16:3

In the end, despite the enormous variety of businesses out there, most of them follow the same basic business models, which center on selling either products, or services, or some combination of both. Hobby businesses have these many major activities in common. What will make your business unique will be your ability to combine these different activities into a business that meets the needs of your customers. A smart business may start in one direction, and as it achieves success, begin to expand in other areas.

To help you decide on the business model that best suits your plans, start with the basics, and then imagine some variations as your business evolves. In later chapters we will explore the execution of these business models in more detail, but for now, start to consider which combination of the following will be the center of your business plan.

Take Custom Orders

Many hobby-driven businesses have started almost by accident, when someone notices a beautiful, handmade object—a painted box, a stuffed animal, a portrait of a child, a beautiful christening dress, a sketch of a house turned into a note card, a creatively decorated birthday cake, a handmade doll, a piece of furniture, a dried flower arrangement, or a piece of jewelry. If someone has ever asked you, "Where I can get one of those?" a light bulb might flash in your mind. With a little word-of-mouth, and some strategic "product placement" in various social settings or local press, you can quickly find yourself in business. Before jumping too quickly some written planning is certainly the best route to follow if you want it to become a real business and not just a one time order proposition.

The key with custom orders is making sure that the invested effort is commensurate with the price. You should never quote a price until you know how long it will take you to make, and until you have folded all the overhead costs into the price as well. I might add here that the price you get for the first sales will not be the prices you get later as the products become much more popular and established. In order to get your products "out there" you might have to sell too inexpensively at first; however don't do that too long!

Trunk Shows and Home Parties, Craft Shows and Street Fairs, Trade Shows, Selling Wholesale to Retail and Consignment Stores

These ideas are great ways to promote a hobby based business. In later chapters I will give more details and suggestions about these concepts.

Trunk shows are a great way to launch a hobby business, because they require a minimum of overhead investment, and build on the social circles that form the core market for your home business. With trunk shows, it is important to strike the right balance between variety and inventory. You should not over-purchase for your first few trunk shows, until you get a clear idea of what sells—a low inventory is desirable, and you can always take orders. On the other hand, a variety of styles and products will allow you to better understand what sells best for your market. If your trunk show is at someone else's house, be certain to choose a hostess who knows how to entertain well, and has lots of friends.

I have several friends who do trunk shows with beautiful designer clothes (for women and/or children) available for order. Others I have known in the sewing business have beautiful custom clothing as samples and take orders at a trunk show.

Craft Shows and Street Fairs

There are literally thousands of craft shows and street fairs around the USA. Some creative research on the Internet will help you find the one that is best suited to your hobby. Make sure that you carefully research the type of event in advance (start with **www.artscraftsshowbusiness. com**, and **www.craftmasternews.com** and then Google the specific fair that interests you for detailed information). It is an incredible waste of time and effort to find yourself trying to sell products to the wrong market. When you prepare for a craft show, you may need to invest in a booth (or share the costs with someone else), and whatever equipment that allows you to easily pack and display your material. You will also need to ensure that you are ready to handle payments and receipts. Of course you will have to have the proper business license and collect sales tax. Have some sort of bag to put the purchase in for the customer.

Trade Shows

A trade show, or wholesale show, is a gathering of exhibitors who sell or showcase similarly themed products to attendees. Trade shows can be a terrific source of sales for a product or service if you target the right audience. If you market effectively at a trade show, you can find lots of opportunities to sell wholesale. Keep in mind that anyone who wants to purchase you products in bulk for resale will need to markup your price. If you can keep your margin large enough to make the transaction you might want to consider selling wholesale as well as retail. The products in my company were always priced with this in mind. I went straight to the factories in Europe for my laces, fabrics and trims. That was necessary for me to be able to offer the best prices to my wholesale customers as well as to my retail customers. I might add here that we also self published all of our books so we could easily wholesale them as well as retail them. It worked for us.

Host Your Own Trade Show, Craft Show, or Street Fair

There is an amazing amount of money to be made in creating your own event. The trick is to have an event where you are sure you will have an audience. One way to ensure an audience is to hire a celebrity to speak at the event. Another is to find a group that already has a crowd—churches, schools, shopping centers, etc.—and offer to host an event for them. Your event will bring them more traffic; their traffic will buy from your vendors! I created fashion show events to help sales. I used my teaching methods to tell a little about how the clothes were made. We then sold our products at the back of the room.

Inviting a celebrity from your field can draw even more people to the event. This celebrity can offer a seminar, or speech. Having a celebrity event associated with you and your business can put you on the fast track to success.

G.R.A.C.E. Keys to Entrepreneurship

A celebrity event will also bring:

- Energy to your business
- Excitement to your customers and staff
- New customers
- New class ideas
- Sales, both at the event and afterwards
- Entertainment (show business) to your business image
- Press interest

Sell Wholesale to Retail and Consignment Stores

Selling your goods or services through someone else's shop is another excellent way to get custom orders, or simply product sales of any type. The big trick is finding stores and settings that are appropriate for selling your product. If you build a strong relationship with a retailer, the shop can take the orders for you, buy and resell your product, or sell them on consignment. When your product is new to a store, the owner might not want to assume the risk of purchasing from you. In such cases, you can ask them to try it on consignment. That means the shop owner exposes the goods in her store, and payment is made only for completed sales. Unsold items are returned to you. If you sell your goods on consignment, you will want to keep careful records of where you have sent your products, and check back periodically to make they are well presented in the store. You also need a written agreement concerning what happens if the article if suddenly "missing from the shop" and cannot be returned.

Always keep in mind that wholesale prices are often one-half of the normal retail prices. If you think that is a huge cut in your profit, you should recognize that fifty percent is a small price to pay for the savings in both the expense and risk of covering phones, employees, advertising, and rent.

Sell by Catalog

The concept of "catalog" has changed drastically over the last few years. Smaller companies rarely send a "paper catalog." The larger companies send them as usual—possibly too many. My first catalogue had laces photocopied onto black paper with the prices typed on little pieces of white paper and glued underneath. My second catalog was printed at a rural newspaper office and actually looked like a small newspaper. It worked. Later we went to very beautiful color catalogs. Today Martha Pullen Company only has a catalog on-line. In the past we had coupons to use if the orders were mailed or faxed. That saved telephone time of one of our employees. Today the orders are placed almost exclusively on-line. We have many online coupons with codes. My, how business has changed!! These are exciting changes.

Today even the simplest computer can create beautiful catalogs that can be made professionally or printed and assembled at home. In addition, there are literally thousands of catalogs that are always looking for new products to sell. Why shouldn't yours be one of them? When you sell your products through another catalog, it offers free publicity, and increases your prospects for future sales. Keep an eye out for catalogs that contain products that might complement your own. Look for publications with a devoted audience, and contact their business offices. Some catalog companies purchase your product at wholesale and resell it at the retail price. Larger catalog companies will purchase your product directly, warehouse it themselves, and resell it at the retail price. Others follow a "drop-ship" model, in which a paid order is "dropped" with you, along with 50% of the retail price, and you ship it to the customer. Some catalogs will simply sell you space in their catalog. Catalog sales work well if you can create your products in high enough quantities to get the wholesale cost down.

Sell Through the Internet

Selling your products through the Internet, also called ecommerce, is now a fully developed industry. I have a very good chapter in this book about taking your business online. This is a critical part of most businesses today.

Sell Through Your Own Retail Store

Many hobbyists dream of the day they can start their own store without considering that this option can involve the most amount of risk and work on your part. Nonetheless, many are ready, as I was, to take that risk and go forth. There are also many small "mall" stores that specialize in things like antiques or crafts. Each vendor has a small space within a larger store, and your rent includes the services of a cashier in the front of the store so you rarely need to be there.

Teach Classes and Lessons

Teaching your hobby by giving classes, seminars, and lessons is a simple and obvious way to increase your income without taking on the expense of renting a space. In a later chapter I will discuss this much more thoroughly. It's also a brilliant marketing tool for your product or service. Many huge companies were started this way. Teach lessons at a local shop, a local junior college, a community education program, your local church, or even in some rare cases your home.

When teaching any home lessons your liability must be considered and you must have proper insurance for this activity. Your insurance agent can advise you on this issue. If you plan to teach children in your home I advise having at least one parent with you for the classes-or one other teacher. I would never teach children in a home setting without another adult present at all times. Always have a form for anyone taking a class with you with name, phone number, emergency contact and email address. If you are going to do children's sewing classes a permission form drawn up by your attorney might be a very good idea. Honestly, teaching in a home is my absolute least favorite place for people to teach classes for many, many different reasons with most of them being liability of many different kinds.

Teaching in stores can be an ideal situation. Just ask yourself, "Where do I purchase the supplies needed to do my hobby? Where do other enthusiasts of my hobby go to shop?" You can approach these retail locations and suggest offering a class. Everyone wins—your class will inevitably increase store sales, and you will gain income from the classes, along with a customer base for future sales.

There are many groups that offer "share-the-gate" classes. In a share-the-gate, you supply the program. The sponsor provides the hall, refreshment breaks, advertising, their list of prospects, postage, printing, and sometimes travel expenses. Usually the sponsor organization sells the tickets, too. Often, you can sell products at the back of the room. The usual arrangement is a fifty-fifty split of the gate, but different organizations work at various percentage levels. Think about: colleges, churches, PTAs, parks and recreation departments, school booster clubs, hospitals, chambers of commerce, and service clubs (Rotary, Kiwanis, Lions, etc.).

Teach With New Media

If you have spent countless hours studying and perfecting your hobby, it is time that you considered yourself somewhat of an authority. As an authority you can teach others through books, magazines, audio, or video recordings. In the Internet age, there is an increased expectation that content should be given away for free. That does not mean you cannot monetize your expertise. First of all, anything you publish can be considered a marketing investment. For example, when you give away a certain amount of your content for free, by exposing it on a blog or YouTube, you increase awareness of any products you might sell. If you build a following, you can sell detailed books or recordings online. Self-publishing requires only a small investment, and guarantees a strong return if you can sell the product. If you are already teaching, your lesson plans can be quickly turned into a how-to book with very little editing. My dear friend Mildred Turner began teaching sewing at a local junior college, and then opened a smocking shop in Asheville, North Carolina. When I saw her lesson plans and her instruction sheets, I immediately remarked, "Mildred, you have three heirloom sewing books already written in these lesson plans!" In a short time she had the first book ready.

Business Consulting

If you find your skills in high demand, you should start considering consulting for a living. The next time someone says, "Will you help me with . . ." very nicely say, "Of course! Would you like to know my hourly rate?" When someone asks you to come over to help them, say, "I would love to. Can we schedule some time? I've begun consulting for my services." Your time and expertise are worth something! Don't be afraid to value it. Consider calling yourself a "personal coach" or a "personal trainer" as a form of consulting. Create a system where you help clients reach their goals in your area of expertise. For a fee they might call in once a week for a half-hour session with you. Most coaches charge around $300 per month for this service. Doing it via phone and/or email will greatly reduce your costs and time.

I Can't Because . . .

Once you know your hobby fairly well, I suggest you let go of all you have learned about why you cannot make money with it. Many people come to me and say, "Martha! I'm ready! I want to start earning income with _____. Help me with ideas of how to do it!"

"Wonderful! Have you thought about giving lessons?" From the looks on their faces I can see that will not do. "How about trade shows? No?"

"Martha you don't understand, I can't because . . . "

"I can't because . . ." How sad. They actually know too much—too many reasons they cannot succeed. The truth is, there are thousands of reasons they can. However, their preconceptions get in their way. If you are ready to gear your mind toward making money with your hobby, empty your mind first. Allow the wonder of the hundreds of possibilities available to you to flow in. Start over as a beginner. Pray hard. Ask God to help you overcome your fears and to give you peace. Make a written plan. Memorize the chapter on planning in this book in your hands. Start writing right now. Right now! Begin your written plan.

Better to Try and Fail . . .

My retail store taught me a lot about what sells and what does not. It gave me many experiences to use in my business seminars with other retailers. I tried lots of things that did not work, but I have become stronger from my mistakes and have become a better consultant by having lived through some whoppers. It is my pleasure to help others not make those mistakes. I made basically NO money (profit) for the first ten years of my sewing career. I had NO WRITTEN PLAN. After getting some consulting help and a written plan we turned the business around to become very profitable.

Even though I had a successful career as a teacher, at age thirty-seven the words of the poets, philosophers, and authors that I had been teaching to others illuminated a path in my life. I realized I would rather try and fail than never to try at all. I had the overwhelming feeling that if I did not try now, I would wake up at age sixty-five and ask myself, "What if I had tried that business?" Would I die with my music unsung? Now that I am seventy I can say that my music is still singing and that I plan for it to sing much longer. I have never been happier in my business career. I think I have more exciting plans for the next ten years of my career than I have ever had before!

I have changed my strategy somewhat since Joe and I sold Martha Pullen Company several years ago. I could not be more excited about Martha Pullen Company as well as my consulting/publishing business, Pullen Press, LLC. I am passionate about helping other women and men achieve their dreams of owning a business. I am passionate about helping them NOT make the mistakes that I made. Once a teacher, always a teacher.

Far better it is to dare mighty things, to win glorious triumphs, even though checkered by failure, than to take rank with those poor spirits who neither enjoy much nor suffer much. Because they live in the gray twilight that knows not victory nor defeat.
—Teddy Roosevelt

Test Your Hobby for Profitability

I wish I could have "tested" some of the great possibilities I tried. To see if your hobby is the sort that you could turn into a business, ask yourself this series of questions:

- **Market Size:** Is there an abundance of people who enjoy this same interest? Is there a way you can do a test of the market? Or get the results from others who have done market tests?
- **Market Interest:** Do you think others would enjoy this hobby if they knew about it? Is it interesting to new people?
- **Market Saturation:** Are there lots of outlets already available for purchase of hobby materials? Are there plenty of shops offering classes in your hobby area?
- **Future Innovation:** Can you think of new products you might develop which you might sell in your business? If your business is sailing, can you write books about sailing or start a sailing magazine? Can you import goods for Americans that are already enjoyed by people in other countries?

- **Uniqueness:** Is your hobby fresh enough that everybody isn't already doing it and getting tired of it? Are there just a few porcelain doll makers in your community?
- **Possibilities for Creative Expansion:** Does your hobby have new avenues after people get tired of the current ones?

The next step is to determine what niche your business will fill. The following questions will help guide you:

- Is your idea practical, and will it fill a need?
- What is your competition?
- What is your advantage over existing businesses?
- Can you deliver a higher/better quality service?
- Can you create a demand for your business?

> *Listen! A farmer went out to plant some seed. As he scattered it across his field, some of the seed fell on a footpath, and the birds came and ate it. Other seed fell on shallow soil with underlying rock. The seed sprouted quickly because the soil was shallow. But the plant soon wilted under the hot sun, and since it didn't have deep roots, it died. Other seed fell among thorns that grew up and choked out the tender plants so they produced no grain. Still other seeds fell on fertile soil, and they sprouted, grew, and produced a crop that was thirty, sixty, and even a hundred times as much as had been planted.*
> —Mark 4:3-8

Passions with Integrity, Joy and Honor

I do not have much patience with people who talk a great deal about integrity and honor. I agree with Ralph Waldo Emerson when he said, "The louder he talked of his honor, the faster we counted our spoons!"

As you explore your own dreams, ask yourself this: "When the business journey is over, will the people who matter most look at me and say, that it was well done? Which of the many choices—thirty years from now—will make you stand a bit taller? I like to believe that the books and magazines we write will be treasured a hundred years from now. For me, the most satisfying part of Martha Pullen Company was being able to bring scripture and spiritual encouragement to readers of our magazines in the "Dear Friends" page of *Sew Beautiful* and other publications, books, newsletters and on our website. I look forward to my new ministry with Pullen Press, LLC and **www.pullenbusiness.com.**

A much more critical question about a business journey's end is of course is whether or not it made a difference in God's eyes. That is my greatest prayer. I know that God does not need me at all. My prayer is always that He can use me. My prayer is that my business always gives Him the glory and that it honors Him. Matthew 28:19 says, "Therefore, go and make disciples of all the nations...." God has through his gracious goodness allowed me through this beloved sewing business to share the gospel all over the world. That has been and will continue to be my greatest business blessing.

Never undertake anything for which you wouldn't have the courage to ask the blessings of heaven.
—G. C. Lichtenberg

Don't worry about anything; instead, pray about everything. Tell God what you need, and thank him for all he has done.
—Philippians 4:6

~ Chapter Four ~

Do Your Market Research. Who is your Customer?

According to the Craft and Hobby Association the hobby industry in the United States is at the $30 billion dollar a year level. Before you leap into your business, you will want to make sure you understand how the market behaves, and how your customers are already being served. As you begin to focus on a specific business model for selling your product or services, you will want to invest time in understanding the market players at a national and local level. This chapter will help you understand where to look for that information.

Thanks to the Internet, there are a huge variety of resources at your disposal to investigate what companies are already serving your potential market, and where potential customer demand may lie. I will list those websites that can help you in the sections that follow. As you are doing your research, you will want to keep in mind some basic questions. You should be thinking about things like:

- How many people practice the hobby?
- How do people spend money on the hobby?
- What are the ages and incomes for people who practice this hobby? In what regions do the most number of people do this hobby?
- What are the business magazines or specialty websites that serve this hobby?
- What type of person is most likely to buy your particular product or service?
- Where would this person expect to find your product or service?
- Why would someone want your product or service?
- How will you be competing with others in the market?

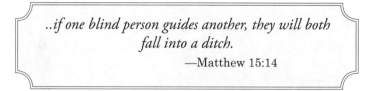

*..if one blind person guides another, they will both
fall into a ditch.*
—Matthew 15:14

As you start thinking about all these questions, what you are really doing is trying to see your business in a practical light. It is far too easy to get caught up in your dreams, and forget that your business might not interest anyone but you.

You need to think about your business through someone else's eyes. You need to step outside of your own shoes, and put yourself squarely in the customer's shoes. Take a moment to stop thinking about your perfect business, and how it will help make you independently wealthy, and start thinking about whether you are really going to be helping someone else. If your business is a "vanity project" that is purely designed to make you happy, without thinking of the customer's needs first, you will discover that your business will be short lived.

There are basically two types of research that you need to perform to truly say that you have a good understanding of your market. The depth of your research is up to you, but the better you understand your market from these two perspectives, the better you will be able to target your product offering to the customer.

---

*Don't be too timid and squeamish about your actions. All life is an
experiment. The more experiments you make the better.*
—Abigail Adams

Primary Research

Primary research is about speaking directly to your customers. When I say customers, I do not mean your sister-in-law and your cousins who are all going to buy something from you anyway. To get a clear understanding of your market, you really want to get an objective opinion from your true potential customers, and learn all about their preferences. When you work directly with your friends or family, they will tend to say things that you want to hear, just because they are afraid of hurting your feelings, or they want to see you be successful. If you keep things professional, and work with real customers in a real business setting, you are much more likely to get to the bottom of the customer's thinking and buying habits.

Getting the names of a group of people can be difficult, especially because many people are not interested in being approached by someone for one more market survey. We have all received one too many telemarketing phone calls during dinner to have any tolerance for another survey.

Of course, you can tap your personal network for names of people with whom you only have a distant relationship, and using that method, you may indeed come up with a dozen or so names. Another excellent method is to post a sign somewhere that people that your potential customers might congregate, whether it is a cafe, church, school or gym.

Lastly, you might consider using the Internet to get in touch with people who represent your potential customers. Try to find websites that allow communities to form, or that host online discussion groups. I have listed some of them below. You can join these easily and just review the topics and conversations that happen in that group. Once you get a sense for the type of topics that are covered, you might feel comfortable carrying on an online chat with regular contributors to the discussion board. Or even better, you can invite them to speak with you offline.

- **Yahoo Groups** is a set of websites that are created and organized by a community that shares a specific interest. Find your particular hobby and join a group. You can learn a lot by engaging in discussions with your peers. (**www.groups.yahoo.com**)
- **Meetup** is a very popular site where different people organize meetings about things that interest them. Browse around to see if anyone in your area organizes meetings around your hobby. Maybe you can meet up and speak to them. (**www.meetup.com**)
- **Craftster** is an online community where members share pictures of their craft projects, and discuss new ideas. (**www.craftster.org**)

Perform a few Google searches, using your hobby's name paired with some of the following search terms, and you should also be able to find any other independent online communities dedicated to your hobby:

- online message board
- BBS (bulletin board system)
- discussion groups

I must admit that I tend to pursue my primary research in a far more improvised fashion. I just go directly up to my customers and ask them point blank what they think about something! Of course this is easy when you have an established business, and lots of conferences that assemble them in one place, where it is easy to approach them. That is just my point. To do proper primary research, you need to find the places where your potential customers go, and you need to be there too.

Few places are better suited for this sort of activity than Craft Shows and Street Fairs. By wandering around and engaging in impromptu conversations with the people you meet, you can learn about exactly what your potential customer base thinks. Watch carefully to see what sorts of people are buying products similar to yours, or what they actually gravitate toward. If you're close to someone's booth, you should restrict yourself to observing people, rather than speaking directly to them. Try to size up the customers, their age and demographics. Above all, make sure, when you are doing this sort of competitive research, that you do not make yourself too obvious. Taking pictures or writing down notes is a sure way to invite the annoyance of any shopkeeper.

Secondary Research

By consulting various written publications, you can better understand your market. There are literally hundreds of options for doing background research through the Internet. Below I have compiled a list of what I consider the best avenues to explore:

- **Google Analytics:**
  Google has a free service that allows you to understand what people on the Internet are searching for, and precisely how much a business will pay to place an advertisement on the result pages. That means that you can use this tool to understand (1) how many people are looking for products or services like yours, and (2) whether the market is saturated or not. Here's how it works:

a.Visit www.adwords.google.com and sign in using your gmail address and password. Click on the "Tools" tab at the top of the page, and select "Keyword Planner"

b. Select "Search for new keyword and ad group ideas". Keep in mind that you'll have better results if you choose specific and narrow terms. "Heirloom smocking dresses" is going to deliver more meaningful results than "Making dresses." You can also select where you want your search to cover. By default it will be set at "United States", however, if you click on the little pencil tool next to "United States", you can type in a city to narrow your search.

c. Your results will show all the related searches that have been made in the past month.

- **Competition** shows whether there are lots of businesses trying to work in this domain. It is listed as High, Medium, or Low.
- **Average Monthly Searches** tells you how many people used that specific search term in the last 30 days both worldwide and in the US.
- **Suggested Bid** shows the "Cost-per-click" and tells you generally how much people are currently paying to advertise their business on the result page of searches for that term. The way to think of this number is to multiple it by 100, and that is how much businesses are willing to pay for acquiring a customer. (In other words, a business will pay $.89 for each ad, knowing that only 1% of their ads will actually create a click to their website).

There's no need to put too much emphasis on the exact figures. You are just trying to get a sense of how many people are actually looking for products in your particular niche and how many people are trying to advertise to them.

- **Business Trends**
The Pew Research Center is an excellent source of information for anyone who is starting a business. They did an excellent survey on how the Internet has impacted hobbies. Although the survey is more than five years old, it provides great demographic information about who practices hobbies and where. I would add that you should browse around the site and you may find lots of additional research about your particular area of interest.

particular area of interest.
(**www.pewresearch.org/pubs/597/hobbyists-online**)

• **Trade Associations**
The Craft and Hobby Association is one of the largest trade associations serving the craft and hobby community. It consists of thousands of member companies that design, build, distribute or sell hobby-related products. Spending some time reviewing the CHA site will pay off immensely. It is worth noting that the CHA publishes an "Attitude and Usage Study" that gives detailed statistical information on the craft industry, broken down by hobby, including sales and size, demographic profiles and shopping patterns. (**www.craftandhobby.org**)

• **Government information**
  • The Census Bureau is a wealth of business and demographic information. By taking the time to study trends and patterns, you can better predict how your customers will respond to your business, and where opportunities can be found.
  • The Statistical Abstract allows you to understand almost anything you would like to know about the United States population, from household pet ownership to the frequency of dining out. Browsing around this site can help you discover exactly how Americans spend their money and time. (**www.census.gov/compendia/statab**)
  • The State and Metropolitan Area Data Book allows you to dig a little deeper and understand the distribution of different populations and activities by city and state. This is the best way to start thinking about the unique qualities of your local market.
  (**www.census.gov/compendia/databooks**)

• **Chamber of Commerce**
Although your state and local Chambers of Commerce are primarily oriented towards passing business-favorable laws, they often have strong directories of local businesses, and their newsletters can give valuable information on state events and resources.

• **SBA**
The Small Business Administration is one of the most comprehensive resources available for small business entrepreneurs. It contains

a wealth of information to help you with every aspect of starting a business. Their Market Research section contains some helpful links. **(www.sba.gov/content/conducting-market-research)** One of the most helpful services that the SBA provides is access to local business centers, where experts will happily sit down with you, and talk you through all the elements of your business. You can discuss your market research strategy, and receive a great number of helpful tips. Check the websites for both the Small Business Development Center, as well as the SBA partner organization SCORE. **(www.sba.gov/content/small-business-development-centers-sbdcs)** **(www.score.org)**

- **General**
You will learn a great deal simply by spending time on the Internet, searching through competitive websites, and reading the trade publications, blogs and newsletters specific to your hobby. **Google** and **Bing** are the most powerful search engines for finding anything on the Internet. Use them frequently, and search effectively for information by using narrow search terms.
(www.google.com)
(www.bing.com)
Wikipedia is the Internet encyclopedia for everything. Most of the information is very accurate, and you can discover a lot of links to other sites that cover your hobby, including this list of hobbies.
(en.wikipedia.org)
(en.wikipedia.org/wiki/List_of_hobbies)

If you're serious about becoming a wealthy, powerful, sophisticated, healthy, influential, cultured and unique individual, keep a journal. Don't trust your memory. When you listen to something valuable, write it down. When you come across something important, write it down.

—Jim Rohn

Summary

By exploring the options for how you plan to make money from your business, and researching the receptivity of the market, you are ready to start building a business plan. During this stage of your business, you should always keep a notebook handy to jot down your thoughts. I would also recommend that you allow yourself to fully explore every possible option in your mind and on paper. By allowing yourself to dream without fencing in your imagination, you will be much more likely to arrive upon a business model that contains the perfect combination of creativity and realism. In the next chapter, we will start exploring exactly how to make that dream start coming true. Turn your dreams into Mind Maps.

Possibilities with G.R.A.C.E.

Now you have lots of possibilities to begin your thinking and planning about your business. You indeed can make money from your hobby. As you are working review all plans with **G.R.A.C.E.**

God: He is first in all things.

You say you have a calling in this business? Who is the Caller?
—Ken Blanchard

Resilience: Get up when you're down. You conquer by continuing.

> *No, despite all these things, overwhelming victory is ours through Christ, who loved us.*
> —Romans 8:37

Problems are only opportunities in work clothes
—Henry John Kaiser

Action: It is not enough to dream; wake up and work at it

Creativity: Allow the unusual to happen. God gave us this gift of creativity and it is OK to use it!

Leonardo da Vinci believed that to gain knowledge about the form of a problem, you began by learning how to restructure it to see it in many different ways. He felt the first way he looked at a problem was too biased toward his usual way of seeing things. He would look at his problem from one perspective and move to another perspective and still another. With each move, his understanding would deepen, and he would begin to understand the essence of the problem. Leonardo called this thinking strategy saper vedere or "knowing how to see."
—Michalko Michael

And I have personally appointed Oholiab son of Ahisamach, of the tribe of Dan, to be his assistant. Moreover, I have given special skill to all the gifted craftsmen so they can make all the things I have commanded you to make.
—Exodus 31:6

Creativity is not determined by the kind of work… but by the kind of approach taken to any job. It is people, not jobs, who are creative.
—Robert M. Fulmer

Enthusiasm: Allow the spirit of excitement to fill you and spread to your friends and your customers. It is contagious and delightfully enriching. Webster's dictionary describes enthusiasm as "intense feeling for a subject or cause." The word comes from the Greek word, enthousiasmos. En means "in." Theos means "God."

So we must learn how to utilize enthusiasm in order to move into that exciting and creative segment of the human race-the achievers. You will find among them total agreement that enthusiasm is the priceless ingredient of personality that helps to achieve happiness and self-fulfillment.
—Norman Vincent Peale

Contrary to popular belief, my experience has shown me that the people who are exceptionally good in business aren't so because of what they know but because of their insatiable need to know more.
—Michael E. Gerber

Here is the bottom line on enthusiasm: it's infectious, and it makes people respond. This is true in the classroom, in the boardroom, and on the campaign trail. It's just as true in the ice-hockey rink. If you are not enthusiastic about an idea or a project, nobody else will ever be. If the leaders don't believe enthusiastically in the direction of a company don't ever expect the employees or the customers or Wall Street. The best way to get someone excited about an idea-or a project or a campaign-is to be excited yourself and show it.
—Dale Carnegie

Whatever you do, do well.
—Ecclesiastes 9:10

~ Chapter Five ~

Making Your Business Plan

"For I know the plans I have for you," says the LORD. "They are plans for good and not for disaster, to give you a future and a hope. In those days when you pray, I will listen. If you look for me wholeheartedly, you will find me. I will be found by you," says the LORD.
—Jeremiah 29:11-14

I have always thought that one man of tolerable abilities may work great changes, and accomplish great affairs among mankind, if he first forms a good plan, and, cutting off all amusements or other employments that would divert his attention, make the execution of that same plan his sole study and business.
—Benjamin Franklin

If I had eight hours to chop down a tree, I'd spend six hours sharpening my ax.
—Abraham Lincoln

Today you are You, that is truer than true. There is no one alive who is Youer than You. Be who you are and say what you feel because You are the guy who'll decide where to go. Today is your day! Your mountain is waiting. So...get on your way. You are you.
—Dr. Seuss

Plan the Work and Work the Plan

Dreams and visions become reality when you plan the work and work the plan. You will find your mind racing with passion in the wee hours of the night, thinking of new and creative plans for additional strategies.

By failing to prepare you are preparing to fail.

—Benjamin Franklin

Most business men generally are so busy coping with immediate and piecemeal matters that there is a lamentable tendency to let the "long run" or future take care of itself. We often are so busy "putting out fires," so to speak, that we find it difficult to do the planning that would prevent those fires from occurring in the first place. As a prominent educator has expressed it, Americans generally "spend so much time on things that are urgent that we have none left to spend on those that are important."

—Gustav Metzman

Business is not about having dreams; it is about reaching them. There is a huge difference between these two ideas. Planning is one of the critical keys to turning dreams into reality. Most people don't plan to fail; but they fail to plan. I can assure you that I planned in my heart for the first ten years; however, I had no written plan and I made basically no profit. God in his gracious goodness kept our business growing and he paid the bills but I made no money. Then, also in his goodness he led me to consultants who showed me the way to turn the business around to a profitable company. Written planning with **G.R.A.C.E.** is now my secret.

May he grant your heart's desires and make all your plans succeed. May we shout for joy when we hear of your victory and raise a victory banner in the name of our God. May the LORD answer all your prayers.

—Psalm 20:4-5

Go From Free to Fee

You have spent your time, money, and energy on your hobby. Now you are ready to make a plan to get from free to fee. Before you are able to charge someone else a fee for anything, you must first believe you are truly worth a fee. I think Jessie Rittenhouse put it best in his poem, *My Wage*.

My Wage

I bargained with Life for a penny,
And Life would pay no more.
However I begged at evening
When I counted my scanty store;
For Life is a just employer,
He gives you what you ask,
But once you have set your wages,
Why you must bear the task.
I worked for a menial's hire,
Only to learn dismayed,
That any wage I had asked of Life
Life would have gladly paid!

I freely gave advice on designing and sewing garments in my store while I was selling customers fabrics and laces. To help sell more products and merchandise, I began giving classes. This is where my paid sewing consulting began. I charged appropriately for my advice through my teaching classes and was able to vastly increase sales in the store. Soon I began traveling doing sewing seminars for which I charged. Not only did I travel to teach sewing I also traveled to teach business workshops on how to start and run a successful business. We began producing larger events which included vendors as well as other teachers.

Putting a value on your time and your knowledge does not mean that you never give anything away. Soon others were looking at my business success and asking me to help them. For many years I gave my *How to Turn Your Hobby Into Money* seminars free to the sewing industry; many new business accounts opened up to MPC because of these seminars.

Selling my advice now falls into two categories: (1) sewing advice and techniques, and (2) business advice and selling techniques. I have spent a lifetime developing these sewing and business seminars and I am able to charge for them. "Free seminars" were a monumental building block to bring about this "for a fee" time in my career.

Another way I was able to go from free to fee was to sell advice through my books, magazines and seminars. I have never resented the price of a book that brought me pleasure and new skills; apparently our customers feel the same way since we have sold more than 750,000!

It will be hard for you to go to those currently in your circle and get them to pay for your services. You have proven to them over the years that your service was one that was not worthy of a wage. I suggest you create a new market for yourself as you strive to go from free-to-fee work.

As you develop this new market, you will need to firmly keep in mind Jessie Rittenhouse's advice: For any wage you asked of life, life will gladly pay! You just need to ask.

Three Critical Ideas

This chapter contains extremely exciting and valuable business planning tools. It is a chapter I wish I had read and studied before I opened my first sewing business, my retail store. It is a chapter I wish I had read and studied after several years into my business when I was working myself to death and making no profit. Before you read the many different and extremely good planning methods I would like to share three things with you.

I. Get a Mentor

One of the best "planning" methods before you start writing your plans is to get a job or an unpaid internship in a business similar to the one you are about to open especially if it is a retail store of bricks and mortar. You might even pay a successful shop owner for two days of her/ his time to be in the business with the owner's giving you advice. If her "coffee shop" or "bakery" or "doggie day care" or "quilt shop" is in another city this might be possible. Some people actually travel across the country to spend time in a business with a successful owner. They usually pay for this consulting on the job.

If you want to open any type of store front (bricks and mortar) another planning suggestion is to get a job in this type of business. Even a part time job will open your eyes as to what is really involved. If you want to open an Etsy store try to spend a couple of days with someone who already has a successful Etsy store. Many Etsy store owners are in every location. If you want to sell on eBay find someone who sells on a regular basis on eBay and pay for some consulting time. It will be very beneficial I believe.

How do you find someone that might be willing to mentor you or consult with you or let you work free for a few days? Go to your Chamber of Commerce or Better Business Bureau and ask for help. Go to a shop owner and just ask. Look on the Internet to find businesses many miles away from your intended location and set up some consulting time. Usually a couple of days will be enough to get started. Ask around in the business community or ask friends. I'm sure you can find a great place to get some experience and some help. Most universities have someone there to help new business start ups. Most states have some help for new business owners or potential new business owners. Write down every place you might go for help and begin your Sherlock Holmes quest. You can find help. Write down all ideas!

II. Get Mind Mapping Software and Use It (iMindMap)

This chapter has a Mind Mapping section. I think this is the most valuable way to plan anything. It is only in the past year that I have found out about Mind Mapping and I think it is the best planning tool on the planet. By the time you read this book I will have traveled to Europe to become an official ThinkBuzan Licensed Instructor. That is how valuable I think this planning skill will be to my customers and students. It is magical in putting together plans that are real and readable and exciting. You will learn more about Mind Mapping later in this chapter but to really learn more go to **www.pullenbusiness.com** and get in touch with me. There are some excellent books available about mind mapping in any book store. Many public and private schools are teaching students this technique to use in many subjects.

III. Read My Now Famous 3/30 Plan Section

I have helped more businesses get started or re-started by sharing my now famous 3/30 plan—the one I used to get my business from total "no profit" to profitable. It is simply to write down the financial goal you have for one year only and proceed to write 3 pages a day for 30 days brainstorming every idea that you can come up with on how that is going to happen. Do not organize. Just write. Check out books from the library. Talk to people. Go to every resource and write down EVERY idea-dumb or exciting-that comes to your mind on how you are going to make that financial goal come true. This is the plan that I have shared for about 25 years in my business consulting. This is the plan that I have used over and over personally in my business. I know so many people who have turned their businesses around using this plan and so many who have planned new successful businesses using this plan. I can share that I have had many others that after having done the 3/30 plan decided not to open the business at all because they saw there was no real possibility of success with that idea.

How To Develop a Business Plan

One of the critical reasons to develop a written plan is to see if your dream has any possibility of becoming a successful business. Some plans will simply tell you "this idea has no financial hope" at all! After developing a well thought out plan other dreams might seem "iffy" at best. The written plan will have served as a vehicle to save you lots of money and grief. If the plan does not seem very good don't open the business!

Thousands of engineers can design bridges, calculate strains and stresses, and draw up specifications for machines, but the great engineer is the man who can tell whether the bridge or the machine should be built at all, where it should be built, and when.

—Eugene G. Grace

You don't create a successful business without creating a pattern. To do that you must create the vision and work on it, or as my grandmother used to say, plan the work and work the plan.

Before you worry about how to get there, you need to have some idea of where you want to go. This starts with a dream. Every dream precedes the goal.

Some men see things as they are and say why.
I dream things that never were and say, why not?
—Robert F. Kennedy

Some self-confronting questions: Where do I want to be at any given
time? How am I going to get there? What do I have to do to get myself
from where I am to where I want to be? What's the first, small step I
can take to get moving?
—Robert F. Kennedy

Life is too short to be little. Man is never so manly as when he feels
deeply, acts boldly, and expresses himself with frankness and with fervour.
—Benjamin Disraeli

Working the Vision Into a Business Plan

I have talked about some of this "history of my company" in earlier chapters but it is important and I will go over some aspects again here in this planning section. I was able to get a small one-thousand-square-foot space at the end of a shopping center. The rent was $500 per month in 1981. I also knew that the space was owned by Joe and I did not have to really pay rent if things got tough. As I stood there looking at a bare room, I was appalled to realize I had already spent all of our savings on the inventory. We dragged all of the fixtures we could spare from our house and bought a few more at antique stores and garage sales. Obviously my original budget for inventory should have included much more than inventory for a retail store. Little did I know how much it would cost to get shelving, wallpaper, carpet, fixtures, a cash register, and a checkout area. Joe paid for all of this—another angel when I needed one. I suggest you do better than I did at creating that first business plan! Actually I should have said "in creating that first business." There was no plan except for my dream of owning a smocking shop. I had no written plan. I just dived in and opened my shop.

A business plan includes the answers to all of the questions asked in the previous section. If you choose to do the 3/30 Plan which will be described later in this chapter, you will have ninety pages of great notes. Take those ninety pages of notes and make a plan! Your local Small Business Administration has forms and guides for business plan outlines. These are also available on the Internet. Do not forget the library and bookstores.

A good solid written plan will benefit you in these ways:

- Writing it all out often unearths advantages, new opportunities, and any deficiencies in your plan. It will assist in identifying your customers, your market area, your pricing strategy, and how to be competitive in each.
- It will help you identify the amount of funds you will need, and when you will need them.
- Lenders and investors will assess your business savvy by your business plan. A solid plan will be the basis for a financing proposal and show you off as a business manager and a good risk. You will find out that I do not suggest borrowing money for your business; however, some people will plan a business which will require financing from outside sources. My suggestion is always to use your own money. If your plan is not solid enough for you to risk your own money then do not open the business. Borrowed money will have to be paid back .
- Putting plans to paper will help you look ahead and avoid problems before they arise.
- The plan acts as a reality check.

A river without banks is a large puddle. Power comes with direction.

—Ken Blanchard

Some people dream, others stay awake and live those dreams! Work on your plan and your plan will work for you. In this section I will give you tips to focus, to organize your dreams and your time, and to overcome procrastination when you start to fall away from working on your plan.

Every single, solitary person on this earth, no matter what his job might be, or what his experience has been, can discover within himself the brilliance, the genius, the captivating and captivated soul of an entrepreneur, once he knows where to look.

—Michael E. Gerber

Focus

> *My heart has heard you say, "Come and talk with me."*
> *And my heart responds, "Lord, I am coming."*
> —1 Corinthians 14:7-8

The first step in working your plan is to work on your focus. Focus with **G.R.A.C.E. God** first in all things, **Resilience, Action, Creativity,** and **Enthusiasm**. Keep your mind on where you want to go. Wayne Gretsky is considered perhaps the greatest hockey star in the history of the sport. He is the only professional player to score more than fifty goals in fifty-or-less games in a single year. And he did it year after year, as well as leading the league in scoring. When asked his secret, Gretsky replies, "I skate to where the puck is going to be, not where it has been."

When you focus with grace on your dream, not only will you walk toward it with a faster and stronger stride, but those around you will be more eager to support you.

> *Even lifeless instruments like the flute or the harp*
> *must play the notes clearly, or no one will recognize the*
> *melody. And if the bugler doesn't sound a clear call, how*
> *will the soldiers know they are being called to battle?*
> —1 Corinthians 14:7-8

You're standing at the cusp of a fantastic opportunity. You've been living with your business idea for a while, and you've convinced yourself that it's time to start moving. You're fully committed — so should you jump right in? The answer is NO without a written plan! Now you can write fast and furiously—maybe 18 hours a day for several days! Don't even think about jumping in without a major written plan!

To map out a course of action and follow it to an end requires some of the same courage that a soldier needs

—Ralph Waldo Emerson

Once you have decided to move forward, you will immediately start noticing new opportunities all around you. You'll be faced with decisions that ask whether you're going to dive right in, or stand back and consider the situation. Maybe a rental pops up downtown in the perfect location, or a friend suddenly wants to partner with you, or someone is going to make you a deal on a piece of expensive equipment. These are never easy decisions, and many of us hobby/craft type peope love to follow our instincts when we feel inspired. The Lord knows how many times I have jumped right into a new business idea without a moment's thought. Over time I have learned through many hard experiences that when it comes to business, it pays to practice some thoughtful planning. WRITTEN planning!

> *For we are God's masterpiece. He has created us anew in Christ Jesus, so we can do the good things he planned for us long ago.*
> —Ephesians 2:10

There are times for diving in, and there are times for standing back and considering the situation. Even in the "diving in" situations such as a vendor's bringing by a greatly discounted group of Swiss embroideries from a factory's going out of business, a written plan evaluating our current inventory, current sales, marketing plan, and so forth is very important. An ability to decide how and if we are going to sell these embroideries even at a greatly discounted price means the difference between financial success and costly losses. The business world is not forgiving, and it will gladly take your money for nothing. If you bet three month's savings on the wrong inventory, no one is going to erase the bill. There is not even a guarantee that someone will take the inventory off your hands at a discount. Second chances usually come at either a steep price, or else through just a whole lot of good old-fashioned hard work.

Written planning is such an important part of creating and maintaining your business. Planning is an exercise that combines imagination, conversation, and discipline to create a roadmap for your future. By standing back and evaluating your prospects, and forcing yourself to prioritize your goals, you can make decisions much easier. By unearthing and coming to terms with some of the basic issues that you may be ignoring, you can free up your creative side to take the right kind of risks.

Many people dislike written planning for any number of reasons. For them, planning falls under the same list as dental appointments and income tax preparation. Actually I like dental appointments even more than income tax appointments. One reason that people want to avoid writing a business plan is because they think it is some kind of formal legal document, like a last will and testament. Nothing could be further from the truth. A plan is simply a way to organize yourself.

In my seminars, I love to use an audience participation exercise to illustrate the need to organize your dreams. I ask everyone to blow up a balloon and hold it above his/her head. When I count to three I ask everyone to release the balloon. Hundreds of balloons whip around the crowd, dashing everywhere. Each balloon is moving with great enthusiasm — but with no plan! Next I ask everyone to blow up a second balloon. This time we take an extra step before just "letting loose our dreams;" we tie a knot in the bottom. Now the balloons go where we want them to go. They can be passed from individual to individual with relative ease. They can even be caught and held quietly. The balloons represent a business with a plan and one without a plan.

A business plan is simply a way of capturing your dreams and enthusiasm so it can become useful. It is a summary of everything you need to consider in order to create your business. Very importantly it is an evaluation tool for you to carefully judge if the business is a viable one. In this chapter, I am going to share with you how planning your business on paper is actually an extremely creative and interesting process for essentially wrestling an idea from out of the clouds onto the ground. If you approach it the right way, there is nothing to stop you from really enjoying the process of planning your business, and more importantly reaping all the rewards that come with it. You will have a much better perspective on where you are going, and you can confidently know your limits when faced with a decision.

A businessman, a Baptist preacher, and a Boy Scout needed to get to Chicago from Huntsville. All the airlines were sold out. A private pilot offered to fly them for a very high price. They agreed.

When they were nearly to Chicago the pilot came on the speaker, "Unfortunately we have a problem and we are going to have to parachute out of the plane. Even more unfortunately, we only have three parachutes. Since I am taking one of them, the three of you can decide who gets the other two."

The pilot jumped with his parachute on. The businessman said, "Since I'm the smartest man in the world, I'm taking one." He put it on and jumped out of the plane.

The Baptist preacher, smiling bravely, said to the Boy Scout, "Son, you go ahead and take the other one. I know that I'm going to heaven when I die. Besides that, I've lived a long full life. I want you to take the last parachute and jump."

The Boy Scout replied, "Oh, Preacher, don't worry about it, we'll be fine. The smartest man in the world just jumped out of the airplane with my backpack slipped around his shoulders."

No matter how smart you are, jumping into your dreams without first becoming a master planner can be a jump into disaster! If you start your business with a random plan, you can expect random results.

Working Without a Plan Is Costly

Imagine you were asked as a personal favor to fill in for a postal worker delivering mail to the neighborhoods. Would you leave the house that morning without access to some kind of local map? A lot of people think they can start a business with no map and skip the planning stage at first. They feel that they do not need to treat the business like a "real business" until things get serious. If you are thinking this way, you are just fooling yourself. Very few people go into business just to quit after a year. If you want to start a business, you should just admit that you have some long-term plans, and start articulating them. Dare to dream—where do you want to be next year? Just because you set down your goals on paper, stating what you want your business to look like in twelve months, does not mean you can not change your mind later.

As I have said many times, a business is not a toy. Your business is a major life decision and it is going to cost you money and time. As much as your emotional connection with your business counts for something, there are some hard, cold facts about what makes a business successful. We have spent a lot of time covering how your business should come from the heart. The ideas and creativity and passion that you feel for your business should indeed have a very close emotional attachment. When we start talking about actually building the business, you need to have a clear understanding of the realities ahead - the money, the customers, the rent, and the supplies.

To be very honest, in my early days, I did not have much use for business plans—and I can assure you that my failure to have a written plan cost me thousands and thousands of dollars. As you already know I basically made no profit for the first ten years that I was in business. To take one example, in the beginning of my business, when I sold sewing supplies from my retail store, The Heirloom Shop, I was always purchasing far too much variety and in far too much quantity. I had core business purchases, consisting of lace, Swiss batiste, embroideries and some solid color Imperial batiste for smocking. Those purchases were safe bets, and matched my customer base.

Had I taken the time to create a business plan, and understand my situation and my customers, I would have been wise to build the business from that core. Instead, I made the mistake of trying to dabble in a little bit of everything. I bought some cross-stitch books and lots of printed fabrics which never sold. I bought an abundance of smocking design plates that found their way to the trash within a year. I even bought some blue rubber cooking pans some of which I still have in my kitchen! Why on earth did I think that people would want to purchase blue rubber cooking pans from an heirloom shop?

Without a planned budget or a researched sense of my customer base, I just bought and bought and bought, praying that I could pay the bills later. Luckily, I never went so overboard to put myself out of business, but inevitably, I threw away or marked down the entire unsold inventory at a complete loss. Each time, I most certainly set the business back a few months on breaking even.

If your instinct is to resist any sort of written planning work, you need to know that fixing a business mistake is not like undoing a few rows in a badly smocked dress! It's one thing to mess up something handmade, but it is entirely another to erase a month's revenue.

Plan To Avoid Disasters

Just a little bit of effort can help you avoid disasters. Well maybe a lot of effort but believe me it is worth it to plan, in writing, to see if a project has a prayer of being successful financially. Let me give you another example of no planning! After several years in which our magazine, *Sew Beautiful,* was doing particularly well, I dreamed up another magazine that would be devoted to hand work and very fancy heirloom garments, to be called *Fancywork.* I felt so sure of myself that I simply dived right in to the idea. My thinking was that *Sew Beautiful* would emphasize smocking and machine "things" and that *Fancywork* would primarily feature hand work. Up until this time *Sew Beautiful* had featured both in abundance. My dream was that our subscribers would subscribe to both publications.

When I look back on it now, I can see so many simple steps I might have taken if I had decided to make a business plan. Did I do a survey with our *Sew Beautiful* subscribers to see if they would want to subscribe to both magazines? Of course not. Did I calculate my bottom line, or what the publication might cost, or how many subscribers we would need? No, I did not. Did I bother to call our advertisers to see if they would like to advertise in two Martha Pullen publications? No, I did not. Instead I just allowed every single one of my unchallenged assumptions to guide me.

Well, I can say with a great deal of joy that the magazine we produced was absolutely gorgeous; however, we did not get nearly as many subscribers as we hoped. Even worse, however, was that we completely cannibalized our subscriber base. Our *Sew Beautiful* subscriptions dropped by about half, while the same number chose to start a *Fancywork* subscription. To top it off, our advertisers simply chose to alternate ads between the magazines, instead of doubling them. What a mistake! We had increased our publishing costs, without gaining any new subscribers, and lost half the subscribers to our flagship magazine. We quickly ended up folding the magazine and brought everyone back to *Sew Beautiful*, but at substantial cost.

As you can see from the above example, written planning is more than just a useless formality. By forcing yourself to carefully investigate and challenge your assumptions, and consider the consequences of your decisions, a written business plan lets you avoid potential disasters. If I had developed a business plan before starting to develop *Fancywork* magazine, I could easily have predicted and planned around some of the difficulties we encountered.

Your Plan Is a Spotlight

Writing a plan has a natural way of forcing you to surface your assumptions. Somehow, when you keep the conversation locked up silently in your mind, you allow yourself to skip over all the nasty details, and stay on the surface of things. Writing down all your ideas will force your assumptions into the bright light of day, so you can not hide a specific oversight under the rug. When you write down your plan and get into a detailed analysis and justification of your goals, the reality principle steps in. It might have been easy to believe that you could base a retail business on your fabulous idea to sell doll clothes, but when you see the numbers staring back at you, and just how many little outfits you need to sell per month, the idea might not sound so clever.

Why a Plan Is Essential

Since I have understood how powerful a business plan can be, and how helpful a tool it can be to focus and target the major goals and requirements for my business, I regularly revisit my business plan and update it almost every quarter. I absolutely consider the maintenance of my business plan one of the most important keys to my success. The business plan is not nearly as important as prayer but it comes in shortly after that!

Here are some basic reasons why a business plan is an essential part of starting a business:

- Planning is the only safe path between dreaming and doing. If you are faced with a complex job and you just jump into action, you are going to blunder your way your way through. When the only loss you are facing is a personal embarrassment, that is no big deal; however, if there is money on the line, you probably want to cut down on mistakes. I have seen so many people invest their total retirement savings on a "dream business" without a plan and see that dream totally gone within a year. I do not want that to happen to you.

- Planning helps you uncover the challenges that lay ahead of you. If creating a business were easy, everyone would work for themselves. A business plan reveals the hidden assumptions and overlooked issues where you need to focus your problem-solving skills in order to be successful. It is like insurance to help you understand and avoid the riskiest parts of your new venture. If your business plan is sound it just might keep you from entering into a financial disaster.

- Planning takes your energy and enthusiasm, and converts it into something real and "actionable." Some people consider plans a pale substitute for the business itself. A plan is a tool. It helps you communicate and share your ideas with others who can help you. It is a living blueprint for the business that you are possibly going to create if the plan really seems feasible. It lays out the parts and pieces you need to consider, the steps you need to take to pull it all together.

It takes as much energy to wish as it does to plan.
—Eleanor Roosevelt

Balancing Exposure and Protection

Apart from sharing your ideas with those who are closest to you, I do not recommend sharing your ideas with too many people until you have developed a working written business plan. Sometimes we get so excited that we immediately want to share an idea with someone. A business idea in its early stages is a very fragile and tender thing, like a seedling. A gust of cold air from some thoughtless criticism is enough to kill it. Just the opposite might also happen when our friends can "over fertilize" our ideas with unwarranted praise, simply out of a desire to be kind.

By focusing on your protecting your idea at first from public exposure, you will allow the healthy ideas to sink roots and start to develop, and weed out the ideas that really do not work. Like a child, you need to give yourself a little time to play "make-believe" before you bring your idea in contact with the real world.

For that reason, you should use written business planning to build a clear sense of where you want to take your business. It is the first step toward eventually sharing it, after you have made your ideas strong enough for exposure to the skepticism and curiosity of others.

> Look here, you who say, "Today or tomorrow we are going to a certain town and will stay there a year. We will do business there and make a profit." How do you know what your life will be like tomorrow? Your life is like the morning fog—it's here a little while, then it's gone. What you ought to say is, "If the LORD wants us to, we will live and do this or that."
>
> —James 4:13-15

God As Master Planner

No section on planning would be complete without my saying that God is the greatest planner and really the only planner who matters in my life. The times when my plans have gone awry have been when I have made them myself without seeking His guidance. I certainly believe in having written goals and dreams; however, these are to no avail if God is left out of these plans. In business as in life God is the Soverign Lord who offers, to those who ask, amazing grace and unmerited mercy. I totally recognize the role God plays in my business as well as my life and the role He has always played even before I gave Him the credit. I understand fully that God knows my future and that I have boundless hope and that I can trust Him. I understand fully that God did not promise a life without problems and troubles which include my business. It is amazing that through the hardest times God has always had a new beginning for me. I could write a whole business book on the times that God has led me down a new path offering a new beginning.

When ours are interrupted, his are not. His plans are proceeding exactly as scheduled, moving us always (including those minutes or hours or years which seem most useless or wasted or unendurable).
— Elisabeth Elliot

Dr. Henry Blackaby is one of my favorite authors and I think one of the greatest Christian writers of the 20th century. In his book, *On Mission With God*, he writes "God wants an intimate relationship with you so that you will know where He's going next by knowing His ways." He then lists four ways of God shown to Moses:

1. He takes ordinary things and people and does extraordinary things with them.
2. He expects you to obey His instructions whether they make sense or not.
3. When you obey, things won't always turn out as you thought they would.
4. God tells you just enough for you to know what to do next.

> *"For I know the plans I have for you," says the LORD. "They are plans for good and not for disaster, to give you a future and a hope. In those days when you pray, I will listen. If you look for me in earnest, you will find me when you seek me. I will be found by you," says the LORD. "I will end your captivity and restore your fortunes...."*
> —Jeremiah 29:11-14

The Basics of a Plan

I have never been too picky about the form and quality of my business plan. The first round is usually just for my own benefit, so I am perfectly happy with a thirty-page plan written longhand with a Ticonderoga and a pad of legal paper. What is much more important is what the plan contains. When I build a business plan, I like to review the following list of questions to make sure that I am answering them in some way. Making a Mind Map is a great way to plan. It is a fun way to plan.

- How much money do you want to make the first year? Write this down FIRST!! You must have a financial goal.
- What is your objective? What is it that you really want to do?
- Give a detailed description of the business.
- Explain the type of business.
- List all possible profit centers.
- Discuss the product/service offered.
- Discuss the advantages over your competitors.
- How is this venture unique?
- List the skills and experience you bring to the business.
- How will you acquire any additional needed skills and experience?
- What name will you use?
- Discuss the ownership of the business and the legal structure.
- Where will the business be located? Why?
- Will this be a store front business or an Internet business?
- What kind of facilities will you need?
- What kind of supplies?
- What kind of equipment?
- To produce your product or service, what steps are required?
- Where will you get supplies?
- Will you need employees? How many? What will your employees do?
- What are your plans for employee salaries, wages, and benefits?
- Discuss how you will hire your employees and discuss personnel procedures.
- Discuss lease or rent agreements.
- What insurance coverage will be needed?
- What licenses and permits will you need?
- What are your potential funding sources? How will you spend it?
- What financing will you need?
- How will the loans be secured?
- What are the tax advantages of owning your own business?
- What are the requirements for making this business a legitimate business for the IRS?
- What is your total estimated business income for the first year?
- What are your total estimated business expenses, by month, for the first year?
- What will the return on the investment be?
- Why do you think this is a good risk?

- Discuss deadlines for each stage of your business. Set timetables. Be realistic.
- Explain pricing strategy for your product or service.
- Discuss your break-even point.
- Discuss how and who will maintain your accounting records.
- Evaluate your personal monthly financial needs.
- Explain your personal balance sheet and method of compensation.
- Explain how the business will be managed on a day-to-day basis.
- Who are the experts you might contact for advice?
- What are the alternatives when things go wrong? Provide "what if" statements to demonstrate alternative approaches to addressing any negatives that may develop.
- Who will your main customers be, the people you will sell to?
- Where might you buy possible mailing lists to reach these potential customers?
- Explain how your product/service will be advertised.
- Discuss how your product/service will be delivered.
- Who will build your website?
- Who will maintain your website?
- Discuss your potential customers.
- Discuss your competitors.
- Discuss how your competitors bring in customers.
- Do you feel that God is leading you to start a business?

As your pages of notes and ideas grow, you will begin to see plans and directions emerge. For instance, you will see you need to talk to the nice folks at city hall, the courthouse, the county government, etc. Include the results of these meetings. Your notes on business licenses and procedures will greatly expand and enhance your plans and directions.

Getting Started

Creating a good business plan is an art form. In the same way that a good story captures your imagination, or a watercolor lets you see the world in a different light, a great business plan should spark your interest. To make your business plan will take a lot of work. You will certainly need to edit several drafts before you get it right.

If this is your first business plan, you should get used to the idea that it is going to take a lot of time—it will not happen overnight. In fact, you should set a basic expectation that it will take a solid window of time, say thirty to ninety days of dedicated work, before you will see something solid.

Too many people rush into a plan. Remember I rushed into a business with NO WRITTEN PLAN! Remember that I worked and worked for ten years before making a profit! You do not want to do this! When you really think about it, the basic premises behind your business are some of the most important pieces. They will determine the fate of your business for a long time. Give these ideas the respect and space they deserve. If you try to rush your plan, you run the serious risk of jumping into hasty conclusions. A good plan is predicated on carefully thinking out all the options, and discussing all the possibilities, and researching all the angles. To do anything less would mean cutting yourself off from a fantastic opportunity.

There are several basic reasons you should give yourself a little while to create a plan. First, you need to give yourself that much time also to allow your creativity to noodle the situation and make it better. Contrary to popular myth, creativity does not come all at once like lightening. The best ideas build little by little, through the careful and deliberate application of thought to a problem that we want to overcome.

Second, your plan should incorporate the collective wisdom from those around you. Do not make the mistake of treating your ideas like mushrooms, locked away in a cold dark basement. Share your ideas with others you trust, let them pop a few bubbles, and dispel a few illusions. If you practice resilience, you can take it. Temper your plan with solid dose of reality by talking with others, and you will always know that your ideas have been reality-tested. Check out books from the library and study them. Many incredible books have been written about small business. Certainly information is available about small business on the Internet.

Third, if you are a perfectionist, you need to give yourself the slack and the patience to let your plan be a mess for a little while. Your plan may start out full of mediocre ideas, and crazy schemes that don't make sense. That is completely fine, and it is a natural part of the process. Give yourself the freedom of stumbling around in the dark until you bump your head on the solution. That is the whole point of figuring it out on paper—you want to make mistakes early and often, when they do not cost anything. If you take that kind of forgiving attitude with yourself—showing the same patience you would offer a little ten year old who wants to start a lemonade business—your plan will get better and better until you have something you can show friends.

Faith is taking the first step, even when you don't see the whole staircase.
— Robert Frost

Planning is a Barometer

Planning has the added benefit of being an excellent measure of your readiness to start a business, because the fact is that if you can not force yourself to sit down and write a plan about your business, and state all the assumptions and elements of how it is all going to work, then you most certainly are not ready to actually run the business. I have saved many people the trouble of starting a business, simply by telling them to work on a business plan first. They never completed it, which helped them recognize that they were not ready to invest their energy in the business either. So, as my final plea to those of you who still want to resist making a business plan, let me just say that **if you are not ready to bring this small amount of discipline and dedication to your business, then you are not ready to start a business.**

You should plan on carving out at least thirty minutes every single day to focus exclusively on the plan. Keep in mind that the required discipline is not simply about the thirty minutes, but even more importantly, the "every single day" piece. No matter how your day has gone, or from where you steal the free time, you need to promise yourself that you are going to sit down and do it. I do not care if you have to lock yourself in the bedroom twice a day for fifteen minutes at a time; you simply need to force yourself to chip away at the plan, just the same way you will need to force yourself to bounce back from setbacks.

It may feel like tough going at first, and you will feel a bit frustrated with your progress, but even when you feel stuck, something is happening inside you. Do not allow yourself the temptation of distractions like the Internet or television when you feel stuck. Remember the written plan? Write how you are going to overcome the difficulty. Remember that even if you feel stuck right now, with a little G.R.A.C.E. you can create your business plan.

If you have built castles in the air, your work need not be lost.
That is where they should be. Now put the foundations under them.
—Henry David Thoreau

Building a Vision

Back in the old days, there were few things that filled me with anxiety more than staring at a blank page on the first day I decided to write a real business plan. As everyone who knows me quickly learns, I have a mind that loves to hop around like a rabbit.

Just because you are getting serious about your business does not mean it can not be fun. The first phase of your business planning—where you start to craft a vision for your business—is designed to be especially playful. In order to tap into your full creativity, you need to keep things enjoyable and light. This is your time to start having fun. Enjoy it. Give yourself the freedom and luxury to play around with all the ideas that you have been entertaining. Think up as many possibilities as possible. Think and WRITE! Write down everything. Mind Mappping is the best possible technique. It is fun.

To cultivate that kind of thinking, I have learned that you need to truly exercise creative methods. Thankfully, I've learned a couple little tricks that I regularly rely on to get me started. These exercises are the perfect way to get started on any new project, because they take better advantage of the way people really think.

For God has not given us a spirit of fear and timidity, but of power, love, and self-discipline.
—2 Timothy 1:7

Brainstorming

As an educator, I have read articles and studied how writing requires the orchestration of so many different parts of our mind—to sequence ideas, to organize grammar, to spell correctly, to write legibly—that the pressure often kills our creativity. Our brains just can not juggle so many things at once and still perform creatively. I know that I do not work like that, and it took me several years to figure out that it is totally counterproductive to expect a fully formed business plan to simply roll out onto the paper from beneath your pen. Brainstorming is the classic method for getting the ideas out, so you can build a big repository of clever ideas, and then start manipulating them into something that makes sense.

There are so many ways to brainstorm and the true measure of their worth is how well they spark your creativity, and unblock any barriers to your free thinking. Whenever I am in a situation that requires some creative thinking, I fall back on two tried and true methods. I highly recommend them, and so I lay them out here in detail.

Mind Mapping - Discovering Your Ideas

What is Mind Mapping? Mind Mapping is a visual technique for structuring and organizing thoughts and ideas.
—Florian Rustler

We are incredibly good at recording images. If you hear some information, then three days later you will remember 10% of it. If you add a picture to it, then 65% will be retrievable.
—John Medina

What is a Mind Map?

As I wrote in the beginning of this chapter I am so SOLD on the value of Mind Mapping in the business planning world that I traveled to Europe to become a ThinkBuzan Licensed Instructor. I think it is the most exciting business planning tool in the world today. Actually if I were to teach school again I would teach Mind Mapping in all of my subject areas. I studied with Tony Buzan the inventor of Mind Mapping, with people from all over the world. I became even more convinced that Mind Mapping is the best technique in the universe for business planning.

Mind Mapping replicates the way our brains think and the way we absorb information. When we think of any idea, our mind instantly starts connecting this to other images, thoughts and concepts. So why do we force ourselves to make notes, plan and create in a way that our brain doesn't like?

—Tony Buzan

Mind Maps look more like pictures than texts. They sort of look like a tree with branches going in all directions. You can Mind Map with colored pencils and paper. Our minds are a funny thing, and many times, we ask it to behave in ways that do not play to its strengths. Sometimes just changing a habit or a way of doing things unlocks all sorts of hidden energy. Mind Mapping is a perfect example, and best of all, it requires little effort and planning. It is simply a different way of recording the relationships between your ideas—much better than a list. Mind Mapping opens up your creative thinking to non-linear possibilities. It helps you build connections. Have you ever heard the statement, "A picture is worth a thousand words?" Well a Mind Map lets you make a plan which is basically a picture. Being an English teacher I think it looks somewhat like diagramming an idea or a business into a picture. I love the iMindMap software.

Mind Mapping lets your mind behave a bit like a puppy dog, running around, sniffing and wrestling with everything in its path. It lets you to pursue every curious instinct that your mind desires. The key to Mind Mapping is that you are not restricting yourself to an itemized, sequential, one-after-the-other style of thinking. You are just allowing your mind to move wherever it likes, and simply recording all the leaps and bounds it takes.

The basic rules for making a Mind Map are simple. You have bubbles and connectors. You start with a central idea, write it down in the center of the page and surround it with a circle. Voila, step one complete. Next draw a branch from the bubble. Now what are some related ideas that you want to explore? Make a new branch for each idea, and link it to the center. Use different colors for each branch. Start to develop your secondary ideas with new branches and connect them. No idea should be floating out in space; it should always have at least once connection.

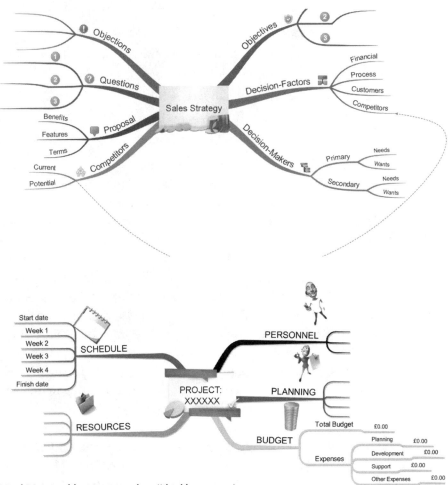

Mind Maps used by permission. http://thinkbuzan.com/

As your Mind Map starts filling out, you might discover new connections—feel free to draw connectors across the page linking distant ideas, but don't go too crazy. Only strong connections count. As you keep building, you will create a bubble constellation of the important ideas that are floating in your head.

What are you writing about, you ask? Well, you could be using Mind Mapping for anything really. I would argue that your main goal is to start recording all the thoughts that pop into your head when you think about your business. The possibilities are endless, and sometimes that can feel a little intimidating. If you need some help getting started, you can turn to the famous example from Rudyard Kipling, who talked about six loyal servants (Who, Where, What, How, When, and Why), who served him well. Turn those servants loose upon your business idea and you'll have created the time-honored **Kipling Business Plan.**

- What are you going to do?
- Why are you going to do it?
- When are you going to do it?
- How are you going to do it?
- Where will you do it?
- Who will be doing it?

Hints for Your Mind Map

- Keep your Mind Map fun, and let yourself be a little zany. Don't censor yourself by saying an idea is silly or dumb, just leave the branch there, it may simply be a breadcrumb that is leading you to a better idea.
- Don't get locked into a specific, narrow idea for your business. Keep your mind open. Simply because you sell sewing machines, doesn't mean that your business can't expand into teaching
- Keep your branch names simple. Don't try to fit too much on a branch. You just need a keyword—enough to remind you of the basic concept.
- Build your branch map in waves extending outward, and keep things spread out. Start with a central concept, and then try to think of all the major ideas that connect to it. Then proceed to develop the major ideas from each secondary branch.
- If you can't fit it all on a page, do not write smaller, just get bigger paper. Go to Staples and buy some large format sketch paper.
- Version your Mind Map several times. For the first few versions you should try to focus on getting everything out there and emptying your mind. For later versions, you should work on the relationships between ideas.
- Treat your Mind Map like a work of art, use colors and pictures. With each new version make it nicer, cleaner, and more symmetrical. Add more detail where appropriate. Notice where there are empty areas, and question why you are not developing this area more.
- Air your fears and concerns. Note the specific details in your Mind Map that make you worry most.

    With a Mind Map, you have two key goals. The first is to empty the storage space in your mind of all those ideas, so you can inventory them on paper. You are trying to unload from your brain all the incredible juggling of ideas that you have been carrying around for too long. The working premise here is that your brain is a great tool for solving problems, but it is not so great at storage. All of us have very fallible memories — it is just a fact of life, and the way our brains were made. The energy we spend on storing and hanging on to ideas ends up gumming up your brain with useless tasks. Mind Mapping takes the pressure off your brain, by letting you quickly get it all on paper in an intuitive way, so your mind can start thinking about bigger and better things.

Your second goal with Mind Mapping is to craft a simple, easy-to-read illustration of your one big interconnected idea in a single view. You are trying to help raise your mind above the full set of your ideas, to an elevation where it can get a "birds-eye" view of them. Just as any map gives you a much better understanding of all the roads and houses in your town, there is something very powerful about getting a map view over your whole plan. It's something that a "street-level" linear list just can't offer. If you are interested in learning more about Mind Mapping please go to **www.pullenbusiness. com**. The iMindMap software is absolutely the best. It is simple and clear and gives users the impression that they are actually drawing a Mind Map and not using software. As I said I am one of the few ThinkBuzan Licensed Instructors in the United States. I felt learning this method, properly, to be able to teach it in my business consulting was critical. So I went to Europe and became a licensed instructor. I think by this time you might have guessed that I am very serious about helping others to plan businesses and grow businesses hopefully without making all of the mistakes that I made. This is a passion in my soul—to help others achieve their dreams of owning their own businesses.

Mind Maps used by permission. http://thinkbuzan.com/

Sticky Planning - Detailing and Organizing Your Ideas

Here is another planning method which is fun. Break out the sticky notes. This method requires a little bit more setup, and you should make sure that you give yourself a solid block of time—at least sixty to ninety minutes—but the results are worth it.

There is a fancy name for this method (**Affinity Mapping**), but I just call it Sticky Planning. By making all your ideas into "stickies" that you can organize and manipulate with your hands, you open up new channels of thinking. In the same way that children learn through playing, you are giving yourself the freedom and the space to refine your business plan, by physically organizing ideas into something that makes sense to you. It is called "multi-sensory processing" and it really works.

Here's what you need:

- An empty wall. Give yourself a large swath of uncluttered vertical wall space, a minimum of six feet wide. Ideally, you can be working in your office, or somewhere where you do not have to clean up right away when you have finished. Maybe you can temporarily take down a few posters or paintings. The more space you will have to spread out, the better.
- Several packs of sticky note pads, in a minimum of three different colors. Do not get the kind with random colors in a single pad— you need to control what colors you choose.
- Do not make the sticky note pads too big or too small—I like the 3" x 3" kind—you want them large enough to be able to write a very brief phrase, like "make pillowcases" or "grow inventory by 50%." (Even though they cost a little more, I would strongly recommend buying the Post-It "super-sticky" kind because they hang on to the wall much better, and will not fall down.)
- A few black Sharpie markers. It should definitely be a thick marker— thicker than a pen—so you can read the writing from a few steps back, but not so thick that you cannot actually write neatly on the post-it.

The first steps are going to feel very similar to Mind Mapping. In fact, if you have done your Mind Map, you can really just copy from it. I want you to take all the most important branches from your Mind Map and put each idea on a sticky note. For this first round of sticky notes, make sure all your ideas are on the same color sticky note—let's say Yellow—these are your **core ideas.** Do not worry about ordering them yet, they should just get stuck up on the wall.

Now after your first flurry of adding things to the wall, it is time to start building greater detail. Now you are going to start using a different color sticky note–let's say Pink—upon which you will start listing even more **business details.** Take a single Yellow sticky note (one of your Core Ideas) and place it on the upper left corner of your space, then ask yourself if you can do a better job adding detail to this idea. Try to start thinking in business terms about some of the following topics:

The product (or the service): Don't lock in on a single product, or a single way of doing things. Think about the options. Why not combine your product offering with other things? Can you diversify the range of products you want to offer? Again, do not cut off any options, that's for later—for now just consider what seems like a good idea.

The market: Who will be buying your product? Can you make it more appealing to other markets? Are you thinking too small? Are you only focusing on local audience when the Internet would let you sell to anyone?

The channel: Are you going to have a retail store, or sell on the Web? Will you make a mail order catalog, or travel to craft fairs? Do you want to do trunk shows? Each of these decisions will have important financial and business consequences.

The financial: How much is everything going to cost? You don't need to be exact, but making some early estimates can help keep perspective.

The personal: Do not be afraid to make this about you. Your instincts are a tremendous guide, and you should let them express themselves. What are you personally worried about with your business? Are you worried about coming up with the cash? Are you worried about managing your finances? Are you worried about the effect of your business on your family? Are you worried about being too busy? These are important things to get out there and confess and admit, so you can look at them squarely.

Reminders

- Keep it to one idea per sticky note—"I want a website and a retail store" are two separate ideas—each one should have its own post it.
- Every business detail is important—if you want to mention that there should be a splash of pink on all your products, then say it. No idea—if

it's important to you—is too small or inconsequential.

- Now that you have laid all your ideas out, in living color, it is time to bring a little order to your wall. Your wall, by this point, should be pretty full of stickies. So what you want to start doing is clustering all these sticky notes into little groups that make sense to you. Feel free to move them all around your open wall—seek open spaces and transfer an entire cluster over there. Be sure to preserve the relationships between your core ideas and business details.
- Once you have created a nice cluster of stickies, take your third color sticky note, and give that entire cluster a name—let's say Blue—these are your categories. For example, maybe you have a cluster that's filled with ideas and details about what you want to sell, so you can call this cluster the "Products" category.
- Go ahead and keep moving all your sticky notes around until you have grouped them all in an order that makes sense to you. The easiest thing to do is put them in columns.
- Give yourself lots of time to move and cluster things in the correct order. Do not feel rushed, this is important thinking.
- Don't fall into the trap of thinking of thinking that you are "wasting your time" or "being silly" by moving stickies around on a wall. See yourself as an artist who is working on her canvas.
- As you are clustering, do not try to hang multiple post-its off a single one, or they will start to fall down.

Once you get the picture, it is pretty straightforward. Like most creative methods, there are no hard and fast rules, so don't feel like you need to do it exactly like I am suggesting. The primary consideration is that you are trying to externalize your thoughts and break through mental blocks.

Once you are done, it is important to preserve your work. The first thing I always do is take a snapshot with my camera—sometimes I need to take several in order to be certain that I can read all the details. After that, you should immediately, or within the next 24 hours, transcribe your sticky-notes onto paper—making sure to preserve the organization you've created. If you have organized your thoughts well, all these sticky notes should easily transfer into an outline format like this:

A. Category
   1. Core Idea

            a. Business Detail
            b. Business Detail
    2. Core Idea

B. Category
    1. Core Idea

By this point, you have managed to construct an outline of your business plan, and you have started to organize all the major pieces. It may still have some gaps, unanswered questions, or unquestioned assumptions. That is alright because we are going to start making your plan even stronger.

SWOT Analysis

Another very productive brainstorming tool is called a SWOT analysis. The acronym SWOT stands for strengths, weaknesses, opportunities and threats. This kind of analysis creates a very simple framework for taking a snapshot of any business situation, and describing the core issues at work. When I am looking at a tough decision that has too many layers and too much complexity—I use a SWOT analysis to understand the heart of the situation. It always helps me arrive at a decision.

Performing a SWOT analysis is extremely simple. You are going to create a grid on a large piece of paper, divided up into four sections as follows:

In the first box, you should write a list of all the strengths that your business has going for it. This should be all the assets and skills that you bring to the business. It should also be any basic financial assets that are going to be helpful contributors to the success of the business. Maybe you have good connections that you can rely on. You should consider both intangible things, like your experience and expertise, as well as tangible things like a savings account, or even a sister who is willing to help you build a website. Think about ways that you can differentiate yourself, and that are clearly under your own control. This is where everything that gives you confidence should go.

The second box is for all the internal disadvantages that you need to overcome with your business. Maybe it is a lack of experience in business, or shyness about selling. It could be a lack of financing, or a poor understanding of retail accounting. These are the simple facts about your business that are under your control, and not living up to your standards. This is where all your worries should go.

For the third box, you want to start looking outside the four walls of your business, and think about the marketplace. These are things totally outside your own control that will still determine the fate of your business. Is your hobby trendy right now, or perhaps there is a lot of interest in home crafts? Think about the local economy and how it is doing. Maybe there is a nearby crafts fair that is held monthly, which you can rely on for building a strong client base. Keep in mind that if you are having trouble filling in this section, because you don't really know much about external opportunities, that is simply telling you that you need to do more market research.

The final box is where you put the threats to your business. Things like high rent or an abundance of local competitors can work against your business. These are areas you need to carefully monitor because they will undermine your success if you do not plan around them.

	Helpful	*Harmful*
Internal	*1. Strengths*	*2. Weaknesses*
External	*3. Opportunities*	*4. Threats*

A SWOT analysis allows you to organize the basic information about your business into a quick diagram, and document exactly where you need to focus your efforts. For each quadrant, you will want to make sure that your business plan can address the challenge or opportunity it presents. You will want to plan your business around the unique set of circumstances for your market and your position within it. With your strengths, you will want to make sure that your business finds ways to maximize their impact, and your business plan should reflect that. For your weaknesses, you need to plan extra hard to compensate for the difficulties you will face. You will want to take advantage of the external opportunities in any way possible, and have true tactical plans that let you walk away from the threats.

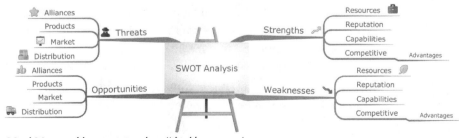

Mind Maps used by permission. http://thinkbuzan.com/

The 3/30 Plan

Those of you who have attended my business seminars over the last twenty years know about my devotion to the 3/30 Plan! Ten years into my business I had a very "large" business from a sales point of view and a failing business from a profit point of view. After ten years of working for no money I was ready to sell the business and go back to teaching in a college which I also loved doing. I was working for nothing and I was working too hard to get paid nothing. I hired an accounting firm to come in to do a "boot camp" and discover what was wrong. What they discovered was that I was trying to be all things to all people and was doing just everything which seemed fun to me and creative. I was wildly buying inventory much of which never sold. I was not concentrating on the things which were always successful in our business but rather was trying to reach out to many unknown very creative territories which were ruining the profits which the successful parts of the business earned.

After realizing that I had to get rid of many "things" in the business and concentrate on what was working I decided to write 3 pages a day for 30 days. First I wrote the dollar amount I wanted to increase my business that year. My goal was to double my sales that year. Actually I did not double my sales that year with the 3/30 Plan but I did increase sales by about 45% which I think is pretty good. I don't think I knew that is fabulous to increase sales in any year by 45%!

Through that 3/30 Plan and the FIRST WRITTEN PLAN I HAD EVER DONE IN MARTHA PULLEN COMPANY, I had a plan and I knew the direction that we needed to go. I wanted to travel in the profitable direction and stop trying, wildly, to do everything that crossed my mind. I was trying to be all things to all people in the name of creativity. I wanted to begin to earn a living in my business!

I have taught this plan for many years. Those who have actually done this 3/30 Plan have learned much and made many decisions based on sound judgment after writing 90 pages. The first step is to write down the dollar amount you need or want to make this year! You must determine a financial goal. Then write 3 pages a day for 30 days.

You might say, "Martha, where in the world will I get enough information to write 90 pages on starting a business?" My answer is go to the library and check out every book on home based business, starting a hobby based business, selling on the Internet, selling on Etsy, selling on Facebook, advertising when you have no money, networking for dummies, planning, entrepreneurship, small business, accounting for small businesses—the list goes on. In any one library there will probably be hundreds of great books on small business and starting a small business. Check them out study them and most importantly write down ideas that look good to you. Notice I said WRITE the ideas!!

Another valuable resource for this 3/30 Plan is to talk with people. Write down their ideas. There are many sources for finding people with whom to talk in other sections of this book. Talk to other small business owners. Write down what they tell you. Get a subscription to the *Wall Street Journal* which has excellent articles on small business on a regular basis.

There are several magazines devoted to entrepreneurs. Some are better than others. Most book stores have a reading area. You might spend some time studying at the book store to see which entrepreneur/small business magazines would be most valuable to you. Study small business websites on the Internet. Write down what you see that is valuable to you. Study YouTube videos about small business. Go to websites of small businesses. Study small business every way you can and most importantly WRITE DOWN WHAT YOU LEARN FROM EVERY PLACE. If you do not write down what you see, you will forget it! Come to www.pullenbusiness.com and join our activities there! I will be constantly looking for new ideas and plans for you. Join our e-mail mailing list! Enroll in my Pullen Business School! **(www.pullenbusiness.com)**

In the 3/30 Plan do not do a lot of organizing. Just write down ideas. After a few pages you might begin to see ideas which look good and those which do not look good. You must address what things cost. Where are you going to get your customers? How do you do a survey? What networking methods are you going to use? By the way, this book has invaluable help in doing your 3/30 Plan on many topics. Go to the IRS and SBA websites and gather information on your needed tax facts. Write them down. Print out brochures and put them in your notebook with your 3/30 Plan.

Now you have created some great resources to draw from as you start actually writing your plan. You have a great outline. You actually have 90 pages of great ideas. If you have allowed yourself to explore your ideas, and created a large universe of options, you are going to be in great shape. The trick now is to convert this wealth of ideas into a solid, reasonably professional document that you can start sharing with others.

In the beginning this 3/30 Plan was my personal method for developing a business plan, which I have used many times. Its primary benefit is that it does not ask you to create perfection from the start. It recognizes the evolutionary quality of an idea, and helps you build it from scratch. But once you are done, you will have a business plan that you are comfortable with knowing that you have done lots of research and that you are a lot more knowledgeable about your possibilities.

He who every morning plans the transactions of the day and follows out that plan carries a thread that will guide him through the labyrinth of the most busy life. The orderly arrangement of his time is like a ray of life which darts itself through all his occupations. But where no plan is laid, where the disposal of time is surrendered merely to the chance of incident, chaos will soon reign.

—Victor Hugo

Writing Is Hard: Be Easy on Yourself

Don't worry about getting a fancy business plan like the big companies have. Former president of France, Charles de Gaulle, said, "It is better to have a bad plan than to have no plan at all." The business plan is a flexible document that will change and get better as your business grows. The more years you spend on it, the better, smarter, and more realistic it will get.

Now I will not pretend that writing is easy. For most of us, sitting down and writing anything takes a lot of discipline. That is one of the reasons I love Mind Mapping so much. It is easy! Great ideas don't magically transform themselves into great writing. But I'll tell you a secret that I've learned from writing or co-writing several dozen sewing books. A lot of people think that what they read in books or newspapers just comes naturally. They get frustrated immediately, because the way they write does not sound as good as what they had hoped it would say.

The truth is that by the time a published sentence reaches you, it has been read, re-read, and corrected by several people along the way. If you can take the big step of lowering your expectations for quality, and raising your expectations for tenacity, you will be much more productive. If you stop trying to write perfectly every time you start typing or writing, and instead happily settle for any kind of writing that gets the basics across, you will have time later to improve it. The key is simply keeping at it every day. You have no idea how many times I have edited and re-written this book!

Write in Waves

Now that your ideas are all out there, you need to make a solemn promise with yourself to plan the time each and every day to work on your business plan. Maybe you will want to buy a writing calendar for yourself. Sit down with it, and spell out the time for each and every day that you plan to write—pretend you are signing a contract for each and every day. For every day that you successfully complete a day's writing, cross it off your calendar.

For the first ten days of your 3/30 Plan, your focus should be on expanding and adding detail to your outline. You can work in a fairly freeform manner, picking various points and trying to develop them further. As you go, continue to allow yourself to exercise your creativity muscles—no idea is too crazy. By the end of these ten days, you should have expanded on all the elements in your outline.

For the second ten days of your plan, you should start bringing it all together. Take all the pieces you have written, and assemble them into a coherent, orderly document. The organization of the document is up to you—but it should make sense. I would recommend trying to organize it along three major sections:

Business
- Describe the business — its products, services, and objectives.
- What are the business risks and mitigation strategies?
- In what directions can the business expand?
- How much time do you expect to allocate to the business?
- Describe what facilities, supplies and equipment are required?
- Describe any production processes required.
- What employees are required?
- What additional services are required (insurance, legal, accounting)?
- What is your timeline for growing the business?

Financials
- Will there be any funding or financing required?
- Give a full inventory of your expected annual and monthly expenses.
- What will be your pricing strategy?
- What will be the different parts of your business to generate revenue?
- State your 1st year financial goals and your "break-even" point.

Market
- Who will be your customers?
- Describe the size of the local and national market for your business?
- How saturated is the market with similar offerings?
- What is the unique value proposition you offer compared to competitors?
- How will you advertise or market your business?

The final ten days of your plan should simply be devoted to the cleanup and polishing of your plan. Focus on trying to express your ideas clearly and simply. Remove unimportant details throughout the document. Reduce your writing to the essential points.

Our life is frittered away by detail. Simplify, simplify.
—Henry David Thoreau

. . joy fills hearts that are planning peace!
—Proverbs 12:20

Ready to Share

Congratulate yourself! You have created a real blueprint for your business that is going to help you make decisions. When that perfect store rental pops up downtown, you are going to know exactly how much you can afford—or by how much you will need to adjust your monthly revenue in order to make it work. Possibly you are ready to hire the web designer for your Internet store. Maybe you are ready to learn how to set up an

Etsy store or an eBay store. Maybe you are ready to rent space within an already established store. Maybe you have found the perfect craft markets for becoming a vendor.

Even more importantly, you have taken the time to actually prove to yourself that you can really do this. You will be able to speak clearly and concisely with others about how you plan to build your business. People will hear in your voice that you have given serious thought to the important questions, and you will feel more confident.

Now you are ready to share your plans with others. Take one more look and make sure that anyone can read your plan and answer the following questions:

- Describe your business idea.
- Name your business.
- How will you make your products?
- Where will you make your products?
- What kind of equipment are you going to need?
- Whose help will you need to make this happen?
- What is the competition?
- Why will your business beat the competition?
- Who is your customer?
- How will you reach your customers?
- How will you sell your products?
- How much will your products cost?

The Master Planner

Look here, you who say, "Today or tomorrow we are going to a certain town and will stay there a year. We will do business there and make a profit." How do you know what your life will be like tomorrow? Your life is like the morning fog—it's here a little while, then it's gone. What you ought to say is, "If the LORD wants us to, we will live and do this or that."
—James 4:13-15

No section on planning would be complete without my saying that God is the greatest planner and really the only planner who matters in my life. The times when my plans have gone awry have been when I have made them myself without seeking His guidance. I certainly believe in having written goals and dreams; however, these are to no avail if God is left out of these plans.

Planning with G.R.A.C.E.

Most people do not plan to fail; but they fail to plan. Planning with **G.R.A.C.E.** has always been my secret.

God: First I ask God to help me see His will in my decisions. Pray all the time for strength and for doors to open. Ask God to guide your dreams and to give you the fortitude and perseverance to plan carefully every step and every day.

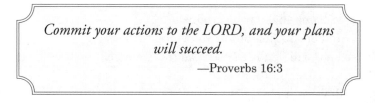

Commit your actions to the LORD, and your plans will succeed.
—Proverbs 16:3

Resilience: With His strength, you will be able to be resilient. Your first plans might not materialize; however, don't quit. Don't ever quit planning for your dreams to become true. "If at first you don't succeed, join the club." Most of us did not succeed with our first business dreams.

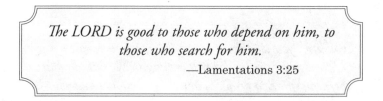

The LORD is good to those who depend on him, to those who search for him.
—Lamentations 3:25

Action: I act. Activity without the insight of a well-thought-out plan provides disaster. But a well-thought-out plan without activity is worse; it is nothing. Planning and action (work!) are probably more important than the dream. Daily you must take action to make your dreams become reality. As Will Rogers told us, "Plans get you into things but you got to work your way out."

> *So take this seriously. The LORD has chosen you to build a Temple as his sanctuary. Be strong, and do the work.*
> —1 Chronicles 28:10

Creativity: I have always tried to think of creative ways to make the plans come true. When God closes a door to me, there is a great reason. I look for the window. I feel great joy when I think of something creative and see that window opening. Then I remember with gratitude whose hand has opened it for me.

> *I rejoice in your word like one who discovers a great treasure.*
> —Psalm 119:162

Enthusiasm: In all levels of designing and executing my plans, I am enthusiastic! The enthusiasm drives my plans forward and God gives me the energy to create better plans.

> *Work with enthusiasm, as though you were working for the LORD rather than for people.*
> —Ephesians 6:7

~ Chapter Six ~

Building a Business Network

Do you remember in Matthew when Jesus gave the great commission to eleven of the disciples? On the mountain? God used a network of people, beginning with a very small network to share the gospel of Jesus Christ. He told them to go not only to their villages but to go tell the nations. Apparently he meant for them to build larger networks, which they did. That is still happening today.

> *Jesus came and told his disciples, "I have been given all authority in heaven and on earth. herefore, go and make disciples of all the nations, baptizing them in the name of the Father and the Son and the Holy Spirit. Teach these new disciples to obey all the commands I have given you. And be sure of this: I am with you always, even to the end of the age."*
> —Matthew 28:18-20

People with goals succeed because they know where they're going.
—Earl Nightingale

If you want to go somewhere, it is best to find someone who has already been there.

—Robert Kiyosaki

It's all about people. It's about networking and being nice to people and not burning any bridges.

—Mike Davidson

Introduction

Joe and I had made the decision to put my new shop in about 1000 square feet of space on the side of his dental building that held some empty offices. After looking through some antique children's story books trying to get an idea of what a little Victorian shop might look like in modern day terms, I concluded that a bay window with a window seat on the inside would be perfect. For display purposes, I knew that some pretty heirloom clothes, possibly mannequins and an antique baby carriage to hold other products would look perfect. Joe hired the carpenter and the entrance to the shop was perfect.

As I toured the empty interior of my new smocking shop, an icy realization came over me. That dewy-eyed vision I had always cherished for my new business, full of decorative possibilities, began to collapse under the weight of reality. We had already spent our planned decorating budget on the bay window! "Oh, what have I done?" I whispered to myself, as a checklist of expenses filled my head: shelving, wallpaper, carpet, fixtures, cash register and a sales counter. I had already spent all my savings and the money Mama had given me for inventory without having seriously considered all the investment required to turn this empty, lifeless, dusty space into a clean, friendly, and welcoming store.

"Now, Martha," I said to myself, "Be creative. You have too much furniture at home anyway. Bring some of it down here." Joe and I brought as many pieces of our furniture and old fixtures from our house as we could spare. Then, over the next several weekends, we scoured garage sales from Huntsville to Scottsboro, driving around in our Buick station wagon, shuffling between the classified section and antique stores (junk stores—we could not afford antiques). By the time we were ready to open the store, we had managed to assemble a rather welcoming environment without completely breaking the bank.

Furniture was just the beginning, because the walls were awful as well as the carpet. "How do I best make this look like an heirloom shop?" I pondered. After looking at some wallpaper books I decided that pink and green were my colors. Laura Ashley had the most wonderful wallpaper with pink and green flowers and pink stripes. There were two versions of this pattern and I chose one for the front of the shop and one for the teaching/sewing machine room. Some nice green carpet finished the look. Joe, once again, dug into his weekly paycheck, and we made it work.

One more bullet dodged. As I look back on the opening of my business, I would probably have had a much easier time if I had consulted more of my family and friends in advance. I failed to gather a network before I opened my business. I failed to gather a network to plan my business before I opened it. As I discovered later, several of my friends had their own friends with lots of past experience running small retail businesses, who might have happily offered advice. I might just as easily asked for a few introductions to some local business owners and heard their tips.

We did get some advice from a few people before opening the shop. I had received lots of advice from my mother's first cousin, Dr. James Erskine Parks, who had a Ph.D. from the Harvard Business School and taught business courses at the University of Mississippi. I loved him dearly and he was always available to talk with me.

My Uncle George Dicus was also a very successful businessman and offered good advice whenever I asked. He had moved back to Scottsboro after retiring from the Sun Oil Company. He had opened and closed two businesses of a wholesale/retail type before opening a Standard Oil Distributorship. His wife, my Aunt Elizabeth Dicus, was a very successful retail shoe store entrepreneur. She was very helpful with advice on running a retail store.

I also talked with Uncle Albert and Aunt Eva Parks, who ran their own successful retail store. It was a small department store that sold all types of clothing, and I had been an employee on the first day it opened, at age twelve. I had always loved working in their store, and my aunt and uncle were always happy to offer me excellent advice.

At the time, I did not know about what people now call "networking," although I had been a networker my whole life. Some call it politicking. This experience of formally identifying networks and realizing how they can help you is very important, and I have taken special care to include it in this revision of my original book.

This chapter concerning networking at the time of the opening of my business is a "do as I say" not "do as I did." Networking became a critical part of my growth of Martha Pullen Company in later years. I could have done much better at the beginning if I had formally networked further than I did for ideas and help. A lot of this book will be to help you from making the mistakes I made at the beginning of my business.

The Value of Business Networks

Mark Victor Hansen, coauthor of the *Chicken Soup for the Soul* series, believes that the two most important skills for business are networking and innovation. What I have learned through many years of business experience is that we all live in a very small world. Without even knowing it, we are surrounded by hundreds of "friends of friends" who are eager and willing to help us. We just need to make the effort to reach out and ask for assistance. So many people can assist us in so many unexpected and undiscovered ways, but we must reach out to them first. In the old days, we called it "keeping in touch" with your neighbors and friends. These days, through the telephone, email, and Internet tools like Facebook, Twitter LinkedIn, and many other social media sites, we call it "networking" with your "contacts." No matter what the label, it simply adds up to taking full advantage of the wealth of wisdom that surrounds you.

Many of us started our businesses seeking greater independence. We placed a premium on autonomy, and adopted a very personal view on how we would make our products and conduct our business. We quickly learned that no matter how much we enjoyed working solo, financial independence rested on the personal network we built around our business. We learned that it is not merely our customers, but our business contacts, that really count. In the end, we discovered that it is our relationships with other people along with God's blessings that determine our success.

Websites like Facebook and LinkedIn have proven that connections count. We are all interlinked, and the ability to take advantage of your social networks will be an important factor in your business success.

Do you remember the movie, *Miracle on 34th Street*? Macy's and Gimbels decided to work together during the Christmas season. Both firms ended up having the greatest Christmas profits ever. This is a great example of networking.

To build and take full advantage of a business network takes time and effort. Many early business owners don't have the experience to approach the process in a structured way. They improvise and hustle and eventually figure out that their friends and colleagues are some of their richest business assets. A mature viewpoint recognizes that it requires a focused effort and a true game plan to build a business network, and it requires dedication to maintain it.

Think about it this way. There are people out there right now whose advice could make a big difference in the shape of your business. Maybe someone has already tried your idea in a different market, and learned some costly mistakes. Maybe someone has begun dabbling with Etsy to sell her products, and she could help you diversify your selling channels. Maybe someone in another part of the country is starting a new retail store and would love to carry your products. There is literally a world of opportunity out there, and you simply need to find it. I am reminded of President John F. Kennedy's Inaugural speech on January 20, 1961 where he said the following:

And so, my fellow Americans: ask not what your country can do for you—ask what you can do for your country. My fellow citizens of the world: ask not what America will do for you, but what together we can do for the freedom of man.

Finally, whether you are citizens of America or citizens of the world, ask of us the same high standards of strength and sacrifice which we ask of you. With a good conscience our only sure reward, with history the final judge of our deeds, let us go forth to lead the land we love, asking His blessing and His help, but knowing that here on earth God's work must truly be our own.

These same principles hold true in business today. No matter how fiercely independent you dreams, once you have made the decision to start a business, and you have begun investing your time and money into its success, there is nothing more foolish than overlooking all the expertise and advice that surrounds you. The people and connections in your business network are assets of inestimable value.

That is especially true in the early days of your business, because you are dealing with so many variables and uncertainties. No matter how much energy and enthusiasm you bring to the table, the simple fact remains that you are inexperienced. There is so much fantastic advice, so many untapped connections, and such valuable experience out there. Especially now, as you prepare to make decisions that will have real financial consequences, things can get confusing. Don't make the mistake of struggling quietly with your doubts and difficulties, when the shared wisdom of your extended circle of friends can help you through many situations.

A lot of people make the mistake of seeing their friends and colleagues as no more than potential customers; however, they are much more than a source of revenue. First of all, your friends are an easy and accessible focus group, if you know how to ask the right questions. Secondly, each of your friends has his/her own personal network of friends, many of them people that you have never met. Each of those strangers, in turn, is either a potential sale, a potential expert, or another valuable contact.

Build Your Business Network Early

I like to define networking as cultivating mutually beneficial, give-and-take, win-win relationships... The end result may be to develop a large and diverse group of people who will gladly and continually refer a lot of business to us, while we do the same for them.

—Bob Burg

Networking is being able to help or benefit from individuals you directly have a relationship with to achieve life's ends.

—Paul Drolson

Now is the perfect time to begin organizing and building your business network in a purposeful way. You have done all the hard work by preparing the business plan. It is all fresh in your mind, and you've assembled all your ideas into something polished and professional. Even better, you are at the very beginning stages of your business, well before you have made any lasting commitments, so you can easily adjust to new information. Your plans are still malleable and can be adapted to new ideas without any additional cost.

By beginning now, you are also investing in something that will serve you for years to come. Over the decades, I have slowly built what I might call my own Advisory Board. Of course, there is nothing formal about it; my Advisory Board is just a network of like-minded business associates, experts and acquaintances, with whom I keep in regular contact. We all reap the benefits of sharing our knowledge, expertise and opinions, so we all do our best to maintain the connection. There are so many people that I have picked up the phone and discussed so many "things." Some of my best advisors, after God, are members of our Martha Pullen Company team. My husband, Joe, has always been my top advisor. I cannot tell you what a mentor my mother, Anna Ruth Dicus Campbell was to me. She was the "mover and shaker" of all times in my view. Although her career was in education, she planned and executed many "businesses" within the framework of her teaching and administration. All five of our children—Camp, John, Mark, Jeff and Joanna—have supported this company and have advised me in so many ways. Camp worked with me for nearly ten years and actually dreamed many of the dreams which have enjoyed much success, including *Martha's Sewing Room* PBS TV series and premiums for subscriptions. Joanna's influence was there from the beginning of this company since she was the inspiration for the whole business. Later she joined the company and worked with me in developing children's sewing books. She also taught at our kid's school here in Huntsville as well as presented kid's sewing segments on our PBS TV series, *Martha's Sewing Room*. I want to thank Alabama Public Television and the University of Alabama Center for Public Television for producing 17 years of fabulous TV shows.

I have talked numerous times with Barbara Spratling, business woman extraordinaire. She had not only her own business experience but that of her father who was a very successful furniture store owner. My business colleague, Kathy McMakin has been one of my best advisors—we worked together at Martha Pullen Company for over 30 years. Phyllis Hoffman DePiano was always willing to listen and advise me almost from the beginning of my company and, in 2004 she purchased Martha Pullen Company. As I mentioned earlier my Uncles George Dicus, Erskine Parks and Albert Parks were always there for me. Uncle George and Uncle Albert had very successful businesses (Standard Oil Distributorship and a retail clothing store). My aunt Elizabeth Dicus was one of my best *G.R.A.C.E. Keys to Entrepreneurship* advisors since she had built a successful shoe retail business following Christian principles. My sister, Mary Nixon, has given me advice not only in the traditional business arena but also in the human relations—understanding people—arena. Mary Nixon's new real estate business has been crafted with lots of creativity from which I have learned much about networking. Margaret Boyles, the first lady of needlework in the United States of America has offered excellent advice on many matters from *Sew Beautiful* magazine to "what to design and print next." My cousin Lewis Page, a prominent Birmingham lawyer, has given creative as well as legal advice. My corporate lawyer, Chris Hinson, has offered much more than normal business legal advice. Sara Domville, President of F+W Media, showed me that an international corporate executive could still have a personal touch for her customers and employees. Rhonda Buescher, Ph.D. has given me advice on many business issues as well as traveled with me to England to become a ThinkBuzan Licensed Instructor.

Several individuals in management with international sewing machine companies were always there to help me. Among these people are Sue Hausmann (Viking/Husqvarna), Steve Jeffery (Baby Lock), Joanne and Rich Gannon (Bernina) and Helmut Ott (Pfaff). Mary Hess, the largest Baby Lock dealer in the country as well as Ricky and Kay Brooks (R&K Distributing) have been invaluable to me with business decisions over the years. Dr. Henry Blackaby opened the doors for me at Lifeway; they published my first business book. Jude Deveraux opened the doors at a top New York agency for me to hire the business author I needed for helping me write parts of this book. Jo Packham has published three major articles on me and my business in her beautiful publications, *Where Women Create* and *Where Women Cook*. Bill Crocker has offered major help to Joe and me along our business journey. From my first trip to Australia in 1988 to right now my dear friend Gloria McKinnon, Australia's most prominent needlework business person, has been a major advisor to me. I must not hesitate to mention the roles Eunice Farmer and the late Clotilde have played in my business development. Patty Smith, Cornelia Anderson, DMD, Kathryn Cashner, MD and Dianne Napier-Wilson have always been there for me with rock solid ideas concerning this business. Joe and I are grateful to Dr. Jimmy Jackson, our pastor of over thirty years for his encouragement and spiritual guidance.

The Benefits

I consider my business network one of the most important assets I have built. The advantages I gain from these relationships include:

- **Perspective**—Many of the people in my business network are peers, and we have experienced many of the same challenges. Keeping in touch and sharing our stories remind me that my difficulties are not unique. Through other people's stories, I can also learn how apparently small problems might indicate a much larger problem hiding beneath the surface.
- **Advice and Feedback**—I regularly use the people on my Advisory Board for feedback. When I bounce an idea off someone, he/she can give me a quick sense of its potential. Depending on who I approach, I can learn what my "ideal customer" thinks of a new product, consider how best to market something, or understand the business impacts of a new approach.
- **Support**—It is tough to be an entrepreneur. It can be lonely and emotionally challenging. While most people have the luxury of walking away from the office, entrepreneurs constantly think about work. My Advisory Board gives me a chance to share my frustrations with others, and keep a healthy attitude toward the business.
- **Accountability**—When I share plans and goals with my Advisory Board, I can better achieve them. By stating my goals and "going on the record," I become more accountable. If I keep my plans a secret, it gives me the room to fall short, but still pretend that everything is fine. By sharing my plans with my colleagues, and speaking with them at regular intervals, I maintain my momentum.
- **New Opportunities**—I don't always have time to keep up with the latest trends and developments in my domain. Keeping in touch with my Advisory Board lets me stay aware of what is important. Because they know and understand my business, my colleagues also tend to call me first when they hear about something that might interest me.
- **Connections**—My business network is constantly growing, and so are my friends' networks. I regularly pass along names to others, and make introductions for my colleagues, and they always return the courtesy. Everybody wins.

Building an Advisory Board

In this chapter I am going to help you create and build your own personal Advisory Board. It is worth repeating that I don't really mean an official Advisory Board whose members you nominate, and who have official duties for your business. There will be no need to create engraved paperweights, and hand out red roses and chocolates to everyone who makes your list. I'm using the term Advisory Board loosely, simply to name a group of individuals who can become important resources for advice and suggestions as your business develops. As I said before, very few of my "advisors" even know that is how I consider them.

This Advisory Board exercise is simply a way of asking you, as an entrepreneur, to begin the lifelong process of creating a loose alliance of friends and experts to whom you can turn for any questions or business concerns. These will be the people who will guide you through some of the the moments of uncertainty that you are going to encounter on the road ahead.

The Right Attitude

Of course, building a business network is really about relationships, and that means that your feelings and your personal attitude will have a big impact on your success. When reaching out to your friends and colleagues, it's worth considering the emotional side of things. Joe has been a lifetime member of the Optimist International of Huntsville. I love the Optimist International Creed which is repeated at each meeting.

The Optimist Creed

Promise Yourself to be so strong that nothing can disturb your peace of mind. To talk health, happiness and prosperity to every person you meet. To make all your friends feel that there is something in them. To look at the sunny side of everything and make your optimism come true. To think only of the best, to work only for the best, and to expect only the best. To be just as enthusiastic about the success of others as you are about your own. To forget the mistakes of the past and press on to the greater achievements of the future. To wear a cheerful countenance at all times and give every living creature you meet a smile. To give so much time to the improvement of yourself that you have no time to criticize others. To be too large for worry, too noble for anger, too strong for fear, and too happy to permit the presence of trouble.

Getting Over Shyness

If you feel too shy and awkward about discussing your business with friends or acquaintances, I urge you to overcome your reluctance. Now you might think, "That's easy for you to say, Martha!" I certainly recognize that not everyone is as socially extroverted as yours truly. We all have strengths and weaknesses. You cannot let shyness undermine your business.

Who Do You Know Who............?

Mark Sheer says this is the most important question to use in asking for a referral. "Who do you know who....?" If you use a closed question such as "Do you know someone who wants to sell her house?" the answer is probably no not now. Rephrasing the question, "Who do you know who might be able to get me some new leads for a listing or a sale?" is much better. The answer certainly is not just "no." The answer might be, "Let me think about it." Or "I know XYZ Company is expanding in a few months and I think there will be new people moving into town. I know the executive assistant to the President. I'll put you in touch with her and you can ask her that question."

Why not use your business as the icebreaker? People love to learn about someone who is trying something new. Whenever the chance arises, just come right out with it: "I'm actually starting a business. Can I talk to you about it?" You will be astonished how differently people treat you when they realize that you are an entrepreneur. Many will be eager to hear more and possibly help you in any way they can.

In the course of your conversation, if you ever reach a lull, just start asking pointed questions about specific elements of your business plan. Would she be interested in the sort of products you would sell? What might she want to do differently? Each person you meet presents another opportunity to learn about your market.

> *Keep on asking, and you will receive what you ask for. Keep on seeking, and you will find. Keep on knocking, and the door will be opened to you. For everyone who asks, receives. Everyone who seeks, finds. And to everyone who knocks, the door will be opened.*
> —Matthew 7:7–8

Letting Go of Perfection

Exposing your plans can be emotionally hard work. After all your preparations, you probably want to get started and prove yourself right. You may feel eager to share your plans, but not so excited about receiving honest criticism, or revising your plans one more time.

Just remember that getting reviewed by others is a very healthy process for both you and your business. If you can listen carefully and accept the criticism, you will walk away with important information. Accept that your business plan has overlooked something. There will be obvious angles that you never even considered. No matter how hard you worked on your business plan, your ideas will need revision, and that is precisely the point. No one ever made a masterpiece without working through dozens and dozens of prior sketches. Rest assured that no matter how much time and effort you have put into your plan, it is only halfway complete until you have bounced it off your friends and colleagues, and heard their reactions.

Be prepared. Some questions may expose a major flaw in your thinking, and your plans may feel like a mere house of cards. Have faith in the amount of time you have invested in building a business plan. By working hard to organize your thoughts, you will look and sound professional, so that people will take you seriously and address your business plan on its merits.

Staying Flexible

Envision children who love to play "restaurant." Imagine that they reinvent the game each time, and add new rules and adjustments. As they talk, they are constantly adjusting to each other's ideas, making new dishes based on the other's suggestions—starting with toast and quickly escalating to ornate chocolate desserts. The rules are always changing from how to run the kitchen to how to serve dishes-all of it is "make-believe." Yet they adapt to each new adjustment. It comes naturally to children.

This is exactly the playful spirit you should adopt when you begin to socialize your plan. Stay flexible and do not be sensitive. Do not lock your mind into anything. You should be eager to present your idea to friends, colleagues, and even strangers, so their ideas can continue to shape and evolve your plans. You want to walk a line between bossy and boring—defending your best ideas, without wincing from criticism.

Any criticism can be constructive, even when it is not delivered nicely. The alternative would be must costlier. If everyone praised your ideas simply to spare your feelings, they have been no help at all. Question every assumption that you have made. Don't get emotionally attached to your own ideas. Allow yourself to be a little wrong. When you feel yourself becoming defensive about criticism, listen carefully and take a deep breath. You can reply gracefully by saying, "You know, that is something I had not fully considered. I am going to reconsider that and see how it impacts my plans."

Remaining Open to G.R.A.C.E.

Remember that your ideas may simply be a starting point for something bigger. Never forget that God is leading you somewhere on His own terms. Only He knows the true path you should follow. Follow your heart, and believe in your ideas, but remain open to the possibility that God may have different plans for you. As you building your business network, keep **G.R.A.C.E** . in mind.

> *For I know the plans I have for you," says the LORD. "They are plans for good and not for disaster, to give you a future and a hope.*
> —Jeremiah 29:11

Trust in **God** above all. If you ask Him he will lead you forward, and present opportunities at every step. Each new connection is a clue to unravel, and a chance to incorporate its lesson into your business. Trust His role in guiding you. Pray a lot.

> *Don't be afraid, for I am with you. Don't be discouraged, for I am your God. I will strengthen you and help you. I will hold you up with my victorious right hand.*
> —Isaiah 41:10

Remember that adversity introduces a man to himself. Negative comments are a form of adversity, and you need to show **Resilience** by refusing to be discouraged. Every new contact is another chance to recreate your business.

Such things were written in the Scriptures long ago to teach us. And the Scriptures give us hope and encouragement as we wait patiently for God's promises to be fulfilled.
—Romans 15:4

Don't be passive about building a business network. Follow the exercises in this chapter, and make **Action** your priority. It takes work to build a strong set of contacts, and you need to put some energy into it. Don't be afraid.

Yes, you came when I called; you told me, "Do not fear."
—Lamentations 3:57

Maintain your **Creativity** through listening closely to others. Do your very best to step outside yourself and see your ideas through another's eyes. Enjoy the exchange. Each new conversation is a chance to expand your creative horizons.

For the Lord your God has blessed you in everything you have done. He has watched your every step through this great wilderness. During these forty years, the Lord your God has been with you, and you have lacked nothing."'
—Deuteronomy 2:7

Your success in connecting with people will be entirely dependent on your attitude. Make sure that you have tapped into your inner **Enthusiasm**, and express it to others. If you are engaged and you believe in your business, many people will be more than happy to help You might say, "I was born excited; however I think I've lost it." Well, get it back! This statement reminds me of a statement Mark Twain once said when asked the reason for his success. He replied, "I was born excited."

> *A cheerful look brings joy to the heart;*
> *good news makes for good health.*
> —Proverbs 15:30

People who concentrate entirely on the material and financial aspects of business fail to realize that in the end all business is conducted through personal relationships.

— Ivan R. Misner

The Process

Hopefully these early words of advice offer a little grounding in some of the emotional aspects of reaching out to socialize your business plans, and building a business network that will help sustain it.

Before you begin speed-dialing all your friends, or dropping in unexpectedly on your neighbor, waving around your business plan, it is worth taking the time to think through your approach. Indeed, you should consider the creation of your Advisory Board just as important a process as finding a location for your business, or deciding what type of insurance you need. You do not want to just go mindlessly barreling into it. This process reminds me of a saying Mama used to have when I called her with a problem or challenge. She would say, "Martha we will just have to think through this."

Different people will have different types of advice and assistance they can offer you. For the same reason you would not ask a plumber for medical advice, you will want to pick the folks on your Advisory Board based on a clear understanding of what skills, expertise, or contacts your colleagues offer. By considering each person's talents, background, and connections, you will be making sure that there are few missteps along the way.

As you begin the process, you can start on paper, but you should quickly transfer your list to a spreadsheet, so you can easily maintain your records. Keep in mind that this is not a throwaway shopping list – it's your future.

There are four steps that I suggest following:

First, **make a list of everyone you know**—and I mean everyone, from the friends with whom you only share a few words every few months, to the close friends you invite for dinner parties.

Second, **add some depth** to the list, so that you can start explicitly documenting how these people are important to your business, and where the strength in your connection lies.

Third, **sort them into different categories.** Each person has a different type of relationship with you, and correspondingly will have a different perspective to offer for your business idea. The trick is figuring out how they all fit in.

Fourth, take the time to **prepare some questions** and speak to them in order to discover who is going to land on your Advisory Board.

Step One: Listing Everyone

Let's start by listing the names of everyone you know. Martha did you say EVERYONE I know? Yes that is right, everyone. You might want to approach your list in waves, by first writing down all the people that come immediately to mind, then going back and revisiting each name to see if that person reminds you of further contacts.

As you compose your list, keep expanding your horizons to consider any other people you know through your daily life—maybe you're friendly with someone at the local coffee shop or grocery store or department store . Possibly you know lots of people at church. Do you have some old business colleagues with whom you keep in touch? Are there old college or high school connections that might be useful? You want your list to be highly inclusive, because you never know where a hidden connection to your business might be lurking. Do you belong to any social clubs that have a directory? When in doubt, put them down.

If you feel like your list is thin, consider making another Mind Map like the one you made in the last chapter on Business Plans. In this case, make all your friends' names as bubbles, and all their connections as branches. This is a great exercise to remind yourself of many connections that you have forgotten. The whole point is to make your list as long and extensive as possible. Even after starting your list, you should keep adding to it over time.

For your final pass at the list, you should add anyone whom you would like to meet in the future. It might be someone who runs a local business, or someone who isnationally recognized. Do you have a personal hero you might like to meet? Don't be afraid to put down a name that seems far-fetched, because you might be surprised how far a little persistence can bring you.

Adding Contact Information

Wherever possible, add contact information for everyone on your list. Fill in as much as possible through some preliminary research, and by combing through your address book. Don't worry about what you can not find right now—so long as you keep adding to your list over time. Keep in mind that this list will quickly become a marketing list too, so your attempts at thoroughness will not be wasted. Things to record:
- Email address
- Phone
- Physical address
- Business address (if applicable)
- Social media info (Are you connected by Facebook, GooglePlus, Twitter, Instagram, Pinterest, LinkedIn or another group?)

Using Networking Tools

We will dig deeply into social media and your business in a future chapter, but it is worth taking a moment right now to discuss the role of Facebook, Twitter, LinkedIn, Pinterest, Instagram and GooglePlus for building your business network. For starters, I'm going to assume that you have heard of both Facebook and LinkedIn, even if you don't have an account on either site. In simplest terms, all of these tools are websites that let you keep in touch with your friends, and rediscover old friends with whom you may have lost touch. The only difference with LinkedIn is that it is designed exclusively for business contacts.

For purposes of discovering names to add to your business network, all of these tools can be very useful. Don't make the mistake, however, of assuming that these sites can actually replace the networking database that you are building yourself.

In the end, these sites are simply communication tools that let you: (1) Easily reach out to your network and send them a message, and (2) in some cases, discover new contacts. These sites will not let you manage your own personal information about each of these contacts. You will need to do that yourself.

If you are unfamiliar with any of these tools, Facebook, GooglePlus, Twitter, Pinterest, Instagram or LinkedIn, I recommend that you take the time now to open an account on each site.

For each of these tools, it is very easy to learn how to use them. They are designed to be simple and straightforward. If you are a bit "technology-challenged" and need some handholding with anything that involves computers, you might try visiting sites like **eHow.com** to learn some of the basics. Or else you can invite your favorite nephew or grandchild over for an afternoon lesson—most kids these days know much about computers.

Once you have an account, you can quickly start browsing around and "linking" or "friending" the people you know. Almost immediately, you will start to see the breadth and power of your personal network.

Please don't jump the gun and begin your business networking yet. There are lots of other considerations that we will cover in the Social Media chapter. We will discuss how you can best take advantage of all these tools.

Step Two: Adding Depth

After you have created your list, you need to give it depth and meaning by adding additional information. This is where your contact list starts differing from both a tradition address book, and social media sites. If you have typed your list into a spreadsheet, you can add a new column and start adding comments about this person's value to you or your business. They should be brief statements to help you situate why this person might be a good connection for you and your business.

For example:
• Is she a close personal friend?
• Is he family?

- Do you admire her taste?
- Would he make a great customer?
- Is she a social butterfly with lots of friends?
- Does he seem to have an especially logical or creative mind?
- Does she have a talent for finance or organization?
- Does he have a particular business experience that could help you?

The point of this information is that it will help you prioritize whom you want to contact first from your list. People with obvious connections to your business will be your first contacts. If you can not think of any immediate connection between this person and your business, that does not mean you should eliminate them from your list. You never know how a connection can serve you in the future.

I have a friend, for example, who was starting a business importing textiles. One evening, she described her plans to some dinner guests, and mentioned her concerns about all the complex importing regulations from different countries. My friend mentioned it only in passing, without any expectations. She knew that her guest was a website designer and her guest's husband was, of all things, a professional scuba diver. What would they possibly know about importing regulations, after all?

To her surprise, however, they explained that one of their closest friends imported spices from the Orient, with years of experience handling customs. My friend left dinner that evening with a phone number and email address of someone who has been an extremely valuable member of her Advisory Board ever since.

Step Three: Sorting Them All

By this point, your list might be quite long. The next steps, after carefully considering the comments and connections of each of your names, is to start categorizing each of your contacts into one of three different buckets. This sorting process is a simple way to define their potential role on your Advisory Board, and help you with a strategy for communicating with them. For purposes of your business, each of your contacts will fall into one of three major categories:

- **Insider**
- **Expert**
- **Connector**

Each of these categories is pretty straightforward. I have created a little table to help you make the decision on the first cut, and we'll go into more detail below:

Category	Who They Are	How They Help
Insiders	Close friends Family	Emotional Support Physical Help (moving, sales, etc.) Administrative Help (letter writing, etc.)
Connectors	Friends Colleagues	Potential customer Introductions to others Word of mouth marketing
Experts	Friends Colleagues Strangers God	Business Advice Business Contacts Immediate Action

> Then Jesus said, "Come to me, all of you who are weary and carry heavy burdens, and I will give you rest.
> —Matthew 11:28

In the sections below, we're going to cover how to approach each of your three categories of contacts. In each case, you are going to need different ways to "interview" them for a spot on your Advisory Board. The ones who are most helpful and engaged, offering the most valuable feedback, are the ones that make the final cut.

Please keep in mind, as we go through this process together, that this is all supposed to be fun! Your attitude as you meet with people will determine your success. If you are excessively nervous or defensive during your meetings, you are unlikely to find many receptive contacts.

Remember the tenets of **G.R.A.C.E.** and let your Enthusiasm shine through. Take the pressure off yourself, and make the journey half the fun.

Enjoy the chance to get in touch with everyone on your list. It is not often that you have such a great excuse to reach out and socialize with so many people.

Insiders: Who They Are and How They Can Help

Your Insiders are your core of emotional and moral support. These are the people that are closest to you, and with whom you have probably already shared your inner thoughts many times over.

Insiders can help you weigh decisions, talk through setbacks, commiserate when you are frustrated, and boost your spirits when you are discouraged. A good Insider is someone with whom you can easily laugh at yourself, and openly share your mistakes without shame. After a good, honest conversation with an Insider, you should feel emotionally recharged, and ready to embark on your next challenge.

Insiders may not be the people with whom you want to debate the particular merits of a specific business idea. Instead, you should consider Insiders a resource for discussing your own personal issues, and getting back some bluntly honest advice. You certainly do not need coddling friends who always think that every single one of your ideas are "just wonderful."

Insiders are also perfect for asking to lend a helping hand. There are many instances in the early days of a business when you cannot afford employees, and yet you need help with simple physical or administrative tasks. An Insider is just the sort of person you should call. My mother was my ultimate Insider during the early days of my business. She was willing to do anything for me.

Insiders: How to Approach Them and What to Expect

Getting in touch with an Insider should be easy by virtue of your close relationship. No doubt, with some of your Insiders, you have already talked a little about your business. While talking with Insiders, it is important to carefully adjust your expectations. In some cases, your close friends or family may not feel the same level of excitement and enthusiasm about your business.

First of all, they have not lived with the dream as long as you, so they may not be quickly persuaded that your business plan will work.

Secondly, they may feel a certain amount of misguided protection for you, and worry about the risks involved in starting a business.

Lastly, they may worry about the personal consequences of your starting a business—which could spell less time and energy for your relationship.

For all these reasons, sometimes your closest allies can be the hardest to win over. Hopefully the work you have put into your business plan will help them see that you have channeled your enthusiasm into creating a serious and practical plan for building your business. If they still seem lukewarm, there is no need to press the point.

On the one hand, the people who are closest to you can offer you very perceptive advice, because they know your strengths and weaknesses. On the other hand, their personal investment in your relationship can bias their feelings. They may want you to stay the same person, and remind you of failed projects from the past.

This is the irony of Insiders. Sometimes the hardest part is creating some distance between you. Because of your emotional connection, you are often looking for emotional support from them. Running a business can be just as much an emotional roller coaster as falling in love or raising young children. These are the people who can help talk you through the day-by-day difficulties of running a business. If their personal feelings about your business get in the way of that emotional support, do not let them slow you down. Your train has already left the station, and you are long past the days of persuading them. They might eventually come around. If they do not then do not worry about it. Remember the train has indeed left the station.

Connectors: Who They Are and How They Can Help

Your Connectors are one step removed from Insiders. They are everyone else with whom you are on friendly terms. Even if you don't know them well, these people will be a great untapped secret for the early days of your business. They will help drive your early sales, and they will pass along word about your business to others. They will get you in touch with their friends, who might have expert advice for you. They are the grapevine along which part of your business will travel. Whenever you speak with a Connector, your primary goals should be:

- To learn how she views your business from a consumer's point of view,

or

- To discover if she has any contacts, whether Connectors or Experts, who could be useful to you.

Never underestimate the importance of someone with whom you share only a small connection. God has a wonderful sense of humor, and loves to remind us how we are all part of His plan. I have known a great number of coincidences in my life, which reminded me of this truth.

Accepting Christ As My Savior

For example, my husband Joe experienced this lesson, and allowed us both to ask the Lord into our hearts to become Lord and Master of our lives, when a series of coincidences left him no choice but to fully embrace the presence of the Lord in his life. First, I want to explain that both of us had been raised in the church, we attended church, we loved God and we were faithful in going to church. We came from Christian families for sure!

One of his new patients, Van Watkins, was a pastor at a local church. He witnessed to Joe as Joe started doing some dental work on him. Van realized quickly that Joe was a "church goer" not an on-fire Christian. Much to Joe's disgust, he returned each day for five days to his office, reading him Bible verses, with the hope of persuading him to accept the Lord into his life as Lord and Master. Do you want to know what he really said every day? "Dr. Pullen if you die tonight you are going to hell!" Joe was mortified that a preacher/patient would say these words to him! Joe resisted Van's "attacks." Joe, only a few days after Van had been hounding him every day around lunch time about the Lord, was on a plane to Italy where he was one of the main speakers at an international implant congress. Little did he know that God had another man lined up to witness to Joe. This time it was an oral surgeon, Duke Heller from Ohio, who was the other speaker at this important Italian dental implant teaching event. By the way, Joe and I know that these two occurrences did not just happen.

When the meeting was over in Bologna they decided to ride the train to Venice for a short tour. They boarded the train and after ordering lunch, Duke said to Joe,"What do you think about God?" Joe was floored! Since Van Watkins had driven him crazy just the week before asking him that same question—every day—he told Duke the whole story about the preacher who had come every day the week before telling him he was going to hell when he died.

Duke told Joe, "He is right. You must accept Christ as your personal savior to live a full life and be born again in order to go to heaven. This is what the Bible says." On that train trip Duke showed Joe passage after passage in the Bible telling about the saving grace of Jesus and about his promises about salvation and about heaven and hell. Duke prayed on that train trip with Joe and Joe accepted Christ as his Lord and Savior. When Joe returned home we went immediately to the church that Van Watkins was pastoring and the same thing happened to me that day. I invited the Lord into my heart. That was the best day of my life, by far! I had found what I had been searching for my entire life. God used two earthly connectors to allow us to make the best decision of our lives. I thank God for Van and Duke!

My Australia Conector

As for me, I have experienced countless number of serendipitous encounters. Perhaps no single encounter has been as fateful to my business as meeting one of the most important mentors in my professional career, Gloria McKinnon, the owner of Ann's Glory Box in Australia, and the premier needlework entrepreneur of Australia. Her empire now reaches all over the world. I crossed Gloria in what seemed to be accidental circumstances when she visited my shop in Huntsville, Alabama in 1988, the year after my magazine, *Sew Beautiful,* had launched. I hardly knew her, but she said to me directly, in her lovely Australian accent, "Martha are you ready to come teach down under? I think you are ready for Australia but I'm not sure Australia is ready for you." At the time, I was not sure that it made much sense to try bringing heirloom sewing to a country where everyone dresses casually and surfs. Thankfully, I listened to her persistent prodding, and as a result, the Martha Pullen Company has an enormous presence in Australia. I have had the pleasure of traveling to Australia twenty eight times to teach since 1988! Gloria teaches frequently at our big Martha Pullen School of Art Fashion events here in Huntsville! For years we had a huge export business to Australia, thanks to Gloria. She is one of my closest friends and business advisoors.

Connectors: How to Approach Them and What to Expect

Probably the best way to approach a Connector is by email. First of all, it allows you to prepare a quick (and re-usable) introductory note, and secondly it gives that person a little time to think over your request. The uninterested people will generally find excuses, and the most helpful people will find a way to meet.

What should your note say?

- Introduce the idea that you are starting a business.
- State that you would like to talk to that person about your ideas and get feedback.
- Propose getting together for coffee and a short chat.

That is it—don't say any more. Your note should not be any longer than about 200 words. Don't make the mistake of going into enormous detail about how excited you are about the business, how long you have been dreaming of doing this, how nervous you are about your business plan, or any of your feelings. Save the details for your actual conversation. Keep your note simple and straight to the point.

If your Connector responds, quickly set up a time to meet. Be as flexible as possible to accommodate her/his schedule.

How to Approach the Meeting

When you meet, you will want to immediately let that person know you appreciate the time he/she is offering you. Make sure that you pay for coffee if you indeed meet in a coffee shop. Depending on how much time you both have, you will quickly want to move past the social niceties, and get straight to the point.

Your conversation should follow the same basic pattern:

- **Give background** on your business. Keep it simple, and cover only the basics—your products, your sales channels, your marketing. You will have time to go into details once the conversation gets going. Here's a good example: "First of all, let me describe the business. I am going to be making handmade christening dresses and accessories for a christening ceremony. I am going to try to sell primarily through my website and Etsy, and I am going to use a blog and a mailing list for my marketing. I am also counting on word-of-mouth and a few placements in some magazines."
- If you have **sketches or sample products** that you can show, these sorts of props can really help get the conversation moving.
- **Get feedback. Write down what he/she says!** Be especially prepared for a certain amount of vagueness. I remember when my

kids were in elementary school. I would ask them about their day, and all I would get in response were monosyllabic replies: "Good," "Yes," "No." Only after posing specific questions, would the kids would finally start chattering and telling me stories about recess or classroom adventures. In your conversations with Connectors, your job will be to guide them into domains where they feel comfortable speaking. The easiest way is to allow them to express their thoughts as a potential customer. Try to consider a quality that you like about this person, or that person's particular talent, and map it to a related question you have. For instance, if your Connector has a creative streak, ask about ways to make your product line or your packaging more appealing. If your Connector is a great organizer, ask if she thinks your plan covers all the bases. If she works in technology, ask her what she knows about building websites. Be sure to emphasize that you are not fishing for compliments, and that you invite criticism. People often find it easier to see faults. Ask what she finds the weakest part of your business, and where the strength lies. What products does she think will sell best?

- **Walk away with a name**. As you prepare to wrap up the conversation, try to summarize in a few short sentences what you both talked about, and the primary "take-aways." Then, without missing a beat, ask your Connector if your conversation reminds him or her of anyone who might be a good contact for you. Jog his/her memory by proposing some different categories of people. Remember to ask "Who do you know who can help me........?"
  - Anyone who has recently started a small business,
  - Anyone who is running a successful web-based business,
  - Anyone who is an expert in your particular craft,
  - Anyone who might be your "perfect customer."

Bad Connections

As you talk with Connectors about your business ideas, there's always the risk that they will be unreceptive, for any variety of reasons. They will say things that surprise, or even annoy you. Be prepared to separate the personal from the helpful, and do your best to react with poise and resilience.

—**Discouraging:** Some people communicate their caring in funny ways. After hearing your business plans, they might only focus on the difficulties you will face. Their concern comes out as discouragement. I find that for some people any kind of risk taking is uncomfortable. Remember that negative feedback does not mean you got it wrong. You may simply be asking the wrong person. If she is not part of your target market, she is not going to be a customer.

—**Indifferent:** Sad to say, some people just do not care. There could be any number of reasons, and you should not take it personally. People may have problems at home or elsewhere that keep them from being emotionally available to others. What you want from your Connectors is interest and a willingness to talk. To discuss your plans and bounce ideas off them, and get unvarnished responses. If they are not interested or engaged, they simply failed your "interview" and will not be a part of your Advisory Board. Please do not let it impact your friendship.

Experts: Who They Are and How They Can Help

You may already have a connection to a few Experts. Your most valuable Experts are probably still out there waiting to be discovered. They will have the most to offer you in terms of professional advice. These are the people with real experience in the business world, either doing similar work as you, or with a deep understanding of a particular niche. Whether it is about marketing, distribution, retailing, or your particular craft, they are subject matter experts with precious knowledge and insider tips that you need to learn.

No matter how many books you read, there will always be "tricks of the trade" that you can learn either by making mistakes or taking advice. Talking with an Expert is the quickest and most effective way to acquire trade secrets for your particular business. Through the expert advice of a local business person, you will get an insider understanding of many of the the unique aspects of your local market. Listening to their war stories and victories, you will understand how personal style influences business. By finding an Expert for each element of your business plan, you will be in a great position to leap ahead, and save yourself months or even years of trial and error.

Experts: How to Approach Them and What to Expect

I have a really good story to tell you about getting in the door of a famous person you really do not know. The background of this story is that we do major sewing events which involve moving into a hotel. Our students rent rooms, we rent convention areas for our classes and banquets, and we purchase food during this event. At the time this story happened we were very happy with the Marriott Hotel which was somewhat on the outskirts of Huntsville and somewhat difficult to get to; however it was gorgeous and new and the people were fabulous to us. I had not even considered going anywhere else. We were satisfied where we were. Now back to my story.

One morning my assistant came to the door to ask, "Martha there is a nice man from the Hilton Hotel here who would like to speak with you. He promises that if you are kind enough to give him two minutes of his time he will not sit down. He will leave after two minutes. He simply wants to say hello." How in the world could I refuse anyone two minutes? I told her of course to let him come in. Indeed he did not sit down. He was very polite and well dressed and simply said, "Mrs. Pullen I'm sure you are happy using the Marriott for your events. It is a lovely hotel. HOWEVER our hotel, The Hilton, is lovely too and we do great events. We are only two blocks from your business. We have large conference rooms and excellent food. I have a brochure for you to look over and we are very competitive with our pricing not only for conference space but also for meals. If you would ever like for us to bid your events, we would be honored to do so."

He gave me the brochure, thanked me and started to walk out—in under two minutes. I said, "No please wait a minute. I am always interested in a bid for a better price than I currently have." Still standing he began to ask about my events. I invited him to sit down. He did. He gathered my information and said he would return after working up some ideas, meal plans and other details. It turned out that I did switch to the Hilton because they were closer to my home and to the homes of nearly all of my employees here in Huntsville. They had a beautiful facility and offered me savings on my total cost for the event. We used that hotel for twenty five years, although it is closed now. We were their largest customer and we had several large events a year there. Please remember how he got into the office of an "Expert." He simply said he would not sit down and he would leave after two minutes. I would also like for you to re-read a very important part of his "sales pitch." He praised the Marriott hotel that he knew I loved. **Praising one's competitor is always critical in establishing intimacy and establishing credibility.**

Finding and approaching an Expert doesn't have to be hard. If you are blessed, a few of your Connectors will get you in touch with several local Experts simply on the strength of your relationship. That might be enough to earn you a meeting over coffee. For others, you simply need to demonstrate your professionalism. A well-written email that combines evidence of having researched your Expert's background and with a clear and well-packaged proposal, followed by some timely phone calls, might get you a quick meeting, no matter how "untouchable" your Expert.

The Internet offers you an incredible advantage by making it so easy to perform basic research on someone's professional background. Using Google, you can discover business websites, blog entries, and local articles that offer a quick history of your Expert's work. Everyone in business wants exposure, and the web is the perfect platform for presenting themselves to the world. Through their Facebook and LinkedIn profiles, you can learn a little bit more. All it takes is some well-crafted search statements, a little common sense, and some digging.

Remember that Internet searches are most effective when you use unique words to describe your Expert's work. Searching for "Sally Smith woodworking" is not going to catch as many results as "Sally Smith Nashville birdfeeders"

Just because Google can't find it doesn't mean it is not out there. Try searching within the website of a local paper or trade publication.

Looking up an Expert in Facebook can help, but I do not advise "friending" someone until you've actually met in a somewhat social setting. If you don't know them, they're not really friends.

Entrepreneurial types might use LinkedIn, and contacting someone through LinkedIn is entirely reasonable. If you can not find someone's email, that is another option.

Don't make the mistake of believing that just because someone did not answer your email, they are not interested in talking with you. When approaching an Expert, your first email is simply designed to get on their radar screen. A follow-up phone call a few hours later, or the next day, is what is required to catch the attention of anyone these days. If that does not work, you should simply wait a few days, write again using the same note, and follow up once more with the phone call. There is really no harm in repeating this several more times. So long as you are polite, persistence is a virtue, and may win the respect of even an untouchable Expert.

Once you make contact with an Expert you should take care to treat that person with the respect he/she deserve. Introduce yourself briefly, why you are calling, and whether she/he might have time for coffee or lunch. If they hesitate, that person is simply trying to ascertain if you are worth his/her time. There is no need to launch into a detailed explanation. Just be focused and to the point, and explain that you would only take twenty minutes of his/her time, then drop a comment about something you learned from your web research, and how it relates to your own business goals. By sounding both professional and informed, they might consider you a good contact worth knowing. If they do not, there is no need to fret, because that person would probably be unhelpful anyway. Remember the man from the Hilton Hotel who only asked for TWO minutes of my time; I gave him twenty.

Be Prepared for the Meeting

When it is time for the meeting, be sure to dress nicely. Dressing nicely sets a good impression and conveys a basic respect for their time. From my research one has about 10 seconds for a first impression. I always dress up! It is critical to have a current hair cut as well as glasses which are the current style. Casual can be OK as long as it is "good looking" casual and not worn out. I think in the vast majority of business settings blue jeans and running shoes are not appropriate. Students at my big events can wear whatever they like; however my teachers must be dressed in "nice clothes." Since they are on their feet for possibly 12 hours, we do say in that instance, "Fashion stops at the ankles." They can wear running shoes with their dress up clothes.

At our events here in Huntsville when men from the corporate sewing machine companies arrive they are always dressed in suits or sport coats and ties when they make their presentations. The second day they might wear a beautiful, woven casual shirt but they always wear dress pants and shoes. For women I would ask that you study Kate Middleton's style of dress. I am not suggesting that any of us could look like Kate Middleton but she always looks beautiful and is always dressed in a classic way. Business classic for me is either a skirt or pants, a shell and a jacket of some kind. Hillary Clinton usually wears this type of three piece ensemble. I am not offering any political forum here but I do admire both of these women for dressing in a classic appropriate manner for the business world. Reflect also on the classic clothing worn by Condoleezza Rice, Laura Bush or Jacqueline Kennedy. I guess if you work for Google or Apple you might be appropriately dressed in jeans and a sweat shirt. If you are trying to build a business network, I suggest you dress appropriately.

For your meeting, you should be prepared to quickly tell your story in about two minutes. You may even want to rehearse your opening, so that it sounds natural but polished—a quick rundown of where you are from, what you have been doing for the past few years professionally or with your hobby, and a conservative description of your hopes for the future. This would be a great place to show a Mind Map of your life. Another Mind Map of your business plans would be helpful also. A picture is worth a thousand words and these two Mind Maps would make it all quick and easy to preview. Explain the connection between your goals and this person's expertise. If you are lucky, that is all you need to say to start that person talking. Most people like to talk about themselves, especially if they have been even remotely successful at their achievements.

If your Expert starts to slow down, or wander into topics that do not concern you, you might need to guide her/him with questions. There is no need to have prepared specific questions like a supermarket checklist. Just use open questions to steer her toward the topics you meant to cover. How did she get into her business? What's does she like about it? What was difficult about starting a business? Would she do anything differently? Be sure you get to the heart of what you really care about.

Equally effective is to pepper your questions with information you have gleaned from your web research. This kind of preparation will make an enormous difference in the quality of your interactions. Being prepared means being able to avoid awkward pauses. The ability to reference specific things—whether it is the types of products this person makes, or the location of her store, or the number of products onher website—shows that you are interested. It demonstrates that you value this person's assistance enough that you decided to take the time to learn more.

Above all, just relax and enjoy yourself. Do not ever lose sight of the fact that most people will be impressed by your initiative and motivation. People love Mind Maps. It takes courage to try to start a business. If you are nervous, you can take the pressure off by pretending that it is a job interview—and remember that you are the one who is hiring.

As the meeting winds down, don't forget to get an address so you can write him/her later. As soon as you get home, while the conversation is still fresh in your mind, take the time to compose a quick thank you note. You should mention something you spoke about, and how much you appreciated this person's taking the time to speak with you. If the meeting went well, be sure to ask if you might continue to keep in touch as your business plans progress. Be sure to write a thank you note right away—it makes a tremendous difference in the impression you leave with someone! I cannot emphasize enough the importance of writing thank you notes! In this world of technology, I recommend writing a hand written thank you note. An email thank you note does not carry the weight that a hand written one does! There was a time that I kept pretty thank you cards with scripture on them to send often. I would buy a handful at the Lifeway book store and just keep them in my desk to send. Many people suggest taking thank you notes and stamps everywhere you go so one can be written and mailed on the spur of the moment while everything is fresh in your mind. I have even received a written thank you note thanking me for the hand written thank you note!

Maintain Contact

Using these guidelines, you can maintain a running list of your business network contacts, and prioritize the people who you want to consider on your Advisory Group. From that point forward, you should make an open commitment to yourself to keep in close touch with them. Either every few weeks, or every few months, depending on the relationship, you should send a quick update on your progress. By maintaining your contact, you will ensure that when you are faced with a difficult challenge or an important decision, you will have someone to call and help you make the right choice. Keeping in touch is almost like sending a thank you note again.

I cannot tell you how many times it has been instrumental to me to be able to call someone and ask his/her advice. I remember at one point, as my reputation had become more established, I realized that I could not maintain my teaching and travelling schedule. Simply put, as flattering as it felt to receive so many invitations, I could not be everywhere at once. But how could I continue to expand the reach of my business? I immediately called my friend, Pati Palmer, who had been licensing Palmer/Pletsch teachers for several years. We had become friends when we were both keynote speakers for the Australian Stitching and Crafts events in Sydney and Brisbane. All I had to do was pick up the phone and ask, "Pati, how would I start a licensed teacher program?" She explained in detail what she had done and gave me many suggestions. Truly her encouragement and advice was crucial in starting the Martha Pullen Licensed Teacher programs.

As another example, the idea of starting a sewing magazine has been brewing in the back of my mind after the huge success of our first two books. I knew enough to realize that I knew nothing about magazines. I picked up the phone and called Phyllis Hoffman DePiano. We had met at a Southeastern Yarncrafters Show, and I recalled that she was publishing *Just Cross Stitch* magazine. I summarized my situation, and she assured me that when she started her *Just Cross Stitch* magazine, "I didn't know the first thing about magazine publishing." Now this was hard to believe from a woman who had already grown her magazine from nothing to more than 300,000 subscribers. Despite her modesty, Phyllis was an endless source of help and inspiration. She offered her advice freely, and encouraged me often. Phyllis Hoffman DePiano was and remains one of my main mentors.

I can list another two dozen examples. I have always considered the friends and colleagues that are part of my Advisory Group as one of the greatest assets I have acquired in business. You could do much worse than try to emulate my example in this regard. By building up a list of colleagues and contacts, you will strengthen your business, and have many people who can help you face new challenges.

I've learned to be on the lookout for opportunities to transform what appears to be mere coincidence into genuine serendipity. After all, isn't that what networking is all about?

Despite being a denizen of the digital world, or maybe because he knew all too well its isolating potential, Jobs was a strong believer in face to face meetings. "There's a temptation in our networked age to think that ideas can be developed by email and iChat," he said. "That's crazy. Creativity comes from spontaneous meetings, from random discussions. You run into someone, you ask what they're doing, you say 'Wow,' and you are cooking up all sorts of ideas.'"

So he had the Pixar building planned to promote encounters and unplanned collaborations. "If a building doesn't encourage that, you'll lose a lot of innovation and the magic that's sparked by serendipity," he said.

—Walter Isaacson, writing about Steve Jobs

More business decisions occur over lunch and dinner than at any other time, yet no MBA courses are given on the subject.
—Peter Drucker

It's not what you know but who you know that makes the difference.
—Annonymous

It's all about people. It's about networking and being nice to people and not burning any bridges.
—Mike Davidson

~ Chapter Seven ~

Taking Those First Steps

> *A final word: Be strong in the Lord and in his mighty power. Put on all of God's armor so that you will be able to stand firm against all strategies of the devil.*
> —Ephesians 6:10-11

A smooth sea never made a skillful mariner.
—English proverb

Business is never so healthy as when, like a chicken, it must do a certain amount of scratching around for what it gets.
—Henry Ford

Choosing a Name

Naming your business is nothing to take lightly. Take your time and choose carefully, because you will be living with your business name for a long time. You may wish to test several business names with the people in your Advisory Group, to see which one wins. As you consider your business name, keep in mind some important factors.

Your business name can span a broad spectrum, from highly creative to deliberately conservative. There is no right or wrong, but you should consider how easily customers will know what you are selling. Your name should set the mood for the entire personality of your business. People should not have to guess too hard what kind products you sell. The name should somehow evoke or allude to the company's business.

"Easy To Remember" Name is a Key Thought

How easy is it to remember? A well-chosen name sticks immediately in people's minds, and stays with them long afterward. Word of mouth marketing, as we will learn, is an extremely important element of your business. If people forgot your name, either because it is too complicated, or a little too exotic, or easily confused with other names, they will not pass it along to their friends.

How easy is it to differentiate from others? Thanks to the Internet, we are all living in the same neighborhood. For the same reason you would not pick the same business name as someone down the street, you should try to adopt an original name, not something too plain vanilla.

Will it grow with you? Your business may easily shift into selling neighboring products. Just because you start with baby dresses does not prevent you from shifting into maternity dresses as well. Pick a name that allows your business some room to expand.

Does it sound too cutesy? Think of your business like a child. A cute baby name can become an embarrassment as the child gets older. Pick a name that you can live with—avoid puns unless they are very clever or subtle.

You can check the government's Trademark Electronic Search System to see if someone else is using some variation on your business name. You should not even consider using a name that has already been filed, because you will eventually receive a cease and desist letter from a lawyer and be forced to find a new name.

I would like to share a personal story with you. How did I choose the name Martha Pullen Company? Joe and I had gone to New York to purchase goods for my little retail store which was to open August 1, 1981. One of our new suppliers who was SO NICE TO US was Herb Stern of Stylecrest Fabrics. Herb invited us into his office to talk about retail fabric stores in general. He asked me, "What is the name of your new business?" I replied, "The Heirloom Shop." He said, "Martha after talking with you just a few minutes, I feel pretty sure you are not going to stop with just a little smocking shop. If you want to expand into other areas you need to name your business Martha Pullen Company and let The Heirloom Shop just be a division. It is easy to remember Martha Pullen Company and The

Heirloom Shop will never be remembered. Besides that there are probably 25 Heirloom Shops in this country right now." He further mentioned how Ralph Lauren, Valentino, Christian Dior and other famous designers frequently use their names for their businesses. My business name became Martha Pullen Company right there in New York City and I have never regretted it. Please choose a name that will be easy to remember.

Your Website Address

From the very start, you should be considering your presence on the Internet. We will cover all the aspects of getting online in detail in later chapters. It is worth considering that while you are naming your business, you should be locking in your website address. Big companies can afford to ignore whether someone already owns a website when they choose their business name. Purchasing the website address from someone for tens of thousands of dollars is simply a startup expense. In your case, I am sure that you will be much happier simply picking a name whose website address has not been taken, at the much more affordable price of $18.00 a year.

There are lots of different websites that let you buy website addresses, also known as "domain names." I consider the simplest and best website for purchasing addresses to be **www.iwantmyname.com**. Their service is very simple. You go to their website and use the search box to type "the whatever website address" you would like to purchase, then click search. The website will immediately tell you whether it has been registered or not. Often the name of the business you pick is already taken. That does not always mean you should abandon a name — for example just because someone has taken "silkandlace.com" does not prevent you from trying to get "silkandlacedesigns.com" or "silkandlacedresses.com." On the other hand, I would not suggest taking a website address that ends in ".net" or ".biz" unless you are absolutely stuck on a name and you simply must have the address. Most people automatically assume that a website address ends with ".com" so you are inviting the possibility that all your customers will visit your competitor's website by accident.

Short and Simple and Easy to Spell is Best

Keep it short and simple—a website address that is too long is difficult to remember. Please make it easy to spell! Word of mouth is important, and if your domain name has a complicated spelling or uses hyphens, it is not going to be easy to pass along. In the same way, do not let a microscopic difference separate you and someone else, like "sallysewingcircle" or sallyssewingcircle."

Make it memorable—do not be too dry and boring, bring some creativity into play; sewingstore.com is less memorable than rainbowsewing.com.

Use keywords. Chances are your basic business name is already taken, so think of a handful of keywords that describe your business and try to mix your business name with them. Examples of this are sunnysidesmocking, or cindyheirlooms.

Brainstorm Names with Friends

If you have too many ideas, and you are trying to decide on the best name, ask for help from friends. You want a name with broad appeal, and many minds often think better than one. Just invite them over and take a vote over some coffee. Ask them to help you think up names. Give them some creative boundaries by offering a list of ten words or ideas that evoke the mental associations you want to conjure in people's minds. Or else, you could create a "moodboard" collage made of pictures you have cut from magazines and newspapers, to depict the values and images that you want your company to represent.

Business Cards

In many ways, a business card is a small and trivial matter. After all, it is just a piece of paper with your name on it. In other ways, however, it is the only thing that you leave behind after meeting with someone. Your card is reflection of your entire business. Even if you do not have all the details for your business worked out, it is worth taking the time to create a small set of temporary cards and keeping several copies of your business card with you at all times.

A business card is quite easy to produce these days with just a computer and printer. You can purchase heavy card stock from a stationary store, and print and cut them yourself, or else buy pre-perforated packages from an office supply store. Beyond the name of you and your business, be sure to include your email address and telephone, and of course a website address if you have one.

Working from Home

It is a natural choice to want to work from home when your hobby is becoming your business. It is exciting to know from the Babson and Baruch colleges poll from June/July 2012 that 69% of new businesses start at home and 59% of established business owners are home based! Separation and structure are keys to successfully working at home. None of us are perfect, and when we are left alone to our own devices, we quickly discover how difficult it is to exercise willpower and discipline. There is a lot of self-restraint and organization required to keep yourself going when you work from home. The key to successfully making a living from your home is being able to clearly separate and structure your work life from your personal life, because allowing that line to drift can undermine your well-being and happiness. When you are a homeschooling mom your work must be planned carefully with your other activities which are also very demanding. This can be done but might involve getting up extra early in the morning or staying up later at night.On the other hand, if you become a workaholic, and allow work to overpower your personal life, you will feel frazzled and overworked, with nowhere to hide.

Tips for Working at Home

The best way to approach working from home is to create clear lines between the two worlds in your home and in your life. Here are a few ideas.
- Create a ritual to help you separate the different parts of your life. Maybe you want to take a walk around the block before you start your work routine, and another walk before your return home to your family routine. Make it clear in your mind that the two worlds should stay separated.
- Stick to a regular schedule. Make specific hours for yourself when you will work, or when you will take care of family obligations, and do not let them slip. It is much more stressful to try doing two things at the same time.
- Use doors and separate rooms to keep yourself truly apart from the rest of the house. Find friendly ways to make it clear to your family that when you are in "work mode" you cannot be disturbed.
- Get dressed as if you were going to work in a different location. I always

put on my make-up, get my hair done and put on my working clothes. It truly makes my work at home easier. This is a trick that Patty Smith taught me from her studies of home economics in college. She said concerning housework, "Get your nice clothes on, fix your hair and put on make-up. That way you won't feel stuck with your chores. Basically in your mind and in reality you can leave and go somewhere else." I have always followed Patty's advice when working at home. Even if I get up at 5 a.m. to begin my computer work, I get dressed before going to the computer. Since I write best very early in the morning, I try to get dressed before I begin writing at my computer. Yes, even if it means putting on make-up before 5 a.m. I always write better when I am fully dressed.

Advantages of Working at Home

With all that said, I'm not trying to talk you out of working from home. There are so many advantages that, so long as you can maintain solid boundaries between work and your personal life, working from home can be a great decision. Here are just a few of them:

- You can spend more time with your family, and be in closer touch with them. You can often turn to a spouse or older child for help, which helps overcome any resistance on their part to your starting a new business. By making them part of the team, your project becomes a shared mission.
- If your children are old enough to take care of themselves for extended periods of time, your daycare needs are reduced. Be careful, however, if you have children who are still at an age where they need frequent attention. You and your kids may find yourselves both very frustrated if you try to do everything at once. If you are home schooling this will be a special challenge but it can be done. Again, it's much better to create clear boundaries, so that you can focus exclusively on the kids and your personal chores when they are around, and focus on work when you can take some time away.
- Working from home means you can set your own hours. The ability to craft your schedule around the times that are convenient for you. That usually means the "off" hours of the day when you are not taking care of your family or other needs, so it is important to watch out for "burnout." Make sure that you keep up healthy work habits, and allow

yourself time to relax and recharge. Since I am an early morning person working very early in the morning-even as early at 4:30 a.m. or 5 a.m. is perfect for my creativity. I frequently work a few minutes during the day at one time and then back for another period of time. I have always believed that I can get a lot done in little "ten or twenty minute segments" of time in-between other things. Of course many times I work late at night. I have always worked on the week-ends.

- You'll incur far less expense. Eliminating the costs of commuting and parking fees can add up to hundreds of dollars savings each month. When you consider the potential overhead costs of renting office or studio space, the savings can reach into the thousands of dollars. In turn, all you need is a business telephone line and an email address. I might add that lunch expenses can really add up if you are working away from home.
- If you have young children working from home even if it means getting up very early and working very late can certainly save on childcare expenses.

A Friendly Workspace

The business side of your hobby will bring its own kind of work. Maintaining a balance between the two sides, your creative work and your administrative work, is crucial to the success of your business. In order to set the proper tone for your business, and ensure that you pay just as much attention to both sides, it is important to create and outfit a workspace that lets you work productively and enjoyably.

Maybe you have already created a space for your hobby. Now that you are starting a business, it is important to be sure that you have a professional setup, with the right tools and supplies. The right equipment can help speed up you productivity and increase the quality of your work. Even a simple makeover of your hobby space will help make you feel like you are a real business person. Take the time to spruce up and organize yourself, or find a way to improve the furniture you work with, so that you are really spoiling yourself. The fact is that you are making an investment in your creativity. My husband used to always joke about how a new pair of running sneakers makes him run faster, but there is some truth in the idea. By investing in your craft, you are not just spoiling yourself, you are laying the groundwork to turn that investment into something better.

Office Space

My first "home office" was my dining room table when I was writing my very first book in 1983. I found that staying at my store was not conducive to writing. The customers always wanted to see me and of course I wanted to see them. The only way I could concentrate on writing the book was to get away from my retail store. I have to admit my dining room table stayed very messy for several months. As impossible as it seems my first books were written on a typewriter and then taken to the publisher who had to turn it into text "pieces of paper" that were literally pasted down.

I was dragging my feet in finishing this book and finally my mother said to me, "I am coming to your house. I will answer the phone and cook your meals. I will pick up any children that need a ride. You will not leave the dining room table until you finish the book." Mama arrived, much to Joe's relief, and I worked uninterrupted for about a week until it was finished. My mother was a mover and a shaker and she liked to finish tasks. I'm not sure that first book, which sold around 50,000 I might add, would have ever been finished without Mama's visit to Huntsville!

Ideally, you will be able to set up your office and administrative space alongside your craft space. This has a distinct advantage by reducing the amount of effort needed to bounce between the two. If your office is set apart in another area of the house, you may wind up avoiding some of the important administrative work that your business requires, simply because it is more enjoyable to just continue with your craftwork. I might add that when writing my second book I turned an extra bedroom into a sewing room/writing room. I had an artist hired for most of the day working with me since I sewed and put the pieces down in front of the artist to draw. It was very helpful to have my sewing and my writing side by side. You might say "Martha you could take a laptop to your sewing room." Please remember what I just said. There were no computers in common use in the early 1980s and I don't think laptops had even been thought about! It was a typewriter for sure! I used the same one that had typed my dissertation before I took it to the final typist and paid her to re-type it for me!

Thanks to technology, the amount of space you need for running a functional office can be as small as a laptop. That does not mean, however, that there is no need to set up a comfortable, productive space that you can call your own. As a point of joy and necessity, you should take the effort to create a real "office" even if it is only a small corner alongside your hobby setup. This will ensure that you give the proper amount of attention and focus to your organizational and administrative tasks.

Create a Real Office Space

If you must locate the two work spaces separately, here are some suggestions for your office space:

- Avoid high traffic areas, such as the kitchen or the living room. There will inevitably come moments when you will need to do some business while others are around, and you should be able to work quietly, in peace and without disturbing others. My home office is in a downstairs bedroom.
- Choose a quiet, brightly lit place, where you can shut the door. If you do not have a spare bedroom or den to convert into an office or workspace, try starting with a corner of a bedroom where you can shut the door, a partitioned section of your garage, or a portion of your basement. Then work toward a separate room for an office or workspace as soon as possible.
- If you expect to see clients or staff, you might try to choose a room with an outside door and separate bathroom, so they can come and go without disturbing your family.
- To save yourself the expense of buying new office furniture from Staples, see if you can find used furniture. Check a local craigslist.com, or look it up on ebay.com. You can also look in the classified section of your newspaper, or a Goodwill or Salvation Army store. For years I used an old but regular sized desk that Joanna had used in high school. It was from Walmart and finally both of the front legs were propped up with a concrete block. Don't laugh. I wrote several books on that concrete leg desk. It worked beautifully! Finally we brought Joe's old dental office desk home; it is much better looking I assure you. It works just fine.
- Make your office space a permanent fixture in the house, not something that moves whenever "company comes to visit." Give yourself and your workspace the respect it deserves, and that attitude will extend into your business. I have a no hands touch rule on my business computer. No matter how much the grandchildren want to work on it the answer is NO. I have another computer they are allowed to use.
- If there is simply no room to convert a guest room, or attic space, there have been lots of businesses that started from the kitchen or dining room

table. Obviously, your working hours will be limited to the daytime hours when the house is empty, and evening when folks are in bed. Perhaps you can find a way to install an unobtrusive fold out desk, and camouflaged filing system. Actually what is wrong with a non -camouflaged desk and filing cabinet? Nothing.

Equipping Your Office

The technology industry has produced a bewildering supply of gadgets and tools. There are so many digital possibilities that it is difficult to know what is needed, from which brand, and how long it will last. What is in vogue today will be passé and outmoded tomorrow. Of course, you can elect to simply ignore all the technology, and run your business "the old fashioned way." I have several friends who have adopted that approach, and become successful enough to hire other people to handle the technology. These days, however, my opinion is that technology offers so many advantages, and most devices have become easy enough to use, that it is crazy to avoid technology.

The Essentials

That said, I would recommend sticking with the essentials.
1. A computer. I would recommend a laptop, especially if you will be travelling often to trunk shows or craft fairs. You can use it both in your office and on the road.
2. A printer.
3. A smartphone, so you can make phone calls or get email anywhere.
4. A broadband Internet connection.

If you are computer-phobic, or a bit computer-illiterate, you should try to overcome that disadvantage. There are so many people out there who can help you, that it is silly to keep your head in the sand. You can rely on relatively inexpensive paid services like Geek Squad **(www.geeksquad.com)** that will come to your home to help set you up. My personal recommendation, however, is to enlist the help of a trusted child, grandchild, niece, nephew or young neighbor, or else bartering with someone who likes your work. I totally recommend taking a course at a community college or other continuing educational program. Many places offer computer classes. If you purchase an Apple computer you can purchase for $100 unlimited private lessons for a year! Believe it or not! I did just this recently. I think most people don't bother to come to those lessons but I am taking full advantage of them.Computers and technology are quite similar to reading, in that once you begin to learn the basics, you can easily expand your knowledge by simply applying yourself. Things that you should learn and understand are:

- Virus software
- Connecting to the Internet
- Backing up your computer
- Setting up and using email
- Setting up a printer
- Using word processing and spreadsheet programs
- Using Google and finding websites on the Internet.

In a later chapter, we will cover all the fantastic marketing that you can do with your computer thanks to the Internet.

Money

Perhaps no other subject has more importance for your business than how you handle money. Your attitude toward money will be a big factor in determining how happy and successful you will become in your business. A casual attitude toward money, in which you avoid dealing with it because it is not as important as your craft, will very quickly prove counterproductive. Tracking your money, watching it carefully, and tracking exactly how it is spent will make a tremendous difference in how quickly you will see a return on your energy and investment. On the other hand, if you are in business solely for the money, your business may lack the charm and personal investment that will actually bring customers. I am living proof that if you are doing what you love, the money might follow eventually. Remember I did not start making a decent salary in my company until about the tenth year. By reading the planning section in this book and following the advice maybe you can make money much earlier than I did! I certainly hope so.

Quitting Your Day Job

Between Hollywood and fairy tales, many of our dreams of starting a business involve a fantasy of suddenly breaking free from the obligations and worries of our everyday life. We all dream that starting a business will allow us to quit our day job. Just like Prince Charming, that day may someday arrive. Until then, it is important to keep a more sober outlook on your prospects. Starting a business is risky, and there's no guarantee of success. Even more importantly, you absolutely cannot afford to lose your health insurance if your current job is offering you coverage. Consider carefully the retirement benefits that you have at your current job. If you have a fabulous retirement coming with just a few more years of work, THEN DON'T QUIT YOUR JOB. Remember you can work nights, weekends and early mornings to have your business as well as continuing your job. You might say, "That is too much work." I can truthfully tell you that owning your own business is 24/7 work. It takes LOTS more energy and hours to build your business than most jobs could ever require. Many of the successful hobby based businesses that I know started as a part time endeavor. Many owners still have their "real job" in addition to a successful home based business.

Rather than putting all the risk on the need for a quick and immediate success, which is what you are doing when you quit your job and stake everything on your new business, you should adopt a slow and steady strategy. Starting a new business should never be an either/or strategy. It should always be a "both/and" strategy. You should be continuing to work your day job AND building your new business at the same time.

The stress will be on you, and it will be difficult. But you can adopt an exit strategy. Keep working at your day job as long as possible, and so long as your mental and physical health can sustain it. As things pick up in your business, and as you find that your small business is able to start replacing some of your day job's income, you might start inquiring about the ability to slightly reduce your hours. If you are lucky, your employer might be willing to allow you to work a few hours less each day, or take Friday off without pay. I might add that it has been said that owning your own business means that you only have to work half time. Choose whichever 12 hours of every 24 you want! Seven days a week!

A Bank Account

Opening a business bank account is a must. Under no circumstances should you mix your personal and business expenses. Any payments from the business to yourself should be clearly recorded as such, and keep in mind that depending on what type of business structure you have made for your business, those payments will be taxed and recorded in different ways.

Startup Expenses

Starting a business is not cheap. If you are lucky, you can manage to avoid a number of expenses by working from your home, and taking advantage of all the "free" overhead and infrastructure that your house supplies. You can also plan on a slow ramp-up period, in which your expenses are spaced out to be only commensurate with your needs. This can often be an excellent approach for a beginning business. A conservative approach that focuses only on the essentials allows you to minimize your expenses, while still delivering products. Far too much money, for example, is spent on useless marketing.

There will be some basic startup expenses, however, that you will need to plan around. If your business plan has not fully developed one, you should articulate a startup expense checklist, and figure out how you are going to spend it over the next few months. Some things to consider, which we will cover in more detail throughout the book:

- **Licenses and permits:** There are some basic licenses you will need just to be able to sell your services or products, and there may be additional licenses depending on your type of business.
- **Rent, phone, utilities**: All these expenses will need to be considered as soon as your business moves outside your house. Even if you have a home-based business, you may incur extra expenses with a new phone line, or because you will be using the heat or air conditioning more often, possibly in the garage or attic space.
- **Insurance:** Health and business insurance are too important to go without. Depending on what type of business structure you choose for your business, you can be held personally liable for the products you sell, so it is important to be financially protected.

- **Marketing and web:** There is lots of room for creative "extra marketing" when you are a small business. There are also some baseline requirements that you should not avoid. The creation of a simple website page, or if it is central to your business, a website that accepts web orders, should be considered part of your startup expenses.
- **Materials and equipment:** My father always said that you cannot do good work without the right tools. Investing in the basic equipment that allows you to work quickly and efficiently, and deliver a high quality product, is fundamental to your success. You should not skimp any more than you need to.

Bookkeeping

Few things can create more anxiety than the unknown. Like walking into an unlit room, the act of keeping yourself financially in the dark is totally unnecessary, and bound to trip you up. Just as easily as you might overspend on a tight month, a failure to understand your cash flow and balance can stop you from making a valuable investment when you had plenty to spend.

As I began my business, I often thought of my grandmother, who learned from the Great Depression to keep close track of the family's expenses. Long after she had passed away, I came across ledgers in which she had noted her every single purchase at the grocery store for years, right down to the last dime, and kept a constant record of her current balance.

That is exactly the sort of discipline will make the difference between a hobby that earns you a little money on the side, and a business that can become a true source of regular and dependable income for your entire family. Nothing speaks to your seriousness and dedication better than the effort you put into your bookkeeping and record tracking.

As you run your own business, this kind of careful attentiveness to detail can become a tremendous asset not merely to your business, but also your peace of mind. Tracking the flow in and out of your business can help you understand the trends that drive your business. Too many people allow their business to proceed along a formula without questioning all the expenses and costs along the way. Look closely at each of your expenses and ask yourself not merely the obvious ones (am I paying too much for these supplies?) but also the hidden ones (how much is my time worth?). Examine each of your products, the costs that go into it, and understand which products give you the highest return.

That is why one of your first investments in your business needs to be a bookkeeping and filing system for tracking all your expenses. At the very minimum, you can buy a simple accordion folder in which any bills or receipts for the month are filed appropriately. This is a convenient solution for storing your expense and incoming revenue. In the end it is only half the battle.

Far more important is working with a public accountant or a piece of software like QuickBooks to track and understand the trends in your spending and revenue. My personal advice would be to find a suitable public accountant for a "start-up" meeting. In this meeting, you can present your plans and he/sheshe can help you figure out the best solution. Explain that you would like to be meeting with him/her infrequently, perhaps once a year around tax time, but you would like their help in setting up a financial accounting system that makes sense for you. I can assure you every penny (sometimes it was a LOT of pennies) that I have spent in accounting help has been worth it. I have always depended on a GREAT accounting firm to keep up with everything concerning my taxes and profits (or non-profits) in my business.

The benefit of an accountant is he/she can bring professional experience to bear on your situation, help you get organized, and help you understand how to manage your expenses. An accountant can be an excellent advisor for helping you understand and plan your startup expenses. It is easy to overlook many of them. An accountant can also help you figure out that all-important "break even" point. They can help you understand how to use deductions and business expenses to your advantage, to reduce your overall taxes. Most of all, an accountant will help you prepare for the year ahead, and help orient you to the important aspects of your business finances. I absolutely without reservation suggest getting professional accounting help from the beginning. To me my accountants are worth their "weight in gold."

Most likely, in terms of setting up a sustainable accounting system, they recommend your using QuickBooks, and they can probably help you get started using it. QuickBooks, which is the most popular business accounting software, makes it very easy to track your records with the incoming and outgoing expenses. You can use the software by paying a small monthly fee that is commensurate with how many features you need, or else you can buy the software outright for your computer for less than two hundred dollars. I consider this money very well spent, and the investment is often enough to get you through the beginning stages of your business—at least for a few years until things get complicated.

Best of all, when tax time arrives, the effort you have made to diligently record your expenses will make it incredibly easy to prepare your taxes. Make sure, in your startup meeting, you cover the subject of taxes with your accountant. Depending on your type of business, and the business structure you have chosen, there may be specific aspects that will require different tax treatments.

Keep Invoices and Receipts

Keeping invoices and receipts is not just a good practice that pays off in the long term, like flossing nightly. Keeping good records is a legal requirement. The IRS section 6001 requires businesses to keep appropriate records, and both the IRS and your home state has a right to request your business and personal records to review your tax return. If they find problems, you could be hit with a serious fine. Far beyond the question of compliance with the law, your financial records are important because you will discover that in the hands of a smart accountant or a smart piece of financial software, the deductions that you can make against your business will be a tremendous help in allowing you to make more money.

Debt

Just as the rich rule the poor, so the borrower is servant to the lender.
—Proverbs 22:7

I believe that thrift is essential to well-ordered living.
—John D Rockefeller

As anyone will tell you, I am not a fan of creating debt for yourself in order to run your business. I'm a big believer in bootstrapping your business through personal savings and personal financing. There are certainly arguments to be made that a bankable business should not be forced to struggle when a loan can push the operation into new areas that will generate even more revenue. From my perspective, however, there is still far too much easy credit available through credit cards and small loans, which can very quickly get you into real trouble later. I believe that the difficulty and struggle of beginning a business under tight conditions forces you to adopt valuable skills that can serve your business well. It also forces you to grow slowly and organically, and take the time to refine and explore the craftwork aspects of your business along the way—to build a creative vision for yourself. I have seen far too many businesses that expanded too quickly, thanks to a business loan or outside investor, and did not have an adequately formed plan to really take advantage of their growth. They found themselves with an excess of inventory, and facing real business losses.

If you do need to borrow money, try to do it privately from family, without the involvement of banks. As a second resort, you can look into personal loans, in which you essentially borrow from yourself. Many 401(k) accounts allow you to borrow from your own savings, and the end result is that the interest you're paying is going back to your own account, instead of a banker. A home equity loan works the same way. I have given many workshops on starting or growing a business. Some have said, "Martha do you really suggest using my retirement funds for a new business?" My answer to that is, "If you have planned (WRITTEN) very carefully, followed all of the proper steps in this book or others on properly preparing before opening a business and think (along with the suggested advisors given throughout this book) you have a very good possibility of success, then go ahead. If it is not worth the risk of putting your own money into it then it is not worth the risk of doing period." A business is not a toy. It is not fun and games. It is a very serious undertaking which if successful will certainly bring gains during your retirement. If you do not, through proper PLANNING, see that it will bring profits to you, don't open the business period. You will only lose money! It will not work. On a brighter note if you have done all of the planning as outlined in this book and if all of the signals and advice look good then my thinking would be that it is worth the risk of your own money. There are never any guarantees in any business I assure you.

Only in the very last resort should you turn to credit cards as a way of financing your business. Although it is ridiculously easy to use them to pay for your business expenses, their interest rates, sometimes as high as 21%, will quickly outweigh any convenience of so-called "easy money."

Instead of looking for ways to borrow money, I always recommend to my friends to find hidden money in your life. If you are really serious about your business, it will mean making changes in your life. An excellent place to look for unnecessary expenses is in your personal life. I am not merely talking about your monthly cable expenses, and whether you need 500 channels of television, although that is a good place to start. You can pose even larger questions to yourself, such as whether you really need two cars, or whether you could refinance your house with a smaller mortgage payment, or even live in a smaller house. Clothing purchases can be based on "need" or "greed."

I suggest you cut back on all with the exception of "need" such as kid's shoes which are now too small. I have observed that eating out is one of the greatest "money wasters" in my life. Cook more at home utilizing convenience savers such as crock pots. I know many families who dress their children and themselves beautifully from consignment stores. I know one family who sold their "larger house" and their "nice new SUV" in order for her to start a home based business on eBay so she could give up her job as a nurse and be home with her three children. She has never been happier!

You don't need to see these savings as a sacrifice. You are simply placing your money where it is most likely to multiply. By temporarily carving these sorts of expenses out of your life, your business can benefit from the savings. The cash you free up can be channeled back into your business where it will start actually making new money.

Read Dr. Ben Carson's Book

In closing this section entitled "Debt" I refer, once again, to Dr. Ben Carson's must-read book *Take The Risk: Learning to Identify, Choose and Live with Acceptable Risk*. He says to answer four questions concerning risk.

- What is the best thing that can happen if I do this?
- What is the worst thing that can happen if I do this?
- What is the best thing that can happen if I don't do this?
- What is the worst thing that can happen if I do this?
- Dr. Carson then says to think, analyze and pray.

Bartering

In the early days of your business, cash is your most precious commodity. Every dollar that you avoid spending on expenses can be channeled back into your business inventory and turned into revenue. Thinking of creative ways to sidestep traditional expenses brings huge advantages to your business. One of the more powerful tools for preserving your cash is bartering for services. Especially as you look toward paying for professional services, like legal and accounting expenses or web design, do not be shy about offering your own products or services instead of cash payment.

A friend of mine who imports exotic textiles wanted to hire a photographer so that she could display and sell all her products online. She managed to find an excellent local photographer who did freelance work for the *Boston Globe* and the *New York Times* taking pictures of food and cuisine, but his fees were far too high to afford. My friend is a very friendly, persistent and persuasive negotiator, and after finally managing to negotiate down his rate by half, they scheduled two half-day shoots. By the end of the second session, the photographer had fallen in love with my friend's textiles, and wanted to use them as backdrop for future photo shoots. The end result was that my friend ended up paying only 25% of the original fee in cash, and she paid the remainder in products. What that really meant, however, is that she was paying far less, because each of her products was counted at its retail value instead of the actual value that she paid for it. By paying with her own products' retail value, she buys everything at a substantial discount.

My friend is blessed, because her products have broad appeal. Hopefully your products or services will be equally popular. Even if they are not, you might offer your custom services. One of my friends in the heirloom sewing custom garment business regularly traded her beautiful garments to her beautician for her hair services.

One final thing to keep in mind is that there are tax implications for bartering, and the fair value of whatever you paid through barter needs to be reported. You can consult the IRS website or speak about it with your accountant.

Permits and Licensing

> *When people do not accept divine guidance, they run wild. But whoever obeys the law is joyful.*
> —Proverbs 29:18

No matter how small your venture, operating a business is a legal matter. Before you begin selling anything, make sure you are operating with the right permits and licenses. It can be a rude shock and a terrible setback to have invested money and effort setting up your business in your home, only to discover that your zoning laws do not permit its operation there. This concern is especially true if your home hobby uses large or noisy equipment, or creates odors or dust.

Unfortunately zoning and licensing regulations can vary from business to business and from state to state, so there are no hard and fast rules to rely upon. For typical small, local businesses, visit the website of your local township, city, or county. Once you have a little background, pick up the phone—or even better—take a trip to the local town offices, and make a friend there. Explain your business in simplest terms, and try to get some help understanding how the rules apply to you, and what offices you will need to contact for licensing and permissions.

The major concerns you will want to address are questions around:

- **Zoning:** You will need to confirm that you can operate your hobby-based business from within your home. Assuming that your hobby does not cause much noise or disruption, most cities and towns will allow you to run a small business from your home. Even if they do not, you can probably apply for a special permit. Take the time to understand the zoning limitations around teaching, advertising, and any other factors that may affect the growth of your business. I had a friend who was an excellent children's swimming teacher. She had a large swimming pool in her backyard and was giving lessons there. A "friendly" neighbor had the city officials come out to inform my friend that lessons with other than one student at a time were not allowed in our neighborhood. She had to quickly rent a swimming pool at a local hotel to give her lessons.

I have a funny personal story about zoning which really is not business related. My husband, a dentist, loves chickens. When he was a child he had chickens in his back yard in the heart of the city. His father, also was a dentist who loved chickens. Joe had a really nice chicken coop built in our back yard and ordered some very expensive and really beautiful chickens to go in our fenced yard in the new chicken coop. He was enjoying this "hobby" when the friendly "chicken police" knocked on the door asking if he had chickens in the yard. Joe answered affirmatively. He then said to Joe, "I am so very sorry to tell you that the zoning in this neighborhood does not allow chickens. You will have ten days to get rid of them." A neighbor had called and reported Joe's chickens. A very sad Joe found a good home for his chickens on a farm with a loving family who would appreciate these very expensive chickens. He would have saved a lot of money if he had checked the zoning first. The abandoned chicken coop still stands in our back yard with ivy growing all over it!

- **Business License:** Operating a business requires obtaining a license from the city or state. You will have to pay a small fee to get started, and an annual renewal fee whose amount depends on your business income.
- **Sales Certificates:** There are often two types of certificates that you will   need to obtain, which are easy to confuse. A "resale certificate" allows you to purchase goods wholesale for later resale without paying the State sales tax. A "retailer certificate" allows you to sell goods and collect State Sales tax.
- **Permits:** Depending on your business, and what sort of materials you work with, there may be additional safety permits that you will need to purchase and file.

Partnerships

Although I am going to include this form of business in this book, I do not recommend partnerships. I have known only a few partnerships that worked successfully. Most that I know about ended with the partners either in a legal battle or life long enemies because they did not work. One of my early mentors, Eunice Farmer of Eunice Farmer Fabrics in St. Louis told me "Martha do not ever have a partner other than Joe. I have never known a partnership that worked." It is important from the very start to understand that a partnership is a precise legal relationship in business, which has many obligations and consequences. It is about as close as you want to get to a marriage without falling in love. When you agree to a partnership, you are agreeing to share responsibility for your partner's actions and mistakes. If your partner, for example, is someone who tends to make bad spending decisions, or act impulsively, you will be assuming the consequences on your own shoulders. Your actions will become entangled with each other, by design, so it can become both costly and difficult to disentangle yourselves. Breakups will be messy, and so as you begin to consider engaging in a business partnership with a friend, you should assume that if a time comes where a disagreement forces you to end the partnership, your friendship will be over as well.

Although it is impossible to state exactly what makes a great partnership any more than any other type of strong relationship, there are some easy principles that you should follow. Most important of all is that you both share the same values and goals. Sometimes these values are implicit and understood, such as how much time and effort do you expect to invest in the business to make it successful? Where do you realistically want to take the business? Do you both have the same vision for where you want to be in five years? Is it intended to be a sideline effort, or the centerpiece of your professional life? Alignment on these values usually translates into the extent that you are willing to invest in the business together. A feeling of unequal contribution is usually what breaks up a partnership, when one person is actually working disproportionately compared to the other, or simply feels like they are.

A second important factor in evaluating whether to become partners is the extent to which you have complementary skills. If you are a creative person and your partner has more business skills, that can make a a good partnership. By covering for the other's shortcomings, each side brings value to the relationship, and together you might form a well-rounded set of skills.

As you might surmise, I don't recommend falling into a partnership. To build a solid and sound partnership can mean investing just as much time in structuring the relationship, as you invest in the business. There are far simpler ways to work together, as independent parties. If you like working with someone, you should consider working with him/ her as an independent consultant. You can together figure out creative means of compensation—whether it is a certain amount to be deducted from incoming revenue and capped at a specific value, or the ability to keep some of the products you're making at cost. Don't underestimate what you are offering your friend. The simple value of learning and experiencing firsthand how to start a business will be giving your friend valuable experience that can serve as a steppingstone on her/his own career.

No matter how you decide to work together, make sure that you are stating and documenting your relationship together in advance. You will want to clarify compensation, as well as create protections for yourself so that your friend cannot simply take your ideas and turn them into a competing business. Do not enter a partnership without a legal contract. A great corporate lawyer will be the best start up expense you will ever have if you are going to go into a partnership. It must be clear how you are going to work and more importantly how you are going to get out. My best advice on partnerships is don't do it!

Business Structure

The question of your business structure can seem very complicated, but it usually ends up being a simple decision. The fact that your business structure can change as your business evolves means that there is no need to overthink — start small and simple, and if you are successful, you can add complexity. The decision on the type of business legal structure revolves largely around taxes and liability. Which you choose will determine how much money and paperwork you will be filing with your local officials. There are three basic business structures that you can choose:

Sole Proprietorship is one of the simplest structures when you are running a small business in the early stages. A sole proprietorship is owned by a single person who pays taxes on the business through her personal income tax returns. The paperwork and expense associated with creating this type of business structure is quite low. What you gain in simplicity, however, you lose in your personal exposure to debt or liability. If your business or products cause any harm, or if your business goes into debt, you will be personally responsible. That makes it important to purchase business insurance.

General Partnerships are businesses that are legally owned by several people. This type of business requires a bit more legal and accounting paperwork, mainly in working out the details of the arrangement between partners. The primary advantage of a partnership is that its income is not taxed directly, but instead through each of the individual partners. On the other hand, each partner is responsible for the debts and obligations of the other, so you will want to make sure that you have a deep trust in your partner.

S Corporations main advantage is their ability to shield individuals from personal liability for any type of business debts. There are additional tax advantages for an S Corporation owner, who can report his/her share of corporate income on personal tax forms, and use their business losses to offset income from other sources. But an S Corporation is a legal entity that requires the participation of a lawyer, and lots of paperwork. It can be a complex undertaking, and probably not recommended, for an early business.

Limited Liability Company is another business structure designed to shield the business owner from personal liability for business debts. The owners of an LLC can freely allocate income among themselves and decide whether to be taxed as a corporation or partnership. The problem, once more, is the legal complexity involved in creating and maintaining such a business structure. You will need to work closely with a lawyer for both the creation and ongoing maintenance of an LLC.

Help and Advice

Starting a business is complicated. There is no shame in reaching out for professional services to help you figure everything out. As I have mentioned before, the Small Business Administration has an excellent website dedicated to people just like you, who are trying to get started. By browsing their website, you can discover forms and worksheets to help you. You can also make an appointment with their local Small Business Development Center, and their partner organization SCORE, to work with an experienced businessperson for help and assistance.

By using professional services judiciously, you can square away some of the most important parts of your business, and allow yourself to focus your energy on the creative aspects. Don't undermine your business, and get yourself in real trouble either financially or legally, simply for the sake of saving money. Knowing when to seek help is its own form of wisdom.

- Chapter Eight -

Marketing Your Business

There was a man named Jabez who was more honorable than any of his brothers. His mother named him Jabez because his birth had been so painful. He was the one who prayed to the God of Israel, "Oh, that you would bless me and expand my territory! Please be with me in all that I do, and keep me from all trouble and pain!" And God granted him his request.
—1 Chronicles 4:9-10

Make no little plans: they have no magic to stir men's blood.
—Daniel H. Burnham

I have been learning marketing skills since I was about two years old from my mother who was in the education arena not the business world. She knew how to make things happen as well as anyone else in the world.
—Martha Campbell Pullen

Groupon as a company—it's built into the business model—is about surprise. A new deal that surprises you every day. We've carried that over to our brand, in the writing and the marketing that we do, and in the internal corporate culture.
—Andrew Mason

Marketing Matters

Who is really going to make it big and stay in business? I will answer first that only God knows who is going to make it in the business world and who is not going to make it. I believe those who wish to make it in business must decide how to create enough visibility to become a legend. They must pray for God's guidance and ask for His blessings and help as did Jabez in the Bible. He reached for a better life and God granted his wish. I must add here that God does not always answer prayers in the way we ask.

How do I define business success? By legend, I believe this is someone who has made a significant contribution in a certain area that brings fulfillment to others' lives in a way that honors God. This statement, above all others, expresses my philosophy of business.

To become a legend one must create a plan to make that business:

More creative than all the competition,
More fabulous in service than the industry standard,
More employee friendly to the customers,
More surprises and fun,
More great products of quality construction,
More personal than the competition,
More—in every aspect of business!

..Like the people very much like us, who want....what?
Who want MORE.
Who want more of what?
Of everything!
But a business can only give so much!
Who said?
And in a free market system, the minute a business forgets these
things, the minute a business stops providing MORE, the minute a
business begins to ignore its sole purpose for being in a free market
system-its raison d-etre-it ceases playing the game called business. It
begins to play the game called good-bye.

—Michael Gerber

All business success rests on something labeled a sale, which at least momentarily weds company and customer. A simple summary of what our research uncovered on the customer attribute is this: the excellent companies really are close to their customers. That's it. Other companies talk about it; the excellent companies do it.

—Tom Peters

Women need to connect. But all over the world, there's been a weakening of community, the original connective tissue of family life....That is what the backyard fence represented when I was growing up spending summers in the south. We want to be a backyard fence that's there twenty-four hours a day for anyone who needs us. We care. Fence me in.

—Mary Furlon

The way to get there is through marketing your business. Marketing is nothing more than the art of selling things. It is all the different strategies and techniques that you might use to sell your products. In practical terms that boils down to making people aware that you exist, and that your product is worth buying.

In today's business world, it is no longer enough to make a great product. People are often too busy and distracted to look too hard for anything. If you want to run a successful business, you must be working just as hard at finding ways to attract customers to your product. You need to get people aware of you, thinking about you, telling others about you, and coming to visit you.

If marketing is not a central part of your business strategy from the very beginning, you're probably missing a great opportunity. No matter how much effort you spend on your products, your business will not grow if no one knows about you. No matter how brilliant your customer service strategy, or how polished your people skills, none of it will do you a bit of good until you get customers in the door. Without customers, you don't really have a business.

I love this thought. I can purchase a Ford dealership and fill the whole lot with brand new cars, have a service department and employ great people.

...til we sell cars. Period.

...at great products are everywhere. Creating a great ...price of entry. You must be much more than great to ...en year after year. People say opportunity will knock on ...u're patient and hard-working. I say that's rubbish! You need to get o... ...ere and knock on everyone's doors yourself. "Knocking on doors" of course can mean the doors of her/his computer! I have found in my business that knocking on doors to meet new people many times means traveling to teach. I love large audiences so I can touch lots of people.

I think my best "knocking on doors" since around 2000 has been my weekly email newsletter. After several years we had about 40,000 subscribers—all of whom signed up themselves to be included. In another part of this book I share what I believe made people open these newsletters every week-at least 35-40% of the recipients-and that is high.

Another wonderful opportunity we had to "knock on doors" was the PBS TV series, *Martha's Sewing Room* which aired for seventeen years all over the country and Canada. One series of thirteen shows was even translated into Japanese for Japanese Public Television. You should have seen me speaking Japanese!

Finding Hidden Doors

> *Listen! A farmer went out to plant some seed. As he scattered it across his field, some of the seed fell on a footpath, and the birds came and ate it. Other seed fell on shallow soil with underlying rock. The seed sprouted quickly because the soil was shallow. But the plant soon wilted under the hot sun, and since it didn't have deep roots, it died. Other seed fell among thorns that grew up and choked out the tender plants so they produced no grain. Still other seeds fell on fertile soil, and they sprouted, grew, and produced a crop that was thirty, sixty, and even a hundred times as much as had been planted!*
>
> —Mark 4:3-8

Marketing is about finding the hidden doors where opportunity waits. With my business, I am always looking for those hidden doors. If I can break into one more market, I say to myself, I will obtain one hundred more subscriptions to our magazine! If I go to speak at one more sewing machine convention, I will win new accounts and more shops will be excited about heirloom sewing. The creative process of finding those hidden doors is what marketing is all about!

As you start thinking about the marketing of your business, you should keep in mind that your work might not directly increase your bottom line tomorrow. Marketing is a much slower process. Sometime marketing can feel frustrating, because you can not quite see how your efforts are paying off. There is less direct feedback. But if you are focused and creative, you will eventually see results.

What Marketing Will Do

- Constantly remind your customers and prospects that you exist.
- Help your customers understand the benefits of your product or service.
- Share with the world the distinct personality of your brand.
- Increase your reputation and credibility.
- Encourage existing customers to buy more.
- Attract new customers.
- Replace lost customers.

Do not take your marketing plan lightly. Your products will not sell themselves. If you are a person who considers herself more of a creative type, and you do not really enjoy the selling side of business, you need to adjust your thinking. If you are secretly hoping that the quality of your products will "speak for itself," and you will not have to focus on the marketing of your product, let me tell you right now that you are sorely mistaken. I have seen dozens of hobby businesses that were making absolutely fabulous products, but because the owner did not pay enough attention to the marketing side, the business failed.

In fact, I would suggest that as you become successful, the marketing of your business will become more and more important to you. You will discover that the health of your business depends on the regular exposure and promotion of your brand to the outside world.

Do not let that intimidate you. Marketing is an extremely creative and gratifying effort on its own. Some of the most clever and creative people in the business world work in marketing. Marketing can truly be fun and fulfilling—but if you approach it like a chore that you need to check off your list, you can be certain that your outcomes will be just as humdrum.

If you can learn to embrace the creativity intrinsic to marketing, and set your imagination loose on the challenge of making your product stand out among all others, you just might have a very successful business indeed. If you can transform all the creativity that you have placed into your hobby, and redirect that energy into spreading the word about your products, your business headed in the right direction.

The best way to predict the future is to create it.
—Peter Drucker

Some Promotional Ideas

Here are more than seventy promotional ideas, some are free, some inexpensive, a few costly. All will give your business exposure.

- Give everyone you meet—EVERYONE—a business card.
- Make a Mind Map with your marketing ideas.
- Get out there and do something. Better to do something for nothing than nothing for nothing.
- Get out and get among 'em!
- Get a good website.
- Create an email mailing list.
- Send an email newsletter as often as possible-at least monthly. Weekly is better!
- Create a Facebook business page.
- Create a Twitter account.
- Ask for referrals.
- Look for new ways to make contact with customers. Write them down.
- Keep in touch.
- Target your market!
- Create a written promotional plan.

- Set dates for when you will accomplish the items on your plan.
- Create a logo.
- Create a mission statement.
- Create a letterhead.
- Create matching business cards.
- Create a great flyer to send by email.
- Send flyers and special offers with promo along with billing statements to your wholesale customers.
- Be smart with your advertising dollar.
- Go after word-of-mouth advertising.
- Go after word-of-mouse advertising.
- Join Internet discussion groups or forums.
- Create a display in the window at your local library.
- Create a presentation/press kit. (These include flyers, articles by or about you, photos, brochures, product samples, anything interesting about you. Have them ready to send by email.)
- Put flyers up in your supermarkets, laundromats, pet stores—anywhere your customers like to frequent.
- Send press releases to the media about your product or service via email.
- Take the press release in person to the newspaper office or television station.
- Call the newspaper office or the television station telling them about your press release that is in the mail or coming by email.
- Create contests or sweepstakes.
- Take surveys.
- Leave a trail of "gifts" back to you.
- Trade your product or service for publicity.
- Co-op with your suppliers for ads.
- Write articles for newsletters and magazines.
- Take professional pictures to accompany these articles. Have copyright permissions on these pictures to give the newsletter, newspaper or magazine people when you deliver the articles and pictures.
- Post information articles on your website and allow people to reprint them in their trade publications and company newsletters.
- Get the media to write and talk about you!
- Get great photos! Have copyright permissions already printed and ready to give to the media.
- Give speeches to civic and service clubs and groups (Kiwanis, PTAs,

Chamber of Commerce, etc.).

- Go to the Chamber of Commerce "After Hours" events. Most towns have something like this. Introduce yourself to everyone there and **give all a business card.**
- Join civic clubs.
- Give programs at your civic club.
- Give free promotional seminars.
- Give demonstrations of your hobby at trade shows, craft shows, and any event happening in your community.
- Team up with other hobbyists for promotions and advertising.
- Start associations and users' groups.
- Create a forum or newsgroup on the Internet.
- **Always carry and give out your business cards.**
- Always get potential customers' business cards or write down their information when you meet them.
- Imprint your company name and logo on giveaway items for your customers:
  - Pens
  - Paper
  - Clocks
  - Calendars
  - Keychains
- My best supplier for giveaways is Cole Industries.
- Give funny bumper stickers.
- Put your message on:
  - Shopping store receipts
  - Shopping bags
  - Your own cars
  - Your team's cars
  - Billboards
  - Bus stop benches
  - Inside buses
  - Vehicle and building signs
  - Point-of-sale displays
- Co-sponsor events with nonprofit organizations and advertise your participation.
- Help give a fashion show for a church related organization to help them raise money.

- Co-op events with related, yet noncompeting, businesses.
- Co-sponsor events with your suppliers.
- At consumer or business trade shows you could:
  - Attend
  - Have a display booth
  - Give educational mini-seminars
- Do telemarketing.
- Train everyone on your team, including your young family members, to be service and salespeople.
- Become involved in your community.
- Create gift certificates.

Promote your business with G.R.A.C.E. with God first in all things.

Think about what people are doing on Facebook today. They're keeping up with their friends and family, but they're also building an image and identity for themselves, which in a sense is their brand. They're connecting with the audience that they want to connect to. It's almost a disadvantage if you're not on it now.

—Mark Zuckerberg

Building Your Brand

One of the core elements of your marketing strategy is your brand. Your brand describes the personality of your products. It's the emotional connection that people feel with your business. Think about some of your favorite brands, and how you feel about their products. Those feelings are a calculated part of that company's marketing strategy.

Building your own brand can help guide your entire marketing strategy, because it forces you to remain focused and consistent. Think about the themes and ideas that fit inside your brand. Are your products quirky, austere, unique, colorful, serious, detailed, formal, or funny? Your marketing strategy should develop those same themes, and begin to tell a story about your brand.

They Buy Your Story

A successful marketing strategy tells the customer a story about your products. When it comes to most hobby-oriented, handmade products or services, people are often just as interested in the time, effort, and ingredients that went into the product as the product itself. They are buying your story. You should make sure that as you design your products, and build your business, everything you do is aligned with that marketing story.

For example, if you are creating dress patterns from old garments purchased at Portobello Road in London your marketing should let that story shine through. Will you choose bright, bold fabrics for your antique patterns, and make "old meets new" part of your story? Or will you look for old European fabrics and make "the past reborn" the story behind your brand?

Your premium brand had better be delivering something special, or it's not going to get the business.
—Warren Buffett

As you consider the different ways to build your brand, think about the reasons you love your hobby, and what motivates you to share your love with the world, in order to allow your marketing strategy to be a celebration of that story.

By staying focused on your brand and building your story around it, you are creating your own specific niche. By that I mean that your business is finding a way to become the first thing that everyone thinks about in your specific field. Once you have created a niche for yourself, and you have found a way to make sure that you are the best at it, success has a good possibility of following.

Do not think small when you start developing your marketing strategy and building your brand. Think big! Think about being the best.

A customer of the moment is the one who buys your brand; a customer for life is the one who joins it....Women want a brand that doesn't say, "Tough luck, that's not our strategy," but that says, "Tell us what you want and we'll make it our strategy."

—Faith Plotkin

Marketing Material

There is no doubt that marketing is one of those parts of your business where you can spend enormous amounts of money. Unfortunately, most early businesses do not have that kind of money. The good news, however, is that you can produce some basic marketing material without much expense. These simple steps will spread the word about your business.

Websites

E-commerce businesses, even e-commerce specialists, have yet to realize that the WWW is first and foremost an emotional experience. Few websites reflect this important priority.

—Grant Fairley

We will discuss websites in much more detail in a later chapter of this book, but it is worth noting here that some kind of web presence has become an industry standard for any type of business. If you are at all serious about starting your business and beginning to market your products, you should definitely have a website.

Of course, it does not have to be anything too fancy. In fact, I would suggest that in the early days of your business, you might consider your web presence like a brochure or a business card. By creating a webpage that allows people to get basic information about your business, and perhaps see some of your products, you validate that you are a legitimate, professional, and reputable business. More importantly, you are creating an "automatic" marketing device that allows anyone to find more information about your business from anywhere at any time.

Business Cards, Postcards and Letterhead

The two most creative business cards that I ever saw stick in my mind today. Jo Packham, publisher of *Where Women Cook, Where Women Create* and *Where Women Create Business*, all fabulous magazines, has the most wonderful cards. Her business card is in a small envelope, which is the color of a tan paper grocery bag. On the outside it is "addressed" with Priority Mail, Air Mail and Par Avion and Via Aerea with an airplane where the stamp usually goes. When you open the card of the same color within you find a tri fold card with lots of information printed front and back.

The other was a rather large card, almost postcard size, with a hole in one corner and a small red Christmas ball attached with a ribbon. There was no significance in the fact that it was a Christmas ball; however I did not throw it away and it was a small happy to receive it. It was so unique I just kept it. Other types of business cards that I like are a double folded with a cut out "window" in the front with a photograph peeking through from the back. There are many places on the Internet that have very creative business cards that you can design using their models.

Although they seem quite modest, business cards and business postcards can be one of the most effective marketing tools in the early days of your business. Once you have decided to start your business, you should always have a few cards on your person, no matter where you go.

Power of One Business Card

Some years ago we had a very successful realtor from San Antonio, Texas who came to be a Martha Pullen Licensed Heirloom Teacher. This is a relatively expensive program which requires a financial commitment. She told me upon arrival, "I made all of the money to come here this week from one business card." When I asked her what she had done she replied, "I did not want to use any of my real estate income to pay for this hobby based venture. I told myself that if I could not earn enough money sewing christening dresses to pay for this trip, I was not coming." She then further explained that she put up one business card on the bulletin board of a predominately Hispanic Catholic Church in San Antonio. The priest had given permission of course. She said, "Hispanic people treasure beautiful christening and First Holy Communion dresses." The first call came shortly afterward and she met with the potential clients bringing samples of finished beautiful dresses and her price lists. The family (grandmothers usually pay for things like this) loved her work and commissioned a dress that day. My friend also had her simple contract she required them to sign. She also required 75% of the money to be paid before starting the dress. On the day of the christening the whole church saw the dress which was magnificent. They asked the family where they bought such a masterpiece which of course would become a family heirloom. The family gladly shared the name of the seamstress; the rest is history! She had fifteen commissions that year and that way more than paid for her whole trip to Alabama to become a licensed teacher. Business cards are almost magic in some situations.

I know at least two businesses where the very successful owners say that handing out hundreds of business cards is their best marketing tool. I mean hundreds. They hand them out everywhere they go and they make it a point of going to lots of Chamber of Commerce type mixers as well as meetings of various kinds.

If I might use one very personal example of a business card's being of the utmost importance. When I was five years old we moved to Greensboro, North Carolina where my Daddy was opening a new Fleetwoood Coffee Plant. My parents went to the First Methodist Church that first Sunday attending Sunday school as well as church. During the Sunday school a very nice surgeon came up to my Daddy and gave him a business card saying, "Mr. Campbell I know you are new in town. If you should have any medical emergencies here is my number." If I remember correctly he also wrote his home phone on this card.

In the middle of the next week I woke up screaming in pain. I had a ruptured appendix and had to be rushed immediately to the hospital for surgery. Of course Daddy called this surgeon; he operated immediately. I am sure this card was given indeed to offer a Christian good deed but it really served to gain a patient almost immediately. Who would ever have thought that the new family would have needed a surgeon three days after arriving in town? Hand out those business cards everywhere. Even if that person does not need your services he/she just might know someone who is looking for exactly what you have to sell. If I were building a new dental, medical, or legal business (yes they are businesses) I would hand out a business card to everyone I came in contact with including church members. Many times church members are more diligent about referring a fellow church member than any other group.

Business cards are easy to carry around and pass along to other people who might be interested in your products. What they offer in convenience and simplicity, however, they sometimes lack in detail. The slightly larger format of a business postcard can often allow you to show more of your products and provide more information about your business than can be fit on a smaller business card. It is critical that your business card tell what you do and how to get in touch with you.

Letterhead Design

A well designed letterhead is equally important for your image. A nice sheet of writing paper bearing your business name and other information lets you to create any sort of information on paper that you can provide to interested clients, like price lists or product descriptions.

In the world of desktop publishing, it is very easy to make your own business cards or business postcards. If you have a computer and printer, you can take a quick trip to Staples and buy a business card kit made by Avery, and print them yourself. If you want to get a little more creative, you can go to the local art store and buy colored card stock for the printer, then design, print and cut the cards yourself.

An easy option is to use an Internet based business card website like Vistaprint **(www.vistaprint.com)**, or Tinyprints **(www.tinyprints.com)**. These sites let you browse from a gallery of designs and create your own business cards, which are mailed to you in very short order.

A final option it to find a local designer and work together on building a set of marketing materials. This will be a more expensive option, but it has the benefit of allowing you to work with a professional to create a logo and design that is completely unique to your business. It also ensures that over time you can create a set of coordinated marketing materials, such as flyers and brochures, with a common look and feel. If you do work with a designer, make sure that he/ she provides you with the "source files" for your logo and design, so that you can reuse it later. Be sure you own the copyright on any work produced for hire; get it in writing!

Keep in mind that in the early days of your business, some of the information on your business cards may change. You may not want to order large quantities until you are certain that all your information is stable. Whatever you do, you should make sure that you cards contain the following information:

- Your name
- Your company name
- Your logo (if you have one)
- Your business address
- Your business telephone number
- Your business email address
- Your website address (if you have one)
- Any other web information you might have (your business Facebook page, your Twitter handle, etc.)

Target Your Customer

No one can make products that everyone likes, and any marketing strategy that tries to appeal to everyone rarely succeeds. As you consider how you are going to market your products, you should always keep your target customer in mind. Try to build a kind of portrait in your mind of your ideal customer. In my business of heirloom sewing, for instance, my products have the most appeal to mothers, grandmothers and great grandmothers of all ages. When I start to think about marketing to those customers, I have to consider that despite their common interest in heirloom sewing, they probably have very different habits and interests. It is CRITICAL to write down everything in your business plan about your target customers. Remember if it is not written down, it will go away! Make a Mind Map.

It is a very valuable exercise, as you start to figure out your marketing strategy, to build these portraits, or "customer profiles," and try to imagine that person's age and tastes. Focus on that ideal customer, and try to imagine how she spends her weekdays and weekends. How are you going to get in front of this person? What sort of magazines does this ideal customer read? What kind of movies does she like? What does she like to do for fun? How often does this person go shopping? Where does she like to shop?

There are some basic ways to target and define your customer. You can use these attributes to build a portrait of your ideal customer. Think about where you target customer falls in these categories:

Demographics
- What is the age and gender of your ideal customer?
- How much money would you expect your ideal customer to earn?
- How is your ideal customer employed?

- How would you expect them to spend their days?
- What sort of residence do they live in—rural, urban or suburban?

Behaviors
- What sorts of products does you ideal customer already use?
- What kinds of activities does your ideal customer enjoy?
- What sorts of magazines or websites does your ideal customer read?

Wants, Needs, and Desires
- What are the kinds of values that your ideal customer believes in?
- What sorts of product features matter most to your ideal customer— price, quality, uniqueness, handmade?
- How does your ideal customer make buying decisions—on impulse, or after thorough research?

By taking these factors into account, and starting to build a customer profile, you can start imagining the best ways to reach your customer, and how to make your products appealing. For example, if you are trying to target customers who are interested in healthy lifestyles, you can find ways to advertise within health clubs or yoga studios. If you think your customers are interested in sustainable or natural products, you can emphasize the fact that you use organic products or get your materials from local vendors.

If you feel uncertain about your ideal customer's tastes and values, you can ask them directly. Make a list in your mind of people who you might consider ideal customers; they do not have to be close friends. Prepare a survey asking them about what appeals to them and ask them to fill it out. You can prepare a survey online using online services like Zoomerang **(www.zoomerang.com)**, or Survey Monkey **(www.surveymonkey. com)**, or Survey Gizmo **(www.surveygizmo.com)** and email it to your acquaintances.

The better you understand your customer's habits and tastes, the more targeted your marketing strategy becomes. That helps ensure that your efforts are spent trying to convince and alert the right people, instead of wasting your time trying to persuade the wrong people.

Types of Marketing

From my point of view, there are about five types of marketing that you can practice, and each of them has benefits and drawbacks. We will walk through them in more detail for the rest of the chapter. I will state here and in other places in this book that my two main marketing strategies for our company have always been meeting people in person (on six continents to date) and my weekly email newsletter which I wrote every week. At one time I had over 40,000 subscribers to this email newsletter.

- **Direct marketing** is reaching out to people either through mail, email, or hand delivered flyers. You are delivering a message directly to a specific person. If it is done well, direct marketing can create a connection between you and the customer. When it is done poorly, your marketing becomes spam and junk mail.
- **Advertising** can be very expensive, but can create lots of exposure for you. You can create print, radio, television or even web advertising. If you do your research and target the media that your customers like, advertising can be very effective.
- **Publicity** is like free advertising. It happens when you reach out to newspapers, magazines, and blogs, and they decide to feature a story about you. You should always be thinking about creating a compelling reason for someone to write about your business.
- **Referral marketing** is about using word-of-mouth from your customers to promote your business and win new customers. You can design special offers and incentives to convince people to spread the word about your business.
- **Event and content marketing** is about using your knowledge about your hobby to attract attention to your business. By presenting your ideas through lectures and seminars, or writing articles, you show your expertise to the world and attract new customers.

What mix of marketing you practice will depend a lot on your marketing budget, and how much time you can afford to invest in marketing. Whatever method you decide, be sure to design a marketing strategy that is sustainable. Do not plan to sink all your money into a single magazine advertising slot and think you can just sit back and watch the customers pour through the doors. You should think of your marketing plan as much more of a marathon rather than a sprint. A steady and focused set of marketing efforts over the long term, spread out over different media, is the best approach

Direct Marketing

People do not just buy from brands; they buy from people. I call this personal branding. More importantly, they want advice, services and even products from people they trust. Much like any form of branding, personal branding is about marketing. It should not be confused with self-promotion. It is about positioning yourself as an authority in a chosen profession or market by sharing your knowledge in a transparent way, earning trust with an audience over time. The rise of the social web is making this possible for a greater number of people.

How to Write Great Newsletters

Keeping in touch with your customers through either email or postal mail is a fantastic way to keep your business on their minds, and keep customers returning. The key is knowing how often to send something to them, and what sort of messages you send. If you are bombarding them with photocopied flyers or uninteresting emails every week, they will quickly tire of your constant communication. On the other hand, if you send them fun and engaging content that is a pleasure to read, or news about new products or sales, they will be much happier to hear from you.

If you want to draw people to your business, you can send them notices about product giveaways and promotions. It is worth keeping in mind the disadvantages of discounting. Any increased sales will be at the expense of your profit margin. You are also training your customer to wait for a promotion before purchasing. Sometimes a better way to encourage purchases is to send a gift certificate to loyal and repeat customers, inviting them to return and spend it at your store.

Email newsletters are a wonderful method to keep your customers connected with your business, and ensure that they continue opening your emails. I cannot emphasize enough what a wonderful and important part role they play in my business. I get scores of responses from every one of my newsletters. I speak about my customers as if they are part of my family, and it creates a wonderful sense of community among all of us. When customers write letters back to me, I sometimes include these letters in my next emails. My customers ARE my extended family.

The trick with newsletters is writing creative and engaging content that will keep your readers interested. That means finding your own voice, and writing about the things that both interest you, and provoke positive responses from your customers. In the Internet Age, people are much more used to an informal style of writing, so don't worry about trying to sound too professional. Just have fun! The more personal your voice, the more your customers will connect with your brand.

Make the Newsletter PERSONAL

Make sure that your newsletter is personal and friendly. Make it an opportunity to connect with your customers and build a community around your brand. Here are some ideas to make your newsletter more personal:

- Put a hobby trick or tip in the newsletter.
- Put a letter from a customer in the newsletter.
- Put a personal letter from you in the newsletter. When I say personal, I mean personal! I write about our family, our dog, our children and grandchildren. I wrote about birthday parties, my mother and her illnesses, our children when they were missionaries in Africa, births of new grandchildren and cute sayings from the grands. On and on. I shared my life.
- Put a thought for the day or a scripture in the newsletter.
- Put in a short devotional. Share what God is doing in your life.
- Put news about your customer's projects which you have seen in the newsletter.
- Put family news about your customers in the newsletter. Get permission.
- Put family news about your employees in the newsletter. Get permission.
- Put new products in the newsletter.
- Put a recipe in the newsletter.
- Put "what's new" to purchase in your newsletter.
- Tell all about a business trip or convention in your newsletter.
- Put pictures! Lots of pictures!
- Put at least one item on sale in the newsletter.
- Make it personal. Make it personal. Make it personal. Make it personal. Share your life. Share your life. Share your heart.

Flyers to Promote Your Classes, Products, and Services

A flyer will be one of the most important items you will need for the first several years in promoting your business. It should be a simple one-sided sheet. In today's cyber-fast world, customers want information now! That means making your flyers emailable.

A Flyer Should Tell:

- What you are selling: seminars? books? dog grooming? This goes at the top of the page and should be small. What is to be emphasized is the benefit of what you are selling, like "Chemical-Free Dog Grooming."
- Title of business or classes: very bold and large, this should stand out.
- What is covered: (short outline and/or bullet points) this gives them an idea of the content. If giving classes, begin this section with "You Will Learn..."
- Who this is most appropriate for. Buyers want stuff that is specific for them. If you are a dog trainer, you are more apt to buy an answering machine that is just for dog trainers, even though it is really not different than other answering machines. Indicate if your products are best for stay at home moms, Ph.Ds, dog lovers, managers, salespeople, front line personnel, etc. If you say your items are appropriate for all, all will think you do not know what you are talking about, even if you are right.
- A few endorsements: These show you are liked by other customers.
- A very short biography: It tells why you are knowledgeable on this subject.
- What you look like: Your photograph or a drawing of you.

Promotional Gifts

Many small businesses create unusual gifts to give their customers and potential customers. This type of gift should be something that can be shared with staff. Your gift should never be embarrassing, crude, personal, or anything that could be considered a bribe. I have sent little key rings which said, "You're Number One At Martha Pullen Company." We have given cups, picture frames, little clocks and other things made especially for our Martha Pullen School of Art Fashion. We have sent "Martha Bucks" with a drawing of me and a discount coupon to be used on a future purchase in the packages. I have given personalized Christmas balls; they are very much appreciated although they cost a little more. (My source is Cole Industries but there are many.)

If you use gifts, keep them fun, inexpensive, and practical! Useable items are kept around. We have sent out soda can covers, key chains, and letter openers with good response. If your business is a "how-to" business, you might send an instructional sheet for a new design. That is much less expensive than plastic goodies from the promotional catalog. We have sent how to sheets as a gift in the past. People love a "lesson plan."

Your Mailing List

Of course, your direct mail campaigns are only as good as your mailing list. Even your best newsletter is going to "junk mail" if you send it to the wrong person. For that reason, I cannot emphasize enough the importance of getting the email and mailing address of all your customers, so that you can add them to your customer mailing address. Whenever you get a sale or an inquiry, capture that information and keep the data! As I have said before–your business is not your product or service, it is your customers. So maintaining a strong customer database is a source of tremendous value. Those who have bought from you personally, and have had a good experience, are your main source of future sales. Always keep track of them in your customer database.

As you start collecting data about your customers, you should make sure that it includes the following information:

- First and last name
- Address, city, state, zip
- Phone and fax number (optional for me)
- Email address (most critical—some only get email address)
- What he/she purchased from you or how you got his/her name
- What his/her special interests are in your product or service

If you do not have a strong customer list, and you want to get the word out to a broad population of people, you can use a commercial service to rent a targeted mailing list. The nice thing about these services is that they allow you to selectively define the criteria for your mailing list. For example, if you only want to mail middle-income families in Georgia with an interest in sewing, your mailing list can be customized to include only those matching families. Experian (**www.experian.com**) is a leading provider of such lists.

In the old days we kept our leads on a 3x5 card system. Today, computers are so inexpensive and easy to use, it does not make any sense to try to keep your database on paper. But once your customer database gets large enough and your email newsletters complex enough, you should think about using an email marketing service.

Fortunately, there are a number of companies that offer very simple marketing solutions for storing your mailing lists, creating emails and newsletters, and automatically sending them out. These services are fairly inexpensive or free, and well worth exploring. Some of the most reputable include MailChimp (**www.mailchimp.com**), Emma (**www.myemma.com**), ConstantContact (**www.constantcontact.com**), Vertical Response (**www.verticalresponse.com**), and Benchmark Email (**www.benchmarkemail.com**).

Publicity

Publicity is free advertising. If you can find ways for local or national media to write a story about your business, it can have the same effect as if you bought an expensive advertisement. Often it is even better, because unlike an advertisement, an article or news story will give your business extra credibility. Every story about your business becomes part of your press kit and adds to your overall reputation.

Publicity takes work and persistence, but it can be a great alternative to paid advertising. The trick is careful targeting. The first step is to go to the library and surf the web to discover the sorts of publications where you would like you products to appear. For print publications, you might want to start locally, and focus on newspapers and magazines. You should also consider specialty magazines.

Keep in mind that by starting small, and getting coverage from smaller publications, you will be gaining credibility and making it easier to win coverage from the larger publications. Most local newspapers will have a Style section that appears once a week, and many specialty magazines will have a section devoted to new and interesting products. You should also target specialized magazines that cater to your particular interests.

Take the time to review these publications carefully and make sure that the products and businesses they feature have similarities to your own. If a newspaper seems to show a preference for gadgets and modern styles, do not bother to propose a feature on your embroidery.

Once you have identified a group of publications that matches your business, do a little more research to find the correct contact address. You should check the masthead to find the email or postal address of the correct editor. Do not be afraid to make a phone call to get the correct contact—it will be a waste of your time to send your information to the wrong editor. You should write a nice personalized note to each contact on your list. Avoid the kind of stiff language that sounds like a form letter. Take the time to comment on what you like about the publication, and how you think your products fit into its style. With your note, you should include a press kit. If your business is not mature enough to have a detailed press kit, just include some photographs and descriptions of your work. Presentation counts! Always make your documents look professional, and packaged in such a way that they stand out. A local photocopy place can make a "press kit folder" for you if you take some information and a picture. A press kit folder is a folder which is printed on the outside and has two pockets on the inside. After getting one printed, put various things in it such as a brief resume, a picture, and some interesting information. You now have a "press kit."

Call Over and Over

Do not be surprised if no one responds right away. You should plan to follow-up with a phone call. Everyone is busy, so it is not a personal insult if someone does get back to you. Just be polite and persistent in asking to speak with the editor. Keep calling back over the course of several weeks. Do not forget to call over and over. Truly the person might not have time to call you back. If you keep calling the timing might just be right. For instance, what if the nightly news person has not called you back? What if you call on a certain day and he/she needs a story for that night's news or for the next night? You just might fit the bill. Do not give up when you get no response on the first call. They are VERY busy; however, sometimes they do need fillers and you just might be the filler they need.

Blogs

In the age of the Internet, blogs are an equally important means of gaining publicity. Blogs, of course, are Internet journals where people post small articles about subjects that interest them. Many blogs attract a greater readership than some larger magazines, so even a brief mention of your products can offer excellent exposure. The way to get blog publicity is to build a relationship with a blog editor by following and reading his/her posts, and making thoughtful comments. Once you have shown genuine interest in that blog's content, you can write the blog editor directly, the way you might write a newspaper editor, and ask if he or she would like to feature your products or link to your store site.

Create Your News Story

A final approach to publicity is to actually create a newsworthy story around your business. Do not be afraid to get creative. I know of a paddleboard business in Maine that wanted to clear its inventory before winter began. The owner organized a paddleboarding expedition two weeks before Christmas. He and several of his friends donned wetsuits and Santa costumes to paddle across Portland Harbor. The story was covered by the local newspaper and television, and the owner sold off his excess inventory within a few days from the publicity.

Of course, you do not have to do something quite so outrageous to get news coverage. Newspapers love stories about volunteerism and community service. By finding creative ways to help your local community, you can create a positive story around your business that will draw the attention of the local press and raise your profile. One Christmas we made Christmas stockings for the babies born at Huntsville Hospital during December to go home from the hospital in. They were adorable and of course the *Huntsville Times* did a story on this. Let me quickly add that they wore clothes and blankets in addition to this stocking! The stocking just went on top of everything else!

Community Involvement

A fantastic way to get free publicity is to get involved with your community. Social consciousness shows that you are a Christian organization that believes in practicing your values. It also sets an example for the rest of the community. We receive hundreds of letters from our customers and colleagues about sewing projects they have created. These projects have often been featured in the newspaper or local television news. Here are just a few examples:

- Mend garments which are donated for resale.
- Make baby quilts for unwed mothers.
- Sew simple dresses, school bags, shirts, quilts baby blankets and toys for Humanitarian Aid. Distribute worldwide.
- Make large stockings at Christmas to put toiletries and other small gift items for long-term care patients. They often like the stockings so much they keep them on display until Easter.
- Make heart pillows for mastectomy patients. Make them the right size for tucking under the arm of patients, helping to relieve pressure following surgery.
- Make wheelchair and walker carriers for patients in a nursing home.
- Sew mittens, hats from fleece for the homeless.
- Sew pillowcase dresses and boy's shirts to send with a mission group traveling to a third world country.
- The lists are endless of people who need your talents to do things for those less fortunate.
- Sew quilts and teddy bears for police to carry in their trunks when the social workers and police pick up abused children from their homes. The child gets to take the quilt and bear to his/her foster care home.

> *So let's not get tired of doing what is good. At just the right time we will reap a harvest of blessing if we don't give up.*
> —Galatians 6:9

Press Releases

Once you have a database of press contacts, you need to work your list. This is done by periodically calling and sending your contacts publicity releases. Publicity releases are short news accounts that you will send to the news media for anything you conceive of that might have a "hook."

There are thousands of PR companies that will help you create and send out press releases, but this is very expensive. On the other hand, it is the easiest way to accomplish getting your name in front of the press. The least expensive and fastest way to send releases is from your own computer. You just take your database and create an email list. Your computer then sends the releases to whomever you wish. Once again I cannot recommend highly enough checking books out of the library on how to write press releases. There is so much information to help you write something which will indeed be taken seriously.

Rules for News Releases

If you follow these rules, the media will pay closer attention to your news release and work with you.

- Put the source of the release in the upper left-hand corner of your paper. This is the name, address, and phone number of the person to contact for further information. The contact person may be you or someone at your PR service.
- Put the release date, typed in capital letters, slightly below the source information and on the opposite (right-hand) side of the page.
- Sum up the most important thrust of the release in the headline in capital letters.
- Sending by email is the best method, I think.
- If you choose to send your news release by mail, use standard 8 1/2 x 11 sheets of paper. Smaller or larger sizes are hard for media people to store. Use only one side of the paper. Keep the length of the release to one page whenever possible. If you must use more, type "(MORE)" at the bottom. Staple all pages on top left. On the last page, type "###" or "END."
- Your releases should be typed double-spaced. Leave a three-inch margin on the top of the first page and leave margins on each side that are wide enough for editing.
- Dottie Walters' journalism teacher wrote the following poem by Rudyard Kipling on the blackboard the first day Dottie was in her class. It has since helped her in every business enterprise. *"I keep six honest serving men, They taught me all I knew. Their names were What and Where and When, And How and Why and Who."* Be sure to get all of your "serving men" in the first paragraph of your news releases. Put the most important and exciting one at the head of the story.
- Use a fine grade of paper. A color other than white may help you stand out in the crowd but stay in the warm spectrum.
- Do not send out news releases that have a "copy machine" look.
- Avoid highly technical language unless the release is for a technical audience.

- Find out how far in advance each contact wants your information. Send it out when they want it.
- Do not pass off nonoriginal material as exclusive.
- Do not try to make an advertisement for yourself out of an article or release. Make it fascinating news for readers instead.
- Give a source for additional information (name, address, email address, website, phone number). Make sure your source knows all the details and does not have to check with someone else for answers if a reporter calls for additional information. This source could be an association or company mentioned in the article.
- Find a way to make your news noteworthy! Give it a twist that is specific to the audience who will read it. A dog expert working with plumbers might come up with a topic such as "Plumbers Use Dogs to Sniff Out Deadly Gas" to catch the attention of a plumbers' publication. Other news media outlets, however, might also find that topic worthy of attention.
- Releases should be the minimum length necessary to present the facts of interest to this audience.
- Keep your news release mailing list up-to-date. Post changes as you receive them. Media people like to see releases addressed to them rather than to their predecessors.
- Make it personal and interesting to read!

Get Those Photos!

Websites and magazines are very keen to print great photos. If you can supply them with a great photo, in a timely manner (usually twelve hours after the event), they will very often print them. If you have someone affiliated with you—a student, parent, friend—who likes to take pictures, you will be well ahead of the game!

As websites or magazines or newspapers inquire about you, you will need good photographs on hand to send along. What would we do without digital photography and email?

PR is Essential

In conclusion, public relations and publicity are necessary events in a successful business. Use a little creativity and the ideas gleaned from this chapter and you will have a good start.

I have never been able to afford an advertising agency, so we have had to be very creative. A few phone calls to newspapers and television stations have opened the doors to getting publicity for my business. In my husband's dental practice, a phone call has brought the medical editor out to see what news was happening in implant dentistry, new equipment, or missionary dentistry around the world. All of these phone calls developed into stories in the newspaper. Never give up on looking for ways to get free or affordable publicity. It is essential.

Advertising

Let me begin this section with my best advertising hint ever. Send frequent email newsletters—MAKE THEM PERSONAL AND FUN—and this advertising is FREE. Advertising people tell me you need to expose your customers to your product **NINE** times before they are apt to buy. The costs of advertising can be very high, and most small businesses cannot afford that kind of early investment. There are some effective strategies, however, that do not have to absorb your entire marketing budget.

If you are looking to advertise in the classic media, like radio, newspapers, or magazines, focusimg on local publications with a smaller but targeted circulation is a good way to keep advertising costs down. You should also look for specialized directories that are focused on your target market. When I had a retail store I always advertised in the Sunday women's section of the *Huntsville Times*. It was very effective for me. You might write a column for a newspaper such as "Ask Martha." Joe did this very effectively for years promoting his dental practice. I think the title was "Ask Dr. Pullen." I truly do not remember the exact title but he put in one dental question and then answered it. Actually he was able to get smaller area newspapers to run this column free since it truly was informational. At the end, of course, he had his name, address and phone number. He requested that the readers send their dental questions to his address. If he did not have new questions he just made them up and answered them!

Internet Advertising

If you want to get into Internet advertising, one of the best and easiest places to start is by using Google or other search engines for paid search advertising campaigns. That means that when someone enters a search term in Google, the search results will feature your advertisement on that page. For example, if you decided to buy a campaign using the words "heirloom sewing," then whenever someone enters those two words on Google, an advertisement for your website will appear on their search results page. You only pay for the advertisement if someone clicks on it. If you pick a very narrow and precise set of words, this can be a relatively inexpensive way to deliver very targeted ads to people who you know are already interested in your products.

Another excellent way to get into Internet advertising is through Facebook. Facebook visitors average over 25 minutes a day visiting the site, and 60 percent of Facebook ad market is made up of small and midsize businesses.

A Facebook ad is perfect in its ability to let you target who gets advertising. Plus they are pretty affordable. There are several ways to pay for your advertising on Facebook. In one case, you can pay for every time someone sees the ad; or you can pay a higher rate for every time someone clicks on the ad. You can also set up spending limits so that once your daily budget is hit, you do not overspend. You can choose by location, demographics and interest, and be certain that your ads are going to only the type of people who match your target profile. That means that you are certain that every penny you spend on ads is going to the right person. It is like doing instant market research. We'll talk more about using Social Media to promote your business in another chapter.

If you want to get into more complex Internet advertising, you should work with a local web design agency, who can help you create your digital advertisements and place them in the right places.

Cost is major factor in any kind of advertising, mostly because of the creative design work that needs to be invested in any kind of advertising. It is not worth skimping on your advertising. A cheap looking advertisement will reflect badly on your products. Once you decide that you are going to invest in advertising, take the time to find a good designer whose work and creative style matches your taste. By working together and discussing your goals, you can both come up with a cost-effective strategy and set of creative designs that you can place in various advertising settings.

Do you not feel like you need to constrain yourself to the traditional channels of advertising? You can advertise your business on any medium that suits your business. Why not use your customers to help you with advertising? Giving away pens, paper, bags, calendars, and stickers will put your marketing material in their hands, and increase the likelihood that they will carry out a word-of-mouth advertising campaign on your behalf. Make sure that whatever sort of advertising product you use, it always contains your website, email address, and telephone, so people can contact you.

Lastly, do not underestimate the power of local advertising on bulletin boards. Supermarkets, laundromats, libraries, bookstores, or pet shops— anywhere you customers are likely to go can be a good location for a simple flyer advertising your services. Creating an informational window in a library is one of the best advertising tools that I can ever mention. It takes some time but it is free. It works.

Referral Marketing

Oh, those glorious referrals! Much of my business has always been referral! Joe's dental practice was almost all referral based. Joanna's real estate business is almost all referral based. There is probably nothing so good for building a business as a personal referral. Referrals help to prequalify the population and get you in front of more interested people in less time with the least amount of expense. A referred customer is already sold on your business, and often ready to buy.

The absolute best way to get referrals is first by doing a good job for a customer. There is nothing like a satisfied customer for building business. Every time a happy customer passes a word along to others, you have greatly increased your chances of getting a new customer. I have a good friend who says that her goal in business is to deliver "wow!" By going above and beyond what the customer expects, that customer walks away with such a positive impression that he or she is much more likely to share it with others.

Great Referral Story

One of my absolute best referral stories happened many years ago in my retail business. An ADORABLE lady, who became one of my best customers, put her head in the door of my shop one day and said, "Where is Martha Pullen?" I heard her and came out and said, "I'm Martha Pullen." She said, after telling me her name, "I have been told by a nurse at Huntsville Hospital that you have a lot of happiness in here. I have just been released from Huntsville Hospital. I have cancer. I have just had a mastectomy. I'm 65 years old. When I was in the hospital my husband of 40 years came to my hospital room and said, 'I do not love you. I want a divorce.'" She said, "I was devastated. I was sick and hurting. I felt very sorry for myself." She then related that a nurse asked her if she knew anything about sewing. She had replied, "I used to love to sew." The next day the nurse brought me several issues of *Sew Beautiful* magazine and said, "I think these might make you happy. By the way, Martha Pullen, the publisher, has a sewing store right down the street. You might want to go meet her and take some lessons in sewing at The Heirloom Shop. There is a lot of happiness in that store."

The rest is history. Not only did she take classes she bought a brand new top of the line sewing machine and serger and lots of beautiful fabrics and laces. All of this business was from a referral from a nurse at Huntsville Hospital who shared her beloved magazines with a very sick, depressed lady. What sets word-of-mouth recommendations and referrals apart from all other types of marketing is that they are based on a network of trust. When someone you trust recommends something, whether it is a new recipe or a favorite television show, you are going to be ten times more likely to try it. It is the earned trust behind a referral that makes it so valuable.

Of course, not everyone is a social butterfly or has a vast network of personal contacts, and sometimes even when you have happy and loyal customers, they do not think about referring your business to others. There are still lots of ways to encourage referrals.

- Try using direct mail strategies, like newsletters, to keep your business fresh in people's minds.
- Politely remind your families and friends how much their referrals mean to your business.
- Send thank you notes to the referrer, and give them small gifts to encourage their referrals. Never be too busy to send a thank-you to the referring person! If you do not thank them, they probably will not send referrals to you any more! Being "too busy" to thank people who take care of your business probably means that you will not have much of a business left in the near future.
- Simply ask your current customers and prospects directly.
- Create a referral program that encourages referrals through discounts and promotion.

- Ask people what you can do to help them. Help them make connections. You get referrals by giving referrals.
- Drop subtle suggestions, like "My clients tend to refer me to others. . . ." and "I am so blessed. Most of my work comes through referrals."

I could never close a referral section without telling you about my friend, Mary Hess the largest Baby Lock sewing machine dealer in the country. Every month she has an "appreciation luncheon" inviting everyone who has purchased a machine or serger in that month to come to lunch. She gives an appreciation certificate and simply recognizes them and thanks them. Of course she sends a thank you note after the purchase but this is one extra way she thanks them. Can you even imagine how many people they all tell about their "special sewing machine luncheon?"

Event Marketing

Event marketing is all about getting out and demonstrating your expertise. By giving a seminar or a lecture, and showing people about your hobby, you are advertising your own qualifications and expertise. There are an endless number of ways to do event marketing, from informal events at a friend's house to seminars at trade shows.

I believe it is better to do something for nothing, than nothing for nothing. That is the spirit of event marketing. There is no need for you to sit around and wait for business to come in, when you can be creating exciting or educational events for people to attend. You will discover that the more generous you are in sharing your expertise, the more likely they will come to you for your business.

The key with event marketing is to offer valuable information to your public, and make your seminar compelling and entertaining. Do not try to overpublicize your business during the seminar or presentation. Instead, a subtle reminder at the beginning and end of your presentation, along with business cards or other advertising on a nearby table, will do the trick. If appropriate, you can offer to sell your products to people after the presentation—but make sure you check with the people who sponsored the event.

You should also consider your event a perfect moment to build your customer database. Make sure to explicitly encourage anyone who would like more information from you or your business to sign up on a clipboard that you keep at your table.

Lilly Walter's hobby is singing. She wanted to find a way to make it pay. She got three of her friends and created a Dickens caroling group. Creating business cards and sending out emails to businesses in the area got them a few bookings. What really brought in the customers was walking up and down the street in full costume at their local village street fair singing the old Christmas tunes. After each song they would say to the crowd, "We are the Holiday Traditions! We do corporate and private parties, and we would love to do yours!" Now each December is full of bookings for their little group.

God is the Master Marketing Planner

There was a man named Jabez who was more honorable than any of his brothers. His mother named him Jabez[a] because his birth had been so painful. He was the one who prayed to the God of Israel, "Oh, that you would bless me and expand my territory! Please be with me in all that I do, and keep me from all trouble and pain!" And God granted him his request.
—1 Chronicles 4: 9-10

When the book, *The Prayer of Jabez,* came out I devoured the book from cover to cover. Dr. Bruce Wilkinson, author , writes, "The very nature of God is to have goodness in so much abundance that it overflows into our unworthy lives. If you think about God in any other way than that, I'm asking you to change the way you think. Why not make it a lifelong commitment to ask God every day to bless you—and while He's at it, bless you a lot?"

Look back at 1st Chronicles to see how Jabez prayed to be kept from harm and pain. Many things can harm a business and truly bad business decisions can be painful. In the marketing arena of bad decisions how about a massive ad campaign in some magazine or on cable TV or radio that brings in no business? I pray before deciding where my main commitments of marketing are to be. Actually I pray about everything in my business now. God is faithful when I truly listen to him and follow his instructions.

God has blessings that we could never even imagine since he owns all the blessings. There is a cute little story in the book about a Mr. Jones dying and going to heaven. He notices a building in heaven which looks like a giant warehouse. The building is a little bit strange since it has no windows and only one door. Mr. Jones inquires of Peter about this building; he asked to enter the building but Peter told him he really did not think he wanted to see what was inside. Mr. Jones assured Peter that he did want to see what was inside; he entered the building. What did he see? There were white boxes tied with red ribbons on the shelves. Each box had a name on it. Of course Mr. Jones asked Peter if one of the boxes belonged to him. Peter answered affirmatively. After finding his box, Mr. Jones opened it. What a surprise when he found many blessings inside. These were blessings that God had for him but he had never asked.

The prayer of Jabez says "why not ask?" There are many more scriptures openly and directly telling us to let God teach us and to ask God for blessings and help. You might say, "Yes, Martha, but does this mean help for our business also?" I absolutely know that it does. Please do ask God for His blessings in your business and you can ask for Him to bless you a lot. There is nothing wrong with asking. He will answer in the way He chooses. Granted, I am unworthy of all the blessings He gives me but He blesses me anyway. I give Him all the praise, honor and glory. God has blessed me WAY more than I deserve I assure you.

> *Keep on asking, and you will receive what you ask for. Keep on seeking, and you will find. Keep on knocking, and the door will be opened to you. For everyone who asks, receives. Everyone who seeks, finds. And to everyone who knocks, the door will be opened.*
> —Matthew 7:7-8

Content Marketing

Content marketing borrows from the same spirit as Event Marketing, in the proven belief that when you share your expertise, you become an authority, and you draw people to your business. You can publish articles in specialty magazines, or simply publish the content yourself on your website.

Thanks to the Internet, there is an endless supply of mediocre content available online. It is much harder to find informative and compelling content about a specific subject. That is where you come in!

A blog is a perfect way to do content marketing. By publishing interesting and valuable insights into your hobby, you draw an audience. Inevitably, a portion of your audience will be interested in purchasing your products. Another way to do content marketing is to create videos of yourself demonstrating specific aspects of your hobby and place them on YouTube. In each of these ways, you start to build your own credibility and help people discover your business.

Whatever form of content marketing you do, make sure that there is always a link back to your business website.

Marketing is You

> *Whatever is good and perfect comes down to us from God our Father, who created all the lights in the heavens. He never changes or casts a shifting shadow.*
> —James 1:17

However you decide to market your business, make sure that it reflects your personal style. In the world of business—huge or small—the personal touch counts. Allow your business to become a reflection of your personal style, and let that come shining through in your marketing. I have always made a point of sharing my heart with my customers, and they have responded with their own love. I always make it clear that mine is a Christian business and that God gets the glory.

Marketing G.R.A.C.E.

God: I could never understand how God has chosen to bless my business so much; however scripture states it perfectly.

> *And may you have the power to understand, as all God's people should, how wide, how long, how high, and how deep his love is. May you experience the love of Christ, though it is too great to understand fully. Then you will be made complete with all the fullness of life and power that comes from God.*
>
> —Ephesians 3:18-19

Resiliance: God's grace has picked me up over and over when I fell down.

> *Whether the cloud stayed above the Tabernacle for two days, a month, or a year, the people of Israel stayed in camp and did not move on. But as soon as it lifted, they broke camp and moved on. So they camped or traveled at the Lord's command, and they did whatever the Lord told them through Moses.*
>
> —Numbers 9:22-23

Action: Action using God's power is the best kind.

> *For God is working in you, giving you the desire and the power to do what pleases him.*
>
> —Philippians 2:13

Creativity: God's creativity is evident in lighting my business paths. He has more creativity than I could ever even dream about.

> *If you are filled with light, with no dark corners, then your whole life will be radiant, as though a floodlight were filling you with light.*
>
> —Luke 11:36

Enthusiasm: God is in control. That should be enough to make anyone enthusiastic! God is the beginning and the end.

> *I am the Alpha and the Omega—the beginning and the end," says the Lord God. "I am the one who is, who always was, and who is still to come—the Almighty One."*
>
> —Revelation 1:8

- Chapter Nine -

Getting Your Business Online

You are never too old to set another goal or to dream a new dream.

—C. S. Lewis

I am constantly amazed at how technology has changed the world of small business. It has been obvious for years about technology in huge companies but tiny companies are now "way out there" with new technological advances. I cannot help but reflect about the first message sent by Samuel S.B. Morse, May 24, 1844. He sent "What hath God wrought." God has guided technology in so many directions and I for one am delighted to have the technology which has helped send Martha Pullen Company to all of the world, literally.

My, how the world has changed! When I started out in business, we didn't even have fax machines—but now the Internet is everywhere. I wrote this chapter because I am absolutely certain that getting yourself online is one of the best things you can do for your business. Actually it is a necessary part of a successful business I believe.

The Email Newsletter

I am starting this whole chapter with this section about the email newsletter. Before I write about the critical nature of the email newsletter I thought I would write about whether it is correctly spelled "email" or "e-mail." Being a former English teacher I began to do research on this very question. After going to about five or six sources I find that both are used correctly and it is six of one and half a dozen of the other. Please know that both are correct! If you have a little time this is a fun topic to research by the way!

If I only had one piece of "Internet" advice for you it would be to gather email addresses immediately and begin to send email newsletters on a regular basis. If you were to ask me what TWO things have been most important for the growth of MPC other than prayer, I would have to say getting to meet and be super nice and loving to as many people as possible IN PERSON and sending VERY PERSONAL email newsletters as often as possible. Before email newsletters I would have told you to send newsletters in the mail. This would have been my number one marketing technique always. People have loved my newsletters. They are VERY PERSONAL and include family news, what's new, pictures, scripture, devotionals, recipes, sales, news of customers sewing, news of our events, my stories and stories of others, sewing tips, other tips—almost anything which is of interest to my sewing family.

Move fast and break things.

—— Mark Zuckerberg

I have always used my newsletter to send out notices of anything new and to publicize events and "things" which were new, sales, things which were not new, fabulous "things" in old products, "things" which people have loved for years and which some people certainly do not know about, and on and on and on and on. Always I told stories about people. Sweet stories. Funny stories. Cute stories. I sent recipes. I sent scripture which never comes back void. I sent devotionals to lift people up always with the hope of reaching people and encouraging them. Actually the newsletters were as much my ministry as they were my sales tool. I truly wanted to take all of my "ladies" on every trip that I traveled, to every event here in Huntsville, on every vacation that Joe and I took and on every special occasion that we attended. I loved to take pictures when we went to a wedding to show the ladies the beautiful dresses, the wedding food, the cake, the tables and on and on. When I traveled I loved to share the beautiful scenery and tell them about the restaurants. In effect I tried to share my life and the life of our business. I knew that so many who got the newsletter would have loved to have been at our events. Our email newsletter list at one time had over 40,000 names and we had a huge open rate. It was long and featured many products. We had a huge sell through.

My first email newsletters were very homemade. I did not have a fancy border at the top. It was simply a personal letter with news and sales. People had to call or mail in to order; there was none of the click and order that we have today. I always had scripture and a devotional and ended with May God Bless You because that was indeed the main message that I wanted the newsletter to convey. I was God's messenger to share the good news that God indeed wanted to bless them. God took the newsletter and indeed took the business to new heights. Heights that I could never have imagined. Before I go any further with all of the Internet chapter you are about to read I had to say above all else the email addresses and newsletter are the most critical. When you get help in planning your website be sure you have a way of gathering your email addresses. There are many different ways.

That All Important Internet

No matter what your business model, whether you are consulting, leading seminars, teaching your craft, making custom products or selling wholesale or retail, you should be on the Internet. As we will discover in this chapter, there is a whole spectrum of possibilities for being online; you can start small and expand slowly or you can just dive right in. No matter how you approach it, you will want to make sure that very early in your business, you start to get a foothold in the online world.

The reasons are almost too obvious to mention. The Internet has changed business forever, simply by making it incredibly easy for anyone to find information about anything through a computer. In little more than a decade, the Internet has become the first and often the last place that anyone needs to go for researching and purchasing any product in the world. Finding it on the Web has become almost everyone's first instinct.

Lack of a Website is a Poor Reflection on Your Business

If you don't have some sort of website, the problem is not merely that you are making it harder for people to find you. These days, the lack of an online presence is actually a poor reflection on your business. A lack of a website or blog says, "My business has not yet graduated to something truly professional. I do not really care about making things easy for my customers. I do not have the resources, know-how, or insight to make it happen."

If you are making your potential customers work twice as hard to purchase something, or even discover you, please be certain that you are losing business on a daily basis. No matter how much local flavor you want to preserve in your business, no matter how much of your business relies on a "personal touch," no matter how much you are counting on word of mouth business—all the same, you need to maintain an online presence. In fact, as we will discover, the Web can allow you to build an even stronger rapport with your customers than you could with just a store. Word of mouth all of a sudden becomes "word of mouse."

Website-Blog-Facebook-Etsy Storefront—Can Be Front Doors to Your Business

Your website, or your blog, or your Facebook page, or your Etsy storefront—all of them can serve as a front door for hundreds and, if you are blessed, thousands of curious customers each week. Invite customers into your "home" and be sure they are welcomed—all online! It will allow them to understand your business and products, and just as importantly, allow them to get to know the person behind it all.

When you make it easy for them to find your site, you dramatically increase the odds that they will pay you a visit, contact you for more information, or simply buy something right away. Even more importantly, when you get them to make an emotional connection to your business through the content on your site, hopefully you will be creating a true customer who will come back again and again.

You might say, "Exactly how does this happen—that I get new customers who do not even know me, just by having them come to a website?" That is a good question with lots of possible answers but I ask you to remember that Jesus was a great performer of business miracles. Do you remember that he produced a huge return on a young boy's investment of offering a few fish and a little bread to feed the people? He turned the few fish and the bread into enough to feed thousands of people. God has performed many business miracles in my company simply by my asking, believing and trusting that He would help me. Believe me, God has always been in the miracle business and He still is.

> *That evening the disciples came to him and said, "This is a remote place, and it's already getting late. Send the crowds away so they can go to the villages and buy food for themselves." But Jesus said, "That isn't necessary—you feed them." "But we have only five loaves of bread and two fish!" they answered. "Bring them here," he said. Then he told the people to sit down on the grass. Jesus took the five loaves and two fish, looked up toward heaven, and blessed them. Then, breaking the loaves into pieces, he gave the bread to the disciples, who distributed it to the people. They all ate as much as they wanted, and afterward, the disciples picked up twelve baskets of leftovers. About 5,000 men were fed that day, in addition to all the women and children!*
> —Matthew 14:15-21

Taking the Right Approach

Attitude is everything in business. Your approach to building an online presence will come through in the results. If you are not convinced how important a website can be for your business, viewing your website like another checkbox to mark off, that sense of disregard will shine through in your website, and your traffic to the site will be flat.

A Good Website is Critical

No matter how small, your website is not just a sign on the front of your door. It is a direct reflection of your brand. No more than you would hire a salesperson with ripped jeans and a sassy, rude attitude, should you allow a mediocre website to represent your business. Instead, you should put as much energy and attention toward your website as you devote to your products. You may not realize just how easy it is to publish on the Web. Once you are set up, with the ability to update your pages at will, you will discover that this is the perfect platform to personalize your business, and express your own enthusiasm for your hobby. Then your business can become a true reflection of your own passions and interests.

Of course, I recognize there are several very good reasons that people either avoid making websites, or have built websites that do not reflect the true quality of their business. Some are simply intimidated by the unknown. They avoid most technology because it is too confusing a world to enter. Others feel outfoxed from their past experiences with technology. Maybe you hired someone to create a website, and now it is impossible to update. Like an unwanted family heirloom it just sits on the mantelpiece gathering dust.

In the early days of the Internet, these sorts of attitudes were understandable, because you really did need to learn a lot to make a functional website. Things have come a long way since then. Now anyone can create a blog. Anyone can create an Etsy storefront. Anyone can sign up for Facebook. Anyone can upload a video to YouTube. Anyone can post a message to Twitter. Believe me, if I can do it, so can you. A little later in this chapter we will look at how to tie it all together. If you are still shying away from using the Internet to promote your business, you are making a big mistake. Beyond the fact that it is a great opportunity to promote your business easily and inexpensively, once you get the hang of these new technologies, your whole attitude might change. You might just discover that you really enjoy working with them.

Your Online Investment

Probably one of the first things to consider as you begin to plan your online presence, is how much money you are willing to invest upfront. That figure will quickly help you determine the scale and complexity of your Internet presence.

The funny thing about the Internet, is that it has spawned a proliferation of options at every level. There are low-cost solutions to everything. You can have a blog for free, you can sell your products through shopping portals like Etsy, and you can make a simple webpage from a template with very little investment. These are excellent solutions if you cannot invest much, but the downside is that they will not be deeply integrated. Your customers will need to hop from place to place in order to interact with your business, and that can confuse them.

On the other hand, if you want to make a customized website that creates a smooth shopping experience and expresses your personal style throughout both the content and the design, your investment will be much larger. Even more importantly, it requires some real planning and work on your part.

One of the first investments you should make, if you are planning to get your business online, is investing in your domain name. That is a fancy way of saying that you'll want to secure your website address, like **www. pullenbusiness.com** or something similar. We covered that step in detail in Chapter Six.

A Word About Technology

Technology is complicated. There are no two ways about it. Everything from VCRs to microwaves to printers to email—they all have a way of tripping us up. Some people choose to walk away from the problem, or pay someone else to fix it. But when we are talking about your own business, it is important that you make the decision to become informed. Even after reading this chapter, you will need to do more research into whatever options you choose. As crazy as it might sound, you should approach web technology with the same type of curiosity that brought you into your hobby. Do not just hand all the decisions over to someone else, or you will find yourself stuck with a website that you do not understand and which you can not modify. Take an active role in your technology decisions. If you know that you are not "tech-savvy," then seek out tools and solutions that are "user-friendly" and "intuitive." Take an adult education class on making web pages, or using social media, so you can learn the basics. Believe me, all those people out there with blogs and websites are no more clever than you. They simply had the drive and the resolve to figure it out.

Stick with the Big Names in Technology

Another golden rule about technology is that it is generally a good idea to "follow the herd." Stick with the big names. Picking the most popular products, whether it is a shopping engine or a blog, is often a strong guarantee. First of all, the more popular a product, the more "dummy-proof" it has to be. Hundreds of thousands of people will not use something that is too complicated. A second advantage of sticking with the herd is that when you have a problem, it is much more likely that you can find help. Either someone will have had the same problem and posted a solution on the Internet, or even better, there will be someone on the other end of a phone who can help you. Lastly, the more popular a product, the more likely that it will "play nicely" with other products, so you will have less trouble integrating it with other solutions.

A last thought about technology is that it gets old quickly. As you start planning your investment in your website, keep in mind that it is not going to be a one-time fee. You will regularly need to invest in the upkeep of your site. Whether it is to expand the site, refresh its look, or upgrade your technology, a website should be considered an ongoing annual or bi-annual expense.

The Big Picture

As you start considering your online presence, you should try to step back and adopt a long-term view. Perhaps you have had the foresight to include your Internet strategy in your business plans. If not, go back to your business plan and ask yourself how you plan to use the Internet over the next few years.

There are really three major questions to ask yourself:

- Can you afford help? Developing a good relationship with a quality web developer or a web services firm can greatly accelerate or expand the possibilities.
- What is your online retail strategy? Do you plan to sell products directly through your own website, or a shopping portal like Etsy?
- What is your online content strategy? How are you going to create unique and interesting content so that people find your website and engage with your brand?

Your ability to answer those questions will help you decide on the next steps. We will cover them in detail in the next few sections.

The number one benefit of information technology is that it emplowers people to do what they want to do. It lets people be creative. It lets people be productive. It lets people learn things they didn't think they could learn before, and so in a sense it is all about potential.

—Steve Ballmer

Getting Help

These days, it is possible to build a custom website all by yourself. If you are unfamiliar with web technology, however, I do not recommend this direction. Too many people have big dreams for their website, and when they try to do it themselves, they get into trouble by trying to do too much. Furthermore, you have far too many other things to worry about in your business. Perhaps most importantly, if you are learning along the way, a mediocre website will reflect badly on your business.

On the other hand, what you can do by yourself is start a blog, or create an Etsy site, which we discuss later in the chapter. If you are planning on doing anything more complicated, I highly recommend working with a professional. Accordingly, you should scale your plans according to the amount of investment you are able to place in your website.

As you start looking around for help, you should keep in mind that not everyone who works with web technologies has the same level of expertise. Different people specialize in different areas, and it is rare to find someone with a full range of skills from top to bottom.

Web Designers

Some people are web designers, and they tend to focus on what we call the "presentation layer" of a website. They help transform your vision into a striking website design. They can also help with the equally important task of defining your website's "information architecture"—which means how all the information in your website will be broken down and presented to your readers. A website designer, however, may lack the programming skills to help you with complex tasks, like installing and implementing a retail store that contains shopping cart software.

Web designers come in two flavors. Some are better at making beautiful websites, and others are great at making functional websites. You will be able to tell the difference when you look at their work. If you end up working with a more "artistic" web designer, you might want to take the opportunity to focus on designing your logo and your overall brand before you start diving directly into the website. This is an important step to consider, because your brand will be the foundation of your business, and you can use these designs for all aspects of your business—websites, print materials and signage.

Web Developers

Web developers are technology experts who are more skilled in some of the more complex parts of website construction, like creating a shopping engine for your site, or installing a "content management system" that lets you make updates to your own website. Sometimes, a good web developer will not have the same strengths in graphic design as a web designer. What you gain in efficiency and the ability to build more complex websites, including integration with shopping cart software, you may lose in aesthetics.

Ideally, you might find someone with a nice combination of the above skills. There are a few easy ways of finding help for building your website. I recommend two complementary methods. The first is what I call the "phone book" method. Just do a Google search using your hometown (or nearby towns) and using some of the following key words:

"Web development" "web solutions" "web design" "brand development" "logo design" "interactive services." Hopefully you will find a handful of good local companies that advertise website design services. Take a look at their portfolios and see if you like the quality of the websites they have produced. If you are going to hire someone to help you build a custom website, I think it is very important to work with someone local, so that you can meet and talk about your goals.

The second method is to simply think of a dozen or so local businesses that you like, and look them up on the Internet. If you like their website, you can usually find out who designed the site with a little searching. The best place to start is in the fine print at the very bottom of any website's home page. If you don't find anything there, or on their Contact Us page, you can simply call the business directly and ask them who made their website.

How I Chose My Web Developer/Designer

With my business of coaching entrepreneurs and small businesses I realized that it was critical that I choose the best web person that I could afford. First I called my friend, M.D. Smith who had been the owner of the local ABC affiliate before he retired. I asked him the question, "Who is the best person in Huntsville to design my website for my new business?" He had one answer. I talked with this individual long before I was ready to develop this business consulting website. I was impressed. When a friend needed to develop a website for his church, he called me to get a suggestion of a very good web developer. Mu friend was very pleased with the help he received from this individual.

Two years later when I was indeed ready for this new website, I called this individual again. We had a great meeting about what I absolutely had to have for the initial website and about what I intended to add at a later time. I asked him to plan a website which can be expanded greatly into other areas. He understood exactly what I wanted and was willing to work with my budget for the less complicated website which later could be expanded. He immediately secured a domain name for me which both of us believe will be easy to remember: www.pullenbusiness.com.

I have to share a funny story about working with him at the beginning. I suggested a domain name which included entrepreneurship since my book has that in the title. He said, "Martha how many people can very easily spell entrepreneurship with no errors?" I laughed and recognized his point of making things simple and most importantly easy to remember. We came up with **pullenbusiness.com** which I believe is easy to remember.

Keep in mind that one of the best guides to any web developer or designer is his/her client list. Take a careful look at the work they have done, and ask them for references. You should absolutely call some of their old clients and ask about their experience building their websites. No one is perfect, so you should try to understand in advance the strengths and weaknesses of your potential web developer.

The person you work with should be very patient and communicative, and eager to help you learn more about web technology. I would mistrust anyone who adopts an "expert" attitude, either by throwing around too many technical words, or who seems unwilling to help you understand how your website will work.

Some topics you should cover with your designer or developer:

- **The process:** Find out if your developer follows a specific, scripted process for designing a website, and what will be expected of you.
- **Content:** The role of content in a website often gets underplayed. Who will be helping decide what information goes where? Who will be writing the content for the website, and will the developer be offering guidelines?
- **Publishing:** A website is never done. There is always new content to be added to your website. How will content updates be performed? Can you perform content updates yourself?
- **Long term plans:** Make sure that you are offering a complete vision

of your website, even if you are not planning to do everything at once.
- **SEO:** This stands for search engine optimization, which is the art of making sure that your website can be found by search engines. What will your developer be doing to make sure that clients can find you quickly and easily?

After my first meeting with this individual he said he needed to do some planning. On our second meeting he returned with a comprehensive outline. I might add that we had one excellent phone conversation (mostly about the "look" that I liked) before the second meeting.

His outline included the HOME page topics that I had requested which included name, text, imagery (slide show with rotating images), navigation methods, and other special features that I wanted to have. He outlined my blog details and my social media linking and sharing abilities. He figured out all of the details for my newsletter and gathering email addresses. He made it easy to use for individuals coming to the website. Issues such as "being search engine friendly" were included. He included website training for me at no extra cost. He outlined monthly fees and maintenance fees and future updates which would fall in the next phase. He clearly stated the initial cost and what would be included. There were no surprises. He listed his fee per hour for future "additions" and revisions. Legal terms for other areas were clearly laid out.

In conclusion to the topic, *How I Chose My Web Designer,* I wanted to tell you exactly how it happened. He came highly recommended by someone in the TV/Internet industry that I trusted completely. He had done an excellent job on my friend's web development for his church. My friend said he had worked honorably and creatively with highly skilled technology abilities.

The commander must be able to see the situation as a whole, attribute to each object its relative importance, grasp the connections between each factor in the situation, and recognize its limits. All this implies a gift of synthesis which, in itself, demands a high degree of intellectual capacity.

—Charles de Gaulle

Your Retail Strategy

The ability to sell your products online opens up a world of possibilities. Suddenly, you have created a store that is open twenty-four hours a day, every day of the week, that anyone from California to Maine and beyond can visit. As long as you have considered all the pieces that need to be in place, both from a marketing and order fulfillment perspective, I heartily recommend moving in this direction.

I am not saying that a retail website will magically double your business with half the effort. You can be sure that you will still need to work for every dime of product that you sell. On the other hand, the style of work is different from selling in a retail store, and it has the potential of reaching a broader set of customers more quickly.

You will need to be prepared to tirelessly and constantly market your website, so that people can discover your products. You will need to be ready to package and ship orders quickly when they come in. You will need to listen closely to comments, and monitor traffic to your website, to ensure that your customers find it easy to order from you. But once you have those pieces lined up, your website can take on a momentum of its own, and can bring in an unexpected number of sales.

At the center of any retail website will be your shopping cart tool, or shopping engine, as it is sometimes called. A shopping cart tool is the software that lets you do the following:

- Organize and arrange the display of your products
- Provide detailed photos and information about each individual product
- Let customers add your products to an online "shopping cart"
- Process your customer payments
- Print shipping labels.

There are a couple ways to set up a retail website. You can either use an existing shopping portal like Etsy, or you can create your own store using a hosted shopping site. We will cover both those possibilities next.

Etsy

If you sell anything handmade, vintage (older than twenty years), or any kind of crafting or commercial supplies, you have the distinct advantage of being able to use Etsy as your retail shopping engine. Etsy is a wonderful shopping site that allows craftmakers and hobbyists to sell their wares through a single portal. It is the digital equivalent of a craft fair, except that someone else handles all the sales.

It is hard to overstate the advantages of using Etsy as your shopping engine. By signing up for an Etsy account, you inherit an incredible amount of Internet traffic that is constantly shopping for products similar to your own. Even better, you save yourself the trouble and expense of processing online payments; Etsy simply sends you a monthly check for your monthly earnings from sales. All you need to worry about is the timely shipping of products when Etsy sends you a notification of a sale.

The disadvantages are quite small. Of course, there's a fee ($.20 per item displayed, and 3.5% of every transaction) involved. Like any other craft fair setting, you have to find a way to distinguish yourself from the competition, which can be accomplished through your own separate website or blog, and marketing efforts.

From my point of view, the advantages of using Etsy are so significant, that the only real question is whether you will use it exclusively for all your online sales, or whether it will serve as a secondary supplement to your own shopping website. If you are just starting a business, and you are not planning to invest in getting help from a web designer, I would recommend starting with Etsy, until your online sales become so significant that it is worth absorbing the extra cost of running your own shopping engine.

Hosted Shopping Sites

Hosted shopping sites are getting easier and easier to use. With a small amount of work, you can set up your site by choosing from a template, add pictures and descriptions of your products, and process credit card transactions from any visitors. You pay a monthly fee, and that is it. This can be a great option for the convenience, and the security of knowing that your transactions are being processed by a highly trusted service.

If you are intimidated by the process, you can hire a web designer to help walk you through the creation of the store and customizing it to your needs. It can be especially helpful to have someone getting you set up for such things as setting up your domain name and designing your look and feel. As you are deciding which hosted solution to use, I would strongly recommend sticking with the herd, and using popular products like Shopify **(www.shopify.com)** or Amazon Webstore **(webstore.amazon.com)** or Big Cartel **(www.bigcartel.com)**

Creating Content To Gain Customers

If you simply want to create a website that serves as an informational website for your business, then your online presence can be vastly simplified, and reduced to several key components. Depending on your goals, you can probably get away with a site that is designed to help people understand your business and the products or services you sell, and where they can be purchased.

The core mission of your website will be to provide the right kind of content for your customers. Beyond being useful, your website's mission will be to capture your customers attention and engage them in your business. Many people have a very shallow and shortsighted sense that the point of their business is simply to sell products. A true business knows that you business is to gain customers. Your website is the perfect place to let this happen.

Of course you will want to create a set of web pages that are designed to be both useful and fun. You should try to think about what someone who visits your site will be most interested in learning. Keep your webpages very simple, because as you know, it is no fun to get caught up and lost in a confusing site.

Many people make the mistake of trying to put too much information into a website, in the belief that it will help their customers. The simple fact is that people do not read web pages in the same way they read a magazine, newspaper or book. You can safely assume that most people are not browsing your website in a casual or leisurely way, as you might while flipping through a magazine. On the contrary, they are much more likely to be looking at your site with a very specific mission in mind. You can be absolutely certain that they are only reading 20% of anything on your page, because they are actually looking for something specific. The top reasons people will visit your website, leaving aside that they want to purchase something are:

- To decide if they want to visit your store.
- To learn more about your business.

- To find your business location, phone number, or email in order to contact you.
- To ask a question about your products.
- To learn more about your products.
- To learn more about you.

Your pages should be designed to help your customers. Forgetting this fact is the number one mistake that websites make over and over again. Businesses who have websites often think that it is an opportunity to show off and impress you.

Those types of websites are like the person who comes into a job interview, and is so obviously trying to make a good impression, that she forgets to relax. Your website does not need to be a major Hollywood production with lots of impressive bells and whistles. In fact, in most cases, a spare and uncluttered site that honors the utility value of your website will be more impressive to your users. It shows that you have thought about their needs, versus showing off your own products with unnecessary ostentation.

As you are starting to think about your site, take the time to list out the main activities or goals that you think your customers will want. Ask people in your Inner Circle what they would want to know about your website. Come up with a list of the five to ten goals that your customers will have, and make sure that your website is designed to meet those needs quickly and easily.

Content Platforms

Of course, your website is just as much about marketing as commerce. You want people to find your website as they browse the Web looking for information about your hobby.

Website marketing is more than a strategy. It is a personal attitude. Promoting your business successfully on the Internet has a different flavor than real-world marketing. Digital marketing is not simply about informing people about your latest sales. To successfully market your business on the Internet means making your business into what's now called a "content platform."

In plain English, that simply means that you want your business to reflect your own personal curiousity and passion for your hobby. By mixing together both your interests and your business concerns, your business is much more likely to be noticed. People will recognize that you are not simply trying to "make a buck," but that you are genuinely interested in spreading the word about some of the beautiful and inspiring aspects of your hobby.

That is how to make the Internet work for you. Be yourself, not just your business. Your goal is to become something of a beacon for your hobby, so that people listen to you not merely to know when you are going to have a sale, but also to learn something new. If you can use the various tools on the Internet to differentiate yourself from all the other businesses that are "just selling stuff," your business will have a very good chance to thrive.

Here's Why Content Marketing Works On The Web!

First, the more content you are creating on the Internet through your website, or your blog, or Facebook, the more likely that your rating on search engines will rise. In simplest terms, the more original content you create about your business and your hobby, and the more attention your content attracts from people who link to it, the more likely it is that people will find your website.

Second, people buy things for a complex variety of reasons. Usually it is a combination of price, convenience, and emotion. You can use all the other levers at your disposal to make your price reasonable, and make it easy to purchase your products. But the emotional side of a purchase comes from how people feel about your brand. If your business is telling a story, and you can get people listening to that story, they will be much more likely to purchase from you.

Blogging

A blog can become the backbone of your content platform. This is one of your best soapboxes for standing up and talking about the things that interest you. If you begin blogging, and put your creative skills toward the service of your business, you will be rewarded for your creativity and diligence. Actually my newsletter has served the same purpose of a blog for many years. Just recently have I started blogging.

A blog, is one of those fancy Internet words for a "web-log." Like a captain's log or a guest register, it's a place for someone to regularly record and publish personal thoughts on a particular topic. If you decide to build a blog around your business, it is like creating an online journal where you can share the trials and successes of your business.

Setting up a blog could not be any easier. In fact, it is probably the quickest and easiest web asset for you to create. There are a handful of very popular blogging tools that run from free to no more than $15 a month. All of them are very reliable and simple to use. In the same amount of time that it takes to order a book from Amazon, you can have signed up for the service, and be ready to post your first entry. Here are a few of your choices:

- Wordpress
- Blogger
- Typepad
- Blogspot

In all cases, there is a very simple process to follow. All of the above services are designed to be quite easy to use. You sign up, choose a template for your blog, choose a layout for your blog, and then you can start posting. All of these sites offer video tutorials, so you can watch a quick instructional video to get an overview of how it works.

The first decision you will need to make, once you sign up, will be to figure out the look of your site. If this is your first foray into the digital world, and your blog is going to be your first web asset, you are probably not going to want to invest too much time and effort (yet!) in designing the look for your blog. You can just pick from one of the many design templates that these blogging software services offer. Take some time to consider the kind of image you want to present for your business, and find something that appeals to you. I recommend staying simple for now. If you find that you enjoy blogging, and it becomes an activity that takes on a more central role in your business marketing, you can always invest more energy in updating the design later.

If you've already worked on your actual website with a Web Designer, and this blog is going to be an addition to it, you will want to work with the person who helped you build the website to incoroporte it seemlessly into your website. It is always better to bring all your web assets under one roof.

The next step is designing the layout of the blog, and determining the elements of a blog page. Again, simple is often the best approach. You can clutter your blog page with too many elements, so it is best to just allow your readers to focus on your latest blog entry, while making it easy to find past entries.

Figuring out the voice of your blog is something that will happen over time, so don't put too much pressure on yourself right away. Here are some important concepts to keep in mind:

- Be consistent. By keeping a consistent publishing schedule, you will be encouraging your readership to keep checking in regularly, and you will be developing the kind of writing discipline that will make you a better blogger. Set up a manageable schedule for yourself and stick to it no matter what.
- Link to other sites. Your blog entries should be a jumping off point for helping others discover and explore the things that interest you. Make it a regular practice to look for new websites and articles that you can share with others. As a blogger, you are part of a community of other writers and hobbyists. Directing your readership to other people's sites is a form of currency and part of the collaborative spirit of blogging.
- Listen to your commenters. The comments will start slowly, but as you build your readership, it is important to listen to what people are saying, and adapt your blogging to their opinions. If they like one of your entries, try to understand why and build on that conclusion.
- Treat each entry like a small speech you are giving to friends. Go ahead and talk about yourself, but make sure it is going to be interesting to others.
- Try to develop a voice and deliver a story. Give people a sneak peek into your business life, with behind the scenes stories, so they can live vicariously through your posts.
- Make your blog entries visual. By adding lots of photos and images, you will attract a bigger following. Do not be afraid to show work in progress.
- Take the time to follow other people and comment on their blogs. The more you see how other people are blogging, and what they are doing, the better a blogger you will become.
- Keep a notebook with you and write down notes to yourself about good blog entries. That way you will always have something to talk about when it is time to sit down and write.
- Do not be afraid to talk about your struggles with the creative process, sharing what inspires you, and telling personal stories.

- Use your blog to help others who are practicing the same hobby. Giving tips and instructions based on what you have learned is a great way to attract readers and create authority.

YouTube

If you do not consider yourself much of a writer, you can still develop a content platform by using YouTube. As you probably know, YouTube is a website that hosts any video that you decide to upload. Video has a great way of allowing customers to quickly get closer to your business. Most smartphones let you record videos, so it is always easy to capture a comment on film. You can create a channel for your business, with your logo, a link to your website and general desctiption of your business. When you use videos on your website, be sure that you link them to your YouTube channel. This also helps your site with SEO. There are lots of ways to incorporate video into your content strategy.

- You could create instructional videos to help other people learn tips and tricks about your hobby; then post links to these videos on your blog or website.
- You could record testimonials from happy customers and post links to these videos on your website.
- If you have a store or if you produce events you could record parties or seminars, so people who could not be there can see them later.
- You can keep a video diary about the creation process of making your products.
- You can make a video with a special message for Christmas, Valentine's Day, Easter, Mother's Day, Father's Day, Fourth of July, Martin Luther King, Jr. Day, Memorial Day, Labor Day, Thanksgiving and a general Happy Birthday.

Business is like riding a bicycle. Either you keep moving or you fall down.

—John David Wright

Social Media

There has been an enormous amount of hoopla over the past few years about the power of social media. Lots of people wonder, and rightly so, whether they should be using social media to help their businesses. The simple answer is "yes," and the only confounding part is just how much time and effort you should invest. This section will help you figure out what makes the most sense for you.

Much of the "buzz" around social media is actually well deserved. Used properly, social media really can help boost your sales and raise awareness about your products or services. There are a lot of people on the Internet, and many of them are using social media. If you can help make them aware of your products, help them understand more about your company, and engage in a conversation with them, your business will benefit. But you need to make sure that you are actually responding to them. Did you know that 95% of businesses don't respond to inquiries that customers make to them through their Facebook site. What's the point of having a Facebook presence, if it is ignoring customers?

Social media is remarkable for its ability to help you perform both customer service and marketing all at once. Most of the confusion surrounding social media is undeserved. The basics are actually quite simple. For precisely that reason, we are going to be taking a little time to dispel some of the mystery around these tools, so that you can decide for yourself just how you want to use them to help your business.

When we use the term "social media," what we're really talking about are a series of new Internet tools that people are using to talk with each other. That is it. Social media is nothing more than a set of tools that let you carry on conversations with people. The fact that these tools have all sorts of unusual names like Twitter, Facebook, Flickr, YouTube, Pinterest, Instagram and Google Plus makes them sound a little exotic. But in the end, once you really learn how these tools work, we could just as easily say that email and a telephone are social media, too. The big difference with the new social media is that they give you the ability to reach a lot more people much more quickly than ever before.

Notice that I said the "ability." It is important to recognize that simply signing up for these tools and using them once in a while does not guarantee an overnight transformation. Just because you sent out a message on Twitter does not mean that anyone is going to listen to what you say. Just because you opened a Facebook account and set up a page for your business, does not mean you will double your Internet sales. But with some time, effort, and little cleverness, you can certainly be using both Facebook and Twitter to connect with more customers than you are today.

So let's start examining these social media tools in detail. In this chapter, I'm going to focus only on the most commonly used tools, because they offer the most significant advantages to you.

Facebook

Facebook is clearly the most popular social media tool in the world. Sometimes I call my self "the Facebook queen." I love Facebook. At our events I keep my iPhone handy and send sometimes nearly 100 pictures over a 3 or 4 day period. My sewing family loves these pictures. In effect I am trying to "take everyone of my nearly 5,000 Facebook friends to the party." I think it is safe to assume that most people have at least heard of Facebook, and many of us have even used it, however infrequently. Facebook is a two-way tool. On the one hand, it allows you to create a web page for yourself, and update it with photos, messages, and anything interesting you find on the Internet. On the other hand, it lets you connect with all your friends, and receive a constant stream of their latest updates. In many ways, Facebook is like having your own family and friends network. Whenever you visit Facebook, you can get the latest news from all of your friends (or at least the ones who post updates), and keep them abreast of your own activities and thoughts.

Here is an interesting thought often mentioned by my friends. Facebook is a great hobby! So how can Facebook help your business? To answer that very reasonable question, we need to take a closer look at how Facebook really works.

Setting Up

Anyone can create his or her own personal Facebook profile which is also called a Personal Timeline. That is the first place to start, of course. If you already have a Facebook account, you know that you can fill this personal profile with all sorts of information about yourself, and include photos. Creating a Facebook account is very easy and adding information about yourself could not be any simpler. Bear in mind that this is information that you will be sharing with others, so don't make it too personal!

Friending

Once you have a Facebook profile, you can start "friending" other people. That means searching by name for other people you know who might have Facebook profiles, and asking permission to be her friend. If they agree, the two of you are now linked. That means that your friend will see any new information you add to your Facebook profile, and you will see any updates from your friend. It also means that you will be able to see all her friends, and you will probably discover some of your own friends on their list. You can keep adding friends as you much as you like.

Sharing

From that point forward, once you make updates on your Facebook profile all your friends get notified. It becomes a "story" on their personal "news feed." Whether you want to share an inspiring quote, write a devotional, make a prayer request, answer a prayer request, offer an old family recipe, or post a recent photograph from your daughter's birthday, all you have to do is post it on your Facebook profile, and your friends will see it too.

Just as you might expect, all the updates made by your friends will be visible to you. Your own personal news feed shows the stories posted by all your friends. That is the core functionality of Facebook—it is a tool that allows people to trade thoughts, stories and ideas among their friends. It harnesses a desire to keep in touch by giving people a forum to share thoughts, while simultaneously letting them see what their friends are up to. The magic of Facebook is its ability to overcome any distance, and keep in touch with even casual acquaintances.

Over time, the usage of Facebook has settled into a fairly common convention. It is obviously not the place to bare your deepest secrets, or share intimate conversation. It is the perfect place to share tips and tricks, inspirational thoughts, family news, and small discoveries, as well as a place where people can announce to their friends what they like and dislike. That is precisely where your business comes into play.

Liking

Now that it has become so popular, Facebook makes it incredibly easy for people to share anything from the Internet on their Facebook profiles, without even visiting the Facebook website. If you start looking closely at all the pages you visit on the Internet, chances are that you will notice a small icon, usually blue with either the letter "f" or "like." Clicking this little Facebook button allows you to instantly share almost anything you discover on the Internet with your friends. For example, if you come across a newspaper article that you want to share with your friends, just find the "like" button on that page (trust me, they are everywhere once you start looking for them). "Liking" is just another way to share an update on Facebook, and any webpage that contains a Facebook icon can be "liked." Instead of cutting and pasting a website address into your Facebook page, you can simply click on the "like" icon. A quick summary of the article will be posted as a story to your Facebook page and shared with all your friends.

"So what?" you might ask, "What's all the fuss? Sharing things with others is something I can already do with email." Well, here is where it gets interesting. Because all of this "liking" and sharing is happening on Facebook, the sharing can multiply very quickly among linked friends. Say, for example, I find a beautiful pattern for a cable knit sweater on someone's web page. I either "like" the page, or I post it directly onto my Facebook profile as a "story." Immediately, this story shows up on my friends' news feeds. Now if a few of my friends, who are also avid knitters, appreciate this design too and they "like" my update, they will be sharing it with their friends. Suddenly, my update is showing up on the news feed of my friends' friends. If my friends' friends decide to "like" this update, it will be shared with their friends, and so on.

That proliferation of what's called "viral marketing," when a message passes through social networks by word-of-mouth, or in this case, through Facebook. To harness the viral spread of ideas is the ultimate goal of all social media.

From the perspective of a business, Facebook offers a great opportunity. In addition to your personal profile, you can create a Facebook page for your business. The practice of posting and sharing links on your business page are the same as your personal profile. You will want to invite all your friends to "like" your business page, so that your updates will show up in their news feeds as well. The benefit of having a separate buisness page is that you can focus on posts that are related to your business, and leave the more personal posts to your profile.

Making a Business Page

The first step in executing a Facebook strategy for your business is to create a Business Page. The process is quite straightforward, as long as you have already created your Personal profile. Just go to **www.facebook.com/pages/create.php**, and start filling in the information that is requested. Just like with your personal profile, you can add photos and profile information so that people can quickly get to know your business.

It is important to remember that your Business Page is not quite the same as a personal page. For one thing, your Business Page cannot go hunting for friends, in the same way you could on your personal profile. What you can do is "suggest" your Business Page to your friends, which sends them a message to look at your page. You can also "share" your Business Page with friends, which puts an update in their news feed. Once your page comes to their attention, they can decide whether to "like" your page so that all your business page updates become part of their news feed. Once you've created your Business Page, however, you can use it as part of your marketing mix.

As you start getting people to "like" your business, take a look to see if there are any patterns among them. Are they mostly young and single, or married and slightly older? Understanding your audience is the key to good business, and helps you know how to orient your business to your best customers. Facebook makes it possible to see the demographics of those who like your page by looking at the *Insites* section of your Page.

This is where you will find lots of additional tools you can use within Facebook. I will be the first to admit that once you start to dig beneath the surface, there is an extensive variety of features to track activity and promote your Page. Keeping track of all this can get a little confusing. Entire books have been written about Facebook marketing strategies, and how to expand your Business Page. My personal recommendation is that during the early days of your business, you not allow yourself to get too lost in all the Facebook options available to your business. Just stick with the fundamentals—you simply want to use Facebook to bring your business to the attention of others.

If you eventually decide that the online portion of your business is a central part of your marketing strategy, then you will want to invest more time and effort into creating a truly outstanding Facebook presence, and perhaps even conducting some business through Facebook, which is called

"F-Commerce." Until that day arrives, however, you should simply treat Facebook as an easy way to connect your business with other people.

Facebook Summary

Your Facebook strategy should focus on four core principles. I strongly recommend purchasing a "how to use Facebook in selling" book and study it carefully. There are many versions on the market and they outline in detail who, what, how, when and where to use Facebook.

1. Create an attractive and informative Business Page that gives your customers a quick overview of your business and helps them see your beautiful work. Your Business Page can direct them to your other Internet channels, such as your actual website, your Twitter pages, or your Etsy site.

2. Post new content on your Facebook Business Page on a weekly (daily is better) basis, whether it is informing people about your business, upcoming events, or just sharing articles and photos that are related to your business.

3. Bring your business updates to the attention of others, by suggesting and sharing important announcements to your friends. Do not over-do it, or your friends might start to ignore your messages.

4. Keep it social. Facebook is not about one-way communication. It is a conversation that you are having with friend and customers through their comments. Use Facebook to post photos about new developments in the company, and keep your customers updated on what is happening. As your customers respond, make sure that you listen to what they are saying and respond accordingly. You are letting them know that you care about their opinions.

Twitter

Twitter is another social media tool that has garnered a lot of attention over the past few years. In comparison to the variety of features on Facebook, Twitter is quite a bit simpler. The best way to understand Twitter is that it is a "texting" broadcast service. You probably already know that "texting" is the ability to send quick messages to other people through your cellphone, rather than calling them. Texting is a wonderfully convenient way to communicate and coordinate with people one-on-one. No matter where you are, you can quickly tell someone that you will be ten minutes late to an appointment, or ask your husband to bring home some milk on the way home from work.

What Twitter lets you do is text a brief message (or a "tweet," as it is called) from your computer or mobile device, but instead of sending that tweet to a single person, you can broadcast it to your followers. At the same time, you can receive and read the tweets of people you follow. Once again, by digging into the mechanics of how Twitter works, you can start to imagine how to use it for your business.

Set Up an Account

To start using Twitter, the first thing to do is go to **www.twitter. com**, and register for an account. Once you have entered your email address, a password, and a username, you are ready to begin. Unlike Facebook, which requires a connection between your personal profile and your Business Page, Twitter allows you to set up separate business and personal accounts. While you are setting up your business account, you can add a short description of your business, upoad your logo and select a background.

Follow People

After setting up an account, the first thing you will want to do is start "following" people, which means that you are subscribing to the messages that these people are sending out. The Twitter website helps guide you through the process of selecting a few people to follow. You can pick a few famous celebrities, or you can search by a keyword related to your business, such as "sewing" or "catering." For each person you choose to follow, you'll be able to see all the recent tweets they have sent. The complete and ongoing set of messages that someone posts is called a "Twitter feed." After scanning a few messages from someone's Twitter feed, you may quickly notice some odd features:

a. All the messages are very short. Twitter restricts all messages to 140 characters. You simply can not write any more, although I suppose you could send out several messages in sequence. While this has the advantage of forcing people to send concise messages, it can also create some very cryptic, telegraphic styles of writing.

b. The messages might contain some strange characters and what look like gibberish words. Don't worry, it is very easy to decode these messages, once you understand the thinking behind them. Basically, the characters are made to help people click on certain words to learn more about the people, the topics and the websites that are contained in the Twitter message:

- The words that are preceded by a "@" are a reference to a person who has a Twitter account. For example, @pullenbusiness refers to my Twitter username. When someone includes a Twitter username in a tweet it is just a way to make sure that anyone reading that message can click on "@pullenbusiness" and see all the messages I've sent through Twitter, and choose to follow me. So let's pretend that @sewinglady wrote a tweet that said, "dear @pullenbusiness, thanks so much for the new #businessbook." Anyone who sees that message can click on @ pullenbusiness, and see all the Twitter messages that I've ever sent.

- The words that are preceded by a "#" character indicate a topic or keyword that is being discussed by multiple people. For example, if lots of people started sending out tweets that refer to a hurricane, they might want to reference it as "#hurricaneirene" in their tweets. That allows any Twitter users to click on that word, and see all the messages that have referenced Hurricane Irene. Including topics in a Twitter message helps organize all the tweets around specific keywords, no matter who wrote it. You can invent your own keywords if they do not already exist. Or if you just wanted to make certain that anyone who is looking for information about #sewingmachines or #woodworking can find your tweets, just make sure to include those words in your message.

- Any other odd looking strings of letters and numbers are just website links that will direct you to a website page. Whenever anyone inserts a long website address, like "http://www.marthapullencompany.com/shopping.com" into a Twitter message, the Twitter system will convert that website address into something much shorter, like "http://t.co/gh20." This helps save space so that a single link doesn't use up your 140 character quote.

Take some time to read through various tweets. Click through to the websites that are referenced in the tweets. Experiment with searching under keywords to find the topics that interest you. Try to discover if there are any particular people whose messages interest you. If someone seems to consistently send out worthwhile and compelling messages, it is probably worth "following" them, so that you can see any future messages they send. Don't worry, you can always "unfollow" them if you get tired of them. Once you start following people, Twitter can recommend other people you might follow who offer similar content.

At this point, you will notice some similarities between Facebook and Twitter. In both cases, the basic idea is that people are sharing information with a larger community. On Facebook, people are sharing and receiving their updates with anyone who is a "friend." On Twitter, people are sharing their little text messages with anyone who has decided to "follow" them.

Send a Tweet

Once have become familiar with some of the unique aspects of Twitter messages, you can start sending out your own tweets. You can send tweets from your computer, and you can even set up your mobile devices to send out tweets. Keep in mind that although you may not have any followers right away, all of your tweets (even the old ones) will be immediately visible to anyone who subscribes to your Twitter feed. Although you can always delete a tweet, you generally shouldn't write anything that you consider too private —Twitter is not a private email.

As you will quickly discover, Twitter is really a very simple tool. So simple, in fact, that many people cannot quite figure out how to use it. "What's the point of sending out brief little quips, especially if no one is listening?" Indeed, using Twitter for your business is like any other marketing effort: the key is getting people's attention. Succeeding at this effort requires a strategy.

Over time, a certain "style" has formed around the correct way to use Twitter. Of course, some people view it as a place to send out all the useless little thoughts floating around in their heads at any given moment. Unless they have celebrity status, such people do not have many followers except their own closest friends, who have probably become used to their tedious tweets. In contrast, the people most worth following on Twitter are those whose perspective is a bit broader. They tend to start conversations about interesting topics that inspire them. They follow topics and join in when they have something interesting to add.

In summary, your Twitter strategy should follow these basic rules:

- Seek out and follow people and topics related to your business. Read postings closely. Start to get a feel for the types of tweets that generate responses among followers. As you will start to discover, the heaviest Twitter users post messages to as a way of starting an open-ended conversation, not as a megaphone to blast out a message.
- Add details to your Twitter business profile, so that people can quickly understand you and your business. The more interesting you appear, the more people will be interested in following you.
- Do not worry about whether anyone is following you or not at first. Just start posting things that you consider interesting and related to your business. Make sure to use topic tags so that people who are searching for particular topics will come across your tweets.
- Go ahead and respond to something someone said. Or you can simply "retweet" it through Twitter to show that you really liked the message. As you become more active on Twitter, and engage with people who tweet frequently, other people will inevitably start to interact with you.
- Include a "Follow me" link on all your marketing material, so that people will know how to subscribe to your Twitter feeds.

Linked In

LinkedIn is the social media for business networking. It is similar to Facebook, in that you have a choice of creating a personal profile or a business page or both. And like Facebook, the content is generated by short posts, shared links and articles. You won't see photos of the family vacation here. LinkedIn has an enormous number of members, and according to LinkedIn, 73% of businesses say that having a profile on LinkedIn can help build credibility. As a business owner, you should take the time to create a profile that reflects your business related skills and experience, in fact it is really an on line resumé.

Create Your LinkedIn Profile

Think of your LinkedIn Profile as an opportunity to establish your professional identity. Use a current photograph, professionally taken, if possible. You will be guided to fill out a summary of your experience, education and any awards you may have received. If you belong to any organizations, be sure to list them. Of course you will want to include a link to your website as well. Be sure and use words that are common to your industry. This will help people find you, not only within LinkedIn but on the entire www! A useful feature LinkedIn offers with their free account is the ability to see who has viewed your profile within a certain period of time. If you want to see every single person who has viewed it, however, you need to upgrade to the Premium LinkedIn account, which has a monthly fee. There are lots of great features available with the free account, though, so become familiar with those before you contemplate the upgrade. For instance, you can recommend specific skills for those in your network, and they can do the same for you. LinkedIn makes this extremely easy to do.

Making connections is very easy as well, and one of the strengths of this network. A panel with names and photos of people you may know stays on the right side of your screen when you are logged in. When you click on the "connect" button, an invitation to connect is sent to that person; and by the same token, when someone sends you an invitation to join their network, you will receive an email notification with the name of that person and a button to click if you would like to add them.

Joining groups is another way to get the most out of LinkedIn. There are groups for all kinds of industries and interest groups. Any organization you already belong to probably has a LinkedIn group as well, which you can find by typing in the name of the group in the search bar at the top of page. Belonging to a group that is within your business industry gives you the opportunity to build your authority in the field. There are group discussions, surveys and polls and general conversations going on constantly. Every time you become involved in any of these, your activity appears in the news feed, similar to Facebook.

Summary

LinkedIn has really kept its focus on being all-business since it began in 2002, and continues to enhance the experience. It may not be as fun to look at as Facebook or Pinterest, but it can help you grow an online network, build your professional profile and reputation, and help with your overall online brand identity.

Pinterest

While Facebook is about words and pictures, and Twitter is based on short text messages, Pinterest is all about pictures. The idea behind Pinterest is to collect and display images that interest you, and allow other "Pinners" to view them as well, "love" and even "pin" them on their own boards. How popular is Pinterest? Well, as of this writing, it is the third most popular way to share something on the Internet, passing up email, and topped only by Facebook and Twitter. You can find fashion tips, hairstyles, recipes, art, decor and just about any kind of craft project you can imagine. "Pinterest Parties" have become popular now; a group of friends get together to make something they have seen on Pinterest. Where you might post photos of your family on your Facebook profile, or your newest product on your Facebook Business Page, on Pinterest you may pin your favorite style of shoe!

Besides being a lot of fun to look at, Pinterest offers a wonderful way to connect with people very quickly and easily. You can have either a personal account or a business account or you can have both. You can even convert your personal account into a business account, without losing any of your pins or followers. I would recommend having a business account whether you have the personal one or not. Set up is simple, and you can start pinning right away.

Set Up Your Pinterest Account

To get started with your Pinterest account, go to **www.pinterest.com** and click on the Sign up with Email button.In the next window, you can decide whether you want to sign up for the personal account by filling in your name and email address, or sign up for the Business account, by clicking on "Are you a business? Click Here."

Once you are set up, you can start creating boards. A board is like a collection or album; you give it a name, then pin images that are relevant. For instance you can have a board for Vintage Dresses, or Favorite Quotes or anything else that interests you. If you have created a business account, you can have boards for your products. With a business account, you can even invite others to collaborate on boards with you. For instance, you can invite some of your associates or customers to pin photos of how they used your products on one of your boards. You can also create "secret boards" visible only to you and those you invite. It is a great way to share ideas and get feedback before you make the pins public by repinning them onto one of your other boards.

After you have set up your first boards, click on the little icon that looks like this: < > under the heading of your Pinterest Business page. You can create a little widget to put on your website that will show some of your pins, and have a link to your Pinterest page. If you click on the "Learn more" link, you will be able to customize the widget. It is simple to just copy the code that will come up when you pick how you want the widget to look, and then paste it into your website, however, if you are uncomfortable doing this, ask someone you know has experience with widgets.

Start Pinning

Anything that is displayed on the Internet can be "pinned" to a board, and most websites today have a little red button with the letter "P" in it. Click on that and you will be asked which of your boards you would like to pin it. It is that simple! Whenever you go to Pinterest.com, if you are logged in, Pinterest will show you all the most recent pins from the people you follow. As you look through all the images, you will also see where your pins have been re-pinned by your followers as well as their followers. As you look at these other pins, you can click on the little heart icon to "love" it, email the link to someone through regular email, or "Pin" it to one of your boards. Any pins you repin will be added to the feed so all your followers will see what you are doing.

I would like to point something out that will help you make the most of all your pinning time. You will notice that every single pin has a link at the bottom of it to the website from which it was pinned. Whenever you are going to pin something for your business, you should pin it from your own website so the link that shows up on the pin will take pinners directly to your website. Even if someone repins it, the link will take them to your website. Remember that little widget you had installed on your website? This is the best way to pin images to your own boards. Simply go to your website and click on the "Pin it" widget that now appears on your pages, and you will be able to choose which images from you site to pin, and which boards you want to pin it onto.

There is one more very handy feature in Pinterest. You can share you pinning activity with your Facebook, Twitter and Google+ accounts, though at this time, you can only share to your personal profile, not your Business Page on Facebook. To tie your accounts together, go to the Account Settings tab which you can access from the very top right of the screen when you are logged into your Pinterest Business Account. You can do this anytime, so get comfortable pinnning first.

People have gotten very creative with Pinterest boards, and businesses are finding fun and interesting ways to connect with them since at this point there is no paid advertising on Pinterest, though "promoted pins" are in development. Pinners have organized weddings, birthday parties and home decor project just through collecting pins. I know someone who looks up recipes while she is at the grocery store so she can buy the ingredients then and there! If you want to dive even further into Pinterest for your business, visit **www.business.pinterest.com** where you can also read some inspiring success stories.

Instagram

The idea with Instagram is to take a photo with your phone or pad, add some kind of filter to it in Instagram and then post it to your Instagram page. From there you can easily share it on Facebook, Twitter, Tumblr, Flicr or email. The main difference between Pinterest and Instagram is that Instagram is for mobile use only. The filters you use give your photo a bit of a vintage look, and will constrain it to a square, which can make a photo look more interesting than it really is sometimes! When you are posting the photo to your account, you can add comments about it, and after you post it, others can also comment on it, so here again, the idea is to engage your "followers" as they are called, in conversation. Instagram uses the # (hashtag) to group conversation topics like Twitter does, which can be very useful for you if you are using it for business. For intstance, say you take a photo of some beautiful vintage lace you are going to use to make a dress, and you want to post it to Instagram. After you have your photo posted, you type something like #vintagelace in the comments section. Now, the next time someone is on her Instagram account, and search for hashtag term vintage lace, your photo will show up. There are actually 4,105 posts with that hashtag right now! You can use as many hashtags as you like, just type them all into the comments area of your photo before you post it. If you want to come back later and add some, you can just add another comment to your photo with additional hashtags.

Businesses are using Instagram to connect with their market in creative ways as well. Like Pinterest, the challenge is to engage viewers in a fun way. Some businesses invite viewers to post photos of them using or holding a product and then adding a certain hashtag. The business will give coupons to those who participate.There are many other ways to use it, of course. This is just one example. This particular flavor of social media is hugely popular with younger people. Even though you might prefer Facebook or Pinterest, if you want to reach the 18-36 age range, you cannot ignore Instagram.

Getting Started

To set up your Instagram account, remember this is for your mobile device, so pick up your smart phone or tablet, and go to the App store. Search for Instagram in the apps, and then download it. Once you have it installed, you can create an account, using your email address, or your Facebook account. Decide whether you want this to be your business account, in which case you would use your business name as the name on the account, or your personal account. Either way, you can add your website in your account information, and everytime someone sees a photo posted by you, your name will appear as a link underneath it, along with comments or hashtags you have assigned it. Your name (or business name) is a link, so when someone clicks on it, they are taken to your profile page, and if you have entered a website in your account information, that will appear as a live link. Getting around Instagram is done mostly by clicking on the little icons across the bottom or your screen. By tapping the little house icon, you can go to the home page, which shows the latest posts by you and people you follow. Next there is a compass icon, which takes you to the "explore" screen. This is where you can type in a hashtag to search, like #vintagelace, or a username. Instagram will then show you all the photos that match up to the search terms you just used. The middle icon on the bottom of your screen is the camera. When you click on the icon, it opens up your phone camera and is ready to take a picture. You can search through all the photos on your camera by tapping to the left of the camera icon. Instagram now allows you to take fifteen second videos by tapping the video icon to the right of your camera icon. To get out of the camera mode, click on the white "x" at the top left of your screen. Going back to the main icons on the bottom of your screen, the heart icon takes you to a screen where you can choose to see the latest posts of the people you are following. The final icon on the very right takes you to your profile page.

Instagram for Business

When it comes down to actually using Instagram, it is really just about taking photos and sharing them, much like Facebook. Here are some pointers to help you understand how you can use this social media in the most simple ways:

- Mix fun photos in with your more serious product shots. A major retail store recently posted a picture showing some cute shoes next to an even cuter puppy, and they also posted a picture of an employee at a company event. Guess which photo got more than twice as many likes?
- When you set up your Instagram account, link it to your Facebook and Twitter accounts.
- When you post to different social medias, use the same hashtag for the photos.
- Follow as many people who follow you. The idea here is to spread the net as wide as possible. It is also why having a business account for your social media is a good idea.
- You do not need to post as often to Instagram as Facebook or Twitter. The newsfeed does not replace things quite as quickly yet, and you do not want to drown your followers in posts. Plan a moderate posting schedule.
- When deciding what kinds of photos to post, think about what other interests your followers might have, and post photos about that, using hashtags. This is how you will be found by people who are not yet your followers. They will be searching Instagram by using hashtags.
- Use hashtags to come up with marketing messages. Search Instagram using the hashtag search for terms that line up with your business. Then use those terms to tag your photos and posts in Instagram, Facebook and Twitter.
- Comment on other people's photos if it is appropriate. When you make a comment, remember that your name is shown and it is a live link to your profile.
- Show photos of you or your employees creating your product. People

love behind the scenes photos.

• Don't forget that Instagram offers video as well.

Tie It All Together

Posting, and pinning and tweeting, oh my! By now your head may be swimming with all of this social media information. Remember what I said earlier in this chapter? Social media is simply talking to people. If you include social media strategy in your overall plan, then you won't find yourself struggling to come up with content at the last minute. Planning also helps ensure that it all flows together. Let us take a moment and recall what social media can do for your business.

• Engage people you already know in online conversations.
• Engage people you do not know personally in online conversations.
• Get instant feedback on ideas, images or content that you post.
• Test new marketing ideas before you spend money on traditional media by measuring the response you get on your social media.
• Go where your market is at any time of the day.
• By posting things that reflect your brand, you can strengthen the identity or personality people associate with your business.
• You can tap into related markets.
• When people re-post your message or image, it is like getting a referral.
• It is free. Though spending money on promoted posts is often a good investment.

So what might a social media strategy look like? Well, let us first take a look at the different groups of people who are online using social media, according to the PEW Research Center. To read the full report, go to **www.pewinternet.org**.

• **Facebook**
Overall Internet users (71%)
Gender   Men (66%)
              Women (76%)
Age   18-29 (84%)
              30-49 (79%)
              50-64 (60%)
              65 + (45%)

- **LinkendIn**
  Overall Internet users (22%)
  Gender   Men (24%)
             Women (19%)
  Age   18-29 (15%)
             30-49 (27%)
             50-64 (24%)
             65 + (13%)

- **Pinterest**
  Overall Internet users (21%)
  Gender   Men (8%)
             Women (33%)
  Age   18-29 (27%)
             30-49 (24%)
             50-64 (14%)
             65 + (9%)

- **Twitter**
  Overall Internet users (18%)
  Gender   Men (17%)
             Women (18%)
  Age   18-29 (31%)
             30-49 (19%)
             50-64 (9%)
             65 + (5%)

- **Instagram**
  Overall Internet users (17%)
  Gender   Men (15%)
             Women (20%)
  Age   18-29 (37%)
             30-49 (18%)
             50-64 (6%)
             65 + (1%)

Most people check Facebook, Instagram and Twitter daily, often more than once. Pinterest and LinkedIn are most often checked weekly or less. This information can help you decide how to plan your posting. Remember, the whole reason we want to use social media is to support our overall plan.

If you have started your blog posting and have your newsletter schedule determined, then you are half-way there with the social media planning! Let those be the main parts of your online plan. Everytime you blog or send out the email, you share that through social media, always with links to your website. In between your newsletters and blog, you can post a little something that is along the same theme as your newsletter and blog for the month. Post to Instagram daily and if you have that tied to your Twitter account as we talked about earlier, then you do not need to worry about an additional tweet! Spend a little time Pinning every other day or so, and when you do, you can use the same image to post to Instagram and Facebook. LinkedIn can be updated the day you send your newsletter or update your blog. The key is to plan the few minutes you will need to keep up. Consistency is key, but do not worry if you miss a day here and there.

Bringing your Web strategy to life will take a little time. Remember that technology is a constant learning process. Make sure that you are getting help along the way. Even a little bit of professional advice as you start developing different web assets will go a long way, and help you avoid unnecessary confusion or wasted time and money

The key with your overall web strategy is to make sure that all the parts make sense together. Pay close attention to the fads, but concentrate on your core message. A simple and elegant shopping site that lets customers buy your products, a fun and engaging blog that keeps people coming back, and a strategic use of social media will create very strong web presence for your business. Being the schoolteacher that I am once again I recommend going to your library to check out books about specific areas of online business. Get books which truly explain in great detail social media, YouTube, blogging and email newsletters. Each topic is really a "college course" if you want to totally and completely understand the true function of using it to grow your business—either a store front business or an online one. There is a world of "how to" information on all of these topics on line of course. Spending time studying and planning (in writing) your online presence before you dive in is critical. As you study every section of this book please remember that I had no WRITTEN plan is the reason, I believe, that I made little profit for the first ten years I was in business. I had "lots of top line" and "no bottom line." I want very much for you to be profitable as quickly as possible and I believe written planning and much study before you dive in is the way to have the best possibility of making that happen.

~ Chapter Ten ~

Customer Service

Do not judge others, and you will not be judged. Do not condemn others, or it will all come back against you. Forgive others, and you will be forgiven. Give, and you will receive. Your gift will return to you in full—pressed down, shaken together to make room for more, running over, and poured into your lap. The amount you give will determine the amount you get back.

—Luke 6:37-38

There is only one boss. The customer. And he can fire everybody in the company from the chairman on down, simply by spending his money somewhere else.

—Sam Walton

Dolly Madison, President Madison's wife, was well known for her marvelous public relations at the White House. She always welcomed people with the words "At last!" showing that she was eager to meet them and had been waiting to see them. When her guests left, her departing phrase was "So soon?" letting them know she hated to see them go.

—Dottie and Lilly Walters

Let your feet do the talking. Walk away from businesses or products you don't like.

—Gloria McKinnon

Old Fashioned Customer Service

The Golden Rule
Do to others whatever you would like them to do
to you. This is the essence of all that is taught in
the law and the prophets.
—Matthew 7:12

My Uncle Albert and Aunt Eva ran a small department store in Scottsboro called Park's Store, and although they were very successful, it was a modest business by the standards of our modern big box stores. Nevertheless, I consider them customer service experts. My first paying job was selling in their store. I was twelve years old. As I was starting my own business, they gave me advice that has stuck with me to this very day. They told me that friends and family would be my greatest customers, and so I should make sure that any new customers quickly became friends. I should take every opportunity to learn more about them, just as I might with a new acquaintance from church. Inquire about their families, ask questions and listen intently. If Uncle Albert or Aunt Eva found out that a customer lived in Pisgah, which is a small community about 15 miles from Scottsboro, they would share a story about someone they knew in Pisgah. I call this establishing intimacy.

They also emphasized the importance of paying attention to every customer and treating each customer well. They always thanked everybody for coming in even if they bought nothing. At Christmas time, or for anyone's birthday, they were always happy to wrap beautiful presents for customers. You could leave your purchases for wrapping, and return to find them on a shelf (a very high shelf) when you came back to get them. You should have seen the beauty of that store at Christmas! All those wrapped presents that filled the shelves behind the counter let everybody know that Park's Store was the place to purchase your Christmas presents. I still do purchase at a store that wraps beautiful presents as long as that present is $15 or over.

Uncle Albert was a lay pastor for the Church of Christ. He preached when needed all around Jackson County. He conducted weddings in small outlying churches, preached funerals, and was always willing to travel anywhere he was needed, whenever someone was sick or had a death in the family. None of these things were done with a business purpose in mind,

I assure you, but of course they did have an enormous business impact. People loved both Uncle Albert and Aunt Eva; everyone wanted to spend their money in that store over any other big name alternative. I think that is one of the main lessons I learned when I was 12 and 13 years old working every Saturday in their store. People loved to spend their money with them knowing full well that they could consider Uncle Albert and Aunt Eva their true friends. They, personally, wanted to be sure that Parks' store stayed in business.

In many ways, my Aunt Eva and Uncle Albert were the consummate networkers. It had nothing to do with business, and that was just the point. They were thoughtful people who loved to share their lives and hearts with the people they cared about. That just happened to be everyone who walked into their store as well as many others. In that respect, I have never known a better example of a truly Christian business than Park's Store in Scottsboro, Alabama. I will tell you about my Aunt Elizabeth's business at the end of this chaper.

The art of treating your customers well is something that will be the foundation of your entire business. This is true if you have a store front or if you have an internet business. There is simply nothing more important than delivering wonderful customer service to the people who purchase from you. If you treat someone respectfully and with consideration, as you might treat one of your friends, they will always return. Not only that, they will likely tell all their friends about you. Customer service is the soil upon which all business growth occurs.

At every moment of every day, you should be thinking about ways that you can treat your customers better. Often it is the little things that count. The way you speak to someone, the way you package their purchases, the friendly conveniences that you offer them, or the way you include extras in their packages. Each of these small touches creates a kind of emotional connection between you and your customer.

In this chapter, I am going to present some of my own ideas about customer service, and offer suggestions on how to make your business more successful by following these ideas. What I have found is that many of these tips are much less about specific practices or technical advice and more about your attitude and approach to customers. So the sections that follow are designed to help you shape the correct attitude toward your customers, in order to keep them returning to your business.

Becoming the Backyard Fence

In the fantastic book, *Eveolution: The Eight Truths of Marketing to Women,* by Faith Popcorn, the author tells us how important it is to let your customers connect to your brand. She talks about the weakening of community bonds in our modern world, and how your business can become a kind of "backyard fence" where customers can rediscover their neighbors and community. I think this is such a true idea, and pray I have naturally built my business this way.

People matter and, in the world of business, how you manage and relate to people is the key to success.

—Dale Carnegie

Always call the customer by her name and always thank her for her loyalty.

—Gloria McKinnon

What Customers Like

In my company, we pay very close attention to our customers. In fact, we collect that information regularly through surveys and other means. Here is a list of what our customers feel is most important when visiting a sewing machine dealership or any store. Several years ago, when I had a sewing machine dealership, I sent out an email (I did not have access to a survey tool like we have now) and asked my customers, "What is the most important 'thing' a sewing machine dealership can offer you?" We received a huge response—maybe 500 out of the 3,000 emails sent. Here are some of the most often repeated answers. Truthfully, I thought "having a fabulous sewing machine, having great service on that machine or offering fabulous classes" might be the top answers. I was wrong. Here are the top answers:

- They call me by my name and ask about me when I walk in the store. This was by far the first choice of the greatest number of people. Just think. The number one response was "They know my name."

- All salespeople love to help me and answer questions.
- They tell me how much they appreciate my business.
- They help me pick out whatever I'm looking for.
- I call them and they help me on the phone.
- They call me when they hear I have a health problem.
- They called me when they heard my mother was sick.
- They treat me like I'm part of their family.
- My dealer has a loaner machine when mine is in the shop.
- I like to be asked, "In your wildest dreams, what would you want your sewing machine to do for you?"
- My dealer has a referral program so I can recommend people to her. If I recommend a customer she writes me a thank you note and gives me a discount on something.
- When I make a large purchase, such as a sewing machine, she gives me a 25% discount off of one smaller item each month for a year.
- They treat all customers the same, no matter how much money they are going to spend.
- They are honest with pricing and other details.
- They always tell customers to call back with any questions or difficulties.
- They ask to see projects or pictures of my projects.
- They know my favorite types of fabrics, books, etc.
- They call me when a new fabric that I like comes in.
- They care about me.
- They call me to tell me about something new which is coming in.
- They have great big smiles every time I walk into the store.
- They are willing to spend some time with me.
- They love to look at my children's (or grandchildren's) pictures.
- The cutest answer we got went like this. "My dealer is the best in the world. When something is wrong with my machine I call him. He says to me, 'Put the phone up to your machine and run it so I can hear it. Let me listen to your machine on the phone to hear exactly what it is doing.' I then put the phone up to my machine and run the machine. If he can tell me what is wrong he does. If he does not know he just tells me to bring it in. Then I take it in. He cares enough about me to listen to my machine on the phone." Can you even imagine what kind of customer service this is? I'll tell you what kind it is. The best!

Love is patient and kind. Love is not jealous or boastful or proud or rude. It does not demand its own way. It is not irritable, and it keeps no record of being wronged. It does not rejoice about injustice but rejoices whenever the truth wins out. Love never gives up, never loses faith, is always hopeful, and endures through every circumstance.

—1 Corinthians 13:4-7

Likeability

Likeability is all about people who have good values and character, I believe. I will go one step more down this path by saying that most of the businesses that I have seen "stay alive" and "succeed" have been owned by people of great character and honorable values. Scripture teaches one how to succeed in life. The Bible has every business principle that I could ever need to operate my business.

Benjamin Franklin, in his autobiography, listed thirteen virtues that he would need to develop his character. Although written in 1726, these virtues, for me, are valid business principles that I would highly recommend if one wants business success. They are certainly worth my time and I believe yours to think about carefully.

- *Temperance. Eat not to dullness; drink not to elevation.*
- *Silence. Speak not but what may benefit others or yourself; avoid trifling conversation.*
- *Order. Let all your things have their places; let each part of your business have its time.*
- *Resolution. Resolve to perform what you ought; perform without fail what you resolve.*
- *Frugality. Make no expense but to do good to others or yourself; i.e., waste nothing.*
- *Industry. Lose no time; be always employ'd in something useful; cut off all unnecessary actions.*
- *Sincerity. Use no hurtful deceit; think innocently and justly, and, if you speak, speak accordingly.*
- *Justice. Wrong none by doing injuries, or omitting the benefits that are your duty.*

- *Moderation. Avoid extremes; forbear resenting injuries so much as you think they deserve.*
- *Cleanliness. Tolerate no uncleanliness in body, cloaths, or habitation.*
- *Tranquillity. Be not disturbed at trifles, or at accidents common or unavoidable.*
- *Chastity. Rarely use venery but for health or offspring, never to dullness, weakness, or the injury of your own or another's peace or reputation.*
- *Humility. Imitate Jesus and Socrates.*

Customer service starts and ends with likeability. Building a strong rapport with each and every one of your potential customers is what will create your business success—much more than any other factor. You might say, "Now Martha how can I do that if I have an on-line business?" I have a very simple answer. Your newsletter can let them know you and your family in a very personal way. I truly believe my email newsletter (which was very long for about 11 years) was the number one way we built MPC to the place it is today. I simply allowed my customers into my life and the life of my family exactly as if they were my family—and they are my sewing family. I always told them on the newsletter about my college letter writing days. Every week I wrote one long letter home to Mama and Daddy telling them everything that was happening. Mama wrote me a letter every week doing the same thing. I always thought of my weekly email newsletter as my "letter home to Mama and Daddy." Of course I always told my sewing family sewing news in addition to my personal news but believe me it was personal.

Did I write this letter just to sell something? Absolutely not, although it did sell certain products that were listed as new or on sale, or events which were coming up. I just wanted to write to them once a week just as I wrote home in college. I never considered this a sales letter although of course it served that purpose if my sewing family needed anything. It let them know that they were my extended family. It was very long and took a long time to write. That was OK with me. I not only wanted to tell them all about products, which I loved to talk about since I loved our products, I wanted to share other things which were going on in my life. Being an English teacher I was always sharing a poem, or a snippet from my antique magazines or sewing tips from our readers or pictures of items that our readers had made or a sweet letter from one of our readers. I always included scripture and a devotional. We included a recipe each week mostly from readers. I loved writing that newsletter and about 40,000 other people loved reading it. In addition to this we gave weekly specials, sometimes only available to our newsletter family! There are samples of these letters on our website (**www.pullenbusiness.com**).

Power of Words

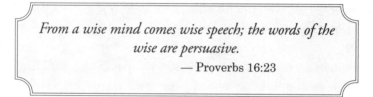

From a wise mind comes wise speech; the words of the wise are persuasive.
— Proverbs 16:23

Of course you can try to win customers by dropping your prices to rock bottom, and you will end up selling your products to all sorts of people. Sooner or later, that strategy will lead to your closing your own doors and putting yourself out of business, because it is not sustainable. In the end, it is not prices that create loyalty. True long-term loyalty comes from the excitement and enthusiasm that you can inspire in people about your products and services. All of those intangible qualities come from your people skills – I call it your likeability – and that is what builds loyalty.

Many of us learned some of our likability skills growing up, and that is a good start. But what if you do not have enough of these skills? Is it hopeless? Absolutely not! I can tell you that I am still learning and growing my people skills. Learning likeability is a lifelong pursuit.

Likable People

Let your conversation be gracious and attractive so that you will have the right response for everyone.
— Colossians 4:6

- Positive thinkers
- Courteous
- Sincere in their caring
- Smiles

- Wise
- Goal oriented
- Joy makers
- Positive thinkers

- Personal with people, intimate
- Great communicators
- Never putting others down
- Not demanding, but rather asking politely
- Good listeners
- Quick to forgive and forget
- Enthusiastic about other people
- Childlike in their joy of the world
- Quick to show appreciation
- Passionate about their business
- Encouraging
- Dependable
- Fair
- Attentive and Sincere
- Self-starting
- Focused
- Energetic
- Resourceful
- Faithful

- Cheerful
- Fair
- Generous
- Careful
- Efficient
- Eager
- Charismatic
- Affable
- Trustworthy
- Clever
- Versatile
- Unselfish
- Other oriented
- Wise
- Warm
- Cooperative
- Adventurous
- Ambitious

Unlikable People

> *But now is the time to get rid of anger, rage, malicious behavior, slander, and dirty language.*
> — Colossians 3:8

- Demanding
- Unkind
- Biting
- Snivelers
- Negative thinkers
- Sarcastic
- Defensive
- Mocking
- Self centered

- Gossipers
- Cowardly
- Cross
- Sullen
- Caustic
- Haughty
- Childish
- Easily angered
- Cold-hearted

- Selfish
- Full of criticism
- Unforgiving
- Quick to point out other people's faults
- Pushy
- Regularly putting others down
- Talkers, and don't know how to listen

- Finicky
- Uncontrolled Anxious
- Thoughtless
- Stubborn
- Foolish
- Mean

How To Be Likeable

> *Don't copy the behavior and customs of this world, but let God transform you into a new person by changing the way you think. Then you will learn to know God's will for you, which is good and pleasing and perfect.*
> — Romans 12:2

Being likeable is often just a matter of your attitude. Often Zig Ziglar talked about an "attitude of graditude." At its core, it is always about **G.R.A.C.E:** asking **God** for guidance, **Resilience** when people do unlikable things, **Actions** that will take one closer to being likable, **Creativity** in the steps we take to being likeable, and **Enthusiasm** in all the steps we take toward others and our goals.

Being likeable is very rich and complex. There are lots of characteristics of being likeable. In the sections that follow, we'll cover different ways to "be" which will help increase your likeability factor.

One filled with joy preaches without preaching.
—Mother Teresa

Be Friendly

> *Don't use foul or abusive language. Let everything*
> *you say be good and helpful, so that your words will*
> *be an encouragement to those who hear them. And*
> *do not bring sorrow to God's Holy Spirit by the way*
> *you live. Remember, he has identified you as his own,*
> *guaranteeing that you will be saved on the day of*
> *redemption. Get rid of all bitterness, rage, anger, harsh*
> *words, and slander, as well as all types of evil behavior.*
> *Instead, be kind to each other, tenderhearted, forgiving*
> *one another, just as God through Christ has forgiven you.*
> — Ephesians 4:29-32

It is amazing to me how often people forget the value of basic friendliness in business. I can think of no other single quality that makes more of a difference in any sort of business situation than friendliness. Many are the times that I have simply walked away from a store because the employees were unfriendly, even though they actually had many products that I actually liked and wanted to purchase. When I feel unwelcome or rushed or uncomfortable in a store, I am not interested in purchasing anything at all.

Friendliness is essential for any hobby entrepreneur. While I was running The Heirloom Shop, I made a point of never hiring a salesperson who did not have a readily available smile for customers. I'm not talking about a Pollyanna, silly grin, but a genuine smile that says, "I am happy to be speaking with you."

Unfortunately, sometimes friendliness does not come easy for some people. I would say that anyone who wants to become an entrepreneur, but does not exude a bright and cheery attitude is in the wrong business. It certainly takes all kinds of people to make the world go round, but all types of people do not make great entrepreneurs. A shy or unfriendly attitude will get you nowhere in business. On the other hand, a bright and genuine smile is the quickest way to welcome someone into your space.

A warm friendly attitude is the best way to win a customer.

The excellent companies really are close to their customers. That's it. Other companies talk about it; excellent companies do it.

—Tom Peters

Be Intimate

> *Dear friends, let us continue to love one another, for love comes from God. Anyone who loves is a child of God and knows God. But anyone who does not love does not know God, for God is love.*
>
> — 1 John 4:7-8

My favorite stores are the ones where I spend the majority of my money. When I step inside these stores, I feel as comfortable as if I were in an extension of my home. The salespeople treat me the same whether I am dressed in a suit or blue jeans. These stores seem to really like me, which goes a long way in encouraging me to like them. They care about whether I am happy with their products, and ask my opinion about all sorts of things. The few times that I needed to take something back, they apologized for the product's not working and for my needing to take the time to bring it back. When I returned something, they never, ever made me feel it was my fault.

Your ability to make customers feel as if they are a part of your life is an important part of intimacy. Sharing parts of yourself is critical in the process of attracting them to you—what you think, who you are, who your children are, and what your business stands for. Just as importantly, you need to express your genuine concern that all is well in their homes. Learn and remember the names of their children and spouses! Write that information down after they have left so that you can keep it in your customer database.

You might say, "Martha how can I be intimate with an online business when I never see the customer?" I have already told you about the weekly email newsletter which is, I believe, one of the best ways to do this. The newsy blog is another. I want to share with you an incident that I will never forget. It was the middle of winter and Suzanne, my missionary daughter-in-law in Africa desperately needed a new swimsuit. Where, in December, does one buy a swimsuit in Huntsville, Alabama? I called Land's End that also did not have swimsuits on their website in December. If they did I could not find them. I explained to the nice lady who answered the phone what my problem was and asked if she could help. She replied, "Certainly." She seemed very interested in my kids who were missionaries in Africa. I told her the size and she began to describe the swim suits they had in that size since they did have several. I told her that Suzanne was a very cheerful and happy person and she said, "Well that does it for me. I think the black suit with big splashy flowers on it is very happy. I really think she might like that better than the solid navy or black. What do you think?" I assured her that she would love the happy, splashy flowers and she shipped the suit to me. It was perfect and I immediately shipped it to Africa for Suzanne. I have never forgotten that dear lady on the other end of the phone who cared about my missionary children and who helped me pick out something that was not available by picture anywhere.

To truly create an intimate business relationship with your customers takes a great deal of work. When you create a client base full of people who know that you care about them, you create a loyal and solid foundation upon which to build your business. Soon you will begin to count your friends among your clients, and your clients among your friends. This kind of intimacy can only occur by diligent effort and understanding of what they like and care about. You will find that the skill you most need to be intimate is to be inquiring.

Be Inquiring

Dottie Walters, the famous speaker and businesswoman, once told me that one of the main keys to her success was to be more interested than interesting. She liked to tell a story about the great actress Sarah Bernhardt to illustrate her point. Late in Ms. Bernhardt's long career, when her theatrical company arrived in Chicago, a newspaper editor told a young reporter that he was assigned to interview her. This reporter was not very impressed by Ms. Bernhardt's career, and told his editor that he didn't want to go. He complained, "She is an old has-been!"

He was forced to go, of course. When he came back, he did not return with a dejected attitude from having endured a long, boring interview. Instead, he flew into the newsroom excitedly, and went straight to his typewriter to write a glowing story about Sarah for his newspaper.

The savvy editor asked the young man, "Well, what did you and Sarah Bernhardt talk about?"

He replied, "Come to think of it, she didn't say much. But every time I said something, she leaned forward with a smile, looked into my eyes, and said, 'And then?'"

The lesson is that we always have a much higher opinion of someone when they show interest in us. The fact that they cared enough to ask questions, and try to learn more about us, is charming and makes us feel welcome.

It is an important thing to keep in mind during the early days of your business, when you are still trying to establish your reputation. Don't make the mistake of always trying to impress someone with how interesting you are. You will find that people's opinion of you is determined just as much by the interest you show in them. Invite your customer to speak, and let them be just as likable as you.

Be Inviting

Wouldn't you like to have customers flooding through the doors of your place of business? Well, did you invite them in? I don't mean something as anonymous as an ad in the paper or something as impersonal as a form letter. I mean, why don't you call everyone in your address book and say, "Now, ya'll come on over this Saturday. There will be refreshments and you can come see our new things!" (That's not bad grammar; we talk that way in Huntsville. And since we are on the subject, "ya'll" means "you all," and that is exactly who I want to come in my doors if I am in business.) I want all of the people I know to shop in my store, and I make sure that I am always giving them a good reason to pay a visit! Email invites are fabulous, too!

When your customers walk in the door, do you invite them to come and see the new items? When they are about to leave, do you invite them to come back soon? If you receive new products, do you call or email them and enthusiastically invite your best customers to learn more about them?

People have busy lives, and it is easy for them to get so caught up in errands and other tasks that they forget to find the time to think of you. Far from taking it personally, you need to make sure that you periodically extend an invitation to all your customers. If they accept your invitation, treat them as if they are special friends which of course they are. Sending an email is an excellent way of telling people about a party or demonstration; however, a personal phone call is still very important!! If your customers like tweeting send a tweet! Or a text if you have their cell phone numbers. Lots of people are announcing lots of things with text messages these days.

Be Enthusiastic

I have never met a successful person—from billionaire to baton twirler—who was not enthusiastic. Stanford University once did a study showing that during a sale, 15 percent of the success was due to product knowledge, and 85 percent was credited to plain old enthusiasm. Think for a second about what that means—your ability to transmit your own personal excitement about a product has much more influence over a person's purchase decision than the product itself! In another "how to sell" book I read that a Harvard Business School study determined that there were four factors critical to sales success: information, intelligence, skill and attitude! How exciting that we can now send enthusiasm over the Internet!

The longer I live, the more I realize the impact of attitude on life. Attitude, to me, is more important than facts. It is more important than the past, than education, than money, than circumstances, than failure, than successes, than what other people think or say or do. It is more important than appearances, giftedness or skill. It will make or break a company..a church....or home.
—Charles Swindoll

Enthusiasm is a keen, animated interest; an absorbing or controlling possession of the mind by any subject, interest, or pursuit. That is what the dictionary will tell you. But look deeper! Enthusiasm is so much more. Do you know the word enthusiasm comes from the Greek entheos? In its original usage, enthusiasm was used to describe people who were so filled (en) with God (theos) that it made them appear divinely inspired.

Today the expression has lost much of its religious meaning for most of the world. But anyone who has been filled with the joy of deep enthusiasm for his/her hobby, or family, or friends, knows that with the genuine expression of this feeling comes an inner state of passionate and sustained elevation of the soul. Enthusiasm actually fills one with a spirit of **G.R.A.C.E.**

In my life, I know this spirit of enthusiasm is a gift from God. It always fills me with joy, and it has the contagious ability to keep filling up all those around me. We are not here on this planet simply to exist, but to live, and to live abundantly. Make sure that you bring your enthusiasm to work every day, and you take the time to share your feelings of happiness with others. By tapping into the ideas that make you feel enthusiastic, you are allowing that energy to spread into all aspects of your business life. You just might pass it along to your employees, colleagues and customers.

The real secret of success is enthusiasm. Yes, more than enthusiasm, I would say excitement. I like to see men get excited. When they get excited they make a success of their lives.

—Walter Percy Chrysler

Be Uncommonly Courteous

The famous businessman B. C. Forbes said, "Politeness is the hallmark of the gentleman and the gentlewoman. No characteristic will so help one to advance, whether in business or society, as politeness. Courtesy is another name for politeness—it costs nothing, but can gain much both for an individual and for an organization."

I can think of no easier way to impress a customer than delivering uncommon courtesy. These days even common courtesy is becoming rare. That means when you go beyond your customers' expectations it will make a dramatic impression. Just saying "Thank you," "You are welcome," and "Please come again" are all ways of offering common courtesy. I am always amazed that when I give a large amount of money at the grocery store the cashier usually does not say "thank you for your business." I believe every cashier at every company in the world should end the sale with "thank you for your business. Please come back again. We appreciate you." How hard would that be in employee training?

What if you went a step further by opening a door when a customer arrived as they do in some restaurants, or offering someone a chair, or proposing a cup of coffee, or sending someone a thank you note? These simple, everyday kindnesses will show your dedication to customer service, and make your business stand out in the minds of your customers. Personally I love to make purchases at Chick-fil-A® where they always end the order with "My Pleasure" from the speaker box!

Good manners have much to do with the emotions.
To make them ring true, one must feel them,
not merely exhibit them.

—Amy Vanderbilt

Be Thankful

Toward the end of each day I like to take a moment and think, "Who helped to make things a little easier today?" When I have a spare moment, I always like to seize on that sentiment and quickly write that person a thank you note. Of course I know to thank God first since it is He that got me through each day.

Saying thank you is one of the most important parts of a business. Everyone appreciates the gesture—it is easy, it helps create intimacy, and, well, it is just plain nice! It is a critical tool for increasing customers' loyalty and sales. I am a firm believer in saying to my customers, "Thank you for buying from me!"

Of course, I say it verbally, but in many cases, I like to find other ways to say it: a small gift, a handwritten note. It always surprises the customer, because it makes them understand how much I value their business, and how much each customer means to me. By writing a thank you note to my special customers, it helps them understand that I feel a personal gratitude for their business and their loyalty.

When SECA executives made the decision to put my television show, *Martha's Sewing Room,* on the national PBS satellite, I was so excited I simply cried. I tried to think of an unusual thank-you gift, that would express just how special and important I considered their decision. In the end, I purchased two big balloon bouquets and sent them a large box. It looked like I was shipping a small cow; thank goodness it didn't weigh much! I later learned that it made a very big impression and went a long way toward establishing a wonderful business relationship between us.

I always keep a stack of thank-you notes and stamps nearby. It only takes a moment to write one, whether I'm on hold for a phone call, or riding in an airplane – anywhere. In an age of email and text messaging, I believe that it is all the more important to communicate your appreciation in a manner that shows your genuine appreciation through a little extra effort. I always have them hand-stamped and mailed the same day. This business principle cannot be overstated enough. Write thank-you cards!

Here are some ways to show your appreciation to customers:

- Train everyone in your organization to treat individuals as an individual.
- Send dear valued customer letters. Postal or email.
- Send birthday cards.Postal or email.
- Send thank you letters.Postal. Email is OK, but stamped is better.
- Call customers after a big sale.
- Email newsletter!
- Send birthday discount coupons for the birthday month.
- Offer discounts while students are enrolled in a class.
- Have a "brag board"in the shop and encourage pictures of children and grandchildren and great grandchildren to be posted for all to see.
- Send Christmas cards with a picture of you and your family. (Joe and I used to have a family picture made every year and print the Christmas story from the Bible on the inside. These were sent to Joe's patients. Inside he also wrote a personal letter telling the patients that next to God and his family they came next in the priorities in his life. He shared a little bit about his commitment to get continuing education so he could be the best dentist he could be for one reason—to bring to them the best dental care that he could. I might add that people kept these cards on their refrigerators for years. They also kept them in their treasures and one of them brought Joe an old Christmas card as Joe was retiring. He said, "I always kept this knowing how much you cared about me as a friend and as a patient."
- Send a Christmas thank you note or email.
- Send a Thanksgiving "I'm so thankful for you" or "when I count my blessings I count you twice " note or email.
- Send a Mother's Day note or email.
- Send an Easter note or email.

- Send an I love America and I am thankful to live here letter on the Fourth of July note or email.

> *Be thankful in all circumstances, for this is God's will for*
> *you who belong to Christ Jesus.*
> — 1 Thessalonians 5:18

Be Sincere

> *The purpose of my instruction is that all believers would*
> *be filled with love that comes from a pure heart, a clear*
> *conscience, and genuine faith*
> — 1 Timothy 1:5

If I can't truly be sincere in caring for my customers and really wanting to be friends with them, than I should not be in the business of selling. My personal and sincere caring for my customers is an essential aspect of my philosophy, because it pervades and permeates every other aspect of my business. The same should hold true for your pursuits.

No matter how much passion you feel for your work, it must be accompanied by compassion for the people you meet. Courtesy without sincerity is hollow. When people feel that you are emotionally sincere, they feel a connection. Always look for ways to speak with kindness to your customers and colleagues, and always make sure that you mean what you say—be sincere! All of this can also be done on the Internet.

Selling is not a profession for individuals who are lukewarm about loving people. I enjoy people. I enjoy hearing about their families and seeing their children. I really care about them and their problems. I never bought anything important from an insincere person who seemed to dislike me. There is always another product brand in another store with a genuine salesperson to present it to me in such a way that I enjoy giving my money to her/him.

If you would be loved, love and be lovable.
—Benjamin Franklin

Be Positive

> *And now, dear brothers and sisters, one final thing. Fix your thoughts on what is true, and honorable, and right, and pure, and lovely, and admirable. Think about things that are excellent and worthy of praise.*
> — Philippians 4:8

There will always be difficulty in life. How you choose to handle that unpleasantness is an extremely important personal decision, over which you can exercise a great deal of control. I certainly don't think I'm alone in saying that I don't really care to be around people who seem to enjoy complaining about one thing or another. When people are having trouble, I like to help and comfort them. There is a large difference between sharing a problem, and complaining about it. I believe it is very important to maintain a positive attitude in my life, and not allow myself the luxury of complaining too often.

In all honesty, out of all the people I have ever crossed in my business dealings, I do not know a single extremely successful person who complains about his/her troubles on a regular basis. The most successful people that I know have a very different perspective on problems. Where we see problems, they see challenges. They see problems as opportunities to rethink and reconsider their assumptions, and perhaps find a new direction to take. That is why they never complain—for the most successful people, problems seem to be just opportunities in disguise!

Many of us may have been exposed to negative thinking all of our lives without even realizing it. We are constantly taught to look on the dim side of things. How many times have you listened to the weatherman say, "We have a 10 percent chance of rain today." Few and far between are the weathermen who will take a moment to praise the positive side of the weather and happily say, "Hey there! 90 percent chance of a sunshiny day!"

So the next time that someone asks you, "How are you doing?" take a moment to compose a proper reply. Rather than saying something that carries a little raincloud, like "I'm fine. A little tired," take a moment to consider what you are really communicating with those words. Can you imagine people of passion using those words? Of course not!

When someone says to me, "I just can't imagine how things could get much worse," I always have to bite my tongue to keep from replying with a snappy answer. Because in truth, I can always think of a good half dozen ways that things could get worse!

Laugh and the world laughs with you;
Weep and you weep alone;
For the sad old earth must borrow its mirth,
But has trouble enough of its own.

—Ella Wheeler Wilcox

Take the time to find ways to praise the positives, both in yourself and in those around you. Sometimes finding the bright side of a situation takes take a bit of creative thinking to find, but just looking for them will help lighten your mood.

Guard your heart above all else,
for it determines the course of your life.
—Proverbs 4:23

Change your thoughts and you change your world.
—Martha Washington

I travel quite a bit for my business, and I have always enjoyed reading the airlines magazines when I fly. They are designed so beautifully and they always have fun articles about different people and places. I have always remembered one specific article that I came across, because the message stuck with me. The story was about a Georgian, named Billy Payne, who was president and chief executive officer of the Atlanta Committee for the Olympic Games. This magazine quoted him as saying, "My father once told me that there will always be people smarter and better than me. But the one thing I could control was my attitude and my work ethic. If I kept a positive attitude and worked harder than the others, I could accomplish a lot."

I have found that my attitude and work ethic changes when I walk with G.R.A.C.E. and choose my thoughts carefully. Prayer can change everything. To get my attitude straightened out (and yes sometimes I do not have the best attitude) I begin to pray asking God's help. He has never failed me.

Don't pray when you feel like it. Have an appointment with the Lord and keep it. A man is powerful on his knees.
—Corrie ten Boom

We have to pray with our eyes on God, not on the difficulties.
—Oswald Chambers

Customers and Friends: Elizabeth's Shoe Box

Although I never had the pleasure of working in her business, my Aunt Elizabeth Dicus was one of the most incredible business women that I ever knew. She ran her successful shoe store with Godliness and love for all who entered. She loved people. She took shoes for any family who had lost their home in a house fire or any other disaster. She took shoes for anyone who had a need for shoes and could not afford them. She baked a cake for families who had lost a loved one and sent flowers to comfort them. She cooked Brunswick stew when there was an illness in a family and delivered fresh food. She showed such love to all who came in her shoe store whether they bought anything or not. None of this was done to increase her business; it was done out of love. As you can imagine it did increase her business. Thousands of people had total loyalty to her and her shoe store. She was an angel of mercy to a whole town and county and God sent her all of the customers she needed in return. She had so many friends. Everyone told their friends about Elizabeth and Elizabeth's Shoe Box. I told her many times when I looked at her I saw Jesus at work.

Getting people to like you is merely the other side of liking them.

—Norman Vincent Peale

- *Chapter Eleven* -

Legendary Salesmanship

*No matter how busy you are, you must take time
to make the other person feel important.*

—Mary Kay Ash

*My dear brothers and sisters, how can you claim to
have faith in our glorious LORD Jesus Christ if you favor
some people over others? For example, suppose someone
comes into your meeting dressed in fancy clothes and
expensive jewelry, and another comes in who is poor and
dressed in dirty clothes. If you give special attention and
a good seat to the rich person, but you say to the poor one,
"You can stand over there, or else sit on the floor"—well,
doesn't this discrimination show that your judgments are
guided by evil motives?*

—James 2:1-4

*From my experience of watching truly successful salespeople I would
say that six critical skills one must have to be a sales rock star are
praying, praying, praying, and listening, listening, listening.*

—Martha Campbell Pullen

A major principle of selling for me is to treat people fairly and equally. That means all people. The biblical principle of "be nice" is truly a life principle for me. My parents taught, no demanded, that we "be nice" to everyone. Many people adopt a very shortsighted view of what their business is really about. They believe that the ultimate goal is to sell their inventory or services. I cannot adequately emphasize how this kind of attitude is a fundamentally wrong starting point. Of course you need to sell products, but that is just the consequence of a much more important goal. In fact, the ultimate aim of any business is to win customers.

"Now Martha," you may say, "you are just talking about two sides of the same coin. Whether you sell a product or gain a customer, it amounts to the same thing."

I disagree. A sold product is just a sale. It has to happen many times over before your business can become profitable. A happy customer is someone who will come back over and over. A handful of happy customers is equal to hundreds of products sold over a lifetime. That is not even considering all the referrals they can bring to your business.

Let me illustrate this point that happened many times in my sewing machine dealership. I would joyfully demonstrate a beautiful top of the line sewing machine in one of my heirloom classes to a young mother or to a grandmother neither of whom could afford the expensive machine. I still insisted that they have the fun of sewing on the machine for the class time just to enjoy the machine. I also told them they could come back anytime to sew on that machine in the store since it was there for their pleasure sitting "lonely "on my demonstration floor. Actually I pointed out that it would help me sell machines if they would bring their dresses back and sew on my demonstration floor so people could see garments being constructed on the machine. They were welcome anytime. Period.

Guess what happened more than once in situations like these? A son or daughter came in and secretly bought the machine for a gift for his/her mother or a mother or grandmother secretly came in and bought the machine for a gift for her/his daughter or granddaughter! I never tried at all to "sell" the machine but simply wanted to share the machine. God had another plan for the joy of this machine to go home with the ones who had enjoyed it so much. Another thing I learned quickly is that I never knew who had thousands of dollars for a top of the line machine and who did not. Do not ever assume that someone cannot buy whatever it is you are selling. Just be nice to all people and share the joy of what you are selling.

Most importantly be nice! Show the love of God to all who enter your shop whether that shop is in a store front or on the Internet! As Mama used to preach, "Be Nice."

No sale of any product is ever worth sacrificing the emotional connection that you build with a customer through friendly service. You should never pressure or persuade or push a sale for any product. It will often be at the expense of a happy customer. A happy customer who feels good about her purchase is someone who will come back again, and probably bring a few friends along next time. This realization should take away some of the pressure you might feel about selling your products. Your job is not about tricking or smooth-talking anyone. Your number one job is much simpler—you are there to help your customers figure out and find exactly what they need. Your products are there to make them have a better life.

If you can communicate that through your attitude, your customers will be astounded and grateful. When they realize that your true interests are squarely in line with their interests, they will appreciate you twice as much.

Top Ten Characteristics of My Customers

My customers:

- Are the lifeblood of my business.
- Deserve the nicest treatment I can give them.
- Deserve to be thanked for their business.
- Deserve to have me listen to their business needs and to try to fill them.
- Deserve to be listened to when they want to talk about things other than what I might sell them.
- Are not dependent on my business when there are plenty of other places to spend their hard earned money.
- Are doing me a favor when they call on me, not vice versa.
- Deserve my being product knowledgeable so as not to waste their time—this shows respect.
- Deserve to be my very honored guests not just someone off the street.
- Are real people who think and feel and have real problems to contend with.

How to be a Legendary Salesperson

There is an art to selling products. Of course you must be likeable and inviting and interested in your customers. Those qualities are only part of the big picture. Over the years, I have learned that there are some specific skills and wonderful techniques that can help a customer get to "yes."

These skills are not necessarily born into a person; they can be learned. Although I began formal study of both management and marketing after opening my business, my teaching career provided me with some of my best lessons in management, marketing, and selling. Have you ever tried to sell Shakespeare to a twelfth-grader in South Atlanta during the spring quarter before graduation?

In this section I want to share a handful of strategies that might help your customer say "yes."

Martha's Commandments of Successful Selling

Whenever I am in a sales setting, I have a set of guidelines that I always follow. These rules are not difficult to follow, nor very complicated, but they best summarize what I believe are the most important aspects of selling. After decades of experience, I believe that these eleven commandments are certainly part of the best path to helping you connect with your customers. Earlier in this chapter I told you who our customers are. Now, let's get down to some of the rules of selling to our customers.

1. Listen. Listen. Listen. Let the customer do 75 to 80% of the talking if you are dealing with the customer face to face. Ask questions. Listen to the answers! Selling is about asking questions.
2. Realize that they are beautiful/handsome/smart/worthy exactly like they are today!
3. Recognize that your customers are smart and special. Treat each of them like the unique human beings that they are, and speak to them with respect and politeness.
4. Become genuinely interested in them and make them feel important. Remember his/her name and encourage him/her to talk about himself/herself.
5. Have a good product that you really love. Don't ever try to sell someone

a product that you don't actually appreciate yourself. You will never find me trying to sell motorcycles or small airplanes!

6. Know your product well, so you can answer any questions for your customer. Be prepared to explain how it was made, what materials were used, and the process for making it. This kind of information will help customers make a decision.

7. Take care of your old customers. A repeat customer is a sign that you are doing something right. Find little ways to let them know you appreciate their business. Keep something nice behind the counter to include in the bags of your repeat customers. Actually a little extra surprise in the bag is great for all customers.

8. Wear a smile and give it away to everyone. Smiles do not cost anything. A friendly attitude will make your customers feel welcome and create a cheery atmosphere.

9. Think positively and successfully. Do not ever complain or use negative words. DO NOT EVER CUSS IN A BUSINESS SETTING OR TELL OFF COLOR JOKES! Many people will never set foot in a business if a cuss word or anything off color is heard, I assure you and they will tell their friends not to go. Bad language is never, never appropriate in any business setting.

10. Become a wonderful listener. LISTENING is more important than talking when selling anything. Ask questions. Listen to the answers. Ask more questions. Pay close attention to the words of your customers and try to help them in any way possible.

11. Always do more than is expected of you. Going the extra mile for your customers will make an impression on them, and keep them returning to you.

12. Sell with **G.R.A.C.E.** *God* always comes first. Be **Resilient** when you face challenges. Don't wait for success to arrive. Take **Action** and create your own success. Be **Creative** in finding way to present and display your products. Let your **Enthusiasm** shine through all the time.

Customer Types

One of the first things I learned about selling is that there are different types of shoppers. Sizing up a customer as she walks through the door is a very important skill. It can help you figure out the best way to treat that customer. I think that customers usually (sort of/maybe) come in four different varieties:

The Arrow is the sort of person who arrives and knows exactly what he/she wants. She will head directly to a specific location, or arrive with a very particular question. This person will often have a busy, brusque attitude that I do not necessarily consider rude, but simply very efficient. I have found that the best way to treat this sort of customer is to speak directly to these questions, and help her be on the way. Prompt and effective service is what they value most. I have found that once this customer recognizes that you are not trying to slow her down, trust will start.

The Browser is usually someone who is between appointments. This customer has no specific goal, and is not in any rush. The Browser is most interested in passing this time "in-between" in whatever is considered a pleasant and enjoyable place. You should return the compliment by giving this customer a warm hello, and a casual introduction to whatever seems to capture her interest, then leaving her alone until she asks for more help.

The Returning Customer is always a pleasure to see, and should be greeted with an effusive welcome. When I see Returning Customer, I always make a point of reconnecting and asking a few friendly questions. You want to establish the point that you remember that person, and are very happy that she decided to come back to your store. Based on your memory of that customer's taste, you should next make a point of showing her something new and special that she might like. Everyone likes to feel recognized, and the more you make that customer feel special, the more likely that she'll keep returning. Sometimes a Returning Customer comes with a friend. Make sure you pay equal attention to this friend. On more than one occasion, I have seen these friends walk out of my store with twice as much merchandise as the Returning Customer.

The **Wild Card** is my last type of customer. I just cannot quite read this person. Often it is because she is introverted and shy. I make a point of never giving up on this type of person too quickly, because these customers can often surprise me. I try to be friendly and available, without appearing too eager. What I find is that behind the quiet façade, the wheels are often turning, and this customer is preparing to make a decision about purchasing a product.

> *"Teacher, which is the most important commandment in the law of Moses?" Jesus replied, "'You must love the LORD your God with all your heart, all your soul, and all your mind.' This is the first and greatest commandment. A second is equally important: 'Love your neighbor as yourself.' The entire law and all the demands of the prophets are based on these two commandments."*
>
> —Matthew 22:36-40

Make Each Customer Feel Important

Take a moment, next time you are shopping in some of your favorite stores, to ask yourself what makes this place so special. In my experience it often comes down to the way I am treated. It is the attitude that comes through in the décor and product selection, which feels unique and thoughtfully chosen. It also comes through in the way the salespeople treat me. I absolutely cannot stand it when I walk into a store and the employees are talking with each other rather than trying to help me. I want to say to them, "The person who owns this business is not paying you to talk to each other. She/he is paying you to talk to me who just might buy something if you were to talk to me."

Now think about places where you dislike shopping. What is wrong with those shopping experiences? For me, one thing might be the lack of thought and care that has gone into the store layout, which often conveys an attitude of indifference. The store seems to say that getting rid of their inventory matters much more to them than how a customer feels. The salespeople are often part of the problem, and they reflect the lack of care that the owner has placed on making the customer happy. Instead of engagement and interest, they often seem aloof or annoyed, as if to say, "I don't really care whether you buy anything or not." Have you ever been in a store where the employees were simply folding clothes to get them straightened up rather than helping you? Don't get me started on the store in Huntsville that always had this happening when I entered with my grandchildren to shop. The ONLY reason I ever went into this store was the grandchildren liked the clothes. That store is now closed. If the owner had been in the store he/she might have figured out why! The employees talked with each other and folded those clothes. They never even spoke to a customer until someone practically knocked them down to get the dressing rooms unlocked.

When I opened my first store, I would look each person right in the eye and convey from the inside out how glad I was to see him/her—and I quickly found that this made people feel welcome. People kept coming back! That is why it became extremely important for me to hire employees who had the same inner enthusiasm and the skill of charm to welcome people as they walked through the door. You might ask if this same relationship can be established with an online business. Absolutely yes. When a person registers to receive your email newsletter you can send a personal reply immediately. You can get a phone number and call this person immediately. If you get the cell phone number you can send a text immediately. With a regular email newsletter you can establish this type of relationship as often as you send a newsletter if you make your newsletters personal. I always felt every time I wrote a newsletter that I was personally writing a letter to my best friends. I believe nearly 40,000 people felt that it was a personal letter written to them.

Pretend that every single person you meet has a sign around his or her neck that says, "Make me feel important." Not only will you succeed in sales, you will succeed in life.
— Mary Kay Ash

Step by Step to Get to "Yes"

I follow a specific set of steps when I am working with a customer. There is certainly nothing remarkable in this approach, except that far too few salespeople actually follow them. What I believe makes these steps so effective is that they follow my basic principle of making sure that your entire interaction is focused and oriented around the needs of the customer, and making absolutely sure that the customer feels both welcome and understood.

• Discover the person's needs by asking and following up on their answers. ASK QUESTIONS AND THEN LISTEN TO THE ANSWERS! Believe me the critical word here is LISTEN!!!

- If the product is something like a sewing machine I many times get out a pencil and paper and write down their answers describing their needs and wants in a new sewing machine. I call this "**pencil listening**."
- Be genuinely interested in the other person.
- Small-talk to gather information about her life. Ask about children or grandchildren.
- Share something about your family, church, hunting trips, fishing trips, or other hobbies, but use these as a method to get her talking about herself. Then LISTEN!!
- Be organized in what you want to communicate (your product, concept, idea, etc.).
- Be enthusiastic about what you want to communicate.
- Be confident that yours is the best, but never put down any other product.
- If they bring up "the competition," praise the competition's products and/or ideas. If the customer says that she likes "brand x" also it is a good idea to say, "You have excellent taste. You are looking at two of the best (products) that are made today. Now let me tell you why I like 'my product.'" End the praise by telling them why you think yours is the best and is worthy of their consideration.
- Look the customer in the eye. Never stare at the floor.
- Always tell the customer what an honor it was for you personally and for your business that she came in to look at your products. Give her your home phone number and your email address in case she has questions that arise during hours when your business might be closed.
- Be sure you get her information to write a thank you note thanking her for the visit and inviting her to come back. Always ask if she can be placed on your email newsletter list.

My greatest strength as a consultant is to be ignorant and ask a few questions.

—Peter Drucker

Stay Positive

Do not ever get too discouraged if you are not having luck with sales. A certain amount of resilience is required to be a salesperson. If you take a lost sale personally, you will be feeling bad much more often than you should. On any day, there are guaranteed to be a certain number of people who will not buy from you.

The fact is that your products reflect a certain style and taste. They might not appeal to everyone. Many of my close friends have taste preferences that do not match my own. This is nothing to take personally. On the other hand, if your products do not seem to appeal to anyone, then you need to adapt to the market, and start displaying products that better reflect your customers' taste.

You should always keep in mind that you cannot really control whether someone buys or not. What you can control is your own attitude. For anyone who decides not to buy from you, make sure she/he leaves with a smile on her/his face. Let them know just how much you appreciated the time they took to stop by and chat. Make it abundantly clear that your door is always open for a return visit. Through your gracious attitude, you should make it clear that you realized that she could have gone anywhere, but she decided to visit you.

On the other hand, it is important to recognize that you can always make adjustments to improve your sales. If you find that something is not selling, or you are having a streak of bad luck, you might need to take a closer look at your selling strategy or your products. Your difficulties may be an opportunity to learn something new. Ask for customer feedback whenever you can, and do not be afraid to take a hard look at how you are presenting your products to customers.

The display of your products can make an enormous difference. You often need to help your customers see the beauty of a product. Do not trust that they will see its potential on their own. You need to help them.

I had a close colleague who was having bad luck at a trade show. Her products were simply not selling as well as she hoped. I took one look at her display and saw the problem right away. She had a beautiful assortment, but an overwhelming variety of colors and sizes to choose from. Quite honestly it looked like a mess. Sometimes too many choices are a bad thing. We worked together to simplify her assortment, and by the next morning she sold more products in the first two hours than she had for the whole previous day.

Lastly, you will want to make sure that your own selling style is working. Ask a friend to come in and quietly observe how you interact with your customers. Are you too stiff, too pushy, too friendly? Some insight from a friend might help you adjust your style and allow you to make a better connection with your customers.

No matter what, do not allow yourself to dwell on the negative while you are selling. This is a surefire way to extinguish your enthusiasm, and further decrease your chances in the future. Think about your ideal customer who is still out there somewhere. Remain confident and upbeat, and take the initiative if necessary to make the odds turn in your direction. Always remember that God has a plan in mind for you, and that His direction will lead you on the path to success. Just keep praying and working in God's plan.

If you try, you may not win every time. If you don't try at all, you will never win. Guaranteed.

—Dottie Walters

What Never to Say to a Customer

Never, never, never, never say, "May I help you?" I'll talk more about this later in this section. The way you greet anyone sets the tone for the whole conversation. I always try to address my customers with great joy, instead of treating them like just another opportunity to make another sale. If someone does not appear to be in a rush, there is no need to dive right into business. Take the time to establish a quick connection, and remove any hint of tension around whether that customer is going to purchase or not. When you make it clear that you are not going to push or pressure your customer, it actually makes you appear more successful. Your willingness to engage on a personal level with the customer tells them that creating a connection is just as important to you as making a sale.

My father told me never to ask a question if I were not ready to hear the answer. One of the worst questions you can ask someone in any sort of sales situation is, "May I help you?" Their automatic answer will always be, "No, thanks, I'm just looking." Meanwhile, what the customer is really thinking is "I wish this person would just leave me alone."

Your opening line to a customer should be an invitation to share your enthusiasm. It should give the customer a chance to smile and feel glad that he/she decided to come visit you. Something upbeat and positive about the weather is always a good way to greet a customer. Or a simple "How are you this morning?" is a good starter. You want your customer to feel as if she has just stepped into a warm and inviting place, not somewhere in which she needs to make a decision about spending her money.

If you're lucky enough to be very busy with other customers, you might say, "Welcome to the world of insanity." Everybody laughs when you openly recognize that the place is a bit busy. Here are some other inviting comments to encourage people to stay and look for a while.

- "Please let me know if you have any questions."
- "I really like that scarf."
- "Is it ever going to stop raining?"
- "Isn't this the most beautiful weather?"
- "I am so glad you dropped by to see us today?"
- "Come on in. We have so many pretty new things."
- "I'd like to invite you to look at whatever you like."
- "Please feel free to come in and take a look around."
- "I really like your outfit."
- "You have a beautiful baby."
- "Your little girl has the most beautiful eyes." (Everybody in the world has beautiful eyes; you just need to notice.)
- "Are you having a good day so far?"
- "Well it looks like you've been busy!" (if you notice she is carrying bags from another store)

Kind words are like honey—sweet to the soul and healthy for the body.
— Proverbs 16:24

Magical Phrases of Language

The difference between the right word and the almost right word is the difference between lightning and the lightning bug.
—Mark Twain

A number of years ago, I thought I wanted to be a school counselor. Consequently I enrolled in a graduate course at the University of Georgia. That summer I found out that I have a tendency to talk far too much to be an effective counselor. Nevertheless, some of the skills I learned that summer have been the cornerstone of my success in sales and management.

As I learned in my graduate class, every phrase we utter has a sort of electric charge, which can trigger either negative or positive responses. By the way these phrases are magical whether in the spoken language or the written language. That is because the phrase often communicates an unspoken attitude behind the actual words. Whenever you say something, no matter how neutral you try to be, you are always telegraphing a message that is living between the lines of the actual words you say. Sometimes these messages are obvious, for example, when someone says, "My, it's getting late!" to her dinner guests, everyone knows that she is actually trying to tell them it is time to leave.

Some phrases will trigger positive responses from the listener. These phrases I have come to call my "magic phrases." They immediately establish confidence and trust with people. These phrases often communicate your personal willingness to go the extra mile for the customer.

On the other hand, there are just as many negative phrases that you might hear in either a store setting, a sales situation or business letter, which indicate a general reluctance to make an effort, or reach out and help the customer in any way. They are phrases with a built-in excuse for laziness, and I call them "strikeout phrases" because they guarantee an annoyed or disappointed customer.

Pay close attention to these types of automatic phrases. Many of us repeat them without even thinking. Even more importantly, pay close attention to your own inner attitude with customers. When you catch yourself trying to discourage a customer whom you might consider somehow annoying, stop for a moment and ask yourself why you are allowing yourself to dislike this person. A good business person should always take her customers seriously. Even if what your customer seems to expect from you feels a little "over the top," your job is not to correct that person's point of view. Instead, you should express an attitude that makes it clear how seriously you take her request. Do not allow yourself to be patronizing and find clever ways to use fancy phrases to disguise the fact that you are basically just saying, "No—and please stop bothering me."

Below, I have compiled a few examples of "strikeout phrases," and the negative message that they communicate to your customer, accompanied by a "magic phrase" that communicates the same message without the negative attitude.

Strikeout phrases: Don't say...	Because they hear . . .	Magic phrases: Do say . . .
"I'm sorry, that's all I can do."	*"I'm not interested in making any effort for you!"*	*"Please tell me, what else can I do?"*
"Can I help you?"	*(It makes her think, "I don't know, can you?")*	*"What can I help you find today?"*
"Thank you for holding."	*(They are already annoyed because they had to hold; don't remind them!)*	*"I'm sorry. Thank you for being patient."*
"We can't."	*"We don't want to."*	*"We will."*
"I'll try."	*"I will make it my lowest priority."*	*"I will."*
"I don't know."	*"I don't care."*	*"I will find out."*
"I'm sorry, there is nothing I can do."	*"I'm not sorry. There is nothing I want to do to help you."*	*"Let me find a way to fix this situation."*
"If we have those, they are on the shelf."	*"You are not important to me; go shop someplace else."*	*"Those should be on aisle four. I will show you."*

Magic Phrases for Communicating in Conflict

Keep these phrases close to the surface of your mind so they will be ready when you need them!

- It seems to me . . .
- I am of the opinion . . .
- You might want to consider . . .
- Have you given consideration to . . . ?
- When you do (or say) that, it makes me feel . . .

"It seems to me"

. . . is the first of my magic phrases. When I want someone to really listen to me, I use these words before I make a statement. Remember that facts are not facts to all people. Many times a fact is true only to me and if I want someone to listen to my opinion, I need to preface it with, "It seems to me" rather than, "You know something or the other is true." The words "It seems to me" are not threatening and possibly will cause another person to really hear what I am trying to say.

This phrase relays that you are looking at a statement not in a black-and-white, absolute way but rather in an open way. Even when I want to add, "but you know that this is true," I refrain if I want to have the other individual give consideration to my thinking.

Let me give an example of how a potential customer might react to two different approaches of presenting facts. If the salesperson is trying to sell a Ford automobile, he/she can say, "This is the best automobile in the whole world." If the customer absolutely agrees with him/her, then this statement is a great statement. However, what if the customer is looking at a Ford, a Volvo, and a Chrysler? The statement about the Ford's being the best automobile might not be true for that customer. If the salesperson wants the customer to really listen to his sales presentation about Ford, he/she should say, "It seems to me that Ford is the best made automobile available on today's market, and I would like the opportunity to share with you why I have found this to be true." Now, the customer is not threatened and possibly will want to hear about the Ford and its wonderful features.

Pronouncing "absolute truth" is bad communication in almost any situation but especially in the world of sales and management of other people. "Truth" always says that I am right and that you may be wrong. I believe that both sides lose when this happens. By using "it seems to me," you can pronounce your "truth" without it being seen as anything but your "truth." That way another person might be more inclined to consider your opinion.

"I am of the opinion"

. . . is another one of my magic phrases to be used when one's opinion is stated. One of the greatest turnoffs to me is someone's making a statement such as, "You know that this product is the best one available." Actually, I do not know any such fact, and my thinking might be that another product is absolutely the best one. To state my thinking on a product and to have the customer at least listen to my opinion, I need to state, "I am of the opinion that this product is the very best one for the job." Once again, I have not pronounced "truth" to another person, and he/she might be able to listen to my ideas with an open mind.

"You might want to consider"

. . . is an excellent way of suggesting that an individual look at your product for purchase. Once again, don't say, "You will love this product," because you can't state with certainty that someone will love anything. That is up to the individual purchasing the product to decide.

"Have you given consideration to?"

. . . is another way of using "you might want to consider" but rather stating it in question form, which is one of my favorite ways of selling anything. Answers might vary from, "Well, no, I have not thought of it in that way" to, "Yes, I have thought about it."

"When you do that, it makes me feel"

. . . is another great statement to learn when one wants to have better communication skills. This communicates what a behavior does to a person rather than what the person does to a person. It is a lot easier to accept that my behavior is not pleasing to another than to accept that I am not pleasing to another person. Instead of "Now, that's a dumb thing to do," I would say, "When you do that, it makes me feel that I do not understand what you intended." I have not criticized another's statements or behaviors but rather told how they made me feel. The communication lines are still open, and I have not offended the other person.

Some other magic phrases to ease you through conflict and build bridges are:

- I hear your concern.
- I see what you are saying.
- I understand your point.
- You are right.
- I really had not thought of that.
- Tell me more.
- That is really an interesting idea. I wonder if we might also consider . . .

No matter how busy you are, you must take time to make the other person feel important.

The Most Magical Phrase in Communication

From the time when we were the smallest babies, what words did we like to hear above all others? Why, our own names! Whenever you are trying to build a relationship, learn your customer's name as quickly as possible, and use it often in the conversation. This establishes intimacy quickly, and helps you remember that person's name for next time.

I am always most impressed by stores like Nordstrom where they teach the salespeople to address customers by name. If I have used my charge card or I have written a check, the salesperson tells me, "Thank you, Mrs. Pullen. You have a nice day and come back to Nordstrom." They know enough to read my name off of the check or charge card and to call me by name.

In Europe, there is a custom that one never calls an individual by his or her first name until that person actually gives you his or her first name. In America, we have more leeway to decide. In any situation I think each person must size up what to call customers. My suggestion when it comes to early introductions with people is to always remain polite, and address them using the more formal Mr. or Mrs. until told to do otherwise. When people call me Dr. Pullen or Mrs. Pullen, I quickly say, "Oh, please call me Martha—everybody does."

When I opened my first retail store, I always referred to my older customers as Mrs. (last name). Those customers who were my age or younger, I usually called by the first name. If there were any doubt, I always used Mrs.

In my husband's dental office, he introduced himself to new patients as Joe Pullen. Everyone who comes into that dental office probably already knows that he is Dr. Pullen. He jokingly told me, "Martha I don't need to call myself Dr. Pullen to patients. It would be pretty silly if someone sat down in a dental chair and did not know that I was a doctor." He has always felt that the title Dr. distanced him from his patients. On the other hand, he and his staff referred to their patients as Mr. or Mrs. unless they requested to be called by a first name. Most of his patients usually called him Dr. Joe which he loved best.

> *Let your conversation be gracious and attractive so that you will have the right response for everyone.*
> — Colossians 4:6

Use Questions to Sell

Asking questions is one of the single best selling skills in the world. In the case of selling sewing machines usually there was a feature on the new sewing machine which a customer had heard about that she was interested in. Sometimes there was something about her old sewing machine which she did not like. Without asking questions about her sewing needs I could not guess what she really wanted in a new machine. When you ask questions, you learn more about your customer, so you are better qualified to help her find what she wants. Questions also get the customer involved. They help set the customer at ease, and help her more easily articulate what she is looking for. Lastly, questions are the first step in establishing a relationship with your customer. Your curiosity and interest in the customer creates a connection, and a customer is much more likely to purchase from someone she trusts. So when you are introducing someone to your product, do not just talk about the product—ask questions! It is a great idea to **write down the answers** to the questions so you can refer back to them as you talk about the product.

You can start by asking questions that will open up the conversation. Try these:

- What specifically are you looking for?
- What about your current product does not fit your needs exactly?
- What about your current product do you love?

- What about your current product do you not love?
- Are you looking for a particular color?
- Are you interested in our current specials?
- How might you use _____?
- What have you heard about _____?
- What is it you don't like about _____?
- Would this be useful to you?
- What has been your experience with it before?
- What most interests you about _____?
- How familiar are you with _____?
- What great things have you heard about (our company) or (our product)?
- What brought you in today?
- Where may I direct you?
- How may we be of assistance?
- What could we do to make this work better?

Questions are a great start, but it is equally important to listen. Listening is an art form, and it takes practice. For someone like me, who tends to talk quite a bit, learning the art of listening has required some dedicated practice. I have discovered a set of practices and habits that best define the differences between good and bad listeners. The good news is that if someone like me can become a good listener, than it is well within the power of anyone to master the art.

A bad listener is easy to spot, because whenever anyone is speaking besides herself, she looks busy. Maybe she simply doesn't look the customer in the eye, or else she is scanning the floor to check on her other customers. I can spot a bad listener simply by noticing whether she seems to be preparing a reply, rather than listening to the words of another. A classic sign of a bad listener is interrupting, or talking over someone else. If you exhibit any of these habits, next time you are talking with someone, just try to focus on their words, without worrying what you are going to say next.

In contrast, a good listener pays close attention to the customer's words, and tries to hear the message behind the words. By using gentle questions, the good listener explores what the customer is asking, and repeats back what she has heard. Smiling, nodding in agreement, and establishing eye contact help affirm to the customer that you are understanding her words. By following these basic practices, you will find that customers are more responsive to you, and more likely to listen to your advice.

Conveying Success

Don't ever brag on yourself! Always brag on your employees! If you have won awards in selling please put the plaques up in your business and mention these awards on your newsletter but thank your employees for a job well done. Give other people the credit! Testimonials are great ways to convey your success. Always let other people convey your success never yourself! Enough said!

Having Fun

Your customers should always be having fun. No matter what the setting, you should always look for ways to make the shopping experience enjoyable for your customers. You want your customers at ease, relaxed, and having a good time. Focus on the atmosphere you provide. Throw parties at your store, or leave out something delicious for your customers to nibble on.

Becoming a Legend with G.R.A.C.E.

> *I create the light and make the darkness. I send good times and bad times. I, the Lord, am the one who does these things.*
> — Isaiah 45:7

Now, who is really going to make it big and stay in business? Who is going to become a legend? First one must decide what is a legend. By legend, I believe this is someone who has made a significant contribution in a certain area that brings fulfillment to others' lives. As far as who is going to make it "big" and stay in business I can assure you that is totally up to God.

By now all of you know my business philosophy. **G.R.A.C.E. God** first in all things. God owns all businesses.

> *Our God is in the heavens, and he does as he wishes.*
> — Psalm 115:3

Resilience: Get up when you are down. You conquer by continuing.

> *So think clearly and exercise self-control. Look forward to the gracious salvation that will come to you when Jesus Christ is revealed to the world.*
> —1 Peter 1:13

Action: It is not enough to dream; wake up and work at it!

> *This is my command—be strong and courageous! Do not be afraid or discouraged. For the LORD your God is with you wherever you go.*
> — Joshua 1:9

Creativity: Allow the unusual to happen. It is God who gives us a creative mind and it is OK to use it.

> *And yet, O LORD, you are our Father. We are the clay, and you are the potter. We all are formed by your hand.*
> —Isaiah 64:8

Enthusiasm: Allow the spirit of excitement to fill you and spread to your friends. It is contagious and delightfully enriching.

> *At last the wall was completed to half its height around the entire city, for the people had worked with enthusiasm.*
> —Nehemiah 4:6

~ Chapter Twelve ~

Retail Sales

> *She goes to inspect a field and buys it; with her earnings she plants a vineyard. She is energetic and strong, a hard worker. She makes sure her dealings are profitable; her lamp burns late into the night. Her hands are busy spinning thread, her fingers twisting fiber. She extends a helping hand to the poor and opens her arms to the needy. She has no fear of winter for her household, for everyone has warm clothes. She makes her own bedspreads. She dresses in fine linen and purple gowns. Her husband is well known at the city gates, where he sits with the other civic leaders. She makes belted linen garments and sashes to sell to the merchants.*
>
> —Proverbs 31:16-24

*Continuous effort—not strength or intelligence—
is the key to unlocking our potential.*
—Winston Churchill

*A mediocre idea that generates enthusiasm will go further than a
great idea that inspires no one.*
—Mary Kay Ash

This chapter entitled Retail Sales encompasses a little of everything that I love from retail stores to producing big events to teaching at home which also involves retail selling. Since we have a whole chapter devoted to online business this chapter will explore the more traditional business avenues rather than Internet retail sales. Of course most of these ideas can be used in some manner in an online business also! Traditional retail sales transition very easily to online retail sales.

Enjoy dreaming with me. As you dream however, always remember to go back to the planning section of this book to see whether those dreams can be turned into a WRITTEN plan which can be turned into a business that will be profitable for you.

Lots of hobbyists dream of running her/his own store. As a child, I used to pass many hours either by myself or with my friends pretending to manage a grocery store. Of course, in my make-believe world, I never worried about any of the true costs of running a store. Fixing broken light bulbs, mopping the floor, or repairing a broken skylight never entered into our childhood imaginations.

If you are entertaining the idea of opening a store for your wares, I recommend that you keep firmly in mind that running a store is a business unto itself. The amount of mental and physical labor required simply to keep the store running can quickly overwhelm your hobby work. The list of things to consider is intimidating—rent, utilities like water and electricity, Internet and telephone bills, insurance, and credit card processing fees—and that is just for starters. For that reason, I strongly discourage anyone from opening a "bricks and mortar" store (as opposed to an online store) without first testing the waters through a slightly less risky proposition. Give yourself a little time to understand your market. Someday you will be ready to go forth. You will know what sells and what doesn't, and be in a better position to make an informed risk.

In fact, there are lots of options for selling your products, without needing to open your own store, which we will explore in detail in this chapter.

Pricing

It is worth taking a moment to consider the pricing of your products. In some ways, pricing is easy, because you simply need to set a price that the market will bear. By looking at the competition, you will get an immediate sense of the range that your products should fall within.

On closer scrutiny, however, you may discover that it is not that simple. For one thing, the range of prices may be quite broad, starting quite low for cheaply made, imported products and drifting into very high designer prices. Another problem may be that your products are unique, so it is hard to really compare them to anything else.

You can build your price from the ground up by calculating your base cost and your markup. Consider the time and materials that go into your product. Do not forget to layer in all the overhead costs, like renting a studio, your supplies and packaging. Next you will want to figure your wholesale rate, which is the price for which you would sell your products to another retail store. This should be enough of a markup to let you cover your base cost, plus the time and materials to make another product. Do not forget that the retailer will be marking it up as well.

Remember that your pricing can scale to the amount you plan to sell. If you have the chance to sell lots of products all at once, you can afford to lower your markup. Finally you should calculate your own retail rate, which is the cost at which you would sell your products directly to a customer. This should be higher than your wholesale rate, but perhaps a bit lower than another retailer's markup.

A lot of pricing is about perception. If you can create a glamour and appeal around your product through its marketing and packaging, people will be willing to pay a higher price. Customers have figured out that they get what they pay for. More and more people are willing to pay a little more for beautiful, handmade products that last a lifetime. Be careful not to start with too low a price, which attempts to undercut the competition, but may lower the perceived value of your product.

Setting Class Fees

We certainly have to talk about pricing classes here also for those of you who are going to have a business teaching classes. First I suggest calling other stores in the area or going on line to see what other comparable stores are charging for classes. You have to figure in the cost of your kits or supplies if you are going to use supplies. If your classes are going to be lecture/demo there might not be supplies. Do a little research to discover what is a fair price if you are a beginning teacher. As you become more in demand you will be able to command higher prices for your classes as well as have more students in your class which of course means more profit for you. Many of our teachers have taught their first classes for only one student. Did they make much money for that one student? Absolutely not but if the class were taught well and the student had fun inevitably she told others that they had to go take a class from "so and so" and the future classes filled quickly. Always start somewhere.

Selling in Stores

Once you have figured out your pricing strategy, and prepared all your marketing materials and packaging, you're ready to start selling! As we covered in Chapter Eight, creating an online store or using an online platform like Etsy is a fantastic way to expose and sell your products. You can complement this channel with old-fashioned retail sales, by getting your products in someone else's store.

The first step is to research where your products might be best presented. This is a fun step because it allows you to do some competitive browsing, and gives you and excuse to visit lots of retail stores. Your objective is to try to find places where the products and personality of the store match your own sensibilities. Pick a day and time when the store will be busy, and spend some time in the store, closely observing the customers and what they purchase.

Do not be afraid to travel a little. Obviously it will be easiest to find a local store and start getting some sales and building your reputation through them. If you can't quite find a match for yourself in your hometown, you should travel to neighboring towns and check out their stores. Eventually, as your products become more established, you can even begin to build broader relationships with stores in different states.

Make a list of the stores that best matched your products, and order them by preference. Many stores will want exclusivity on your products in their local market, so you should always target your favorite stores first. Call each store and introduce yourself. Set up a meeting with the store manager. Most retail stores are interested in seeing new products, so they should welcome the opportunity.

For your appointment, you should be ready to bring some samples and a set of marketing materials, including pricing information, that you can leave behind. Be prepared to sell your own story, as much as the products. Don't be surprised if the manager does not want to make a decision right away.

You can expect your conversation to turn around some common topics. The manager will be most interested in how well your products have sold in the past, and under what circumstances. She will also want to know if they are currently being sold in other stores or online. Of course, you will want to discuss your pricing. You should be prepared to offer volume discounts if the store plans to purchase a large number of products. Keep in mind that some stores may operate by consignment, which means that they are offering to display your products in their store in exchange for splitting a significant portion of the sale price with you, which can run anywhere from 30% to 50%. A consignment check is usually issued monthly.

I might issue a word to the wise here. Things can get stolen from a store. In your written arrangement I would definitely state that if by some chance the garment or product should disappear the full wholesale cost of the product will be paid to you. My suggestion also is that your things, if they are items of clothing, be hung so high that they can just be looked at not handled. If someone is really interested then it can be taken down. If your consignment items are heirloom flower girl dresses or christening dresses you really don't want them handled unless the shop keeper is there with them. This is only smart business with very expensive consignment items. Be certain you photograph the items you are leaving in the store preferably in the spot where they will be displayed or with the shop's owner holding them for display.

If the store is interested in your products, and wants to carry them, you will need to create a written agreement that covers the details of your arrangement, which can be supplied by the store. Be sure that you discuss important subjects like how returns will be handled, as well as how your products will be displayed and promoted. Don't ever feel pressured into an arrangement. The deal has to work for both sides, and you have the right to walk away and think about it. You can also influence how you would like your products to be presented in the store. It will not do you much good to sell your products exclusively through a store that hides them in the corner, so make sure you discuss their display.

Cooperatives and Partnering

Two variations on the classic retail store present excellent alternatives for hobby sales. The first is to join a cooperative store, in which many different producers join together to share the overhead costs of a retail space. The benefits are obvious—by joining a cooperative, you become part of a larger hobby community that will draw all sorts of customers. Cooperatives usually require a fee to join. You will be allotted a certain section of the retail space, where you can create your own "mini-store" to display your products. In exchange for membership in the cooperative, you may be asked to help out by staffing the shop occasionally, or helping to maintain the premises.

The second possibility is to find a partner who wants to open a store in a similar or complementary line of products. This allows each partner to split his or her expenses. I have seen a beautiful children's clothing store in California, where the back corner of the store is rented out as an open studio for another woman who creates handmade children's dolls and clothing. She is often creating something during business hours. It is the most delightful store, because it allows mothers to shop for lovely clothing for their children, while the kids are either being entertained by a doll-making lesson or looking for doll outfits. I would add here quickly that I think partnerships only work if each partner has her/his own business and only shares space. Trying to intertwine money and decision making usually does not work. Sharing space and rent and utilities just might work very well.

Trunk Shows and Pop-Up Stores

There are several alternatives to selling your products through a classic retail store. One option is to organize trunk shows. Trunk shows can happen anywhere. I have heard of trunk shows being organized within an existing store, after normal business hours, or else at homes. The trick with a trunk show is making sure that you announce it broadly and invite as many people as possible. You should work closely with your host to organize the arrangements. The two of you can create a warm and welcoming environment. Your host can be responsible for food and drinks, and you should be certain that you can display, package and sell your products. A few of my friends have done very well taking their trunk shows on the road, and spending several weeks visiting all their friends across the country, while putting on trunk shows at each of their friends' homes.

A popular variation on the trunk show is the "pop-up store." In this arrangement, you briefly lease an unrented space and set up a temporary shop. There is no deep investment in your overhead, and you can quickly walk away from the space. The drawback is that you must make a great effort to let your customers know where you are before you disappear again.

This "pop-up store" concept is happening more and more with selling slightly used clothes. I believe there are even computer programs teaching how to price the garments and run these shows. I know about a young woman who rents an old armory several times a year, has all of her friends bring their slightly used children's clothes in already priced and computer taged, and the business is brisk. It is all checked out on the computer and the checks are delivered to the owners of the used clothes and all do well. Mostly the lady who organizes this huge event does well. This is a great hobby based business. You might research consignment shop software to find options if you should want to consider this seriously.

A third option is to sell from your home. In this case, you should be careful that you are not violating zoning laws. Keep in mind, however, that even if your zoning laws do not allow a home retail business of this type, you might be able to have samples and take orders from home. You can arrange with your suppliers to ship the product directly to your customers. Some very famous people brought their hobby to profit by starting in their own homes. Henry Ford started in his garage. Mrs. Knotts started her jams and Estee Lauder her cosmetics, all from the comfort of their homes.

I guess the most famous business ever to start with home parties is Mary Kay. She built a whole industry on them. Another very successful home party company was Stanley Home products. My Aunt Bessie earned her living with very successful Stanley parties all over Jackson County in the 1950s. Stanley had fabulous products and her customers were very loyal to her.

Craft Fairs and Trade Shows

I have noticed a revival of craft fairs in the past few years. Lots of young people are turning their hobbies into businesses, and using these craft fairs to sell their lovely products. From antiques to teddy bears to stamps, from woodcarvings to painted items, from baseball cards and toys to art, a craft show is one of the best forums for any type of hobby-related business. People love the festive and eclectic feeling of craft shows.

Trade shows are slightly more structured and professionally oriented, but present just as many opportunities for you to present your wares. I have known plenty of hobby-based businesses that have built their entire business plan around selling their products through the annual cycle of major trade shows.

The rules of the game are pretty similar for any of these types of shows. You reserve and pay for a booth or a space within the show. You will be sent passes and various instructions about the set up and breakdown of your stand.

It takes a lot of work and effort to attend a craft show, so try to choose the best ones you can. Use the Internet to discover the best ones. Follow popular blogs. Talk to local crafts people or ask around among friends or colleagues. Join online communities and post your question to the group. Contact your local Chamber of Commerce concerning all the shows in your area

Some shows are hard to get into, so you will want to reserve your booth space early. Ask the organization people which are the best booths for traffic and placement. If booths are offered in various sizes, I would not recommend taking too large a booth for your first time. I believe that it is better to try several shows in a small space and see which ones are most profitable rather than to spend all of your money on a big booth at the first show you try.

You may, in fact, want to simply attend the craft show as a customer for your first time. It will give you the opportunity to observe how people present their products, and what are some of the most successful strategies for drawing business. Don't be afraid to talk to people and ask questions. Explain that you are interested in starting a business and strike up a conversation. I have found that the hobby community is very open and welcoming, and always happy to help others.

For your first show, do not feel that you need to have a large inventory of products to sell. If you have samples, you can just take orders and ship the products to any interested customers. In such cases, make sure that you receive payment (or a substantial deposit) from the customer, you are very clear about the expected delivery date, and you write everything down on a receipt for both parties.

Tips for a Successful Show

We have sold very well at most shows, even those with low attendance, and I am certain it is because we followed some of these guidelines.

Use Giveaways

Give something away at your booth. It can be as simple as a nice piece of marketing content, like a postcard, with some interesting content on the back: recipes, instructions for making something, anything crafty! When people get home and look at your material, some of them will follow up, and perhaps visit your website if you have one.

Create a Mailing List from Attendees

Create a prominent email and snail-mail list at your booth for those who would like to receive your newsletter, catalog, or other mailings. Add these people to your mailing list as soon as you return, with a note about how you acquired her/his name. Thank that person in an email for signing up, to reinforce your personal touch.

Teaching Opportunities

Research if there are seminars or other teaching opportunities at the craft show where you can teach. Presenting at a seminar gives you great exposure. When I am able to speak in a seminar, I can sometimes address up to 250 attendees at one time. Many of these people walk right out of the presentation and into my booth to buy. I pass around a legal pad for an email list for each person to sign if they would like to be on my email mailing list. If you have a large crowd start that legal pad early in the seminar. It takes a while for people to sign up and pass to the next one. If giving a lecture is not possible consider finding ways to offer brief presentations from your booth during off hours. I have seen successful "in booth" presentations "go on" all day long drawing a crowd of people the whole day watching a great presentation. Giving "in booth" presentations all day long is VERY HARD WORK but it is very effective. For instance we have done lace shaping demonstrations all day long and kept a crowd of people at our booth when many vendors only had what they call "tire kickers" come by and look and walk on by their booths without paying much attention. You don't want "tire kickers" at your booth but interested people who learn something and truly get to "know" you a little bit.

Dress Appropriately

When you are at a show, your first impression makes a difference. I have been to shows where the dealers' clothing and hair were dirty, they smelled bad, and they had on worn-out blue jeans. Obviously these things are not good. Take the time to look your best. It will be a long day, so bring along a toothbrush or other such toiletries so you can refresh yourself when you have a free moment. Even if most of the attendees wear blue jeans and sweats to the show I suggest you wear beautiful clothes, look fashionable and appear stylish.

Smile and Enjoy Yourself

A big, beautiful smile spreads joy. Smile at everybody who comes by and say a little pleasantry, such as, "It looks like you've shopped until you dropped." Smile at all of your customers while they are in the booth. Only if there are no customers nearby should you lower your standards of "booth etiquette" and allow yourself to sit down. If any customers are passing by, be on your feet to speak the inviting comments or just to say, "How are you today?" Stand up and walk over to greet any customer. I find that it is fatal to sales if we sit on our backsides without greeting someone who is looking at our products. If there is a chair in your booth please offer it to the customer who comes by to rest a few minutes. Usually it is a very welcomed little rest for those who have been walking the floor for hours. It also gives you a chance to get to visit with a potential customer for a few minutes. It is just plain good manners.

Never Complain!

Laugh and the world laughs with you; weep and you weep alone.
—Edna Wilcox

Don't complain about anything. Don't say, "I'm so tired I could drop," or "I'm glad this is the last day. I'm about dead," or "I wish six o'clock would come soon," or "I wonder why the promoters didn't advertise this show better. There are no customers here."

Complaining and griping have no place in any business setting. Leave your personal problems at home and smile no matter how you feel. Don't tell anyone how stressful the show has been.

For anyone who asks, tell them it's been a great show. Nothing is less interesting than gripers and complainers who whine because they didn't get rich during this show. Whether you sell something or not, you have learned very valuable lessons, and probably gained some great contacts. If you have sold nothing you can still answer when someone asks how the show has been, "It has been great! I don't think I have ever met such nice people. I have also made some fabulous contacts that I cannot wait to follow up on. It has been truly great."

Thank Everybody

Thank everybody for their business and comment on what good choices they have made. Tell them that you believe they will enjoy their products and tell them where your name and address can be found in the materials they have just obtained in case they have further questions about the product. Be sure they have your business card, which of course has your website listed! Your best customers probably should be given your home phone also. I have almost never had a customer call me at home; however, it is a great way to let your customers know how much you value them.

I have a cute story to tell you. I have been to Australia 28 times now to teach sewing. I always gave the ladies, yes in Australia, my home phone also. One morning very early, say about 2 a.m., the phone rang. I fumbled and answered the phone, "Hello." On the other end was the sweetest voice of one the lovely Australian ladies that I had met on my last trip down under saying, "Hello, Martha. My name is Dianne, do you remember me?" What could I say since I was hardly awake and I had met about 1000 people on that trip? I said, "I think I do, Dianne how are you?" "Fine," she replied. "Martha I know you said you would help me with any sewing question I had and I absolutely love this puffing wedding dress in the *Sew Beautiful* magazine that I bought from you. It is on page 88 of Issue _(something). Can you tell me how that puffing was made? I have never made puffing and I want to make that wedding dress for my daughter." Now I was awake. I fully realized that I did not have any issue of *Sew Beautiful* beside my bed. I did have a paper and pencil beside my bed. So I said, "Dianne I would love to take your telephone number and tomorrow morning I will get in touch with the lady who made that dress and have her call you with all of the details. I am sure she would love so much to help you. I, by the way, love that dress too. And thank you for coming to my workshops in Sydney. And be sure to come to Huntsville when you can." She said, "Thank you Martha." We hung up. The next day I did indeed have the designer of the dress call her to help her with the construction details of making that gorgeous dress. I paid for the international phone call of course. So do not be sure who will and won't call you when you give people your home phone!

Packaging

It seems silly to mention, but sellers often forget that they will be selling a product that needs a bag in which to send it home. This is poor business. We always have extra bags in case someone else has not provided a bag. Use your bag, and any other packaging, as a marketing opportunity—put your name, logo, website, business address on it. If you don't want to go to the expense of printing custom bags at least get some of those "Thank You" bags at a business supply place.

Producing the Big Event

We have been extremely successful by creating a celebrity event—The Martha Pullen School of Art Fashion. We have about 220–300 people at one of these four-day events. We have produced other celebrity events called Extravaganzas in the past. You can apply this "big event" concept to your business whether your business is a bicycle shop, a bakery, a construction company, a real estate agency, a physician's office, a dress shop, or any other type of business. Once again, this big event is a hands-on, educational experience. The formula is as follows:

- Create an event, with at least one celebrity to pull in attendance.
- Get the best teachers, preferably authors.
- Have lesson plans required by all teachers.
- Get the schedule ready.
- Be well organized.
- Make it personal.

Details for a Big Event

Usually we do events on Thursday, Friday, Saturday, and Sunday. As an added personal touch, we have an optional Sunday school early on Sunday morning for all those who would like to attend.

The following "how-to" information for a four-day big event can be used for any number of people, and you divide the people into four sections.

Teachers/Celebrities
- Getting four celebrity teachers is fairly easy and not too expensive. "Celebrity" in many industries means someone who has written a book or been published in magazines or taped a video.
- You might use two celebrity teachers and two excellent local teachers. However, hiring celebrity teachers usually is better than hiring local teachers. We have had a funny statement in the sewing industry that says you have to cross the Mississippi River to become an expert.
- Have a teacher contract drawn up so both of you can sign it.
- Cover things such as teaching fee per day, meal per diem allowed and how it will be paid, transportation to and from the airport, who will pick up your teacher and return him/her to the airport, and having the teacher give the hotel a personal credit card upon arrival so the teacher can cover all expenses not covered under your arrangement, and other things which you will not be paying for. Many contracts cover dress code for teachers for the event.

Hotel or Convention Facility
- Get a hotel or other venue that will handle your classes as well as your lunch and dinner meals, if you choose to include meals in your event.
- Usually a hotel will give you discounted teaching rooms if you have at least one meal a day in the facility. Bargain and look around for hotels or conference centers.
- Negotiate with your hotel for discounted lodging rooms for a certain number of student rooms rented.
- Check on security for your rooms from the hotel. We leave sewing machines in the rooms, so we can't be lax about security.
- Know who will have the teaching room keys at all times.
- We prefer to use average-priced hotels or convention centers.

Electricity and Audio Visual Equipment
- You must know the electricity requirements that your teachers and students will need. Check with the hotel electricians to be sure the electricity is adequate. We do sewing seminars, so we need electrical outlets for each person to have a sewing machine as well as a light. I might add that sewing seminars require irons that pull a lot of

electricity. Knowing the exact amount of electricity that each piece of equipment pulls is critical. Getting that information to the engineering staff of the venue before the event starts is even more critical. We had a large event in a conference room in a large condo building in Orange Beach, Alabama where we had to pay to have electricity added to the room before the event.

- Work with the audio equipment people to have things such as screens, microphones, laptops, overhead projectors, Power Point projectors, or shades on the windows for correct lighting all properly planned. These things must be in proper working order. Two times I have arrived on Saturday morning for a major fashion show and slide show, and the projector light bulb was burned out.

Pre-Event Promotion

- You have to let your prospective students know well in advance about the event.
- I think planning a big event at least a year in advance is advantageous. This gives people a chance to plan their schedules and to plan for the cost of the event.
- Advertise in your usual places. Internet is certainly best now. Rent email lists.
- Get brochures ready to email.
- Snail mail brochures to selected lists.
- Snail mail postcards to selected lists.
- Create a website page and email information in your newsletter. Your newsletter is one of the best places to inform people of the exciting event that is coming up.
- Get a deposit of at least one-fourth on the event admission to hold someone a place. Be specific about refunding a deposit and when you will refund the deposit. Have a computer program of some type for entering the people and their deposits. Clearly state the date when the rest of the tuition will be charged. No refunds will be made after that date. It is better to collect whole tuition at first if possible.
- Send out reminders and happy news about the event to inform them what supplies to bring, about the discounts you will offer while they are there, and anything else you would like to tell them. This keeps them excited and wanting to tell their friends about the event.

Insurance

- Check with your business insurance to see if it covers events like this in a hotel for personal injury and other possible events. Your business agent must be given details and dates of all of your outside events. You need a written contract with your agent stating what is covered in an outside event and where the event will be located.
- Check with your hotel or facility about their insurance coverage in the event of an accident. You and your hotel or civic center should have some written understandings about their hotel coverage of your guests.
- Do not transport business guests in personal vehicles unless they are insured specifically under the business policy.
- It is good to state that all personal equipment will be the personal liability of the owner. We tell students to insure equipment (sewing machines, computers, etc.) on their home owners policy before bringing it to an event.

Classes

- We run our classes from nine to twelve and from two to five.
- We have scheduled breaks in the morning and afternoon.
- The teachers need good lesson plans if these classes are hands-on.
- Kits need to be ready and neat.
- Room lighting needs to be good.
- Tables need to be adequate for the projects if the projects are hands-on.
- All supplies need to be either in the kit or available to buy in the store.
- We send supply lists to the students several weeks before the classes.

Retail Store in the Hotel

- You need to sell things during "off hours" while the students are with you for the event.
- We use a teaching room in the hotel or a suite with the furniture moved out to set up a retail store.
- Always give the largest discounts that you can possibly afford to give when the students are there. Remember people love to buy while they are at events and have this hobby on their minds. People love discounts.

Lunch Activities

- We give door prizes at lunch.
- Getting everyone's name into a bag is easy. Either run them off from

your computer student list or get everyone to sign in the first day on a little slip.

- Draw from the same bag each day so one person will not get more than one door prize.
- If there is to be a grand prize on the last day, get another bag with everyone's name in the bag.

Other Evening Event Possibilities

- A tabletop clinic is a fun night where teachers, as well as other business people, present a tabletop demonstration of many different types. We usually have a potato/salad buffet bar for the evening meal. Students just walk around from table to table and learn something from each demonstration. I got this idea from dental conventions.
- I use a combination power point and fashion show for my evening large group presentations. Fashion shows can be done with things other than clothing. People can walk with the latest in equipment and simply have a microphone narration about the new product. We have had sewing machine fashion shows where the machine was carried while the commentary was going on about the new product. These are fun and very unusual. Vendors at shows have walked with other new products including fabric paints, new cutting mats, lots and lots of zippers, blank articles for embroidery—the list goes on.
- Students love to participate in evening "show and tells," whether it is in "modeling" or in a "drag and brag" time. It is fun to include students' work in the evening fashion shows.

Banquet Night

- Banquets are fun and festive even if you don't have entertainment such as a fashion show.
- Don't plan on a band and dancing if you just have women or men in attendance. Besides, bands are expensive. I once went to a large sewing machine consumer convention banquet with a fabulous band. Nearly all of the attendees were women! I was asked to lead the women in the bunny hop and other "line dances" since there were no men for dancing! We had a wonderful time but it was a little peculiar to have a big dance planned with only women there!! Mostly we sat at the tables and talked while enjoying the music of a wonderful band. That was fun too.

Teaching to Sell

If you are talented enough to be selling your beautiful products, chances are good that lots of people would be very interested in learning from you. Teaching is a great method to increase your reputation as an authority, market your products, and open up immediate opportunities for direct sales. When I opened my store, I immediately realized that teaching could increase my sales.

People who learn a new skill are immediately excited to learn more and immerse themselves in the hobby. They will love the opportunity to own something made by their teacher. They will be equally excited by the prospect of pursuing their own projects. If you can show them your own products, or even the specialized supplies they will need, it is almost certain that your students will purchase from you after class. It is really fun for me to teach sewing. Many people love to teach their hobbies and by the way teaching has become a GREAT business for many people.

In-Store Teaching

One of the best places to teach will be an existing store. It's a "win-win" because the store owner will draw more customers into the store, and you will have the chance to expose your talent and your products to a larger base of customers.

The best sort of arrangement will combine the store's theme with an actual workshop in the back. I have seen, for example, a store full of fine stationary and other writing and printing products. In the back of the store is a full letterpress workshop, where customers can come and learn the art of letterpress printing. The store has become a hub for all types of hobby activities, and the workshop has expanded to include scrapbooking and papermaking classes.

If you can find a store whose products match your own hobby interests, perhaps you can convince them to allow you to teach classes either during store hours, or after hours. As you work out the terms of your arrangement, be very careful and clear about how you will sell your own products while in the store. Perhaps the store will simply carry them directly.

No matter what your final arrangement, you must be totally loyal and supportive of everything the store sells. Once a fabric store owner said to me, "Martha, I have a wonderful smocking teacher in my store, but we are not selling any smocking machines. Is that common?" Upon further investigation, the owner found that the teacher was asking her students to purchase smocking machines directly from her at a cheaper rate. That teacher not only lost her job, but she earned a reputation that extended throughout the state, thanks to that store owner's extensive network. The teacher would have done much better to renegotiate her contract with the store to include a commission for her on each machine sold.

Share-the-Gate Classes

Another teaching option is to create "share-the-gate" classes. In a share-the-gate arrangement, you supply the program. The sponsor provides the hall, refreshment breaks, advertising, their list of prospects, postage, printing, and sometimes travel expenses. Usually the sponsor organization will sell the tickets. Often, you will be allowed to sell products at the back of the room. The usual arrangement is a fifty-fifty split of the gate, although different organizations work at various percentage levels.

Before you approach any business or organization, you will want to have an appropriate lesson plan and a flyer that details what your program will cover. Bring a current resumé with references from past classes if possible. If you have never taught anything, then use personal references. Make an appointment to see the director and make your pitch.

To identify share-the-gate opportunities, look for any business or association that might want to increase their visibility, or offer something interesting to their community. Some examples might be:

- Colleges
- Churches
- PTAs
- Parks and recreation departments
- School booster clubs
- Hospitals
- Chambers of Commerce
- Service clubs (Rotary, Kiwanis, Lions, etc.)
- On-line seminar classes
- Associations

If you manage to book a share-the-gate class, you should do some preliminary research on the space where you will be teaching and plan your class in advance. Check ahead about supplies that might be needed, including electrical outlets, tables, chairs, easels, or whiteboards. Look into their liability insurance coverage for teachers in the event of an accident. Find out if you can sell materials on the premises to your students, and how students will get supplies in general. You may want to discuss whether there will be a materials charge to every student as the price of entry, so that you can supply the necessary materials to students when they arrive.

Teaching from Home

Although I briefly mentioned teaching classes from your home earlier in the book I would like to go into much more detail in this section. There are MANY important issues to consider very very carefully if you decide to teach at your home. Teaching in one's home is really not the place I recommend most highly for teaching a hobby. There are many reasons which I will try to list below. If you can handle the influx of students into your house, teaching your hobby directly from your home might be a good way to begin teaching. You will quickly start to learn what works and what doesn't in a teaching environment through the feedback of your students. There are many red flags to investigate before even thinking seriously about teaching in your home.

I have to add before I talk about the actual teaching some words of advice. In today's world one simply cannot be too careful about anything. First you must check with your zoning to see if you are zoned to teach in your home. I know piano teachers are usually zoned to teach one piano student. One sewing or painting student might be allowed but more than one might not. You must check with zoning before taking another step at all. If you are in a zoned area that allows teaching one or more students in your home then you are ready to do further investigation into other very critical issues.

Before bringing students into your home I would personally get about an hour of your attorney's time to go over the legal questions of having business guests in your home. If you plan to teach children's classes this is even more critical. I personally would never advise teaching a children's class in a home without an adult assistant or a parent present. In other words do not bring children into your home without two adults present at all times! If you cannot afford to pay an assistant usually a parent will assist. I suggest you might give her child free classes for her time to be your assistant.

If you do decide to teach at home, you will want to establish some clear ground rules for both you and your students. It is OK to create a relaxed atmosphere, but remember that you must rise to a certain level of professionalism if you are charging for classes.

Get the email address of everyone who signs up, so that you can send them a confirmation and introduction to the course, where you can include start and end times, rules, needed materials, safety tips, important phone numbers, anything they might need to know. You will want to charge your students in advance for the classes, perhaps as a block of classes, and make it clear that you do not offer refunds for missed classes. This is very important that they pay for the class and the kit at the time they sign up. If they call saying someone is sick or something has come up, here is your answer. "I am so sorry about this emergency. You remember on my contract it stated that no refunds would be made but I can transfer your tuition to the next available class. Your kit is available for you to pick up." Do not start refunding class fees or about half your class will have a last minute excuse not to come. Whether valid or not you must realize that you have planned on this income and have planned your time and your business to run this class. Be firm from the beginning. This is the only way to run a teaching business that will be a business not a toy.

Make sure that you have all your supplies out when your students arrive, and plan to start classes promptly. When the classes have begun, take care to eliminate all possible disturbances. All cell phones must be off— yours and all of your students. If you have young children at home they must have baby sitters. It is unprofessional to have your children present in the classroom unless they are older and can indeed assist in the sewing classes. I have certainly seen older teens who were excellent assistants. Some students will want to hang around long after the lesson is over. One way to discourage this is to offer a private consulting rate after class time is up in the information worksheet that you send. This helps students understand that your time is not free, and it is less rude than simply forcing them out the door. Your initial contract might say, "The class time is from 6-8 p.m. We will start and end promptly at these times. If you would like more time I am available at $65 an hour for private consulting. For this consulting time you will need to inform me in advance of the lesson." I cannot emphasize enough how you need to put everything in writing before the students arrive. Then there are no misunderstandings.

Lastly, be sure to consult your homeowner's policy or your insurance agent to clarify your liability for business guests in your house. You may even want to layer in "release from liability" language into your application form that students fill out to purchase the course. Perhaps you might think I have gone into too much detail about the legality of teaching in your home. I assure you I have not. I am not a lawyer and I cannot offer legal advice. I truly think you need legal advice before teaching in your home. I have not even covered issues here that you need in your contract for teaching in your home especially concerning children's classes. Included need to be that children will not go into any rooms other than teaching room and restroom. In closing this section probably I want to say that I really do not advise teaching in a home. With that being said, I know that many people do have successful classes in their homes. The ones that I know have followed all of the legal and safety rules and have all of the bases covered.

Tips for Making Classes Fun and Successful

[The Golden Rule]
Do to others whatever you would like them to do to you. This is the essence of all that is taught in the law and the prophets.
—Matthew 7:12

- Give everyone an A+ for her/his grade! I give this A+ before the class begins because all of my students are A+ students!
- Tell the students there are no mistakes in your class. Only "holidays." What they call "mistakes" are only opportunities to learn what they might not have had the chance to learn.
- Assure everyone at the beginning of the class that no one in the class rode a bicycle the very first time he/she got on the bicycle and it might take a little bit of practice getting your class to his/her level of perfection. Assure them that you will consider their work perfect even if they don't! Everyone has to start somewhere and you are so happy they started with your class.
- Thank them for trusting you as their teacher.
- Tell them it is an honor to have them as a student.
- If possible show them your very first project. Especially if it were horrible! Let them know that you know all about "holidays" since you have made every mistake that there is to make! I always assure them

that I still do make mistakes all the time!
- Assure everyone right as the class begins that she is going to graduate!
- Have a beautiful graduation certificate for everyone. These are easily found on the Internet or you can draw up one for yourself.
- Have a graduation ceremony to present the certificates at the end of the class It is really fun to actually sing the graduation song and have each student come to the front as the rest of the class sings the song. Make a picture of each student receiving her/his award/certificate.
- If possible plan your graduation class around a meal. Each person could bring a sack lunch or you could make some soup by opening cans and heating in a crock pot. If a meal is not possible bring purchased cookies or something for the graduation ceremony. Remember do not serve homemade food in a business setting. Health laws do not allow homemade food for customers in any business setting. You only have to call your local health department to verify this. I remember all of those years I cooked homemade food for my students! I was violating all health laws and did not even know it. I do not do that anymore.
- Have a candy bowl in the classroom. Some teachers think everyone works better with candy kisses available.
- Have coffee or at least ice water to drink. Do not allow drinks at the table where the projects are being made. Drinks can be placed on the floor or enjoyed in another location.
- Serve a package of peanut butter crackers or purchased cookies for breaks. Fruit is always a great snack.
- Save time each day for "What I loved best about today's class!" from each student.
- Save time at the end of each class for "What I thought I could not do but I did!" from each student.
- Have some kind of written evaluation at end of class allowing students to tell you what they enjoyed best about the whole class and how the class could have been improved. Read them very carefully and try to implement the suggestions for the next class.
- If the students will give you their consents use these evaluations in a testimony book for your teaching.

Explore Your Options

There are so many options for selling your hand made products. Don't be afraid to explore a variety of them. The first options I suggest for today's world are Etsy stores or eBay. Getting a website is fabulous. I also know everyone is not interested in a computer based business! There are many traditional ways of building a business. Experiment with a trunk show, open a booth at a craft fair, or try giving a class. Many individuals who sell gorgeous christening dresses rent booths at elegant bridal fairs and baby fairs. Each effort will bring its own reward. You will learn more about your customers and your market niche. You will broaden your network of contacts. The diversity of feedback you will get from each event will help you refine your business plan and strengthen your brand. Every new lesson brings a richer level of professional experience to your business. Please, please please don't forget to make a WRITTEN plan before doing any of the above! You need to plan what will work and what will not work before investing time and money into your business no matter how large or how small.

The reward for work well done is the opportunity to do more.
—Jonas Salk

When you get into a tight place and everything goes against you, till it seems as though you could not hang on a minute longer, never give up then, for that is just the place and time that the tide will turn.
—Harriet Beecher Stowe

A business absolutely devoted to service will have only one worry about profits. They will be embarrassingly large.
—Henry Ford

Taste and see that the LORD is good. Oh, the joys of those who take refuge in him!
—Psalm 34:8

Chapter Thirteen

Leading Others

> *After washing their feet, he put on his robe again and sat down and asked, "Do you understand what I was doing? You call me 'Teacher' and 'Lord,' and you are right, because that's what I am. And since I, your Lord and Teacher, have washed your feet, you ought to wash each other's feet. I have given you an example to follow. Do as I have done to you. I tell you the truth, slaves are not greater than their master. Nor is the messenger more important than the one who sends the message. Now that you know these things, God will bless you for doing them."*
>
> —John 13:12-17

Take away my people, but leave my factories,
And soon grass will grow on the factory floor.
Take away my factories, but leave my people,
And soon we will have a new and better factory!

—Andrew Carnegie

Still the question recurs "can we do better?" The dogmas of the quiet past are inadequate to the stormy present. The occasion is piled high with difficulty, and we must rise with the occasion. As our case is new, so we must think anew, and act anew.

—Abraham Lincoln

With God's blessings, your success will quickly make your time very scarce. You will find yourself overwhelmed with work, and struggling to keep up with demand. There will come a point when you will realize that your time has become too valuable to do everything. That is the moment when you should start considering your options for hiring and leading others.

As I discovered very early in my career, one of the greatest secrets of business success is the ability to identify, hire, and motivate other people. No single person has ever built a successful business without others. As John Donne put it, "No man is an island." Teamwork and collaboration are one of the foundations to any effort.

Martha Pullen Company today is built on the work of an outstanding group of people. We are blessed with a great team. God has sent certain people to us who do more than they are asked. They say, "I can," not "I'm just too busy." They uplift others on the team. They create new ideas for the company and help implement them. They are polite to others on the team and to consumers. They are positive thinkers, not gripers. Our team reminds me of the words of Vince Lombardi, coach of the Green Bay Packers, who said, "The achievements of an organization are the result of the combined efforts of each individual."

Hiring and Interviewing

If you hire good people, you can delegate. I hired the best accounting people inside my business and the best accounting firm outside my business. I need to know the big picture about our finances each month and perhaps each week. I depend on the team to make good decisions and to bring me into it when I'm needed or for necessary major changes. I always keep up with sales by the month and major financial challenges.

Other than that, I just check monthly for sales, trends, and other details that interest me. For the rest, I rely on a wonderful team that tracks cost and quality at all times.

Hiring someone is an important decision. Mistakes can be costly in time and money. I have learned from experience that it is worth following some guidelines during the interview process.

- When you are hiring someone, always get the opinion of others. Even if you do not have any other employees, ask a friend to help you evaluate this candidate. Check references carefully. I depended on Joe's interview skills early in the business.

- Be entirely clear in your mind what type of person you are looking for. Take the time to create a qualifications checklist before you hire someone. This will help you determine areas in which the applicants are strong and weak.
- Your initial impression of the candidate is critical, especially in situations like sales, customer service, and management where a great deal of interpersonal interaction is the mainstay of the position. Remember, your customers will be making the same quick judgment.
- Let your candidate talk. Don't get so excited talking about your business that you don't listen to the applicant. You need to find out about her/him; he/she doesn't need to know much about you yet.
- Use open-ended questions in your interview. If you ask a question like "We are looking for someone who is outgoing and enthusiastic; are you outgoing and enthusiastic?" she/he will of course say yes. A better question would be "What two adjectives best describe you?"
- Hire, if possible, on three month trial period.

Praise

As a schoolteacher and later as a college professor, I found that praise got better results than criticism. Criticism crushes motivation, and you want your employees feeling happy and excited. The more I encouraged my students and sang their praises, the more they performed. Giving a student an opportunity to get extra credit after a bad test grade did lots more than saying, "Tough luck. You just didn't study."

Praise means noticing improvements and encouraging them. It matters. I believe praise for good things done is indicated even when you have to point out mistakes or improvements that an employee needs to make. Building on the good attributes while stating what is wrong helps make the criticism easier on both the employee and on me. Even while asking for changes in your employee's actions it is important to treat her/him like a valued adult.

War may be fought with weapons, but they are won by men. It is the spirit of men who follow and of the man who leads that gains the victory.

—General George Smith Patton, Jr.

Expect Greatness

*We awaken in others the same attitude of mind we hold
toward them.*
—Elbert Hubbard

*It is the nature of men to rise to greatness, if greatness is
expected of them.*
—John Steinbeck

A man's reach should exceed his grasp, or what's a heaven for?
—Robert Browning

*Good leadership consists of showing average people how to do the
work of superior people.*
—John D. Rockefeller

Many people will perform well if you expect them to perform well and then
praise them for it. I have high expectations of our team. Sometimes we all
have to put in some extra time, but I expect no more from our team than I
would ask of myself.

I think most people don't realize their greatness. Leaders can help each
team member actually see their abilities in a new light. Leaders can point
out strengths that a person might not even know he/she even has. Once
they learn how good they really are, they will not easily settle for their old
standards.

In Chapter One, I mentioned my high school home economics teacher
Mrs. Ingram, who assigned us the task of making some curtains. She gave
us a small budget and sent us to buy the necessary material and rods at The
Mill Ends Store in Scottsboro. We had no idea how to measure for curtains,
make curtains, buy material, buy rods, or install rods. When I boldly asked,
"Mrs. Ingram, how do we do all of this?" she quietly thought a few moments
and answered, "Girls, just do it."

Mrs. Ingram believed we could make those draperies, and she made her expectations clear. Guess what? We did it! That was a lesson that I never forgot. She knew we could do it—so we believed her.

Be Flexible and Fun

A cheerful heart is good medicine,
but a broken spirit saps a person's strength.
—Proverbs 17:22

Employment is a two way street. If you want the personal respect of your employee, you cannot treat her/him like a robot. If you are clear about your work values and expectations, you should allow for some flexibility with your employees. I maintain an interest in my employees' family and health. Our team members know that I am someone who will meet real emergencies with special considerations.

Most importantly, we do our best to maintain some fun in the workplace. We like to have parties at work to celebrate success. We do have covered dish parties where employees bring dishes. We never serve home made food to customers; however we have cook outs for our employees in the parking lot which are fun and we have brought in pizza for a party. We love little parties at our office.

In things relating to enthusiasm, no man is sane who does not know
how to be insane on proper occasions.

—Henry Ward Beecher

Never Take Credit, Give It

By now you know I was a cheerleader for the University of Alabama when Bear Bryant was the coach. I never heard of Coach Bear Bryant's saying, "I am a great coach," yet he, in my opinion, was one of the most wonderful coaches who ever lived. If only there were more like him. He taught values to his players, and one of the most valuable lessons attributed to him is: "When everything goes bad say, 'I did it.' When things go in an average or mediocre way say, 'We did it.' When things go especially wonderfully say, 'They did it.'"

Giving other people credit for successes is absolutely necessary in my leadership philosophy. Taking full blame when anything goes wrong is always my leadership responsibility. Everybody makes mistakes, and the buck stops with me when any in my organization make a mistake. I take the blame when things go wrong and I praise my employees when we are successful. When people say, "Martha, you do so many wonderful things and I don't see how you do it all," I reply, "I serve a great God who knows how to make any business a success. Joe is the greatest advisor in the world. Our team at MPC is wonderful! God, Joe and our team at MPC are the ones that make me look good."

A boss drives other people; a leader coaches them.
A boss loves to use authority; a leader prefers goodwill.
A boss always says 'I'; a leader uses 'we.'

—Unknown

The Art of Delegation

Surround yourself with the best people you can find, delegate authority, and don't interfere.

—Ronald Reagan

In the early days of Martha Pullen Company, I did almost everything. I wrote every word of my books. I sewed every stitch and put the sample in front of the artist at each step. In the middle years our company could not have published as many books if I had still written every word. At that point I started working with artists who actually sewed well and with writers who wrote fabulous instructions. Usually I still wrote parts of the books but I left the sewing and instruction writing up to others. We certainly would not have written over fifty books if I had continued doing all the work.

So I have a little advice for you. There are all kinds of tasks that others can easily do as well as you. There are many tasks that others can do better than you. Delegating your responsibilities to others helps everyone. You allow your employees to grow and become more valuable members of your team. For many years I had difficulty delegating tasks. I invented myths and legends in my mind that I was the only person who could perform certain tasks. OK, OK I still think that way sometimes a little bit.

My perspective certainly changed. Our employees at Martha Pullen Company are living proof that I am surrounded by excellence. There is nothing so vain as assuming nobody can do it as well as you do! The only way for a business to grow is through the increasing responsibilities of its employees. Delegating lets you unload work, so you can focus on the parts that need your attention. Don't be afraid to ask for help, and don't be afraid to invest the time in training your competent employees.

Communication Skills

Communication is a people skill. Without good communication habits, your business will struggle. Let me be more blunt. It will probably die. Most adults are not equipped with perfect communication skills, but they can easily be improved.

The easiest place to start begins with recognizing that everyone has a different perspective. Sometimes what I consider a fact is only true for me. If I want someone to listen to my opinion, I need to preface it with "It seems to me" rather than "I know for a fact that," or something similar. By stating your opinion as your own viewpoint, and not the objective truth, it is much more likely that your words will be heard.

Pronouncing "absolute truth" is bad communication in almost any situation but especially in the world of sales and management of other people. "Truth" always says that I am right and that you may be wrong. I believe that both sides lose when this happens. By stating your opinion as a personal truth, instead of an objective truth, the other person might be more inclined to consider your opinion.

Similarly, when you are talking to someone about her/his behavior, it is important to be clear that you are not criticizing her/him as a person. Often you are trying to let them know how their behavior impacts you or your business. So instead of saying, "that was a terrible thing to say," you can say, "when you do that, it makes me feel terrible." It is a lot easier to accept that my behavior is not pleasing to another than to accept that I am not pleasing to another person. You have left the communication lines open, and you have not offended the other person.

Martha's Magic Phrases

In the same way I have magical phrases that help me with sales, I keep a few handy that I find very useful for managing conflict with my colleagues and employees as well as our customers. I would suggest memorizing these phrases and have sessions with your team to be sure they know how to use these phrases with your customers not only in speaking with customers but in writing notes to customers.

- It seems to me..
- I am of the opinion...
- You might want to consider...
- Have you given consideration to?
- When you do (or say) that, it makes me feel...
- I hear your concern.
- I see what you are saying.
- I understand your point.
- You're right.
- I really hadn't thought of that.
- Tell me more.
- Could we also consider?
- Exactly right. You are exactly right.
- That is an interesting idea.

It's not about me.

—Rick Warren

People Skills with G.R.A.C.E.

In my life most of the time I need to stop being so busy and pay much more attention to God's voice. I need to listen to God more. I need to seek Him with my whole being not just when I have time. I need to rest in

Him not rush through life so much. In those moments, I hear God saying, "Martha, remember the entire population of the universe, with only one tiny exception, is composed of others." These small reminders help me keep my perspective. The people I work with are a blessing from God. Their loyalty is worthy of respect, and I try to do everything possible to communicate with them in an open-minded way.

God: First in all things.

Any concern too small to be turned into a prayer is too small to be made into a burden.

—Corrie ten Boom

Resilience: Get up when you're down. You conquer by continuing.

> *I have told you all this so that you may have peace in me. Here on earth you will have many trials and sorrows. But take heart, because I have overcome the world.*
> —John 16:33

Action: It is not enough to dream; wake up and work at it!

It has been said that success can come only working half days. Choose either twelve hours per day that you like.

—Martha Pullen

Creativity: Allow the unusual to happen. God gives creative minds for us to use.

> *Intelligent people are always ready to learn.*
> *Their ears are open for knowledge.*
> —Proverbs 18:15

Enthusiasm: Allow the spirit of excitement to fill you and spread to your friends. It is contagious and delightfully enriching.

> *I will exalt you, my God and King,*
> *and praise your name forever and ever.*
> *I will praise you every day;*
> *yes, I will praise you forever. Great is the Lord! He*
> *is most worthy of praise!*
> *No one can measure his greatness.*
> —Psalm 145:1–3

Sermons We See

I'd rather see a sermon than hear one any day;
I'd rather one should walk with me
than merely tell the way.
The eye's a better pupil and more willing than the ear,
Fine counsel is confusing, but example's always clear;
And the best of all the preachers
are the men who live their creeds,
For to see good put in action is what everybody needs.
I soon can learn to do it if you'll let me see it done;
I can watch your hands in action,
but your tongue too fast may run.
And the lecture you deliver may be very wise and true,
But I'd rather get my lessons by observing what you do;
For I might misunderstand you
and the high advice you give,
But there's no misunderstanding
How you act and how you live.

When I see a deed of kindness, I am eager to be kind.
When a weaker brother stumbles
And a strong man stays behind
Just to see if he can help him,
* then the wish grows strong in me*
To become as big and thoughtful
as I know that friend to be.
And all travelers can witness
that the best of guides to-day
Is not the one who tells them,
but the one who shows the way.
One good man teaches many,
men believe what they behold;
One deed of kindness noticed is worth forty that are told.
Who stands with men of honor
learns to hold his honor dear,
For right living speaks a language
which to every one is clear.
Though an able speaker charms me with his eloquence,
I say, I'd rather see a sermon than to hear one, any day.
—Edgar A. Guest (1881)

Telling employees what to do is a far cry from showing them. I have always made sure that I roll up my sleeves just as much as anyone else. In the early days before we had a cleaning service I took my turn running the vacuum cleaner, emptying the trash, and cleaning the bathrooms. I do not expect our team to do anything that I am not willing to do myself. That does not mean that you cannot make mistakes. You should show your employees the same forgiveness that you allow yourself. The key, as a good leader, is simply to demonstrate the same work ethic that you ask of your employees. "I will do my best, and keep getting better and better."

But those who trust in the Lord will find new strength.
They will soar high on wings like eagles.
They will run and not grow weary.
They will walk and not faint.
—Isaiah 40:31

~ Chapter Fourteen ~

Personal Business Skills

> *And if the bugler doesn't sound a clear call, how will the soldiers know they are being called to battle? It's the same for you. If you speak to people in words they don't understand, how will they know what you are saying? You might as well be talking into empty space.*
>
> —1 Corinthians 14:8-9

> *If you need wisdom, ask our generous God, and he will give it to you. He will not rebuke you for asking. But when you ask him, be sure that your faith is in God alone. Do not waver, for a person with divided loyalty is as unsettled as a wave of the sea that is blown and tossed by the wind.*
>
> —James 1:5-6

Focus

In business, I believe you always need to keep your mind focused on where you are heading. This helps you achieve your goals quicker. I know too many people who chase their dreams like they are butterflies. I believe this is the wrong approach in business. I think creativity can be a butterfly, but I need to keep my business mind focused like a hawk. I could have saved myself a lot of heartache, not to mention money, by always making sure that my mind stay focused on business not on chasing creative butterflies!

Don't confuse focus with obstinacy! Your business will not and should not move in a perfectly straight line during the first few years or ever. It is perfectly reasonable to discover that you need to adapt to the market, and change your business plan. You will make mistakes! You will misjudge your consumers' tastes and make some bad choices. If you spot a problem, do not make the mistake of ignoring it.

You should always be ready to re-evaluate your business plans. A great way to stay focused is to constantly ask yourself what business are you really in? As Tom Peters pointed out, railroad companies almost went out of business because they did not stop to ask themselves this vital question. If they had only realized they were in the transportation business, instead of the train business, they would have gone into air transport as it grew.

I hear you saying, "Martha, should I have asked myself that question before I got started?" The truth is that you can not really know what is going to work until you get into it. Only in the midst of your WRITTEN plans will you discover both errors and opportunities. As you work and rework your WRITTEN plan, ask yourself, "What business am I really in?"

By stopping to ask yourself fundamental questions, you will notice ways to change your plans in profitable new directions. No matter how brilliant your written plan may be, it will have to shift and adapt to your market. That is the fun part of business, whether it is driven by necessity, because something was not working, or driven by success, because you can afford to expand. Adapting to new situations lets you apply your creativity to new challenges.

You might need to create more products, or open up a new line of products. You might need to expand your circle and break into new markets. This allows you to meet new people and learn more, while you apply all your past experiences. Each new opportunity opens up a new dimension to both you and your business. Never, never forget to write a new extensive written plan for any new idea which seems possible to you. Only with a written plan can you really evaluate if it might work well.

Business Plans Change

Just look at the path my business followed. It was anything but a straight line. My plan in the beginning was simply to have a small retail shop. To help sell in the store, we started teaching classes. Students would buy all of their supplies right there in the store, which greatly increased sales. As I saw new opportunities, my plans began to change. I had been frustrated by having to go to New York to purchase my supplies for my shop since there were no catalogues available. You might also remember from earlier in this book that the New York people were rude to Joe and to me when we were purchasing our goods! I realized that I could start a wholesale business by going to France and Switzerland and importing French laces and Swiss batiste and embroideries. I knew I would figure out how to make a catalogue of some kind and get to trade shows so others would not have to travel so far to get supplies. We also knew that we knew how to thank people for their business and how to be nice to people. We traveled to both France and Switzerland and bought a whole warehouse of lace and batiste! The wholesale division of Martha Pullen Company was born about six weeks after I opened the doors of my tiny retail shop.

Teaching is in my blood. I wanted easier ways to share my knowledge. There were no books on heirloom sewing by machine. Suddenly the books and the magazine, *Sew Beautiful*, were born to meet that need. Big seminars grew out of little ones in the store. We grew into a traveling sewing school and seminar company. We traveled all over the world teaching sewing. When we discovered we still could not reach everyone we wanted to touch, we created a television show, *Martha's Sewing Room* for PBS which quickly grew to airing in all 50 states in the United States and Puerto Rico. Thirteen of the shows were actually translated into Japanese. The shows aired in many places in Canada. These shows ran for over 17 years. Even after the television shows began we still could not reach everyone with our classes. We started licensing other people to teach Martha Pullen Licensed Classes. We now have a team of teachers literally in every state in the United States and in fifteen countries teaching Martha Pullen classes. Plans change as opportunities arise.

In planning your business dreams, do not try to take short cuts. Much prayer should come before any major change or new directions. I wish I could tell you I went after all my goals in a smart way. I did not and I paid the price many times over. If your idea has an impact on your business plan, you owe it to yourself to think it all the way through and plan for it. Make written plans! Determine the objective of the idea. Size the idea. Share it with others for feedback. Forecast the expected results in the short term and the long term. Make a written plan for each idea. Notice I said WRITTEN. Determine what is going to be needed in terms of people, time and money. What is the fallback position? Can you exit the decision gracefully without too much loss of time or money? Once you have convinced yourself that the new plan is reasonable, you will want to adjust and update your business plan. Carefully plan the details, set a timetable, and make it happen. Pray hard.

> *Trust in the LORD with all your heart; do not depend on your own understanding. Seek his will in all you do, and he will show you which path to take.*
> —Proverbs 3:5-6

Momentum

> *This is my command—be strong and courageous! Do not be afraid or discouraged. For the LORD your God is with you wherever you go.*
> —Joshua 1:9

Part of the importance of always dreaming new dreams and refocusing on what your business needs, is that it keeps up your momentum. MACMILLAN DICTIONARY defines momentum as "progress or development that is becoming faster or stronger." Momentum is an essential, and often overlooked aspect of business survival. What do I, personally, mean by momentum? Well, it is simply that feeling that things are going your way. It does not mean necessarily that everything is perfect. On the contrary, you could be in the middle of a hectic week, but in the back of your mind, there is a feeling that you are doing something good and worthwhile. You feel like you are making progress. You are slowly making visible and concrete steps toward realizing your dreams. That is what I call momentum. I also call it peace which comes from God.

In the early days of your business, keep track of your momentum. Keep a daily diary and just briefly note how you are feeling. Write down some of your setbacks and victories. Take time at the end of each week to review these notes and evaluate your momentum. If you are feeling more discouraged than excited, you need to find ways to rebuild momentum. One of the best ways to gather new momentum is to get out there and start talking to people.

Truthfully the best way to keep momentum going is through prayer. God is the giver of all gifts including momentum.

> *Don't worry about anything; instead, pray about everything. Tell God what you need, and thank him for all he has done. Then you will experience God's peace, which exceeds anything we can understand. His peace will guard your hearts and minds as you live in Christ Jesus.*
> — Philippians 4:6-7

Those who are blessed with the most talent don't necessarily outperform everyone else. It's the people with follow-through who excel.

—Mary Kay Ash

Problem Solving

I am grateful for all my problems. After each one was overcome, I became stronger and more able to meet those that were still to come. I grew in my difficulties.

—J. C. Penney

Dreams of being an entrepreneur are so lovely and simple and peaceful when they drift like clouds through our imaginations. I dreamed that I would open my doors and customers would casually drop in all day long. I would sip tea with them, cut their materials, and offer suggestions. I would have time to sit and smock with some of them. As the business grew, I would hire good teachers to teach the classes.

That bubble popped on the day we opened our doors for real. All my customers came in a single flood and I could barely keep up. Business boomed, and I quickly had to hire an assistant for the busy parts of the day.

The dream was lovely and peaceful. The reality was thrilling madness. Every day brought a whole new set of challenges and problems. It was very difficult, and I came home each night exhausted. I learned so much in such a short amount of time. Solving each one of those challenges brought me a secret joy and excitement that I will always cherish. Then the reality hit. We had lots of success. Lots of business. In reality I worked very very very hard for ten years and we made almost no profit. We invested nearly all of our savings into the business and we were getting nowhere. I was exhausted. Basically I had no written plans and I was totally ready to hang it up, pay the bills and quit.

Stop to Analyze

When things go wrong, stop to analyze what is wrong rather than just trying to do more in the same mode. Problem solving requires a cool head. Problem solving requires a written plan! If you panic, and make emotional decisions, you create confusion and make mistakes. I should have stopped early in this stage of my business asking "What is wrong? Why am I making no money when I have a large wholesale/retail catalogue business with best selling books, when I am traveling all over the world, when we have fabulous events here in Huntsville which people love and when things 'appear' to be going so well?" I just kept on chasing the rainbow, working harder and harder and making no profit. I should have created a written plan at every stage of the journey.

Problem solving and decision-making are the two crucial qualities that allow you to move forward and maintain momentum. Stop and pray hard asking God to help you figure out what is wrong. That is the first and most critical step. The second step is always to create a written plan! Take each problem as it comes. Learn to prioritize and deal with the most pressing issues first. The mistake of many early entrepreneurs is to gravitate only toward the problems they can solve best. Do not allow yourself to only take on the exciting challenges, and ignore the others. I should have stopped early on to analyze why we had all of this business and no profit. I just kept working harder and harder. I traveled more and more. I should have sought financial help and analyzed why the business was booming without profit much earlier than I did.

A smooth sea never made a skillful sailor. Challenges make us better. Use the difficulties that you encounter as opportunities to improve your people skills. Great relationships often form from the camaraderie built while getting through difficulty. Use these challenges as an opportunity to build relationships. The following verse from the book of James has over the years become one of my most recited. I have recited it in airports, while writing books, while dealing with almost every situation in my business and in my family. I think it is well worth memorizing if you are going to start and run a business.

> *Dear brothers and sisters, when troubles come your way, consider it an opportunity for great joy. For you know that when your faith is tested, your endurance has a chance to grow. So let it grow, for when your endurance is fully developed, you will be perfect and complete, needing nothing. If you need wisdom, ask our generous God, and he will give it to you.*
> —James 1:2-5

Today as throughout this whole journey of over three decades I rely on G.R.A.C.E. to help guide me through a problem. I look at the problem objectively, perhaps discuss it with someone I trust to get another perspective, then use G.R.A.C.E. to guide me. That means I do the following after much prayer asking God to guide my thinking

First, I frame the problem. I try to strip myself of preconceived notions and opinions, so I can look at the challenge objectively and without bias. If other people are involved, I try to get their opinions.

Then I write things down. It is amazing what the simple idea of writing things down can do to clarify your mind. By putting it on paper, you remove it from circling your head, and things are often simpler than you had believed while it was troubling your mind. I put down my assumptions first. By stating my assumptions on paper, I can start to see the gap between what I hoped and what actually happened. Finally, I state the decision that I need to make, and my possible options. I cannot state strongly enough what just writing down things does to clear my mind. If you have never tried this I beg you to do so.

If I am still confused, I create a matrix as follows and fill each box :

	If I do nothing	*If I do something*
Positive Impact		
Negative Impact		

> *Even when I walk*
> *through the darkest valley,*
> *I will not be afraid,*
> *for you are close beside me.*
> *Your rod and your staff*
> *protect and comfort me.*
> —Psalm 23:4

With most big problems, it is best to sleep on it, and allow God's answer to come to you in its own time. Prayer and a good night's sleep will help solve many of our most difficult challenges. Through prayer I get the right guidance. When I try to make decisions on my own, they tend to fall flat. Instead I tell myself that God is sovereign, and that He is in control, and He does not make mistakes. He knows what I need long before I know that I need it.

I have not failed. I've just found 10,000 ways that won't work.

— Thomas Edison

Organization

Those who make the worst use of their time are the first to complain of its brevity.

— La Bruyère

You cannot escape the responsibility of tomorrow by evading it today.
—Abraham Lincoln

Work hard and become a leader;
be lazy and become a slave.
—Proverbs 12:24

Organization will have to be the heart of your business. No matter how creative your products, if you do not maintain a great level of organization, your business will suffer. In the end, organization is an effort to help you manage your time more efficiently. Every moment you spend hunting for phone numbers or frantically looking for an invoice that you misplaced, you are wasting your energy. In the early days of a business, when you need to accomplish as much as possible every single day, you can not afford to waste time. Ask me how I know! I was not very organized in the beginning.

The best way to get organized is to create and adopt a personal system for managing your time and information. Now that everyone has a smartphone and a computer, there are a whole variety of ways that people can organize and manage their lives. I have seen very efficient people use their iPhones to manage their calendar, daily tasks and address book.

Some very smart people I know keep their daily to-do lists on paper. Some people prefer using an electronic system. Truly the choice is personal. I have all of the gadgets. Mind Maps are magical for planning.

As I was working on the final edit on this section I asked six of the most organized business executives that I know how they organize their daily to-do lists, short and long term goals, and calendars. The answers varied from using Microsoft Outlook calendars to Google calendars to iPad calendars to Evernotes to Planner Plus to plain old spiral notebooks! All said they do use paper to-do lists in addition to computers. One does not use a computer to-do list system at all but rather just a notebook. All of them said for people to use whatever they are comfortable with. One very smart friend said for people not to waste time trying to learn a new computer system rather than concentrating on the details of the business. Another says she uses a computer system and always keeps a spiral notebook in her purse for other notes. How smart is that?

Whatever you decide, be sure to keep it simple and portable. Part of being organized is developing good habits, and if you have a complicated system that is hard to work with, you will not make it a habit. As you will quickly see, if you begin to use a comfortable system faithfully, it will provide enormous benefits. Not only will you be able to accomplish more in less time, you will feel better. People who are organized worry less, because they have a clear understanding of what needs to get done, and a clear plan for accomplishing it. Organization is like anti-stress medicine.

That is not the only advantage. I believe being organized will actually make you more likeable to customers and business partners. People just might trust organized people more, because they can find things quicker, pay on time better, and respond in a more timely way. No matter how great your products, if you are disorganized, people might feel a little reluctant to do business with you.

Your personal system for staying organized should cover:

- **Your daily tasks:** Keeping a constant list of to-do's is one of the most critical factors in my business life today. Without such a list, I lose track of what is important, and I quickly lose momentum. Some people keep their daily tasks on a 3 x 5 card that they create every morning. That is an excellent idea, although I should mention that the daily tasks that I mark and cross-out in my planner are also a nice historical record. Many times, I have referred back to an older list to remember when I completed something. Both of these methods are rather old fashioned. The computer systems are much newer if you are comfortable with these systems; however, don't snicker about the 3X5 cards. I personally know a top international corporate executive, who is very young, who prefers these 3x5 cards. It is almost refreshing to think about this type of system when the whole world is busily watching a computer screen for every move in life! To tell you the truth I use an iPhone, a mini iPad and a notebook which I keep in my purse at all times. Then of course I have my computer! My daily task list usually consists of:
    - Emails and phone calls to make
    - Errands to complete
    - Meetings to set up
    - Problems to solve
    - Things I should delegate to others

- **Your short-term and long-term plans:** It is always important to raise your head from the daily struggles that keep you busy, and take a look at the horizon. Keep your short-term and long-term plans firmly in mind to help you prioritize. If you know that you want to start building a website in the next three months, you will give higher priority to the daily tasks that promote that goal. I use my calendar to track my short and long term plans. With my short-term plans, I track:
  - Deadlines on projects I want to complete.
  - Deadlines on getting source materials or inventory.
  - Marketing deadlines or goals.
  - Meetings to advance my marketing plans.
  - Meetings with lawyers, accountants or other professionals.
  - Internal administration and bill paying that needs to happen.
  - Potential plans for new markets.
  - Possibilities for new marketing or publicity plans.

Whereas my short-term plans are usually written as specific deadlines on specific days, my long term plans are written as looser goals for a specific month.

One of the most common patterns in my life in getting organized is to start strong, by keeping track of everything for a week or so, and then slowly tapering off until I'm just as disorganized as when I started. I have to work on staying organized. Getting organized is a habit, and it takes discipline to stick with it. Here are my suggestions for getting and staying organized.

- When you make plans for anything, put a date next to it. Make it a realistic date that you can actually meet, or you will find yourself constantly adjusting your calendar. It is important to get in the habit of keeping your commitments!
- Prioritize constantly. You can not do everything all at once. Figure out each day what are the most important things to do. Make your daily task list a combination of pressing items, and other tasks that have longer term benefits.
- Spend the first few minutes of every day planning. Figure out your goals for the day and the week; get these things done. If anything from yesterday did not get finished, bring it into today's list.
- Use planning as stress relief. Ideas take up more space in our minds

than they deserve. Writing relieves anxiety, by allowing us to take big problems and break them down into smaller, bite-sized tasks.

- Whenever you are in a meeting, always jot down the key "action items" and the dates that they are due. Plug those dates into your calendar and plan around them.

- Reserve a part of your planner to capture even crazy ideas. Never let a good idea get away. Sometimes a great idea grabs me in the middle of the night and I reach over to my trusty list and write it down! No idea is too crazy to write down. If an idea is not written down I guarantee it will be forgotten. Always have a notebook and a pen with you and write it down. One of the top international corporate executives that I ever knew in my life kept a small spiral notebook in his suit pocket along with a pen. Even during dinner meetings he would pull out that notebook, write down an idea and put it back in his pocket. He never let an idea go without writing it down if it had merit.

- During moments when you are stuck waiting, take out your planner and scan through your calendar. Take stock of your progress toward long-term goals, and where you would like to be focusing more.

- Create specific times in your day to handle communications like emails and phone calls. Do not let communication constantly interrupt you, because it breaks your efficiency and concentration.

- Keep your workspace clean and uncluttered. Clean things up on a regular basis. Put everything in its proper place. I have to remind myself of this constantly!

- Give yourself some wrap-up time at the end of each day, and each week. Take a moment to figure out what you want to do next, and summarize what you got done today. While problems and solutions are fresh in your mind, write down notes on your to-do list. Put a date due on your tasks. Deadlines matter.

- When you are preparing for a meeting or a phone call, write down your goals for the meeting–what you want to talk about, and what you need to get from the meeting.

- Pray for God's strength in having the discipline to organize your life and your business. Without organization your business won't go very far.

Mind Maps are Perfect for Organization

Mind Maps are the perfect way to simplify your "list making," your everyday planning, your long term planning and your "crazy, brainstorming planning." Turn your paper sideways. Simply put the main idea in a circle in the middle of the page, draw connecting branches (lines) away from this circle naming each of these branches (key words) and draw connecting branches from these key word lines. These are the details of your plan. It is helpful to use colored pencils or pens for each branch; it makes it easier to remember. I LOVE the iMindMap 7 software which is very inexpensive and easy to use. Mind Maps, either hand drawn of computer drawn, are so much fun to make. A Mind Map takes the work out of organization. Go to **www.pullenbusiness.com** to get a free seven day trial.

> *And may you have the power to understand, as all God's people should, how wide, how long, how high, and how deep his love is. May you experience the love of Christ, though it is too great to understand fully. Then you will be made complete with all the fullness of life and power that comes from God. Now all glory to God, who is able, through his mighty power at work within us, to accomplish infinitely more than we might ask or think.*
> — Ephesians 3:18-20

Overcoming Procrastination

Many of us are experts at avoiding the unpleasant. Whether we consider it boring or difficult or inconvenient, there is no end to the variety of excuses we can invent to avoid doing work. Although we make wonderful plans, we can always find a hundred little reasons to put off the small steps that let us realize them. Soon we find ourselves discouraged and wondering why our dreams have not come true.

Overcoming procrastination is a simple question of ignoring excuses, and making a commitment to yourself to begin working, no matter what. Tackling a task often takes no more than the decision to dive right in, whether you are in the mood or not. Begin writing plans immediately. Pray for God to help you tackle the task.

I procrastinate because I fear something. My undergraduate degree is in speech and theatre. I performed in many plays while I was in college. While I was in undergraduate school Dr. Marion Gallaway, my drama coach, at the University of Alabama told me, "If you ever prepare to stand in front of an audience and you don't have butterflies, then don't go on; it means that you don't really care about your performance." I have remembered this advice for the last fifty years since I have spoken before audiences of a very small size and those which numbered in the thousands.

When I am preparing to speak to a new audience, I tend to procrastinate, because I am anxious about giving the talk. I guess you would say I am afraid. Would you like to know something? There is a scared little child inside of me which says to me, "Martha this time they won't like you." This is truly foolish because I have entertained so many audiences and I know that most likely they will like me. I am not being egotistical but every audience to whom I have spoken has liked me. I am a speaker and a very good one. BUT that scared little child still loves to tell me that this time they won't like me.

Even after more than one thousand presentations, I still get nervous. I have learned that unless I force myself to prepare, I will procrastinate during the few hours before my speech for as long as possible. What I have learned is that I always give a better performance when I ignore my excuses and take the time to thoroughly prepare, no matter how I feel about it. I have to admit that after hours of preparation I still take my red pen and re-work my presentation right up to the time I walk on the stage. Knowing I am well prepared, I then forget about the "fear" and give the audience the very best I have. I love to speak. One reason I love to speak is because I am so well prepared and I know what I am going to say. By the way, once I see my audience the fear goes away and I love speaking. I truly love speaking before a large audience—well actually any audience.

This first business book was written in the late 1990s. My fears allowed me to procrastinate in writing that first book. Even though I knew that I had a lot to say about starting and growing a business, I had a terrible time starting to write. Day after day I procrastinated, telling myself, "Oh, Martha, you don't know how to write this type of book. You only know how to write sewing books. Wait until you have learned more about business. Maybe take a course in business at the university." I seemed to forget that

I have an earned Ph.D. in Educational Administration and Management and that I did most of my research out of the business and commerce library at the University of Alabama for my dissertation. I seemed to forget that I am a former English teacher who had taught writing for several years to high school students! Mainly I seemed to have forgotten that I had indeed started "from scratch" a business that had become quite successful! I was indeed an entrepreneur.

Finally, I had the good sense to purchase a book on "how to write a book." I read the silliest section which said in very simple terms, "To write a book, just begin to write. Write three pages a day no matter if you have an interesting thought or not. Don't try to organize or plan anything. Just write three pages per day for one month. It doesn't matter what you write, just write."

I began to write three pages a day. I took my computer with me and wrote on the airplane and in hotel rooms. I wrote on Sunday after church. At the end of the month I had ninety pages. Soon I began to like what I was doing. Even when I was not "in the mood to write," writing actually put me in the mood! The first book (copyright 1999) would not have been in your hands way back then if that had not happened. About twelve years later the first book, of course, was out of print. People began to ask for the book again. By this time so many things had changed about the business world and about my business. It became necessary to re-think the whole concept of re-writing the "business book" including the story of my journey but developing it to fit this world today with all of the Internet commerce which has totally changed not only my business but all small business. I realized that I would have to get some help writing this time—expert help with the "new business of Internet commerce" and all that goes with it. This is exactly what I did. I contacted the best talent agency in New York City. I hired an outstanding writer who was very experienced in helping business authors with the "new business" writing. This book is still my story although I had some help with parts of the book. This book would not be in your hands right now if I had waited until I felt like writing.

Tips to Conquer Procrastination

- Write down the things that you need to do. It magically turns them from secret wishes into direct commands.

- When faced with a job that I have been avoiding, I make a two column list and write down the reasons to avoid the job, and the reasons to do it. This kind of thinking helps me sort out what to do next. If the positive reasons are more powerful than the negative, I can usually convince myself to get started.
- Break down a task into smaller parts if you have been avoiding it. Sometimes just taking the first few steps helps you build enough momentum to finish it all.
- If you really do not want to do something, do not beat yourself up. Look for creative solutions. Can you hire someone to make the job go away? As much as I like my house very clean, I don't like to clean my house! Rather than condemning myself for that, I will gladly pay someone else to clean it.
- I had to hire some help for the technical writing parts of this book. That is exactly what I did.
- Use **G.R.A.C.E.** Give the problem to **God**. He'll give you ideas and the ambition to get it done. Be **Resilient** and work to push past your inner roadblocks. Go around them, go under them—whatever it takes. Take **Action**. By pushing yourself you will make progress. Be **Creative** in finding something about the task that will capture your interest and spark your mood to begin. Be **Enthusiastic** and find the energy to push yourself through.

Have a plan. Follow the plan, and you'll be surprised how success-ful you can be. Most people don't have a plan. That's why it's easy to beat most folks.

—Paul "Bear" Bryant

Balancing Family and Work

When you turn your hobby into a business, it stops being a hobby. Your family will feel the impact before anyone. My family has not had as many home-cooked meals as they deserved. Joe and I have spent a lot of time apart, and I do not do lovely little dinner parties for eight anymore. Nor do I get to spend as much time with my grandchildren as I would like.

During the high school years of our youngest child, Joanna, I missed some events that she would have liked for me to attend. Until Joanna was in high school, I made family time my top priority, after God. Once Joanna entered high school, Joe and I decided that it would be reasonable for me to travel about twice a month. During the weeks I was home, I put all my energy into taking care of my family, especially evenings and weekends. I have always done my writing at home for several reasons. I cannot write anywhere else. Many times I am get up around three or four in the morning simply because I write better early in the morning. That makes it possible for me to get two or three good hours in before anyone else wakes up and needs anything.

During the middle years of my company when I was traveling so much, Joanna and her dad developed a wonderful relationship, making up for the earlier years in her life in which I tended to monopolize Joanna's time. They became best friends during her high school years. My mother said that my traveling was the best thing that ever happened to the two of them. To this day they are best friends.

Planning family time into your business life takes hard work. When you are working hard on your business, your family must adapt as well. Plan ways to let them know they are loved and important. The easiest way is to get them excited about your new project. But, if they can't, or don't want to, find ways to keep them feeling warm and loved while you are busy. Joe and I always went to church as a family, we had family sit down meals and I always drove Joanna to her dance lessons and picked her up. Joanna is ten years younger than our four boys. Our boys still remember having family meals together and their cleaning up the kitchen afterward. I cooked and set the table and they loaded the dishwasher afterward. There was lots of talking time at dinner. Our boys were in college when I started most of the major travel with my business. I have found that car pool travel time is a great time to truly visit since you really can't do much other than talk. Car travel time is a great time to put the cell phones away, turn off the radio and just talk.

Sacrifices

During those first growing years of my business, we were a very thrifty family. We did not buy new cars, I certainly did not buy clothes for myself, we did not do "wonderful vacations," and we did not paint the walls or get new carpet. When some friends were talking about new wall paper I remember just staring at them. We couldn't even afford to hire outside carpet cleaners so I rented one at the local Winn Dixie. Our "exciting place" travel was always either with Joe's dental business or with my sewing business. Actually we loved this since we both love working vacations. I have to confess that we did go to Gulf Shores, Alabama twice a year to relax on the beach with our kids. We owned a condo which we rented most of the year. Joe went purely to relax; I took my computer and this was one of the places I wrote books with the greatest of creativity. You have to know with red hair and fair skin sitting on the beach has never been a favorite activity of mine; however I love to sit in air conditioned comfort behind a little computer and create while looking at the gorgeous ocean!

I also chose to make some social sacrifices. When I opened my retail store, I realized that I could not maintain all my former activities. If I were to put God first, family second, and business third then some things had to go.

We quit giving parties and going to most of them. We eliminated almost all social activities other than family ones, even on Friday and Saturday nights. We realized that family time meant just that—TIME. There was not much time after working the way we were working, and almost all non-business time must go to family. If we went to a movie, we took our youngest, Joanna, and her friends. We loved to stay at home on Saturday night, read books and spend time with Joanna. Since the boys were teens at this time, they certainly did not want to go to a movie with us or stay home and read on a Saturday night!

Let me hasten to add that I did not start the massive international travel until Joanna was in the ninth grade. Our boys were then grown and away from home. Several good things came from my intensive travel. As I said Joanna and her dad became best friends. Actually Joanna and Joe went on my first Australia trip with me. My social friends became the people with whom I worked. My ministry became bringing joy to women through teaching and sharing our beloved sewing. Part of this joy came from supporting and listening to people who were hurting. I know God does not need me; however, I hope he chooses to use me through this business in the world.

When the Honeymoon Is Over

> *I will lead blind Israel down a new path,*
> *guiding them along an unfamiliar way.*
> *I will brighten the darkness before them*
> *and smooth out the road ahead of them.*
> *Yes, I will indeed do these things;*
> *I will not forsake them.*
> — Isaiah 42:16

It happens to everyone. You wake up one morning and discover that the thrill and excitement of your business has begun to fade. Whether it is over financial difficulties, rude customers, or an unsupportive family, there are never a shortage of difficulties in business to make it less wonderful. If you find your enthusiasm waning, and struggling through hard times, it can be hard to hang on.

When Thomas Edison invented the lightbulb, he is said to have tried more than 2,000 experiments before he got it to work. A young reporter asked Mr. Edison how he felt—to have failed so many times! Edison said, "I never failed once. I invented the light bulb. It just happened to be a 2,000-step process."

That is the sort of attitude that will get you through tough times. Prayer is really what is needed along with that "keep on going don't quit" attitude. God's strength can keep you going when nothing else can.

> *But now, O Jacob, listen to the Lord who created you. O*
> *Israel, the one who formed you says, "Do not be afraid,*
> *for I have ransomed you. I have called you by name;*
> *you are mine. When you go through deep waters, I will*
> *be with you. When you go through rivers of difficulty,*
> *you will not drown. When you walk through the fire of*
> *oppression, you will not be burned up; the flames will*
> *not consume you. For I am the Lord, your God,*
> *the Holy One of Israel, your Savior.*
> — Isaiah 43:1-3

Believe in Life, Not Stress

At one time, I had a vision of my life as a successful business person. I sipped my Diet Coke in a posh office. My trusted employee brings the final set of proof sheets for the upcoming issue of the magazine or a new book. When she arrives I languidly glance at them and nod my approval before I pick up the phone to check on other aspects of my business that my able and ample staff has totally completed. I only have to check and approve each person's work.

"Dorothy, honey! Wake up! It's Auntie Em."

Let me tell what my life is really like today. "Financial stress" takes on a whole new meaning when you start working in the millions. Deadlines haunt my dreams. For years I traveled at least part of thirty-five weeks in any year. I need to plan new directions for the company and make sure the old plans are working. I always have jet lag, it seems. I try to do some things with my gorgeous husband, my grandchildren, and my children. I have Diet Cokes but no leisure anything when I am in my office.

Yes, I believed in stress!

Then, in Chicago, one of my seminar students changed my life. At lunch I sat down beside a lovely lady. As we got to know each other a little better, I found out that she was a managing physician for a practice of ninety other physicians.

I said, "Oh my, you must have the most stressful job in Chicago!"

She replied. "I don't believe in stress."

"Uuh . . ." was my first witty reply. After picking my thoughts up off the floor, I asked, "What do you mean?"

She explained that stress is a state of maladjustment. We all choose what we do with our lives. We choose how we handle those events in our lives. It doesn't matter what business or occupation one is in, that person can be "stressed out." Recently she had taken her two children to buy shoes and she asked where her usual salesperson was. The answer was, "He had to quit. The stress was too much for him." How stressful can selling shoes be? As stressful as one wants it to be.

After that I began to simply eliminate the word stress from my life. I just don't believe in stress; I believe in life. I believe life is fast. I believe my

Father will not send me any task that He and I together cannot handle. I just call it by another name, and it looks a great deal better than it did before.

When people say, "I don't know how you do what you do," I reply, "I have a loving God, a wonderful supportive husband, and a fabulous team with whom I work. I pray a lot. I have the same twenty four hours a day that everyone in the world has access to. By the way that is the only prayer that God has simply said no to me. He refuses to give me any more hours in the day! With all of that help, I don't have much trouble keeping up." I just believe that I am not stressed. It works.

OK, OK, it doesn't work all the time. When I feel really down, which isn't often, I get some professional help from a Christian counselor. After a few hours, I am back on target again and I try to wipe negative words out of my vocabulary. But sometimes I want to scream, "I can't stand the stress any longer!" Joe allows me this privilege and I appreciate his understanding. The difference is now I don't allow those words to cross my mind often. I just think of my physician friend in Chicago who taught me this valuable lesson.

Surround Yourself with Enthusiasm

Whatever you put in your mind comes out as words, thoughts, and actions. Your mind tends to absorb things from the environment around it. If you surround yourself with negative people, you will become negative. Even if your life forces you to be around people who are dismal (perhaps because of your current job), take charge of the other areas from which your mental computer is absorbing data: the music you listen to, the television you watch, the books you read, the friends with whom you socialize. I find my main source of comfort in hectic times to be my Bible. God is my main enthusiasm source.

As I read the words [1 Timothy 1:17] there came into my soul, and was as it were diffused through it, a sense of the glory of the divine Being; a new sense, quite different from anything I ever experienced before. From about that time, I began to have a new kind of apprehensions and ideas of Christ, and the work of redemption, and the glorious way of salvation by Him.

— Jonathan Edwards

> *All honor and glory to God forever and ever!*
> *He is the eternal King, the unseen one*
> *who never dies; he alone is God. Amen.*
> — 1 Timothy 1:17

Enthusiasm groups can keep you inspired and on track. Benjamin Franklin created a small group of like-minded individuals who wished to seek solutions to various issues of importance and offer possible solutions. It met once a week, posing a question or problem each time and then accepting the reports of the members the following week after their reflection and research into the problem and possible solutions.

Bring positive thinkers into your life. You might actually assign one of them to help you be more positive by reminding you when you slip into negative thoughts.

You Get Out What You Put In

> *Don't be misled—you cannot mock the justice of God.*
> *You will always harvest what you plant. Those who*
> *live only to satisfy their own sinful nature will harvest*
> *decay and death from that sinful nature. But those*
> *who live to please the Spirit will harvest everlasting*
> *life from the Spirit. So let's not get tired of doing what*
> *is good. At just the right time we will reap a harvest of*
> *blessing if we don't give up. Therefore, whenever we*
> *have the opportunity, we should do good to everyone—*
> *especially to those in the family of faith.*
> — Galatians 6:7-10

My Grandmother Dicus (my beloved Nannie) told me "You get out of life what you put in." I can assure you in the business world I have found that to be true as well as in my personal life. I've learned that every day you should reach out and touch someone. People love a warm hug, or just a friendly pat on the back. I've learned that I still have a lot of learn. I've learned that people will forget what you said, people will forget what you did, but people will never forget how you made them feel.

Respect your fellow human being, treat them fairly, disagree with them honestly, enjoy their friendship, explore your thoughts about one another candidly, work together for a common goal and help one another achieve it.

—Maya Angelou

Even when your heart is heavy, or you are discouraged, send out messages of enthusiasm. Soon they will echo back to you a bit stronger than what you sent out. Before long you, and those around you, will find yourselves walking lighter, faster, and with passion.

—Senator Bill Bradley

Don't go around saying the world owes you a living. The world owes you nothing. It was here first.

—Mark Twain

Importance of Passion

Enduring passion is one of the things you will need to bring your dreams to reality. I combined all the things I was truly passionate about and God, through me, created a multi-million-dollar business. Creating beautiful things for my family and friends, working with people, teaching, sewing, sharing my love for God, and sharing my love of heirloom sewing still are my passions. The result is a flourishing business and an abundance of friends, and a lifestyle in which every day is joy. This is something I didn't realize was possible!

People look at our multimillion-dollar business, the international ecommerce, magazine and seminars, the national TV show, and think, "That must have been easy! She just took her hobby and simply started making money with it!"

In many ways it is simple. Simple in the sort of single minded way that anything great happens. With God anything is possible. That is the way it all happened. He did it.

Creativity

Allow the unusual to happen. God gave us this gift and it is OK to use it.

Creativity is not determined by the kind of work . . .
but by the kind of approach taken to any job.
It is people, not jobs, who are creative.
—Robert M. Fulmer

Enthusiasm

Allow the spirit of excitement to fill you and spread to your friends. It is contagious and delightfully enriching.

Meeting Setbacks with G.R.A.C.E.

So we must learn how to utilize enthusiasm in order to move into that exciting and creative segment of the human race— the achievers. You will find among them total agreement that enthusiasm is the priceless ingredient of personality that helps to achieve happiness and self-fulfillment.
—Norman Vincent Peale

When you are down and worried, look at your situation with **G.R.A.C.E.** I always remind myself of these three sentences when my plans seem to go wrong:

1. God never fails.
2. God is sovereign.
3. God is in control.

As I have said of my quest to walk with **G.R.A.C.E.**, resilience is one of those important characteristics of success. I do not believe that many things come quickly in the business world. In my life that has certainly been true.

Yet I am blessed in many ways.

As an advisor to many individuals who are considering going into business, I am quick to point out that the national business statistic is 85% of all new businesses fail. Although that statistic is depressing, it should not be overlooked when deciding whether or not to take the plunge. I think 85% of the people in this world just give up too easily. I also believe that those 85% had no written plan! Some of your plans will get fouled up; it is normal. Just do not think of them as failures, think of them as "SNAFU's"—a World War II Army saying, meaning "Situation Normal All Fouled Up." Harriet Beecher Stowe said, "Never give up, for that is just the place and time that the tide will turn."

I have been driven many times upon my knees by the overwhelming conviction that I had no where else to go. My own wisdom and that of all about me insufficient for that day.

—Abraham Lincoln

We do make a difference -- one way or the other. We are responsible for the impact of our lives. Whatever we do with whatever we have, we leave behind us a legacy for those who follow.

—Stephen Covey

Success is the ability to go from one failure to another with no loss of enthusiasm.

—Sir Winston Churchill

My Father and Mother as Role Models

Love is patient and kind. Love is not jealous or boastful or proud or rude. It does not demand its own way. It is not irritable, and it keeps no record of being wronged. It does not rejoice about injustice but rejoices whenever the truth wins out.

— 1 Corinthians 13:4-6

One of my greatest blessings is that both my father and my mother are great heroes to me. My mother and father were devout Christians. I thank God daily for my parents. Let me elaborate a little. My parents were such incredible examples of selfless people. They always put God first. They always put other people first. They were disciplined and worked hard. They did what they were supposed to do with **G.R.A.C.E.** They never bragged nor mentioned their many accomplishments.

During the hard times of my business life, especially in the beginning, I would often remember how my father faced difficulties with a **G.R.A.C.E.** I hope to achieve some day. I never heard him say an unkind thing about another person in all of his eighty-one years. I never heard him complain about having to travel to earn a living or about having to spend most of his life in a hotel room. My father had many things to "brag" about but he never even mentioned them. I thought you might like to know that my Daddy is indeed "the father of all instant bullions and seasonings." That's right—in the whole world. He invented instant broth/bullion in his kitchen in 1937. He gave the rights to this invention, free of charge, to the company for which he worked. He never bragged or told people about his invention. It was just part of his job as far as he was concerned. I have permission to print the information which was printed from the G. Washington Coffee Company which is now owned by the Homestat Farms company to share with you.

G. Washington's Seasoning & Broth

In 1908, Mr. George Washington, a distant relative of General George Washington, established the G. Washington Coffee Refining Company, the pioneer of instant coffee, in Morris Plains, New Jersey.

Having successfully marketed instant coffee, the company was interested in developing additional products. In 1937, headquarter staff member, Paul J. Campbell, was served an exceptionally delicious dish while visiting friends. Impressed with the flavor, he complimented the hostess, who in turn showed him the seasonings she had used in its preparation.

Mr. Campbell discovered these seasonings mixed with water produced a pleasant meaty taste. His idea was to add dehydrated onion, celery and other vegetables to the mix, in the hopes of creating an instant broth that could be sold as a companion to instant coffee.

Working late night hours and having tried numerous failed experiments with the ingredients, Mr. Campbell awoke one night at 3 A.M. having had a dream in which he made certain changes that produced a successful formula. Going to his kitchen, he recalled the changes made in his dream thus creating today's recipe for the broth.

In 1938, G. Washington's Seasoning & Broth was originally marketed as "Broth," It was distinctly packaged in tin foil packets called "Aces" with 50 Aces to a box. Advertising on the radio and thru other mediums, G. Washington's Broth was successful from the very beginning.

Initial distribution was confined to the New York City area. This changed after the product was featured at the New York World's Fair of 1939 as the "Soup of Tomorrow."

During World War II, G. Washington's Seasoning and Broth was packed in "K" rations for the Armed Forces, replacing bouillon paste. Today it is recognized as the first of the "Instant Seasoning and Broths."

In 1945, American Home Foods acquired the G. Washington Coffee Refining Company. Under American Home Foods, packaging was improved and the product name was changed from G. Washington's Broth to Seasoning and Broth. This classification change added versatility and has contributed greatly to the product's success.

International Home Foods purchased the brand from American Home Foods and then sold it to ConAgra in August of 2000.

October 2001, Homestat Farm, Ltd. purchased the brand from ConAgra.

These brands continue to have a strong brand equity and loyalty with consumers.

Daddy never bragged about this invention. He never even talked about it. As a matter of fact when I wrote my cookbook I had to do some research to even get the facts straight.

His never complaining spirit was a tribute to his love of God and his influence from his grandfather, the Reverend Dempsey William Ward, a circuit riding Methodist minister who came from Tennessee in 1870 to help establish the Methodist Conference in the State of Alabama. Daddy told me that his grandfather Ward told him, "Paul if you can't say something nice about someone, don't say anything." Daddy lived by this teaching his whole life. As soon as my father retired from traveling he was elected to the city council in Scottsboro. He began to travel over the country to promote Scottsboro, Alabama to large companies in an attempt to get industry to move to Scottsboro. Several companies did indeed build plants in our small town bringing many jobs to Scottsboro. He taught Sunday school at the

First Methodist Church for many years always spending his time during his travel during the week studying his Sunday school lesson at night while in the hotel room.

Once I remember going to visit my father in the nursing home after he had many strokes and was unable to walk alone, get up alone or do anything much for himself. He was frowning a little as if he were in pain. I kissed him and said, "Daddy, do you feel bad?"

Rather than complaining about his very difficult lot in life, he replied, "No, I'm just a little lonely and I'm so glad you have come to see me." Despite his failing health, he only talked about positive things, such as how sweet the nurses were to him and how good and warm his room was in the winter. He looked around under the worst of circumstances and found beauty, joy and goodness. He always thanked everyone who came to see him and always asked if we had eaten when his tray was brought to his room. He wanted to be sure everyone else had eaten before he ate his food. God lived in him and in his actions his whole life. I never saw Godly ways more evidenced than I did when he suffered so for the last five years of his life. I might add that my mother, although she had a full time job as a junior college administrator came every night to eat supper with Daddy in the nursing home and stayed for a long visit with him. Sometimes she went twice a day to spend time with him-before work and after work. On the week-ends she had the helpers load him in the car and she took him for wonderful rides to see all of the places he loved to see in Jackson County. What a wonderful source of strength he has been in my life. He lived with an attitude of **G.R.A.C.E.** daily, in the good times and the bad. Daddy was my hero until the day he died. He still is.

My mother was also a hero to me in many ways. Mama, like my Daddy, never bragged on her accomplishments. Mama had earned not one but two graduate degrees from George Peabody College for Teachers (now a part of Vanderbilt Univerity) traveling on week-ends and summers to Nashville while teaching full time in the Scottsboro Schools. I have to add that after her death I found her transcripts in her "trunk of treasures" and she made all A's in her graduate work. She never bragged about that either. I would think that she had more education than any woman in Scottsboro at that time. Never in a million years would she ever have said that even if it were true.

She always taught me that we are tough and that we do not quit. She taught me that we had been given blessings far beyond what we deserved, we must never waste them and we must give back to others less fortunate. She was the epitome of resilience since she always got up when she fell down. She never quit a difficult task and she would not allow us to either. Moral and ethical standards were always kept in my family and she required action of me in all situations. I can hear her saying to me now, "We do not shun responsibility." She never allowed self-pity. She was fabulous right up to the very last days of her life, on figuring out a new plan if Plan A did not work. My mother was a champion of poor people and of those less fortunate. As a junior college administrator she was instrumental in helping people, especially women past the traditional young college age, discover that they could get a college education. So many believed that they were not smart enough or that it was too late for them. She was the first woman appointed to the hospital board of Jackson County, Alabama. She was a mover and a shaker her whole life, always working to make lives better for those around her. Both of my parents always taught Sunday school in addition to working full time jobs.

One of my earliest memories of her "giving back" was when my mother was an elementary teacher when I was a little girl. So many of the children were very poor in Scottsboro and had no medical care. When children in her room were sick Mama would put them in her car after school, take them to the doctor, buy their medicine and take them home with the instructions on how to use the medicine. Many times when children had no shoes that fit or clothes or underwear, Mama would take them to town, purchase what they needed and once again drive them home. If she found out that there were no groceries in the house she would then go to the grocery store and bring groceries back to the home. She did all of this on her Alabama teaher's salary which was low to say the least!

I lovingly say that the only two excuses for missing church and Sunday school at our house were "throwing up" or a very high fever. Any other ailment was absolutely inexcusable. We went to church under almost all circumstances! I even remember walking when the snow was so bad that we could not get the car out. In Scottsboro most people stayed home that day I might add. But not the Campbell family! We were on the third pew where we always sat! Mama and Daddy taught their Sunday school classes!

One of the greatest gifts my mother ever gave to my sister and me was choosing to move herself into an assisted-living apartment when she could no longer live alone without twenty-four-hour help. She was falling frequently. Her weakness and walking problems, caused primarily by mini-strokes, got worse and worse. When we approached Mama about considering assisted living, she replied, "I'm one step ahead of you. I've already reserved myself a room in the brand new facility here in Scottsboro. I'm just waiting for it to open."

This was one of the most courageous moves my mother could have taken. Once again, she proved that she was tough and that she was not afraid of making difficult decisions without any help from us. I think my sister and I cried more about her leaving her home than she did. She only shed a few tears the last day we were packing her personal belongings to move. She announced immediately upon moving that she loved her new home and that she got excellent care. She even said that the "girls" who live there had decided that it was like living in the college sorority house again except everyone used walkers! Mama looked on the positive side of everything. Mainly I think she did not want Mary and me to worry about her. She never looked back and she never complained about not being in her own home. Mama was my hero until the day she died. She still is. So you see I was given all the business skills I would ever need by my Mama and Daddy as well as by my grandparents. I thank them for that. I thank God for giving me my family.

> *So let us come boldly to the throne of our gracious God. There we will receive his mercy, and we will find grace to help us when we need it most.*
> — Hebrews 4:16

G.R.A.C.E. Once More

> *For nothing is impossible with God.*
> — Luke 1:37

God first: Open your mind to the lessons God is trying to teach you with setbacks, and you will learn as much or more from these so-called "failures" as from your successes. A college professor was trying to perfect a hearing device so his wife, who was partially deaf, could hear better. He gave all to this passionate dream, and failed. God had another plan for Alexander Graham Bell.

> *If you fail under pressure your strength is too small.*
> — Proverbs 24:10

Resilience: When you make mistakes, there is always another chance for you. You may have a fresh start any moment you choose. Face it with **G.R.A.C.E.**

> *For I can do everything through Christ, who gives me strength.*
> — Philippians 4:13

Action: The only place where success comes before work is in a dictionary. Many times we hesitate because we are afraid. With God's help we can take action and make dreams come true.

> *God has given each of you a gift from his great variety of spiritual gifts. Use them well to serve one another.*
> —1 Peter 4:10

Creativity: A seed will only germinate if it dies. Our failures are usually the seeds to our most brilliant successes.

> *Oh how great are God's riches and wisdom and knowledge! How impossible it is for us to understand his decisions and his ways!*
> —Romans 11:33

Enthusiasm: Allow the spirit of excitement to fill you and spread to your friends. It is contagious and delightfully enriching.

> *I will exalt you, my God and King,*
> *and praise your name forever and ever.*
> *I will praise you every day;*
> *yes, I will praise you forever.*
> *Great is the Lord! He is most worthy of praise!*
> *No one can measure his greatness.*
> —Psalm 145:1–3

Conclusion

It is difficult to make a man miserable while he feels worthy of himself and claims kindred to the great God who made him.

—Abraham Lincoln

God owns Martha Pullen Company and Pullen Press, LLC. Actually God owns all businesses. He has opened doors that my eyes could not even begin to see. Asking God to guide me has been more effective for my business success than anything I could have done on my own. He has provided miracle after miracle keeping our doors open when I saw no way for that to happen. He still opens "Red Seas."

I have no doubt that you have to believe in yourself and work hard to accomplish your dreams. Remember the book, *The Little Engine That Could* with the famous statement, "I think I can; I think I can?" In reality I know that God had the keys to doors that I never dreamed would open. I would like to rephrase that little book by saying, "I know God can; I know God can." Working hand in hand with Him has been the true miracle of our success. All of the glory for all we have achieved goes to God and God alone. May God bless and keep you as you begin pursuing your dreams of a hobby-based business.

*But those who trust in the LORD will find new strength.
They will soar high on wings like eagles.
They will run and not grow weary.
They will walk and not faint.*
—Isaiah 40:31

*Now all glory to God, who is able to keep you from
falling away and will bring you with great joy into
his glorious presence without a single fault. All glory
to him who alone is God, our Savior through Jesus
Christ our LORD. All glory, majesty, power, and
authority are his before all time, and in the present,
and beyond all time! Amen.*
—Jude 1:25-25

About The Author

Over the course of her career, Martha Campbell Pullen, Ph.D. founder of the prestigious Martha Pullen Company Inc. and of Pullen Press LLC, has enjoyed numerous and varied vocational pursuits. Early in her career, some of those pursuits laid the groundwork for future entrepreneurial success. She has been a salesperson (dresses, shoes and jewelry); community teacher (dance, baton, cheerleader coaching, speech, modeling, etiquette); church pianist; pageant judge or coach for adults and children; and professional educator (college professor, middle school educational curriculum developer [University of Florida's Project F.A.I.S.], English teacher at the middle and high school levels [Charlotte, Atlanta and University of Florida's P. K. Yonge Lab School], and second grade teacher [Scottsboro, AL]. She honed her presentation and speaking skills through such activities as performing with the Tuscaloosa (AL) Little Theatre (Annie in *Annie Get Your Gun*) and in Boone, NC (in *Horn in the West*). She was a model (photographic and runway), government contractor (washed shopping carts at a grocery store on a military base), alterations seamstress, tutor, and event speaker (leader of Christian women's conferences).

At one point in her career, Martha was even offered a position as host of *Miss Romper Room* TV show. But when she discovered that the salary was not even enough to pay her baby sitter, she sadly had to decline the offer. Martha actually loved the concept of "Do Bees" and "Don't Bees" taught by *Romper Room* and has considered those concepts as she has worked in the business world. For example, customers having fun in the hobby business world is a critical concept in growing their loyalty!

All of these experiences grew her personally and professionally and laid a strong foundation for her move to national and international prominence as an entrepreneur. She was a television personality (host of *Martha's Sewing Room* for 17 years on PBS), founder of *Sew Beautiful* magazine (readership of over 100,000), author (more than 50 sewing books, two business books, and two cookbooks), and consultant (educational consultant, newspaper in education consultant [*Ft. Worth Star Telegram, Rocky Mountain News, Lubbock Avalanche-Journal, Charlotte Observer,* and *Colorado Springs Gazette*],business consultant, DISC Licensed Trainer, and Think Buzan Licensed Mind Mapping Instructor).

Martha also recognizes the importance of her unpaid vocations and commitments— wife, mother, grandmother, daughter, daughter-in-law, sister, friend, encourager, Bible teacher at sewing events, prayer warrior and volunteer. Most everyone reading this book realizes that these roles are the most time consuming and that an entire book could be dedicated to listing specific tasks in each of these important roles.

With all the interesting and varied vocational directions Martha pursued along the way, she is most well known for her success as an entrepreneur, which all began when she was age 14 in Scottsboro, AL and started her first business: the Martha Campbell School of Dance. By the company's fourth year, she was a senior in high school with 100 dance and 50 baton pupils enrolled in the School of Dance. In the entrepreneurial world, Martha is best known as a leader in the heirloom sewing industry, which began in a tiny retail shop in Huntsville, AL. In 1981, two months after opening that shop, Martha began importing laces and fabrics to sell wholesale and retail by mail order. Next, the Martha Pullen School of Art Fashion was launched in Huntsville, AL which eventually brought 400 women to Huntsville twice a year for a week of sewing education. For many years, Martha Pullen Company brought more "tourist nights" to Huntsville than any other business in the city, with the exception of a religious group's annual national convention in Huntsville. As a result, on April 5, 2002, the Huntsville/Madison County Convention and Visitors Bureau presented Martha with the Pinnacle Award "In grateful recognition of your place at the pinnacle of loyal Huntsville meeting planners. The number, size, frequency and economic impact of your meetings, conventions and events is truly substantial."

The success of the School of Art Fashion prompted Martha to venture out of her local market, conducting full scale Martha Pullen schools in Australia, England, Mexico, Sweden, Canada, New Zealand, and Puerto Rico as well as in 45 states. She has made 28 trips to Australia to teach. Since Martha could not travel everywhere, she expanded her base of influence through training Martha Pullen Licensed Teachers to teach Martha Pullen classes. These licensed teachers are now conducting Martha Pullen-developed classes around the world.

For sixteen years, Martha Pullen Company produced a consumer event, Martha's Sewing Market, in Arlington, TX, which then expanded to Orlando, FL and Pomona, CA. For three years, MPC produced Martha's Quilt Academy in Huntsville and Orlando. Martha's Sewing Extravaganzas were produced across the United States in collaboration with one sewing machine company featured per event. Five of these Extravaganzas were produced at the Pasadena Convention Center in Pasadena, CA. Martha Pullen Company trained sewing educators from Pfaff and Husqvarna/Viking to conduct Martha Pullen Events. In one year, Husqvarna/ Viking conducted 37 of these events across the United States with their Martha Pullen Viking Licensed Educators. While working with Martha Pullen Company, Martha developed and wrote a weekly email newsletter which included sewing tips, information about sewing events, a personal letter, a recipe and a devotional. This free e-newsletter was sent to over 45,000 opt-in subscribers, and the newsletter had a very high open rate. In 1999, the Internet Embroidery Club was launched with the purpose of sharing heirloom machine embroidery designs through an online club. Today, Martha Pullen Company is fully digital, with the Internet Embroidery Club, digital books and magazines and even online Martha Pullen Licensed Teacher Training.

A project that "makes her heart happy" is *Sew Beautiful*, an heirloom sewing magazine she founded and began publishing in 1987. In 1992, public television audiences across the United States and Canada began receiving the benefit of her love of heirloom sewing through the *Martha's Sewing Room* series, which aired in 85% of PBS stations in the United States. Thirteen shows were translated into Japanese and aired by Japanese Public Television. Martha wrote her first book in 1983, *French Sewing by Machine, The First Book*, which sold more than 100,000 copies. Martha now has more than 50 sewing books to her credit. Martha's first business book was titled *Turn Your Hobby into Money* and was published in 1999 by Broadman & Holman (LifeWay). In 2010, she and her daughter-in-law, Suzanne Crocker, authored a cookbook titled *Recipes...Reflections... Remembrances.* This cookbook was revised by Adams Media in 2012 and released as *Martha Pullen's Southern Family Cookbook: Reflect on the Past, Rejoice in the Present, and Celebrate the Future Gatherings with More than 250 Heirloom Recipes and Meals.* With the publication of those cookbooks, Martha has realized the dream of turning her two favorite hobbies—sewing and cooking—into entrepreneurial business ventures. In 2004, Martha Pullen Company became a subsidiary of Hoffman Media and then in 2012 became a subsidiary of F+W Media.

Martha was born in Morristown, NJ but grew up in Scottsboro, AL. After receiving a degree in speech and English from the University of Alabama, she taught those subjects at almost every level of middle school and high school. Later, in 1977, her studies led to a Ph.D. degree in educational administration and management from the University of Alabama. Prior to receiving a Ph.D., Martha completed graduate courses at Vanderbilt University, the University of North Carolina at Charlotte, the University of Florida and the University of Georgia. She completed post-doctoral work at Vanderbilt University, Alabama A&M University, and the University of Alabama in Huntsville.

Martha's work as an entrepreneur and business leader has been recognized widely. In 2005, Martha was inducted into the American Sewing Guild Hall of Fame for her many contributions to the sewing industry. She was named a national Daughter of Distinction of the Daughters of the American Revolution, the ninth person to receive this honor, which she shares with Elizabeth Dole and Janet Reno. In 1995, she was named Huntsville/Madison County Chamber of Commerce Executive of the Year—only the second woman in the history of the organization to receive this award. She has been a nominee for *Inc.* magazine's Executive of the Year and is a Paul Harris Fellow of Rotary International. Martha was presented with the Golden Needle Award from the Schmetz Needle Company of Germany and Euro-notions. In 1987, Agape of North Alabama, Inc. presented Martha with the Special People Award "For Special Interest in and Concern for Homeless Children and Troubled Families Being Served through AGAPE." She was presented the Merrimack Hall Performing Arts Center's 2011 "Dream Big" Honoree Award. In 2011, her classmates in the Scottsboro High School Class of 1961 presented a beautiful crystal plaque to her at the 50th class reunion, "For Humanitarian Service."

In addition to time spent building businesses, Martha has also prioritized giving much time and love to her family and community, to philanthropic endeavors, and to mission work. Martha has served on the boards of the Huntsville Symphony Orchestra and Huntsville Community Ballet. She is a member of the Daughters of the American Revolution, the Gothic Guild, the Chi Omega Alumni Association and the Optimist Club. For many years she has been involved in fund raising efforts for St. Jude Children's Research Hospital and for Africa New Life Ministries which serves families in Rwanda, Africa. She is the wife of Joe Ross Pullen, DMD, a retired implant dentist; mother of five; and grandmother to 18. An active member of Whitesburg Baptist Church, Martha has served as a volunteer with the Southern Baptist Convention International Mission Board and Whitesburg Baptist Church in Africa, Jamaica, and Brazil. She and her daughter in law, Suzanne Crocker, have led Christian women's conferences in Alabama and Texas.

Martha's goal is to spend the remainder of her career helping others build successful businesses. She has been very blessed and gives all credit for her business success and personal blessings to God and God alone. Martha can be contacted at **painlesspullen@aol.com** or **www. pullenbusiness.com.**